AF521928

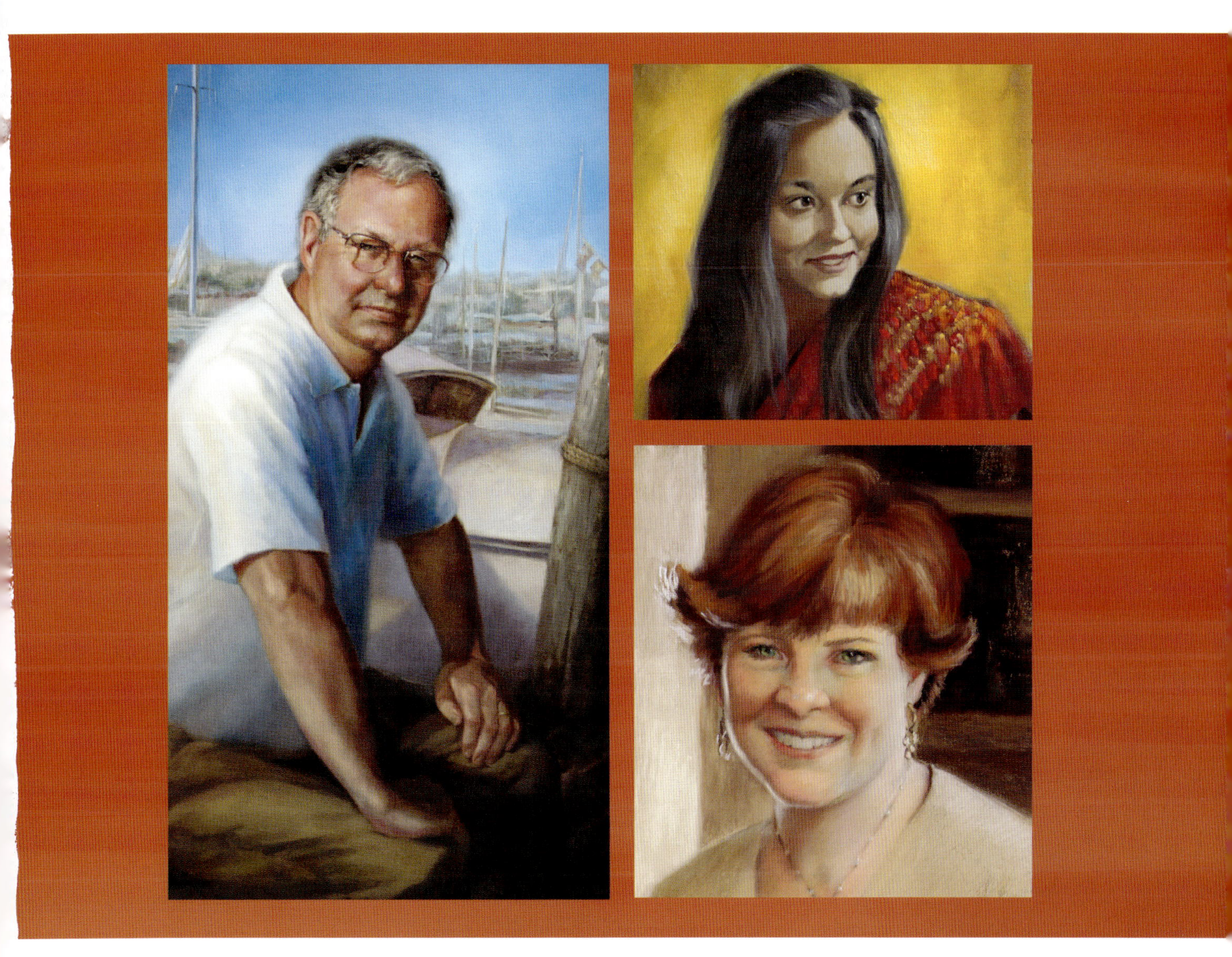

PAINTING CLASSIC PORTRAITS

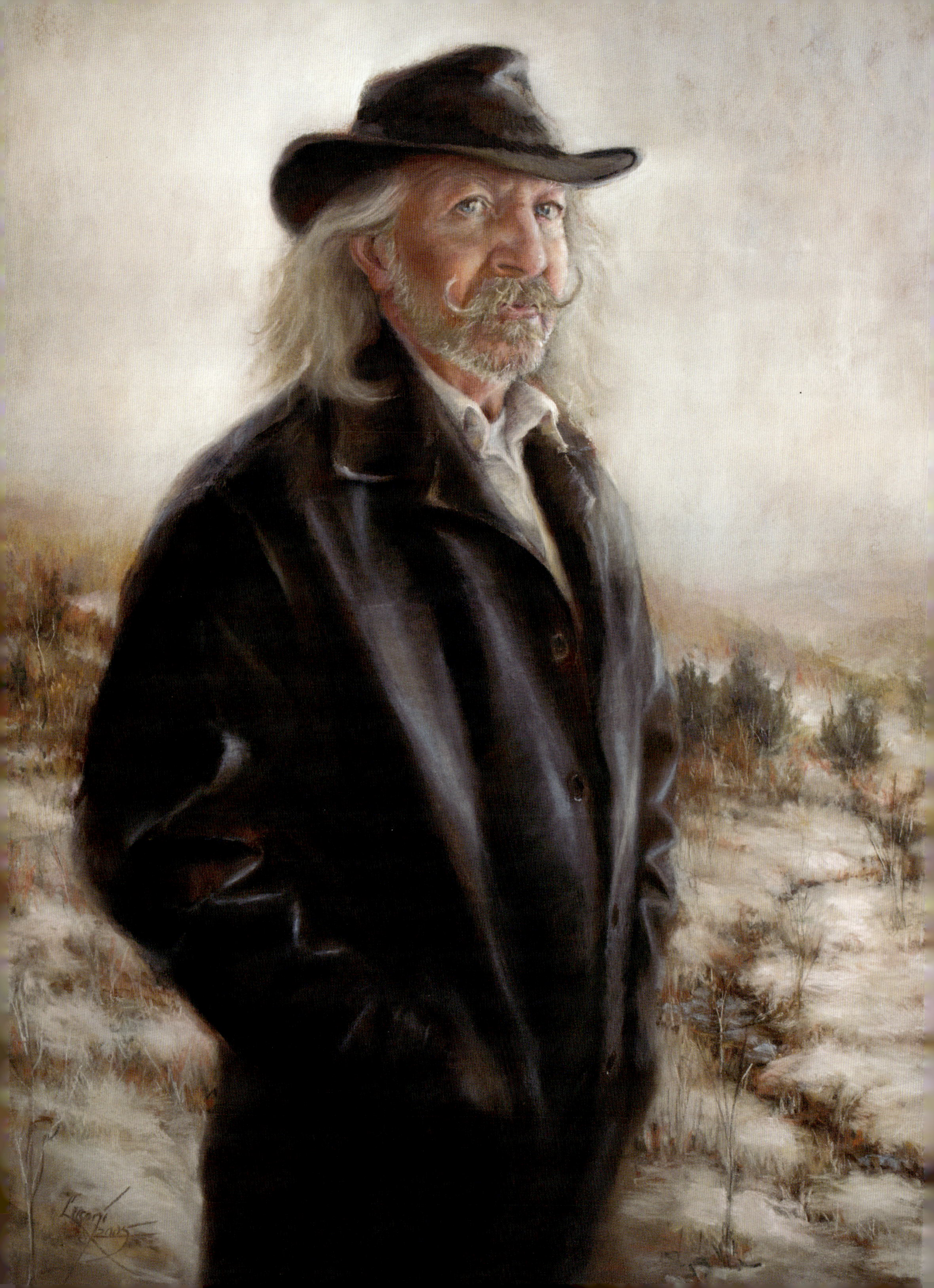

PAINTING CLASSIC PORTRAITS

GREAT FACES STEP BY STEP

LUANA LUCONI WINNER

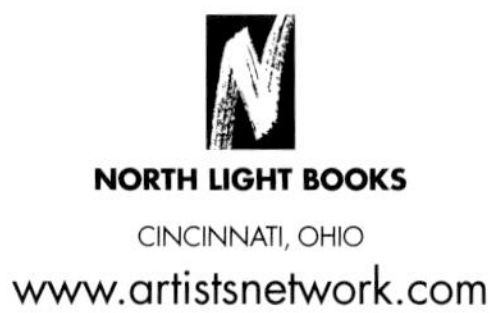

NORTH LIGHT BOOKS
CINCINNATI, OHIO
www.artistsnetwork.com

CONTENTS

INTRODUCTION 6

MATERIALS AND GROUNDS 8

CHAPTER 1
REFERENCES, STUDIES & COMPOSITION 12

CHAPTER 2
CONSTRUCTING THE HEAD & FEATURES 36

CHAPTER 3
THE COLORS OF PEOPLE: SKIN & HAIR 76

Color Reference Charts for Oils *80*

CHAPTER 4
DESIGN DECISIONS 100

CHAPTER 5
DEMONSTRATIONS 114

COLOR REFERENCE CHART FOR PASTEL 140

INDEX 141

ABOUT THE AUTHOR 142

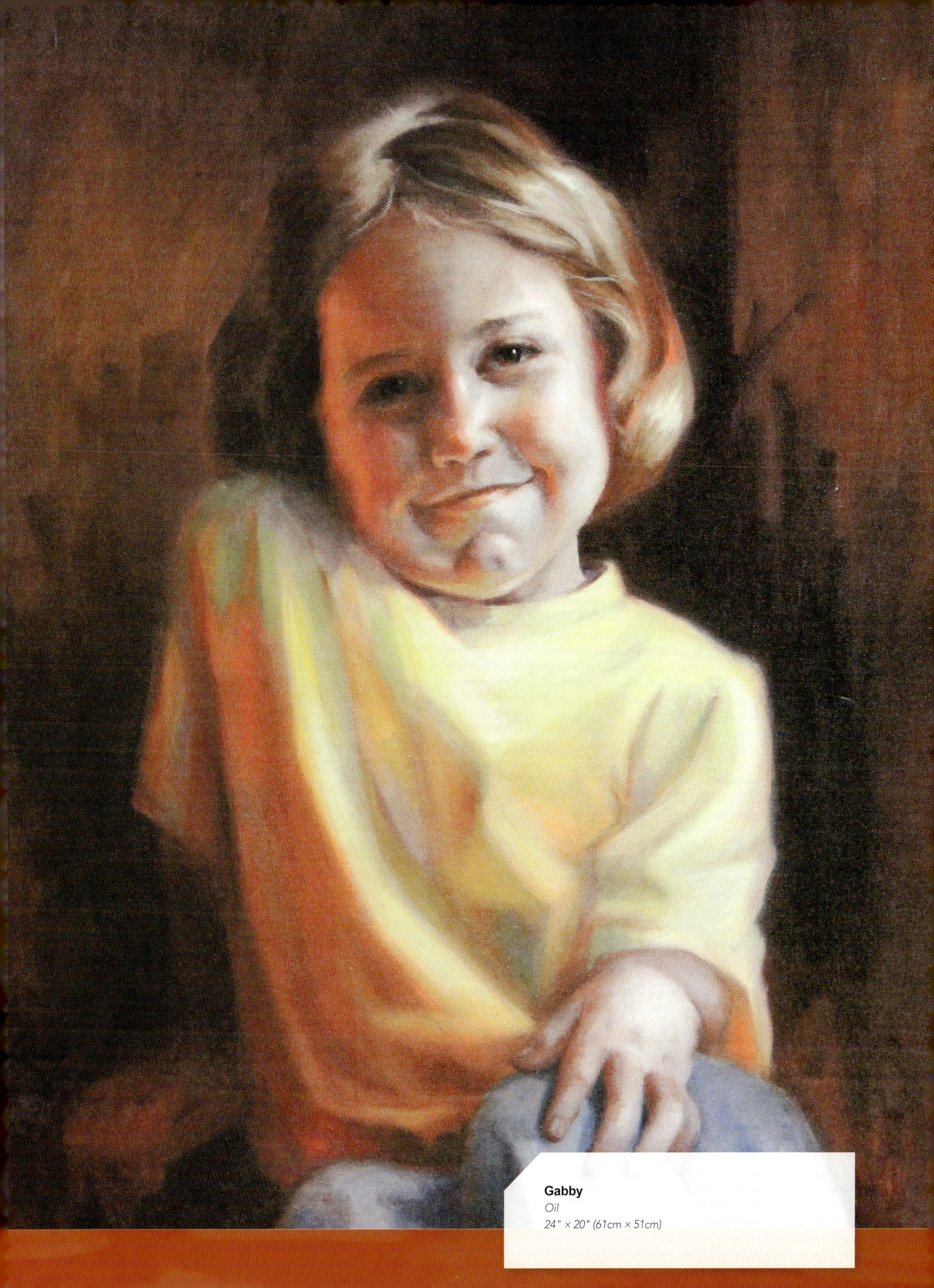

Gabby
Oil
24" × 20" (61cm × 51cm)

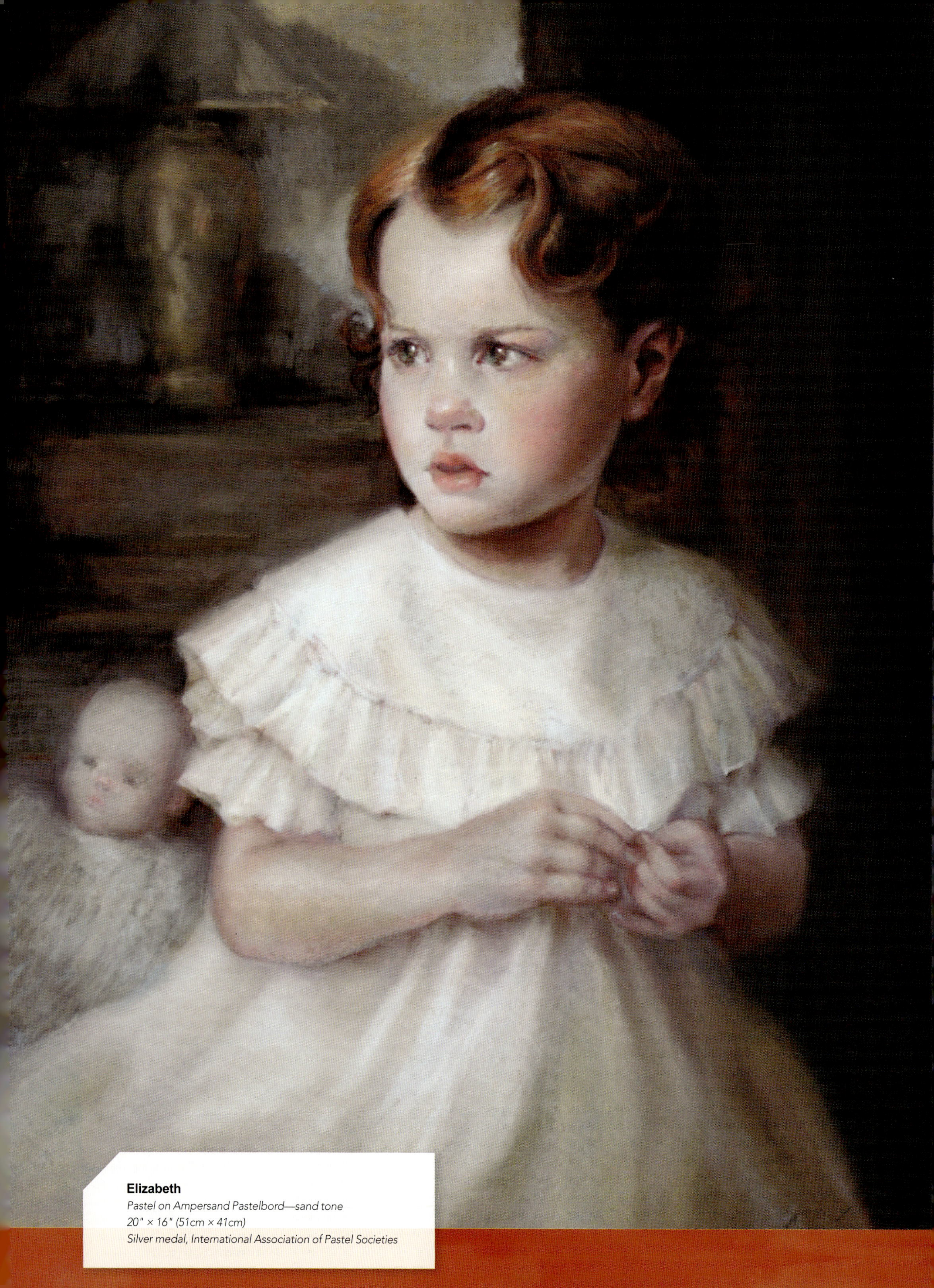

Elizabeth
Pastel on Ampersand Pastelbord—sand tone
20" × 16" (51cm × 41cm)
Silver medal, International Association of Pastel Societies

INTRODUCTION

Art should make us sense something, whether it's sympathy, anger, satisfaction or love. It should make us question or evoke a memory. Paintings and sculpture should encourage us to react to more than the mere material from which they are created. The portrait must depict a singular, particular life, one with heart and soul and memories and feelings of its own. Can we paint that into a portrait?

Painting great faces never loses its intrigue or challenge because even with a set, repetitive, mathematical pattern—two eyes, one nose, one mouth, two ears—the slightest change of a line or movement in the shadow will create an entirely different face. Think of it: There are seven billion people on the planet and no two people look precisely alike.

We have our work cut out for us.

While an artist finds an effective way to collect pertinent data required to tell the sitter's story, the preparatory sketches become key to linking the subject, her history and the accoutrements of their life into one beautiful composition. The portrait tells a story. Don't ignore or rush this vital element when you have the opportunity to get to know your subject.

Remember that during the initial sketch sitting, the subject is often fighting nerves worrying about how to remain still, how he really looks to others and how to remain comfortable and self-confident as this stranger stares and studies him in detail.

The artist, in turn, is concerned about making the subject comfortable and less self-conscious while collecting pertinent information. To paint the person, get inside his persona to tell the truest story. Do this in the time allotted and with the highest level of skill. Do not cut corners. Do the work.

Artists should always be reaching further, delving deeper, stretching wider as they attempt to attain a new level of truth and wisdom.

Here are some thoughts before we proceed:

- **Decisions at the start affect the finish.** At the beginning, the artist should have a clear plan. There will be minor changes of the movement of a skirt, the tilt of the flower in the vase or a touch of sunlight that has moved slightly. This *does* mean that if the painting is planned as a seated person with one hand on a dog, we do not, in the middle of production, take out the dog, put in a desk, and move the hands and arms. We begin a new canvas for the new image and design. It needs to always stay fresh and feel spontaneous, not overworked.

- **There are no disclaimers displayed on paintings.** No opportunity to explain what it should have been, what it could have been. If you are the type of person who should not be rushed, don't set a deadline. A painting that is rushed, or repeatedly changed or repaired, reveals all of that. The viewer will see the struggle. Step away and make a plan. Do a drawing again and again until you can really see the finished painting in your head—then just lay it on the canvas.

- **You have looked at faces since the moment you were born. Now it is time to look into faces and souls.** Do not distract the viewer with unskilled anatomy. We will simplify things into straightforward, uncomplicated, geometric shapes. Nothing will be too intimidating to tackle.

- **We live in a world of amazing color, but people's skin needs to be painted true to their ethnicity or blend of ethnicities.** The color charts will give you the confidence to dive right into the painting, but remember, no one chart is going to be perfect for anyone. Take the theory, the color family and the process, and adapt it to suit your particular model's needs.

- **We will learn together how to tell stories in our images.** How can you succinctly tell the viewer two hundred years from now who this person was and what he felt? You are recording his history. Make it count.

- **Does the final painting match your perception of perfect? No? Move on!** There is always more blank canvas out there just waiting for you. You will hear repeatedly, "You will only be as good as the miles of canvas you have covered." So let's get started!

MATERIALS AND GROUNDS

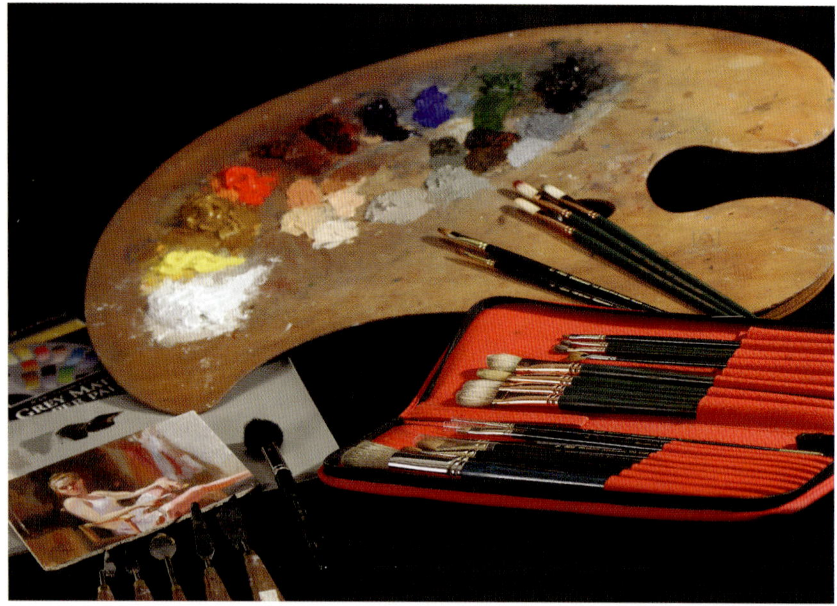

Tools of the Trade
This arm palette by MABEF in Italy is weighted on the lower right near the thumb hole to help balance it on the arm rather than strain to keep it upright.

A working artist needs to master the medium. Because we each have little idiosyncrasies, it is important to work with different materials to determine what the best fit will be for the envisioned artwork. When beginning to draw and paint, try many new things. Go to classes and become comfortable with new techniques. Buy whatever is affordable, and as time passes and skills improve, replenish materials with better-quality pigments, brushes, pastels, grounds, etc. Once the use of materials becomes second nature, all that is left to attend to is the inspiration and creativity.

SKETCHING ON PAPER

Work on paper all the time. Keep an 8" × 5" (20cm × 13cm) ring-bound notebook everywhere there might be a moment to sketch. Put an 8" × 5" (20cm × 13cm) Moleskine notebook in a carry bag, in the glove compartment, in a briefcase. Have something available all the time so you have no excuses not to sketch.

Strathmore has a wonderful array of papers that suit many opportunities. All of the 14" × 11" (36cm × 28cm) graphite sketches in this book are on Strathmore bristol Vellum. The oil color charts were painted on Strathmore Canvas Paper. Multiple tonal studies were done in charcoal and chalk or pastel on Strathmore Gray Scale. All are easy to carry and easy to store with glassine paper in between images.

Pencils vary from 9H as the hardest (lightest lines) to 9B as the very softest (dark as charcoal lines). Most of the studies shown use a limited number to create the values: 4H, 2H, HB, F, 2B and 6B. More can be used when completing a polished graphite drawing instead of a quick planning sketch.

A variety of charcoal from General Pencil Company and other companies provides a wide range of soft and hard qualities that provide a wide range of techniques and finishes.

PAINTING IN OIL

There seems to be a misconception that oil painting is both smelly and messy. Neither needs to be true.

Consider the first: Most people think of the odor of turpentine. However, turpentine is only used to clean brushes, rarely to mix into the paint. Now that there are multiple products that have no odor, like Turpenoid by Weber or Gamsol by Gamblin Artists Colors, that is no longer a problem. When thinning paint for application to the image, try Galkyd Lite by Gamblin or Jack Richeson's Everett Raymond Kinstler Medium.

As for the second, oil painting does not have to be messy. Set good habits in the beginning and stay determined to only put paint on the brush and the canvas—not on the handles of the brushes, the easel, the taboret, the table, the hands and arms or the clothes. Think of the money you will save! This will also prepare you to work in people's homes with silk furniture and white carpets or in boardrooms and offices at major corporations. Set good habits early to maintain a clean and orderly working environment.

PALETTE

Find a palette that is large enough to work with when painting a large portrait. Jack Richeson makes good wooden palettes, and Turtlewood is creating a palette that is a beautiful thing. Have a few small and medium-sized Jack Richeson Grey Matters Paper Palettes around for the occasional individual mixture that needs to be isolated and held up to the painting while mixing and matching.

OIL PAINTS

Oils vary from student grade to the finest-quality pigments with no fillers

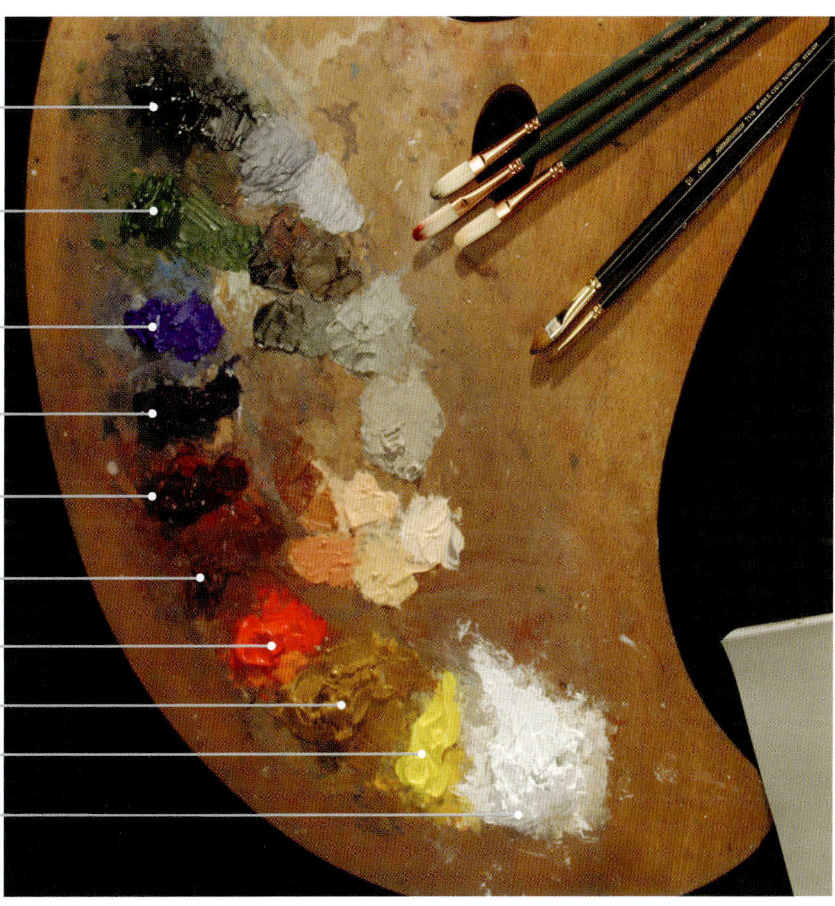

Maintaining Order
I suggest that you try this order for placing your colors. Place the paint across the outer edge of the palette, leaving the large center area free to mix. This palette includes a white, black, and warm and cool version of each of the primary colors. With the addition of two colors to temper the brilliance of some mixtures, you will have success in building a series of charts of skin, hair and lip colors.

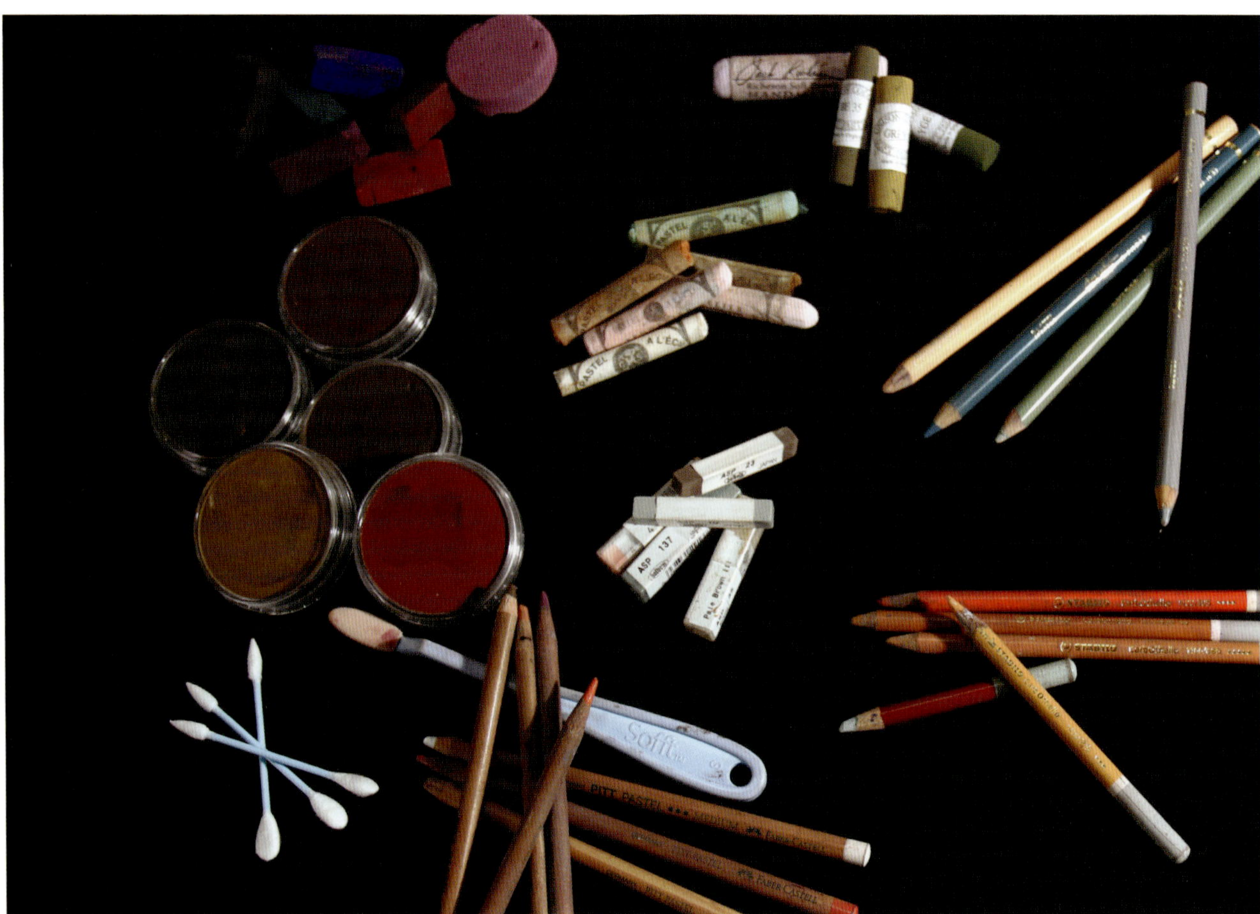

or additives, making them both stable and archival. Buy what you can, but replenish with higher-grade paint as skills improve. Sennelier Finest Artists' Oils are lovely paints that require no mediums to push the paint around in thin, beautiful layers. The transparency allows beautiful optical blending in layers for some of the pigments. There are many others that provide tubes heavy with pigment and radiant color—Old Holland, Gamblin, Maimeri, Jack Richeson's Daniel Greene Professional Oils and some Winsor & Newton.

BRUSHES

Remember, oil paints have no odor—only the cleaners for your brushes do. Be gentle with the brushes, and they will last a long time. Silver Brush has a series called Grand Prix. They are responsive bristles, and in combination with a few Silver Brush Renaissance Sables, the artist can paint anything. Use the Silver Brush mop (traditionally a watercolor brush) with soft natural hairs to knock off lumps and edges where none should appear. Have a few synthetics around for long-lasting rough work. Silver Brush Ruby Satins are nice and affordable. Richeson has put out a new line of brushes that are very nice. Try lots of brushes to find the touch that works.

Do not forget to have some painting knives for nice, textural statements.

WHEN WORKING IN PASTEL

- Start with hard pastels.
- Enrich new layers, strengthening darks.
- Add lights with softest pastels.
- Finish with pastel pencils. A great trick is to use these instead of a blending device like a tortillion (rolled cardboard blending stick) or a cotton swab. Pastel pencil used with a light touch over the layered color allows a bit of pastel to be moved around with the benefit of the slightest adjustment in temperature or value.

These are wonderful for certain approaches to landscape portraits. The delicate Italian painting knives by Demco are slightly more flexible than the stiffer palette knives used more for cleaning the palette and mixing paint.

PASTELS

The delightful problem with pastels is that one can never have enough. All the different degrees of hard and soft display the most dazzling colors. Ampersand Pastelbord has tooth that permits layer after layer of application. The boards are archival and available in four pre-toned colors and white. Here, white is not a negative, as it can easily by toned with watercolors, inks, thinned acrylic, thinned oil or pastel dust, or sticks liquefied with pastel fixative or alcohol. A bottle of liquid fixative by Winsor & Newton or Latour, offered by Sennelier, makes quick work of putting a tone down on the canvas by pushing the liquefied pastel around with an old brush.

Using fixative is controversial. As a finish spray (aerosol or atomizer), fixative damages the images as the ingredients darken the lights and lighten the darks, changing all the carefully planned values of the hues. However, using fixative while laying out the underpainting or in the very earliest layers of color is a great tool. Learn to use all materials that will help achieve the desired final goal.

Many working pastel artists collect several full sets of a variety of brands. After acquiring several sets, fill unmet needs by buying individual open-stock colors later.

Learning to use pastels is, in a way, much the same as painting in oil. Applying the hardest pastels to the surface first will not fill the tooth too quickly, allowing the addition of softer pastels as darks transition into lights.

The juicier, heavier applications will be in the final layers. This equates to the "fat over lean" rule in oil painting, where the thin paints—typically the dark greens, blues, browns and black—are on the bottom, while the fattest paints are on top—the lights, typically the oranges, yellows and particularly reds. Holbein hard pastels are great for this; all of the pastel pencils work well, too. Be cautious not to incise the surface with pencils. Unison soft pastels, Terry Ludwig soft pastels (particularly the darks) and Sennelier soft pastels mid- and high-key ranges offer an amazing array of hues.

PAINTING IN WATERCOLOR

Watercolor is a terrific, versatile sketching medium. Always travel with a small portable set and waterproof ink drawing pens or flexible nib brushes like the ones made by Faber-Castell. The ease and simplicity of use, as well as cleanup, make it great for portraits and sketching.

Try different paints and brushes, but the ground is the most important thing. How the ground receives the paint makes all the difference. Pocket sets by Winsor & Newton or Sennelier are perfectly portable; some even have a water bottle included, making sketching in color anywhere very simple. Besides the brushes included in any of the sets, a couple of Silver Brush Black Velvet rounds, Cat's Tongues and a mop

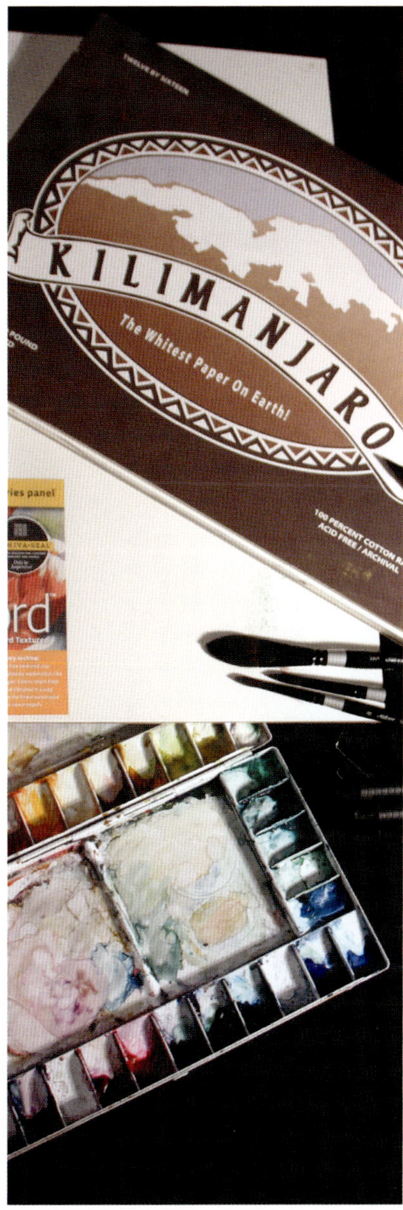

are most useful. Watercolor tablets and pads, like Kilimanjaro, are available in any size. If you want an archivally sound surface and choose to work vigorously with many layers of color or multimedia, Ampersand Aquabord holds an amazing amount of pigment and yet wipes away right down to the white surface when necessary.

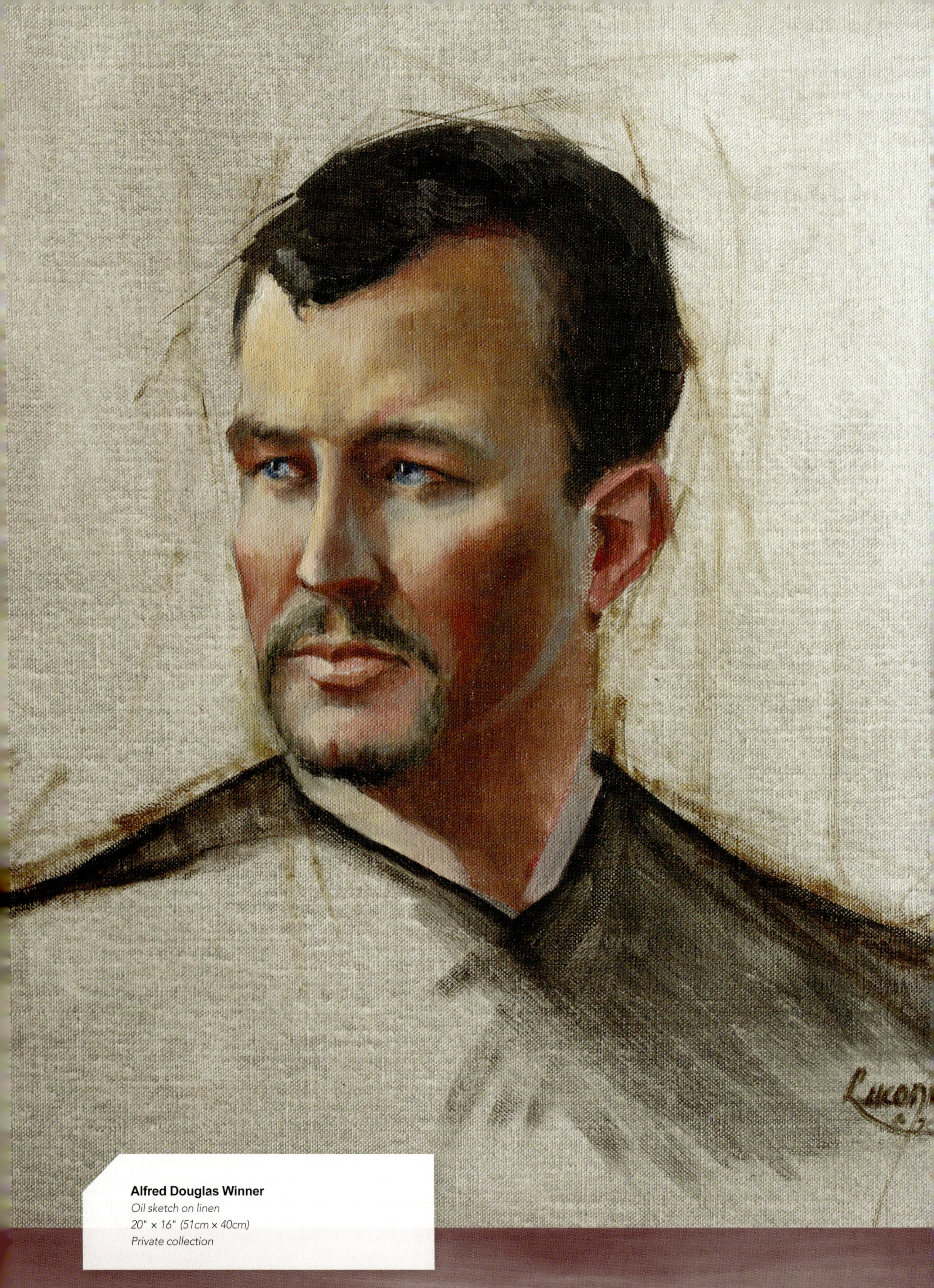

Alfred Douglas Winner
Oil sketch on linen
20" × 16" (51cm × 40cm)
Private collection

CHAPTER 1

REFERENCES, STUDIES & COMPOSITION

Drawing, painting and conversation are the key skills needed to succeed at portrait painting. Distracting and calming the sitter by initiating relaxed conversation about subjects that interest them will keep the sitting enjoyable for them and efficient for you. Without worry of stilted, awkward expressions from the "snapshot syndrome," trust your eyes and hands to gather beautifully rendered reference sketches. Make them fluid with comfortable, natural expressions.

Do not rush this essential stage of developing the painting. The key components of a functional sketch, to be used while your subject is away, are to control the focus and draftsmanship, and to mold the form into a believable three-dimensional representation.

"Speed, is there anything more stupid?... People will tell you in the most natural way: In two days you must be able to draw... But there is nothing that can be done without the patient collaboration of time."
—Edgar Degas

The Eyes Have It
This quick sketch leaves no doubt that the focus is the eyes.

CONTROL THE VIEWER'S ORDER OF SIGHT

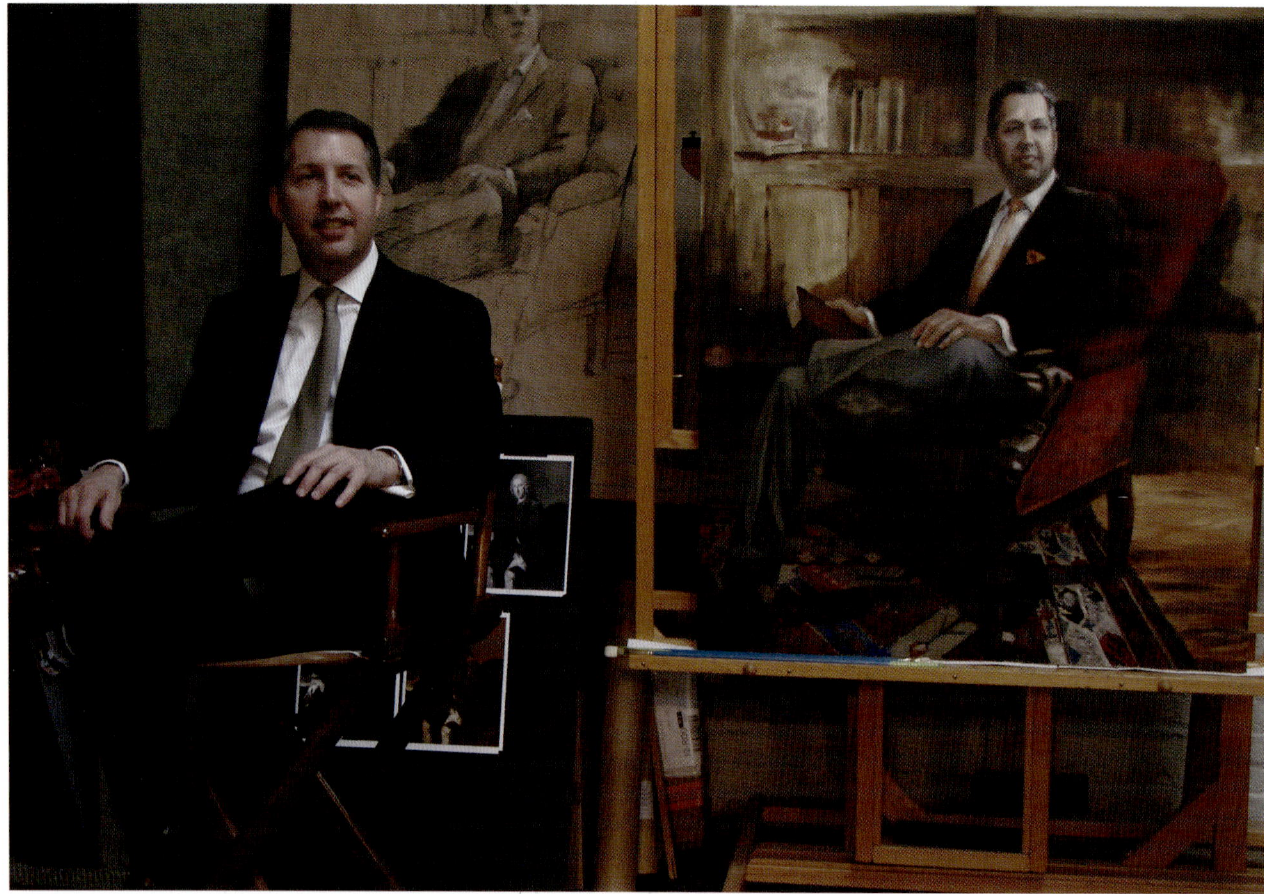

Abundant References Act as a Model
The importance of reference collection comes in the studio when all the graphite sketches, the accurate head sketch and the full-size charcoal/chalk sketch act as your models for the laying in of the tonal underpainting.

Your eyes are sensitive and intuitively perceive things automatically. The eyes seek out light, bright color and hard edges as they focus rapidly on objects. Knowing this, the artist can control where the viewer looks. The painting needs to grab the viewer's attention so they will stay a while and wander through the image to really see what you are expressing.

There are three ways to control where and in what order the viewer will observe your painting. This is true for all paintings, whether portrait, landscape, still life or abstract. These methods are:

- Capture the viewer's initial glance by placing the highest contrasts of value side by side.
- Place the highest contrast of complementary colors side by side.
- Use the sharpest lines in one concentrated place so the viewer will focus there first.

But before we can create a great representative painting of the subject, preliminary studies are the best way to study mannerisms, expressions, interactions and body language.

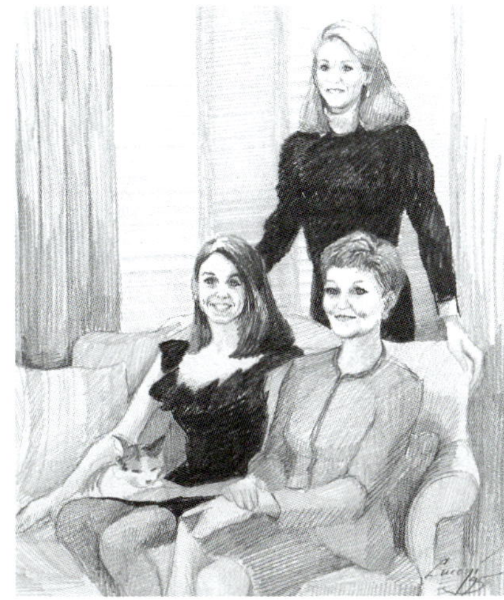

Control the Viewer's Focus

This sketch was done in preparation for a 46" × 38" (117cm × 97cm) oil painting. Strong triangular design allows travel of the eye and movement all around the composition. High value contrast from the black velvet dress on the elder daughter in the background to her mother's soft pink skin and blonde hair in the foreground frames her face and brings focus to her.

Doggett Women
Graphite sketch on bristol board
14" × 11" (36cm × 28cm)
Private collection

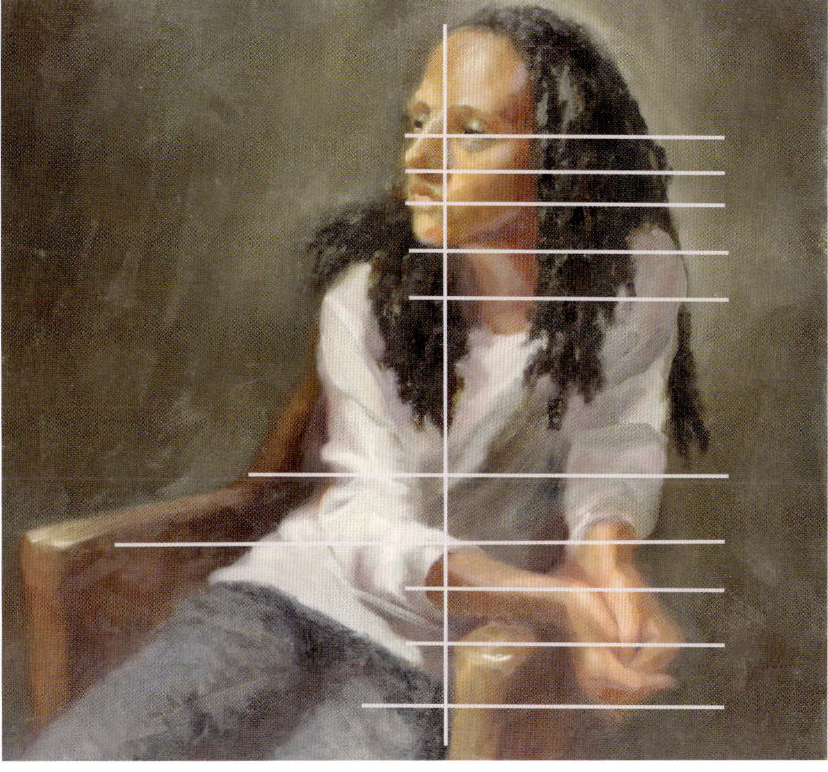

Find Intersecting Reference Points

Use a vertical line as a base from which you can locate various key points. Using intersections, locate the eyes, nose, mouth, chin and outside shapes, including shoulders, hands and the chair.

Dana, the Artist's Intern
Oil on linen
20" × 24" (51cm × 61cm)
Private collection

Keen observation is the key to strong values and accurate color mixtures. Whether sketching in color or only in tone, this is the time to study and see how everything relates.

Everything is relative. Every line relates to the adjoining edge, and every plane relates to the ones touching it. Every shadow relates to the light it hides from and every color relates to the surrounding colors.

Be patient as you sketch. Slowly alter minor refinements as you adjust an edge here, change a direction line there and strengthen a value. Slowly, the image will appear. Consider every move you make, as each approach to the paper should improve the image.

Keep economy of line, plane, tone and color in mind. Every stroke must count. Each one should be there because you deliberately meant it to be.

A painting or drawing is simply a series of corrections and every new stroke brings you closer to the most exact expression and representation of the subject.

Draftsmanship is the key to a solid foundation. These skills include outline, shadow line, shadow pattern, background and modeling.

THE OUTLINE

Leonardo da Vinci taught us that the two chief elements in the expression of form are the outside shape (outline) and the edge of the shadow.

Collect drawn data taking measurements by using the sight-sizing method or geometric shape

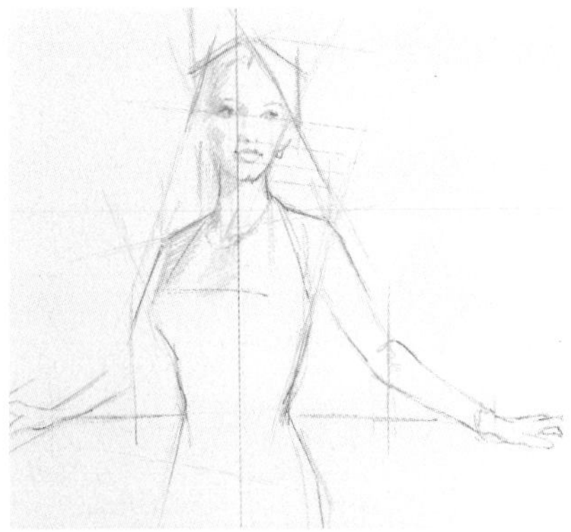

Build From a Center Axis
An additional variation of this method is shown here in a detail from a 11" × 14" (28cm × 36cm) graphite on bristol board. The vertical line is intersected by angled lines delineating the tilt of the features on the head, the opposing tilt of the shoulders and the opposing tilt of the hips, all while still helping to locate the outside shapes.

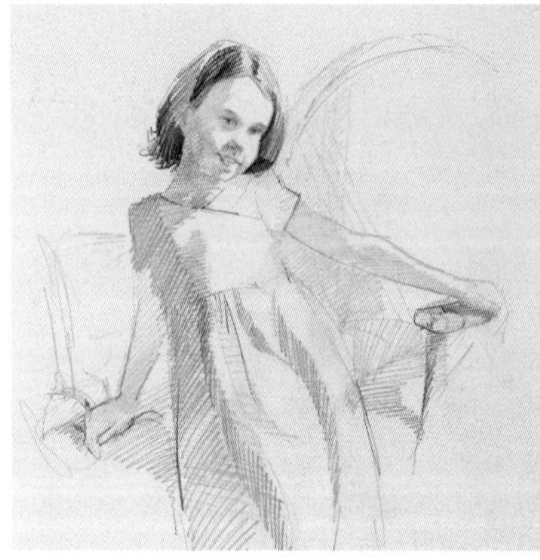

A Continuous Shadow
The shadow travels in one continuous form down the side of this child. If drawn in two values, there would be a light side as she extends her left arm into the sun and a shadow side from the top of her head to her right knee.

Amelia
Preliminary graphite on bristol board
14" × 11" (36cm × 28cm)
Private collection

analysis for the outlines of the largest shapes. Then proceed in this order:

- Establish points of reference on the vertical line.
- Hold a plumb line at arm's length, and choose the necessary horizontal notes.
- Place these intersections on your vertical mark on the paper or canvas.
- Measure with the plumb line from the vertical to the outermost contour points.
- Using these marks as a guide, create an outline.

THE SHADOW LINE

This is the line dividing the light and shadow because it falls across the form. This is one of the most important elements of the drawing because it describes the topography of the form.

If the outline or footprint has been drawn reasonably well, the next step will be simple. Study only the larger shadow shape and create only a flat mass keeping the shape simple. Maintain the edge of the shadow sharp until the shape is correct. Then model to the appropriate degree of softness as needed.

Do not confuse this area by breaking it up into halftones and reflected lights.

THE SHADOW PATTERN

In nature, there are thousands of variations of values between black and white. For our purposes, start with three and then build to about eight value variations.

Three values of dark, middle and light are easily accomplished in a heightened charcoal and chalk study. Using toned paper as your middle value, establish the form with charcoal as your darkest value and complete the dimensional quality by placing the light in with chalk.

Simplifying every quick sketch in this manner realizes quicker, more accurate results. As skills develop, expanding to a working knowledge of eight to ten values will bring refinement to the work.

By massing values, we connect all closely related values by organizing all of these areas into larger, simpler shapes or groupings. This process of massing not only simplifies the painting but can give the final design a powerful punch at the focal point.

Always work dark to light. The painting loses its vitality of values and colors if you apply them in reverse order. The rich darks are drained of their life when applied over the lights. However, the light shimmers and sparkles over the rich dark tones that are applied as a foundation.

BACKGROUND

Transform the linear drawing into a tonal drawing by blocking in the background. Try to keep the background slightly lighter or higher key than in nature to play off the aerial perspective. Using a tortillion, stump or chamois to efficiently push the charcoal or graphite is the same as using a brush to push buttery paint around the background. Again, maintain simplicity. Do not rush. Complex background tones often

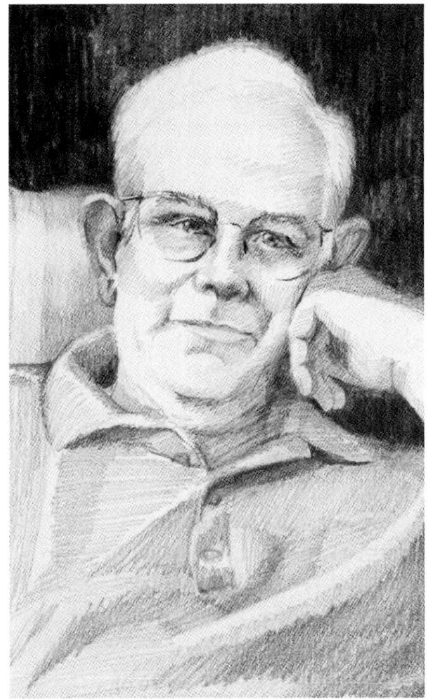

Tom Campbell: The Relaxed Expression
Strong values and a comfortable expression make this a great reference tool when the model is not present.

Tom Campbell
North Carolina Hall of Fame broadcaster, producer and television host
Detail, graphite on bristol board
14" × 11" (36cm × 28cm)
Private collection

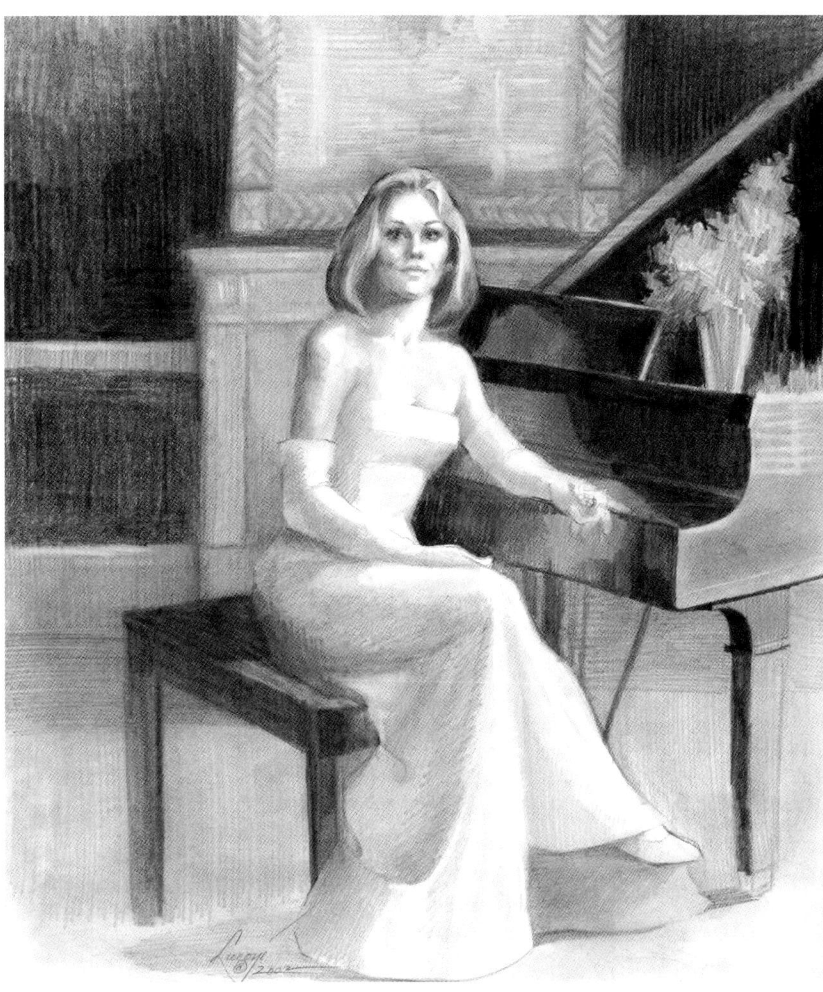

Jaclyn: The Reliable Sketch
This strong sketch can easily "sit in" when the model has left.

Jaclyn
Graphite on bristol board
14" × 11" (36cm × 28cm)
Private collection

detract from the subject. Details are best saved for the focal point in the drawing.

MODELING

With the foundation drawing established and the basic shapes designed, an introduction of simple, broad values is now in place in the light, shadow pattern and background. More modeling can carry the drawing into a more complete form.

Halftones can be carried out a shade lighter so the transition from light to dark does not become muddy or dirty looking. Go into the shadows to darken and increase the value range and thus create a more dramatic effect.

Building the form takes shape with the slow development of values as they move the form in and out of the light. The halftones carry the form from dark to light.

Create depth and perspective by modeling values. Softer values, hues and edges will give the form roundness and dimension.

The ability to neutralize color, control values and maintain controlled edges adds up to the most successful rendering. This is our goal.

SIGHT SIZING VS. GEOMETRIC SHAPES

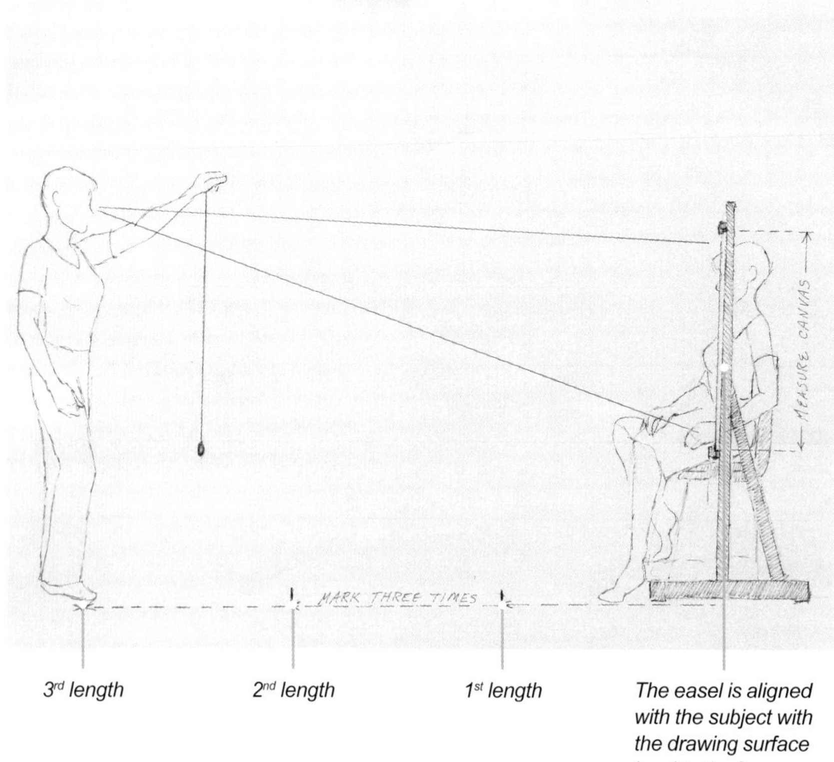

The easel is aligned with the subject with the drawing surface level to the face.

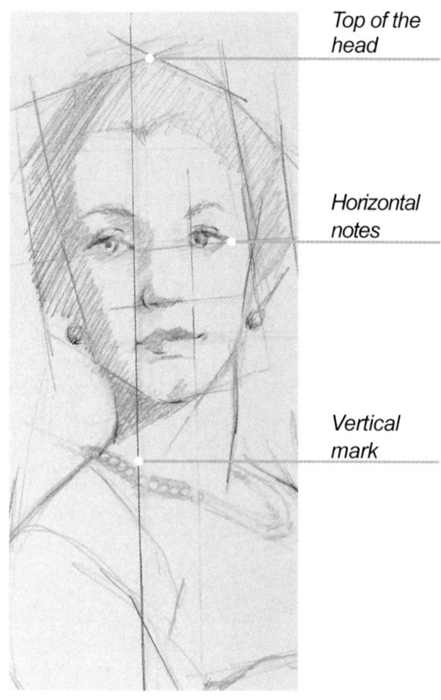

Use the plumb line to determine where at least three or more horizontal notes intersect the vertical mark. Mark the top of the head on the canvas.

For hundreds of years, the academies in Europe have been training students to draw accurately from the cast or model by sight sizing. Art and science are inextricably intertwined, and this process involves a method that has been passed down for generations.

SIGHT SIZING

- The easel is aligned next to the subject with the drawing surface level to the plane of the face.
- Make a vertical mark down the canvas with thinned paint or charcoal on paper. It is from this vertical line that all measurements will be determined.
- At the Florence Academy of Art in Italy, a thin cord is used, heavier than thread but not as heavy as thin rope, with a lead weight like a plumb line. Using this method, measure the greatest length that the painting will encompass—head and shoulders, half body with hands, etc. Measure three lengths on the floor, starting from the surface of the canvas, and tape or mark the floor at this point.
- Standing on the third mark with your arm fully extended, hold the plumb line out in front of the model so that at least three or more horizontal notes will intersect the vertical mark. Make a mental note of the top of the head. Advance to the canvas and mark it on the vertical line.
- Return to the mark on floor. Observe the next intersection and make a mental note, advance to the canvas, place the mark. Repeat this until all vertical markings appear along the original vertical, and then continue the process with horizontal marks outward from this vertical line.

The resulting drawing is painstakingly slow, but extremely accurate and life-sized. And the exercise of back and forth movement will keep you fresh and alert.

It works.

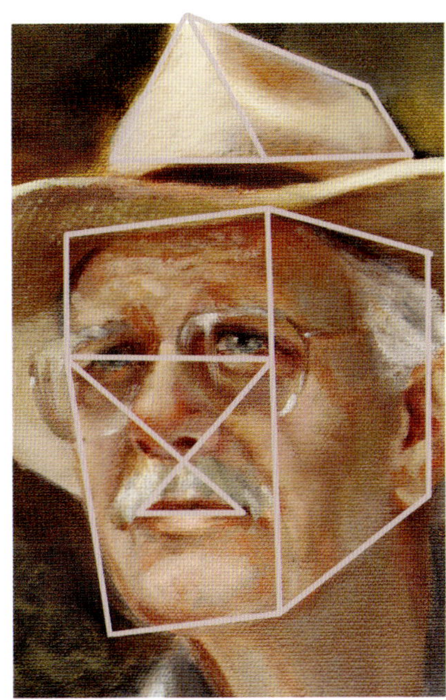

GEOMETRIC SHAPES

An artist can translate any complex composition from landscape to still life to figure by simply breaking down large elements into simple geometric shapes. Somehow this makes the process much less intimidating. When all the large objects are placed on the canvas with circles, squares, rectangles and triangles, consider how these shapes expand to three dimensions by adjusting them to spheres, cylinders, cubes and cones. The organic feel of these natural shapes and the simplicity of this approach make easy work of the most complex design.

THE SHAPE OF NATURE

"May I repeat what I told you here: treat nature by means of the cylinder, the sphere, the cone, everything brought into proper perspective so that each side of an object or a plane is directed towards a central point."
—Paul Cézanne in a letter to Émile Bernard, April 15, 1904

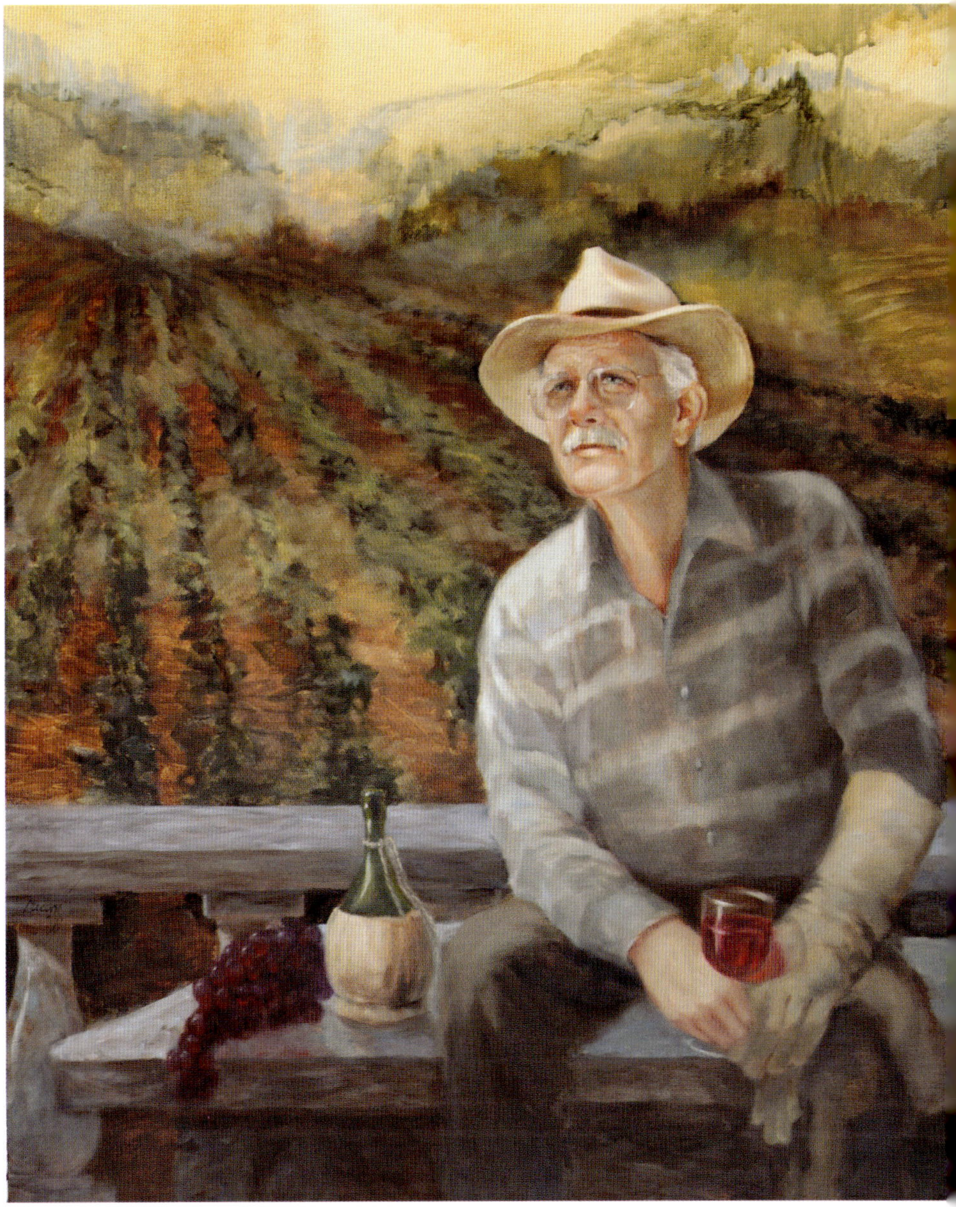

The Vintner, Tuscany
Oil on gallery wrap canvas
40" × 30" (102cm × 77cm)
Private collection

VALUES CONTROL FORM

Everything is relative. Value to value, color to color, nuance to nuance. Keep values strong and distinctly different. Make a statement; don't wimp out. Think in planes.

The head will always appear more three-dimensional when you use powerful value changes from dark to light. If the shadow line carves the correct shape, the likeness will appear. Values are the biggest key to your success with likeness.

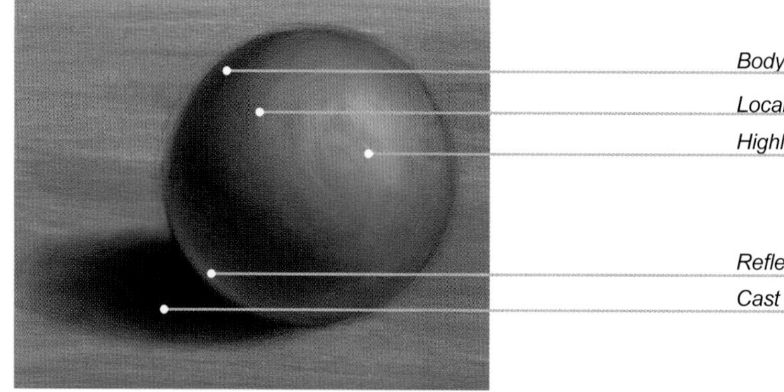

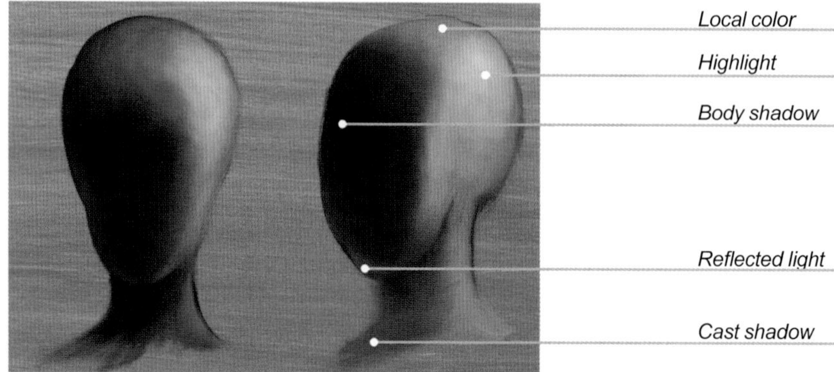

VALUE SCALE

A value scale is of great help in clarifying a problem in a painting. Often, to push or pull an object in or out of the picture plane involves only the correct value in a monochromatic painting or drawing. In color work, the problem may be solved with correct value and/or the correct color temperature.

A wonderful exercise for beginning to advanced students is to create your own value scale in your favorite medium. Using a piece of bristol board, rag board or illustration board, mark off ten one- to two-inch squares in a single row. Make the tenth square the darkest black you can achieve with your medium. Move to square number nine and reduce the value by ten percent. Continue across the row until you reach number one, which will remain white.

The second tool to determine correct values is a sheet of colored acetate (red or blue are most commonly used). In antique photos of old-time movie directors, you see them with a monocular hanging from their neck to check scenes; this was a blue lens that gave them a clearer understanding of how the scene would look on the black-and-white film they were shooting. It works for us as well.

THE FIVE ELEMENTS OF EVERY FORM

Every item in a painting has five elements. This is true whether you are painting or drawing a single object, a building, a mountain, a tree in the meadow or a person. Look for these:

- **Highlight:** The highest key spot at the point where the light strikes most directly and intensely. This will be the highest, lightest value.

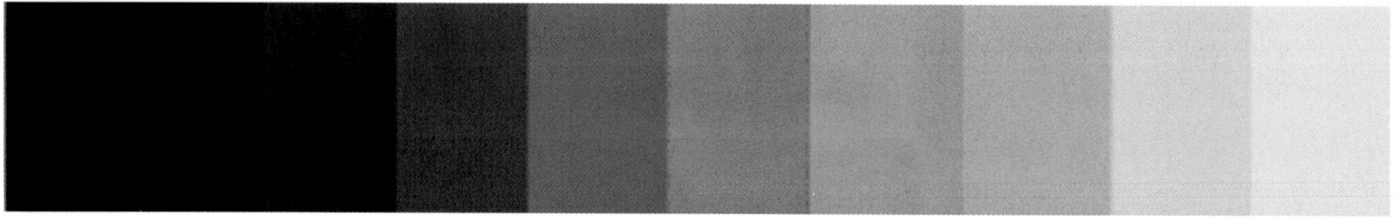

Ten-Value Scale

- **Local or body color:** The body tone flooded with light where we can observe the truest color and value. This may be in a mid-range value.

- **Body shadow:** The area of the form that turns away from the light. A dark value.

- **Cast shadow:** The shadow created by the object blocking the light and throwing a shadow on an adjacent surface. A dark value affected by the texture of the surface.

- **Reflected light:** Light bouncing off nearby surfaces back onto the shadow side of the object. This will be lighter than the body shadow or the cast shadow but not as light as the highlight or local body color.

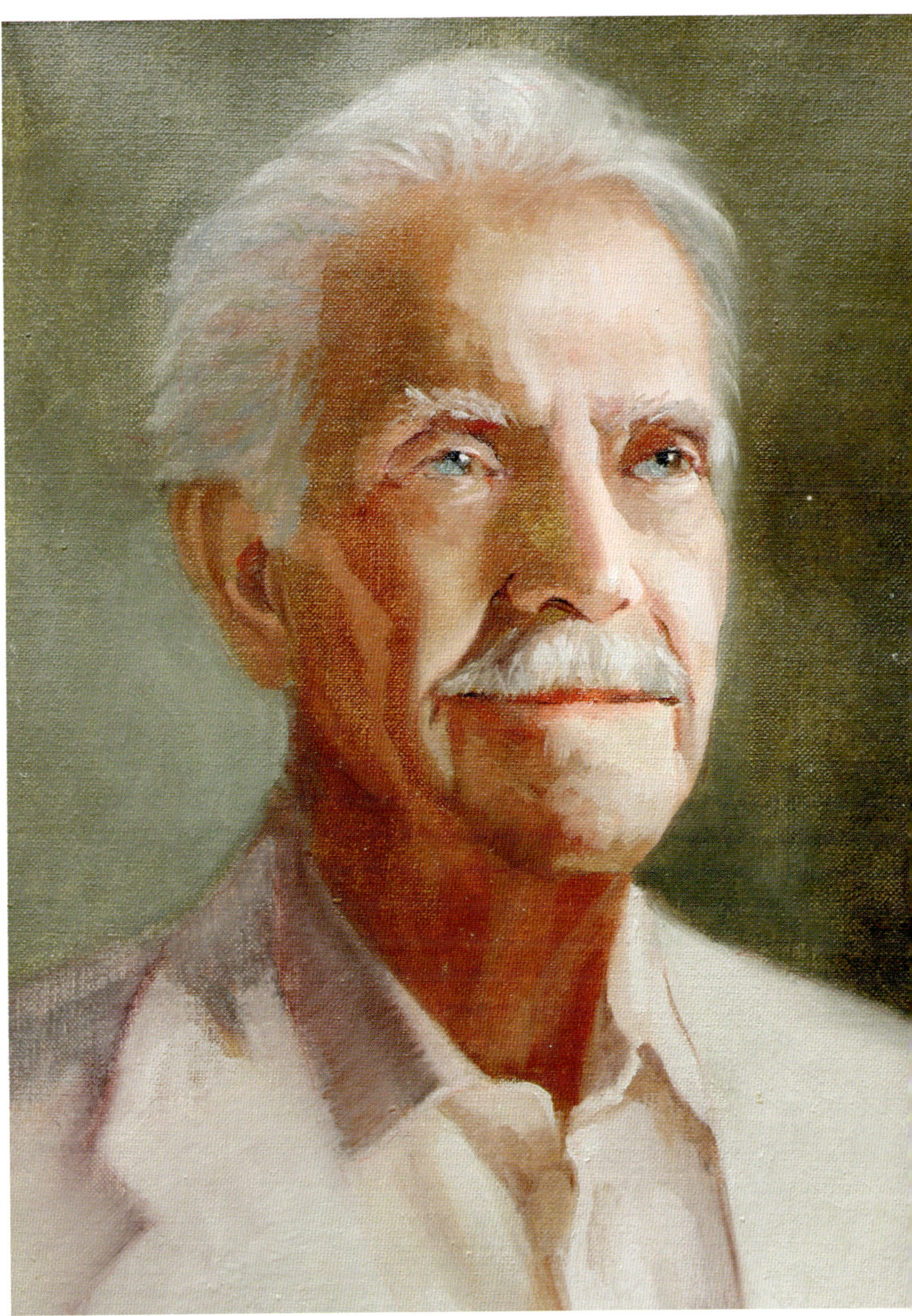

Five Elements of Light and Shadow

Find the highlight, local color, body shadow, cast shadow and reflected light on this gentleman's portrait.

Alfredo
Oil on Claessens linen
20" × 16" (51cm × 41cm)
Private collection

COMPOSING THE STORY

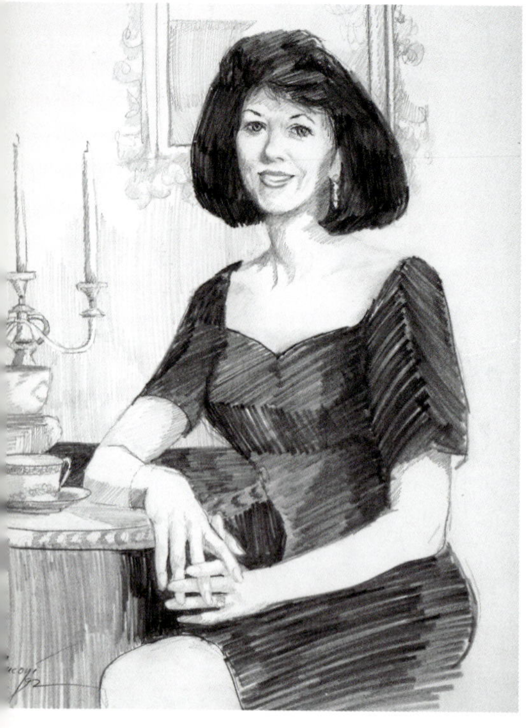

Elegant Style
Though sketches were started in a beautiful living room, this client's stories lead to the dining room with antique silver and china—the perfect background to tell her story to future generations who will eat from that same china.

Mrs. Michael Patterson
Preliminary graphite on bristol board
14" × 11" (36cm × 28cm)
Private collection

NATURE'S MATHEMATICAL BALANCE

Fibonacci was perhaps the greatest mathematician of the Middle Ages. Fibonacci recognized a series in nature: 1, 1, 2, 3, 5, 8, 13, 21, etc. where the third number is the sum of the two preceding numbers. This is called the Golden Ratio, or phi. It is the foundation of math and design from trigonometry to architecture and fine art.

The Golden Ratio, or the Golden Mean, is the ratio of 1.618 and can be observed throughout the basic design of nature. The individual bones in the hand from the tips of the fingers to the base of the wrist increase by the proportion of 1.618. The length from the shoulder to the fingertips, divided by the length from the elbow to the fingertips, is also 1.618. Scientists have found this ratio in the branches of trees, veins in leaves, the geometry of crystals and more. This universal relationship or ratio offers the most pleasing arrangement of design in our paintings as well.

When painting groups of things, look at that group as a unit with a unique silhouette and a rhythm of movement. Don't lose sight of maintaining the person or persons in the portrait as the main focal point. The smaller, multifaceted details may help to tell the story, but can easily overwhelm the subject. Use these extraneous objects with caution and care.

Find a new way to say what has been said before. This is the hardest part of the job to create the painting. You have to think! How can there be one more painting of a little Southern girl in a white dress and bare feet? Well, getting to know her and her personality, her likes and dislikes, her family's likes and dislikes will help a great deal. But ultimately, it is up to you to guide them to a beautiful resolution of design.

Play to the whole. Draw the viewer in. Smell the fragrance of the garden. Don't count the flowers behind your subject. Capture the giggle in the siblings without staring at their teeth. Share the warmth of the sun on the rocks by the brook without losing focus on the boy leaning on the tree with his dog beside him. Draw the viewer in and expose him to the environment of the painting.

Stir emotions. Remind the viewer of a time long ago in his life. Give great-grandmother's china teacup a place of importance in this family heirloom portrait. Give the viewer a taste of something new and interesting in an old landscape on the farmland in the background. Show the boardroom, library or office in a manner that encourages the viewer to enter and see more. This is more than just about the person. It is a painting about the person and her life. Make the viewer feel that.

This involves work and dedication, practice and failure—and above all, persistence.

BASIC ELEMENTS OF DESIGN

Here are some basic elements to keep in mind:

- **Placement** Use the rule of the Golden Mean to design beautiful compositions as all of nature has designed. A simple explanation is to divide the picture plane into thirds in both directions. At two of those intersections, you have the opportunity to place a focal point and an opposing secondary focal point with beauty and balance.

- **Focal Point** Never place your subject in the direct center. This should be the controlling solo spot that all other elements in the painting support.

- **Unity** Unity of line, design, movement and color will produce a more harmonious painting.

- **Variety** Allow objects to overlap to create additional depth, or separate them completely. Variety of texture, value and surface add interest. This should include contrast of light and dark patterns—use cast shadows to tie the composition together and allow the path of light to connect and travel through space.

- **Rhythm** Movement through the painting should direct you from the primary subject to the secondary subject. It should allow you to travel with the light source through the painting as the light gently touches each of the important areas and dissipates as the light moves farther from the focal point.

- **Harmony** There should be harmony of color, line and movement. There should be nothing jarring to take the attention away from the main subject.

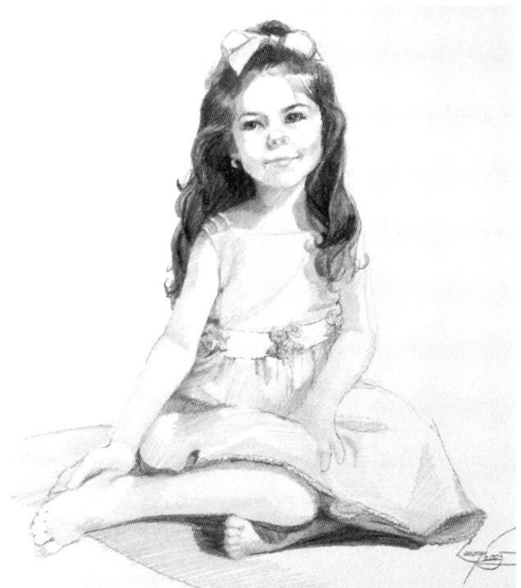

Personality

This little lady with the big bow could not have been more charming. The simple, elegant triangular design of this sketch provided a straightforward rendering to help build the painting.

Teagan Haskin

Graphite preliminary on bristol board
14" × 11" (36cm × 28cm)
Private collection

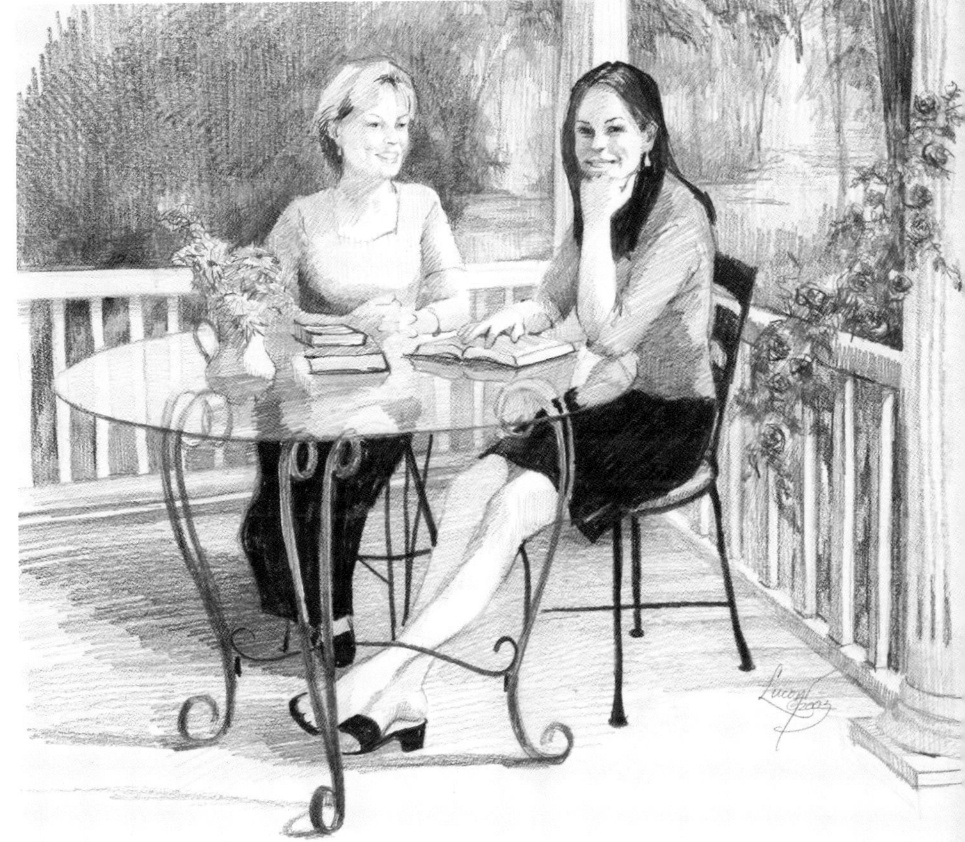

Sharing Time Together

Dr. McLaurin and her daughter share the love of reading and said that when together, they often find themselves on the front porch of their antique home reading.

Dr. Anne McLaurin and Daughter Emily

Graphite sketch
11" × 14" (28cm × 36cm)
Private collection

MAKING TONAL STUDIES

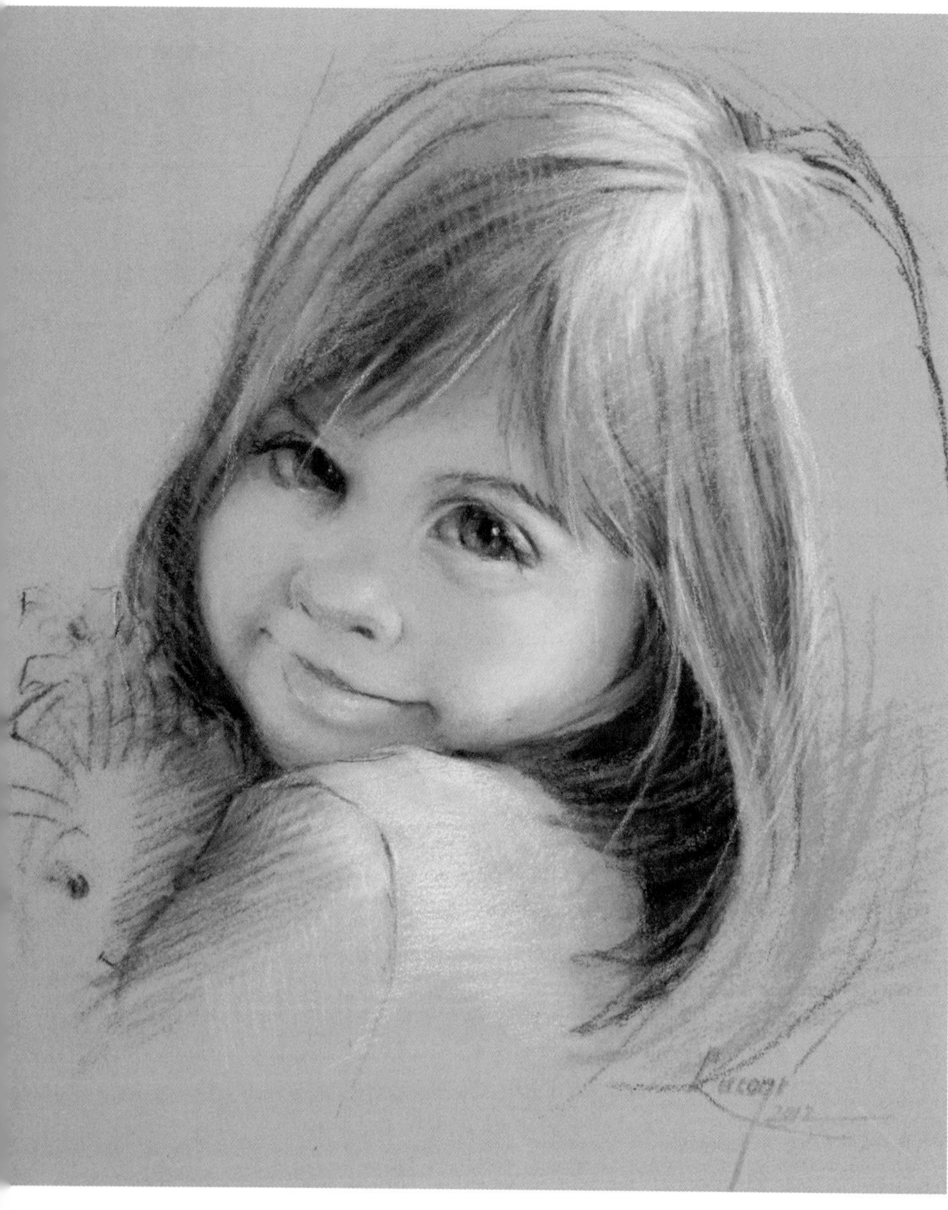

Quick Tonal Sketch

Put down your darks in charcoal first. Highlight with a few lights in chalk. Let the toned board do the rest of the work, and you're done!

Kiri
Charcoal and pastel on Ampersand Pastelbord—sand tone
10" × 8" (25cm × 20cm)
Private collection

Draw the way a sculptor sculpts. Begin with the large masses and refine down to the specific details. Learn to think in planes instead of lines. When carving the head and face out of the empty canvas, use large, distinct values to create the movement of one flat plane to the next.

Simplify everything: your subject, design, your planned layout and your sketched lay-in. Be bold in the start. Block in the darks as single large masses. Work from dark to light—proven through history to be the strongest approach.

Placing the painting or drawing on the canvas should never take more time than a few bars of music takes to play. Find the rhythm of the form quickly.

Everything is relative. Every line relates to the edge next to it. Every plane relates to those touching it. Every shadow relates to the light it hides from, and every color relates to the colors it is surrounding and is surrounded by.

CHARCOAL AND CHALK

Work on a variety of surfaces to find the ones that give you the results you expect. Work with a variety of hard and soft charcoal to achieve different textures and effects. Hard charcoal is useful for certain effects, but be cautious as it may damage the surface of soft papers if used too vigorously.

Start a drawing with vine charcoal on any ground. Using a middle-value tone will permit you to apply your darkest darks first, then your lights. Place the drawing on the surface with vine charcoal, which is very easy to

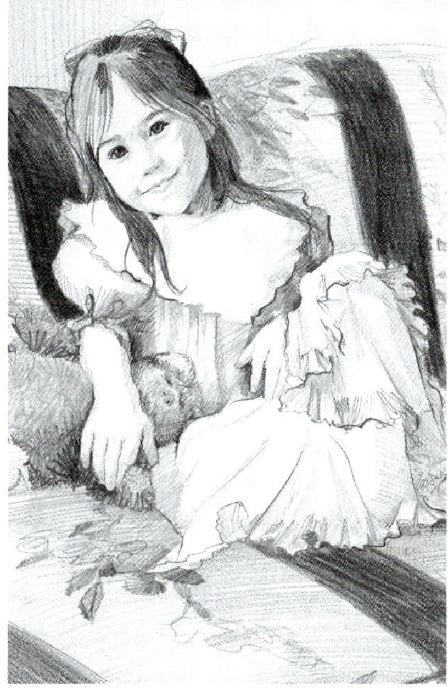

Charming Children

The charming child is often the most relaxed and cooperative. Be truly interested in what they have to say. When you gain their confidence, they relax into poses you would never try to set up.

Sarah Grace Latham
Graphite on bristol board
14" × 11"(36cm × 28cm)
Private collection

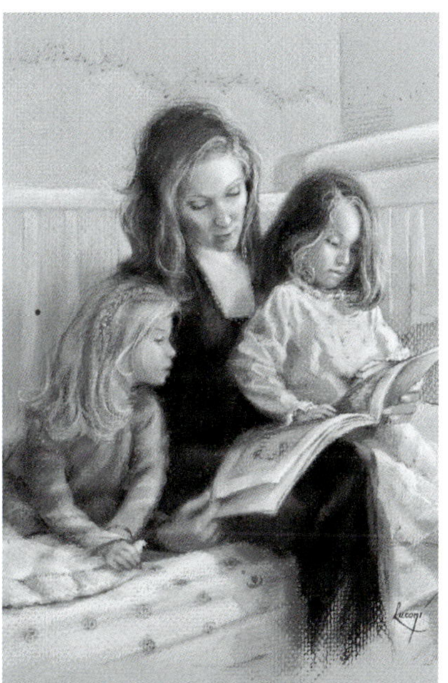

A Natural Diversion

To paint active, healthy children, use natural ways to slow them down, as in this engaging storytime scene.

When preparing the preliminary sketch, take time to finish a few to a finer level. This may lead to an additional income stream.

Story Time
Charcoal and chalk on Strathmore Grayscale paper
16" × 12" (41cm × 30cm)
Private collection

FINEST THREADS

When a parent worries about the child's insistence on a favorite outfit, whether as a cowboy, a superhero, a ragged shirt, a bathing suit or oddly mismatched clothes, do a few sketches in that outfit for the child first. You will gain the children's confidence and cooperation, have some fun and then be able proceed in traditional street clothes for the parents.

manipulate and remove, then build the values with different layers of soft and hard charcoal to get the desired effects, and finish with a few choice highlights in chalk. Use stumps, tortillions, chamois, felt, rags, cotton swabs and kneadable erasers to achieve variety in line and texture.

GRAPHITE SKETCHES

Graphite is quick, extremely portable and clean in comparison to charcoal. Use a variety of hard and soft graphite pencils to produce drawings that have the strength and richness of charcoals. Most of the graphite sketches in this book were done on white Strathmore bristol vellum finish unless otherwise listed.

Start with a hard 4H and a very light touch so as not to incise the paper. As you sneak up on the placement and design, change to the darker and softer pencils to design the shadows. Come back into the light to develop the high middle tones. The white of the paper remains your highest value.

Smudge and blend with tools—never your fingers—or try value variations with hatching and crosshatching marks of distinct, clear parallel lines across and with the form. Woven layers of lines become stronger and deeper in value, giving a cleaner, etching-like effect. The more you work, the sooner you will find a rhythm of your own.

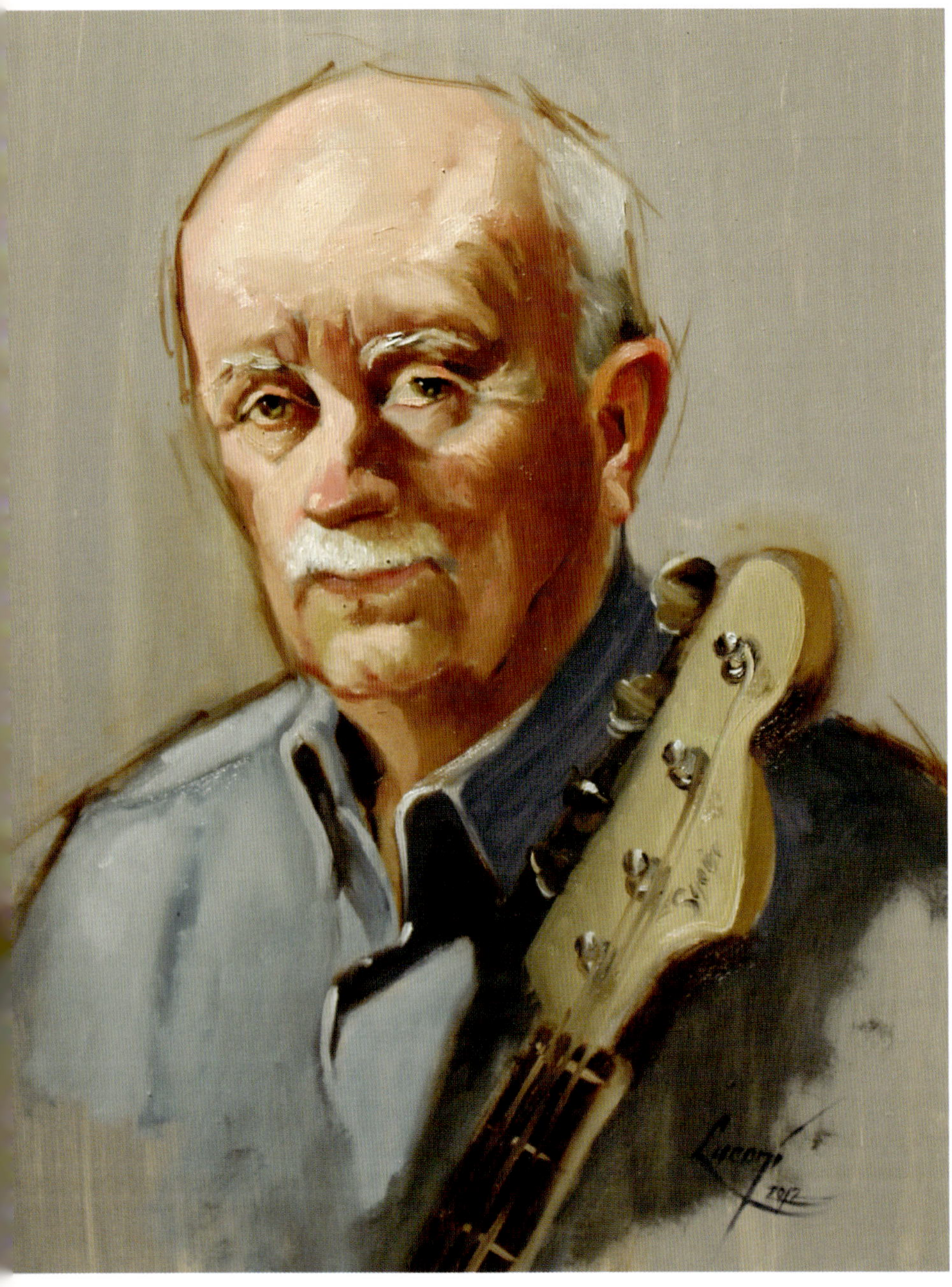

The 90-Minute Oil Study

The beauty of the quick color study is that the sitter has little time to be self-conscious. By the time you have discussed the pending portrait, discussed locations, talked about back stories and potential props, the study is done.

Edward B. Williams, Jr.
Director, Food and Drug Protection Division, NC Department of Agriculture
Oil preliminary study on Ampersand Gessobord
20" × 16" (51cm × 41cm)
Private collection

STUDIES IN OIL

Everything is relative: value to value, color to color, nuance to nuance. Color is where the magic comes together. Working from dark, thin paint to light, thick paint, all the elements come together to build a believable, three-dimensional world on a two-dimensional surface. Magic!

Make a conscious decision to create a painting in high-key tints or low-key darker shades. Set the tone and mood of the painting by choosing the quality of the color, whether highly saturated pigment or muted tones. Use your color studies to experiment with these properties of paint and color.

Whether working out a color plan for an overall composition or collecting specific color data for the construction of the head, hair, skin and eyes, react to the subject, setting and locale. Everything around you is sending off color responses. Respond. React. Record it.

These are the notes you collect on color at this stage, regardless of medium. As if you were taking shorthand notes in color and most often with limited time, choose a carefully limited palette, react to what you have before you, move with confidence and some speed, and the results will be valuable when you return to the studio.

Give the painting harmony throughout the canvas by the use of a unified color theme. Often this can take a good-quality painting into the realm of a great painting. As an exercise, consider doing a color sketch with a limited palette of three or four colors and black and white. The overall results will be more harmonious, elements will relate better, and the color design will flow with a lovely rhythm.

STUDIES IN WATERCOLOR

Watercolors always bring out the child in us. Remember the excitement of that first water-soluble set? Why be inhibited as an adult? Using water-based paint affords us freedom and speed to sketch in color and try out different ideas.

If you are more comfortable using toned grounds with opaque mediums, experiment with tinted papers or try floating a tint all over a page and letting it dry before beginning the image. It provides a richer finish and an overall harmony to enhance the color plan. Use this especially if preparing a low-value, dark, rich-finished (tapestry-like) watercolor with the look of an oil painting. Try using a surface that can take a beating and still continue to receive and release pigment as needed. Ampersand Aquabord has given watercolorists a grand, durable and brilliant surface to play on.

Although traditionalists will tell you to work transparent watercolors from the white of the paper building outward to the very darkest shade, try this: After applying a tint overall, determine your dark passages and go into them first with a medium dark approach and very soft edges. Build the structure throughout with medium values leaving your lights alone. Then plug in the really rich darkest values at the end to complete the image.

And remember, just have fun! Bright and bold or quiet and somber—use your watercolors all the time. They are the perfect sketching medium with minimal travel, cleaning and usage issues. With or without graphite under drawings, just sketch and color away—let your intuitive inner child artist out!

SOME KEY TERMS

High key: Colors and values on the lighter high end of the value scale with value 1 as white and down to only middle 4 or 5.
Middle key: Very closely related values all falling in the middle range of the value scale and never using extremely light or extremely dark values. A painting could contain as few as three or four values from value 4 to 7.
Low key: Created all in dark values. No light values (values 1 to 4 or 5) appear anywhere in the painting, and all values are contained on the low end of the scale using values 6 to 10.
Tone: Refers to a color's intensity or saturation, strength of color/pigment.
Tint: A lighter, less intense value or saturation of color/pigment.
Shade: A medium or darker, grayed color.
Chiaroscuro: Italian "chiaro" = bright, clear; and "scuro" = obscured, dark. Used in describing effects of light and shadow, and the design of the light/dark pattern in an artwork.

STUDIES IN PASTEL

Pastels are the most amazing medium. The variety of loose sketch quality to full painterly finish gives it a wonderful versatility. If you want to see how the oil painting will turn out, do a small finished sketch in pastel. Or use it to

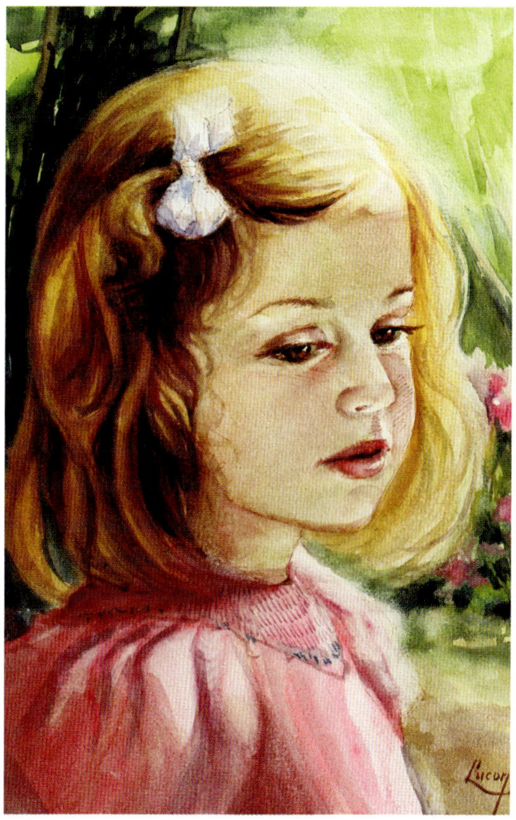

Watercolor: A Natural for Children

The clear, transparent color and speed of watercolor make it a natural match when working with children. When planning a larger oil, pastel or watercolor, the 10" × 8"(25cm ×20cm) quick sketch will hold all the key elements.

Leighton Livengood
Watercolor on Ampersand Aquabord
10" × 8" (26cm × 21cm)
Private collection

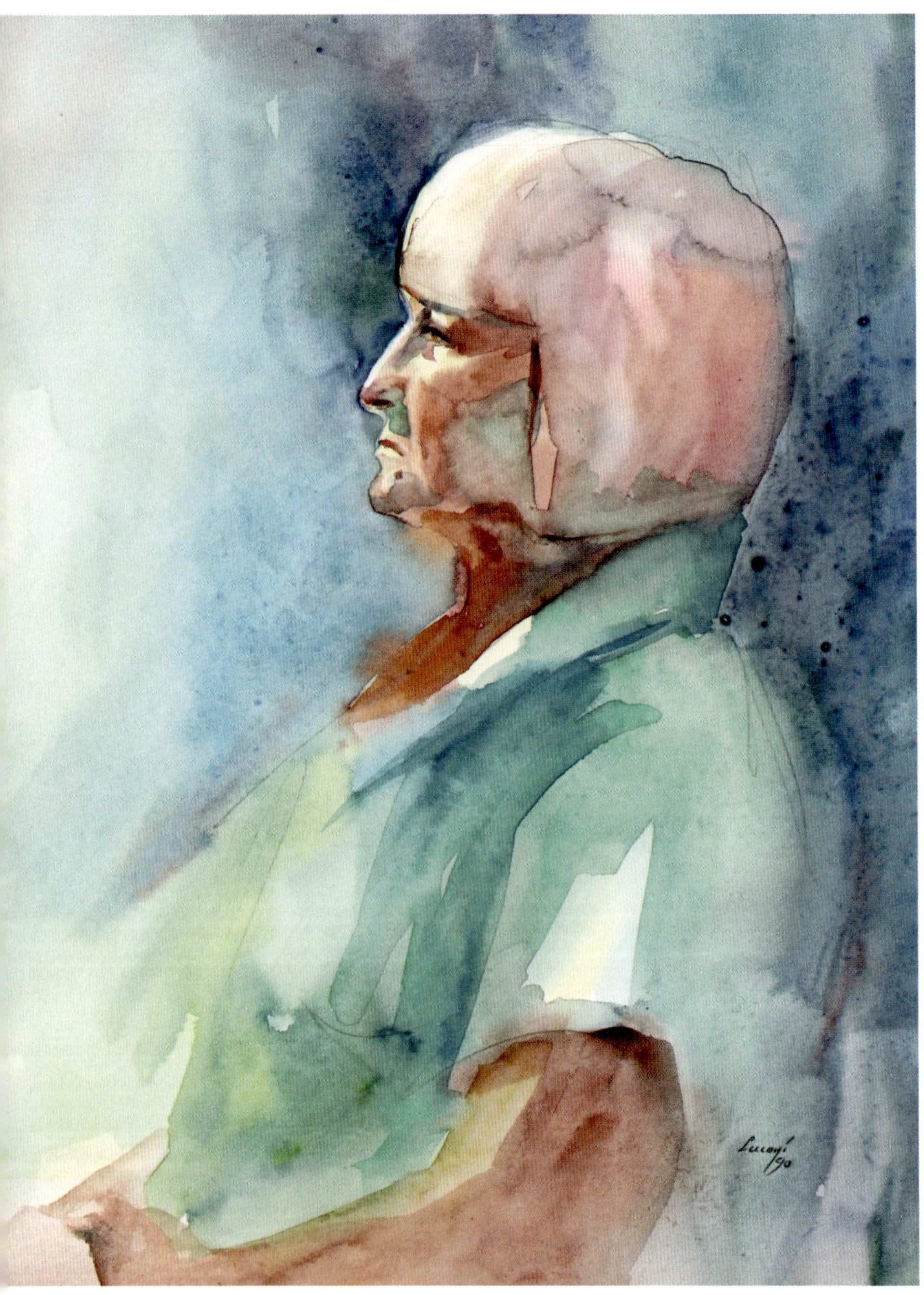

expand a monochromatic sketch into full color. The possibilities are endless.

The richness of saturated color, the stability of its archival quality (no oil to oxidize) and the ease of use are all special qualities of pastel. Now that we have so many manufacturers of colors, there are endless possibilities of what we can accomplish with the pigments. Take time to build a collection of color. Purchase all different degrees of hard and soft sticks in stores where there are drawers of open stock. Be adventurous. Be the kid in the candy store. Respond and react to the colors. Experiment and find what suits your hands and temperament best.

Start with hard pastels or pastel pencils to lay out the painting's footprint and establish the darks without filling the tooth of the ground. Then move on to layers of subsequently softer and lighter colors. This is the same as painting thin darks to thick lights in oil. It is a natural transition—same mindset.

Thin strokes in delicate tints and subtle patterns or bold, lively, saturated crayon-box colors—determine what suits your nature and personality best and develop it.

The Joy of Watercolor

Each medium has its own idiosyncrasies. I particularly love it when the medium is used as it is intended. In this quick sketch, the slap-dash technique really helped capture this German model/actress/artist's true colorful nature.

Breezy
Watercolor on Arches 300lb (640gsm) hot-pressed paper
14" × 11" (36cm × 28cm)
Private collection

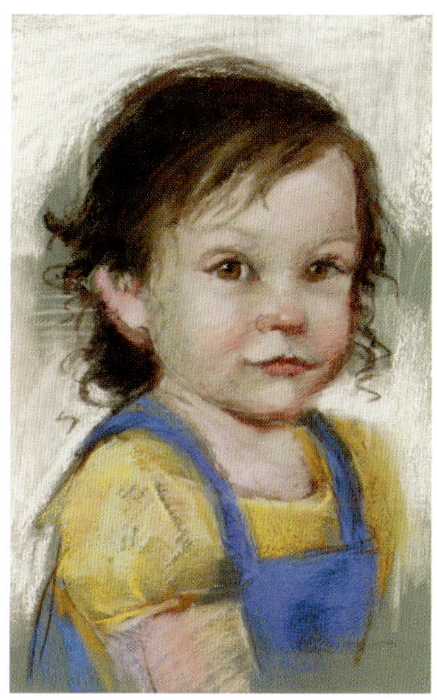

Children in Pastel

As students of the Impressionists, we are all captivated by the children done in pastel in that period. Working quickly, like you can with chalk and charcoal but with the boost of rich color, we can reach an appealing finish in the length of time their curiosity wanes and they are off to other things.

LCB
Pastel on Ampersand Pastelbord
20" × 16" (51cm × 41cm)
Private collection

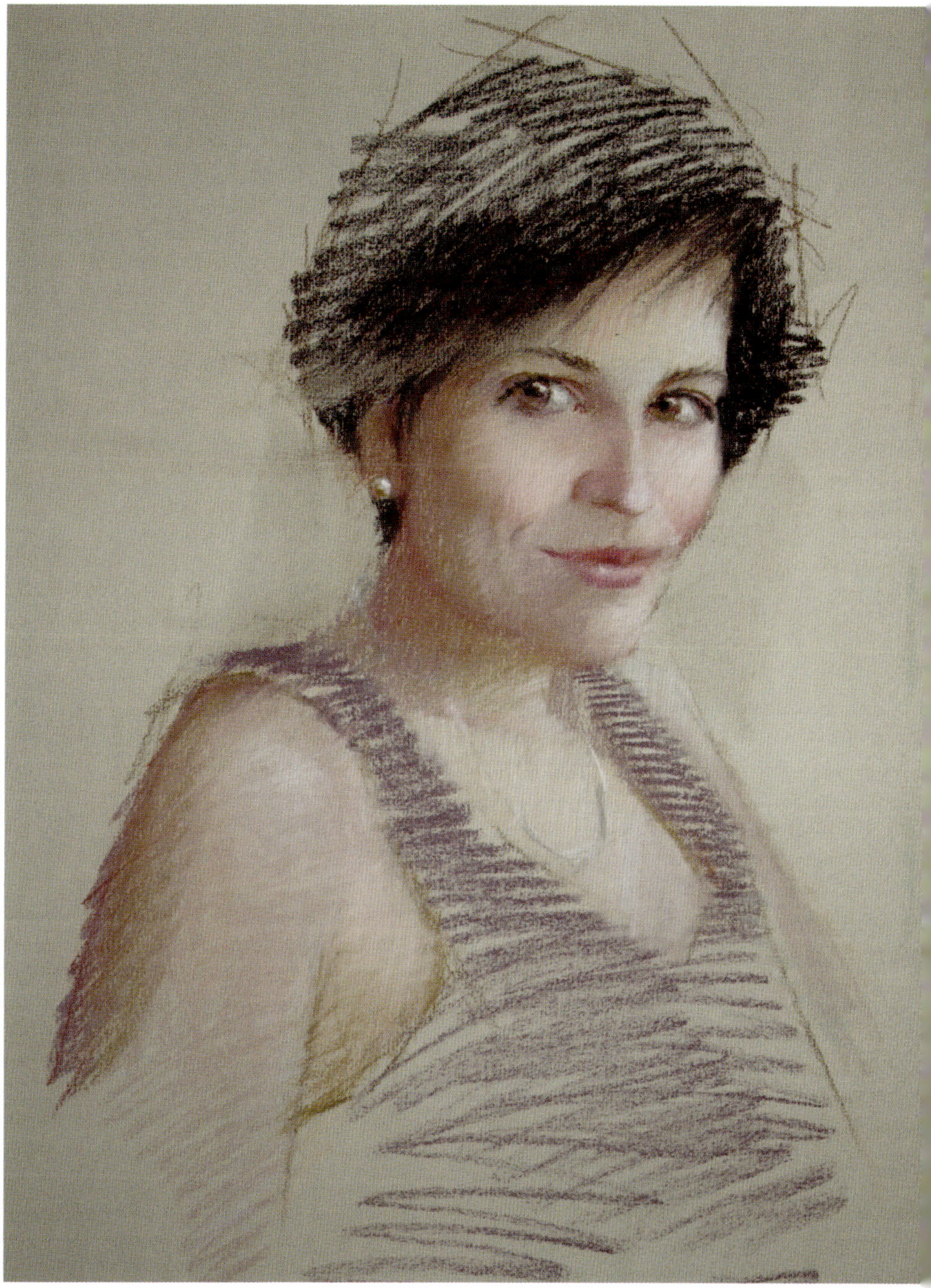

The Strength of Pastel

This woman looked so much like her French grandmother in a portrait the family had prominently displayed, that I had to try to quickly capture the same expression.

Caroline Huffman
Pastel Sketch on Canson Mi-Teintes
22" × 19" (56cm × 49cm)
Private collection

QUARTER-SIZE STUDY: THE COLOR PLAN

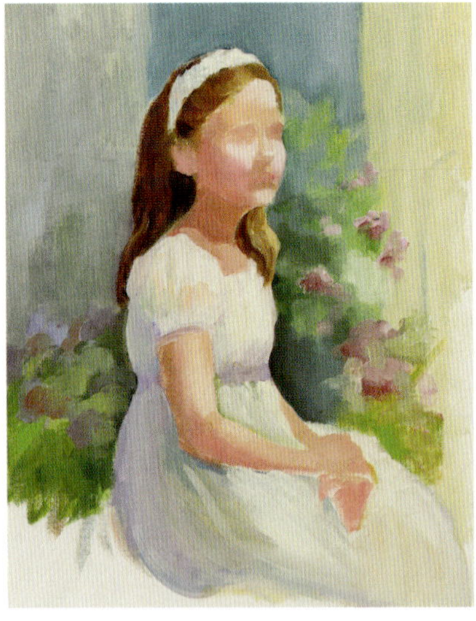

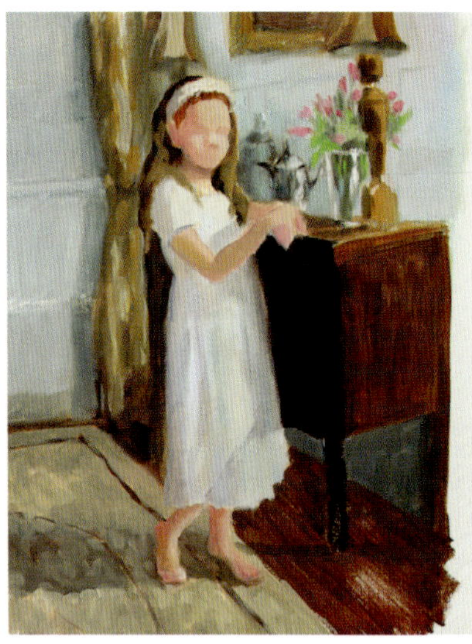

Indoor and Outdoor Color Studies
These are two of several 14" × 11" (36cm × 28cm) oil sketches that were completed to test the overall color plan for this young girl's painting. This is particularly helpful when comparing indoor and outdoor backgrounds and lighting.

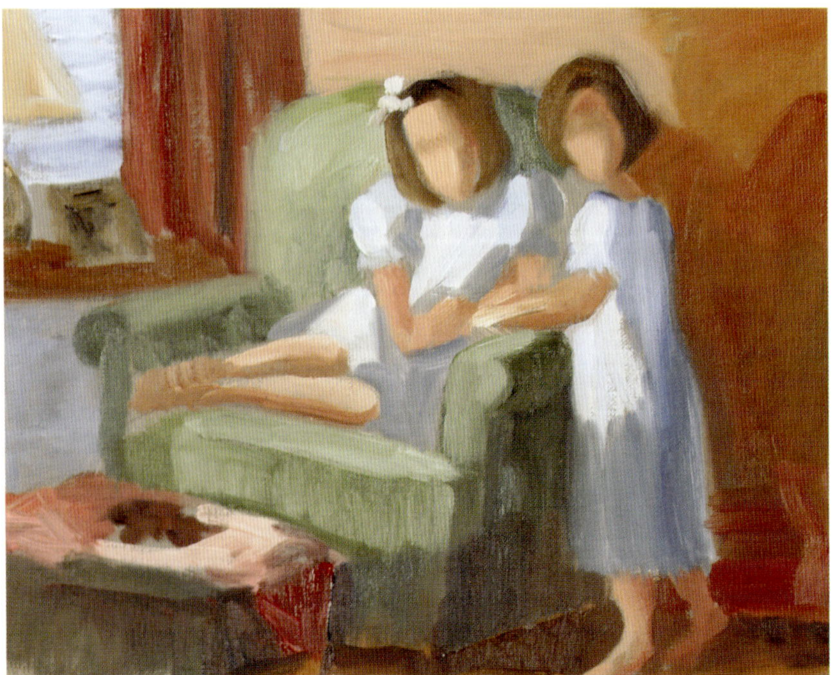

Choosing a Temperature Plan
When working with these two delightful young ladies, I felt that the warmth of the home was well represented in the warm colors surrounding the girls and decided to play on that even more in the final canvas.

In preparing a very large painting, it is a common practice among portrait artists to paint a quarter-size study in full color to test the overall design and harmony of color. If, for instance, the final canvas is to be 48" × 36" (122cm × 91cm), the quarter-size study would be 24" × 18" (61xcm × 46cm).

Sometimes it works well enough to create this color study in an even smaller, but proportional, size. This may be done when presenting the preliminary sketches, head study and color plan to a business committee or a large family who will make final decisions on a portrait. Keep in mind that you may be contracted to do a portrait for a person or persons who have very little art background or understanding of the process. It is then up to you to make them see what you are envisioning as choices for the final composition.

Using very large flat and filbert brushes, the colors are worked very quickly and loosely with a broad approach and no attention to detail. The smaller the study, the less attention to detail. The colors are applied in large flat masses and planes of color in appropriate temperatures and values.

It may look like a blurry jigsaw puzzle with only a flat oval in shadow and light to depict the head as there will be no attempt to create a likeness. Its purpose is a rapid method of determining pigments, overall color interaction and general placement for the final painting on the large, full-size canvas.

HEAD STUDY: A QUICK SKETCH IN COLOR

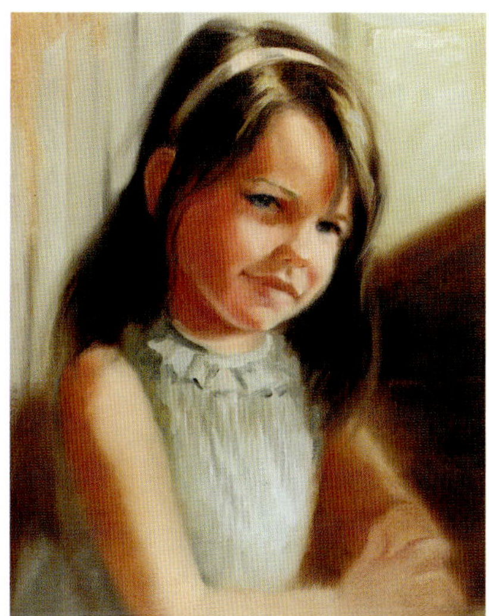

Ellie Stoltz
Oil study on linen canvas (unfinished)
20" × 16" (51cm × 41cm)

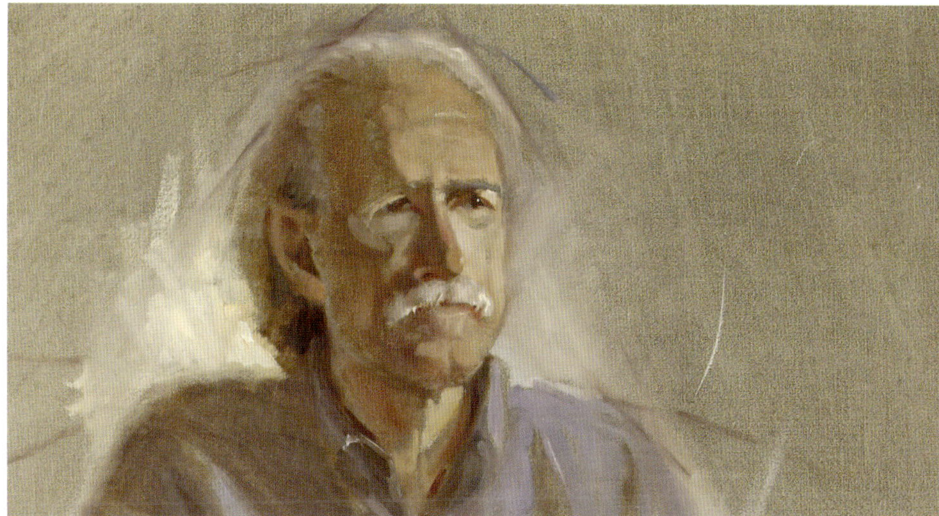

Time Is Relative
The oil sketch was done as a demo in 1 hour in front of a workshop. The second, more considered 3-hour study was started with Ellie and finished in the studio, where I added clothing details and background information on a second approach to the canvas. This is still an unfinished painting, but it is most useful as a color study.

Dick Wayne, Man With Mustache
Retired advertising executive and artist
Oil sketch on canvas
20"× 24" (51cm × 61cm)

Stare, study and sketch. Establish the head as a whole unit on the painting ground first, beginning with the placement of a vertical from which all measurements will be evaluated. Map out the placement of the features next and refine the details last—never reverse this order. Paint dark to light. Think of painting from inside the shadows and work your way out into the light.

Work mostly with darks and middle values. Use lights sparingly and soft edged to avoid the "shiny apple" look. Highlights with soft edges depict soft textures and surfaces. Highlights with sharp, hard edges depict hard, solid, shiny surfaces and are therefore less appropriate for skin, hair and clothing.

Particularly when working with people who are from out of town, out of state or out of country, the artist needs to collect as much data as possible. One such reference piece should be a quick sketch of the head in full color—regardless of mediums.

This study can be done very quickly with fluid strokes for only the purpose of color notes in shadow and light. Or with slightly more time and consideration, the rendering can be more accurate so this canvas may sit in as your model between sittings. In either case, this is the perfect opportunity to scrutinize natural skin, hair and eye colors. Formulate the mixtures, intuitively respond to the sitter and then make notes of what you used so back in the studio you can move forward.

Once you have made notes of these color mixtures, add the information to your file for this painting project. Do not rely on your memory of the color mixtures. Later with more experience, your eye will tell you what you have used. This is why for centuries, artists have continued to do copy work at museums and ateliers. Eventually you will see the hue and recognize the pigments that created it.

Work a life-size head of 8"–10" (20cm–25cm) on a 20" × 16" (51cm × 41cm) or larger board or canvas. Add information on the jewelry, shirt, tie, sweater, pinstriped suit or any additional clothing on the upper body. The temperature of the lighting used and the colors worn will reflect into the skin tones and require careful consideration.

PHOTOGRAPHY AS NOTE-TAKING

Everyone has their own ideas, concerns and uses for photography in their painting studios. Degas used this new medium as an aid to his study of life around him. He certainly benefitted from the stopped-action images at a time when his eyesight was failing. It was a new medium and a new tool—something to assist with his paintings, pastels, monotypes, drawings and sculpture. He took advantage of modern tools.

If we artists use photography solely as another tool in our paint box, we can benefit from it greatly. Using the camera for note-taking in a journalistic fashion will provide data collection that can augment your sketches at the first sitting. Trust your eye to record the person with slow deliberate studies. Use your camera to gather up all of the extraneous details needed to complete the story.

In this hurry up world, the camera is a huge benefit for collecting information on objects that cannot be taken from the client's home or office for reference. Using a close-up lens to capture the smocking on a little girl's bodice, an antique brooch, the intricate design on an embroidered neckline—all of these are painstakingly time-consuming to draw on the spot. When there is limited time with a sitter due to their business stature and demands or simply their physical distance from the artist, the camera becomes a powerful record keeper to augment your carefully crafted monochromatic sketches and your full-color sketches.

Many artists prefer to go to the subject with a fully portable photographic studio set up with multiple lights, strobes, wires, filters, lightboxes and other paraphernalia. This is the very

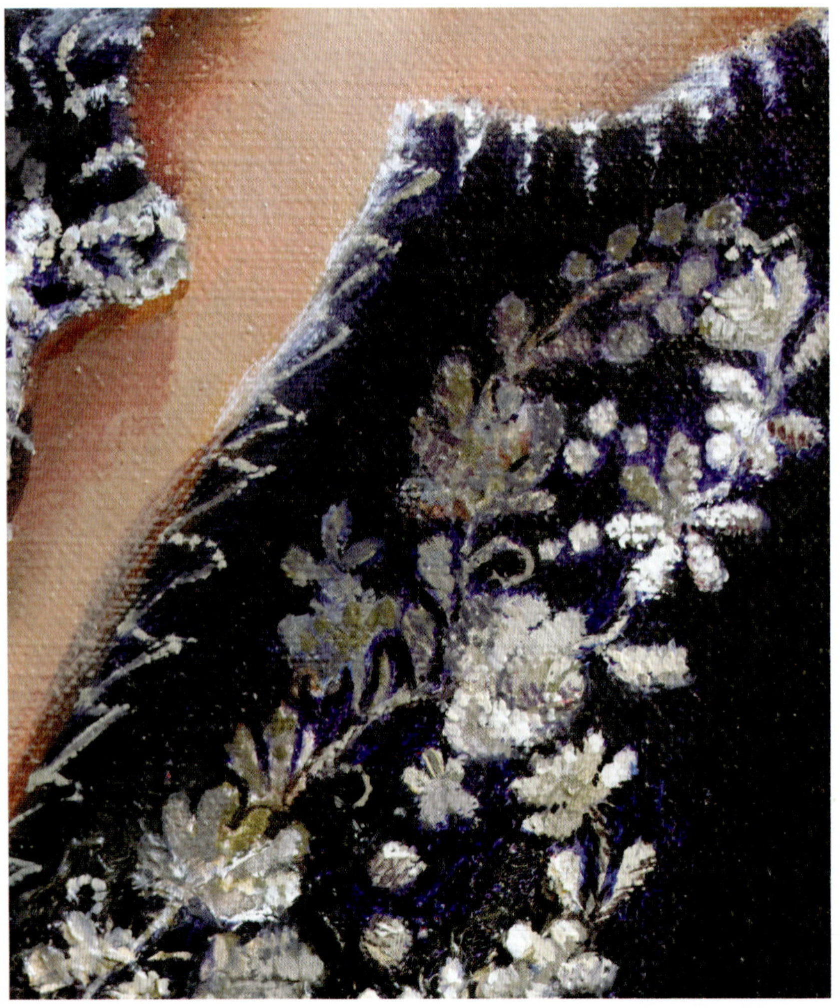

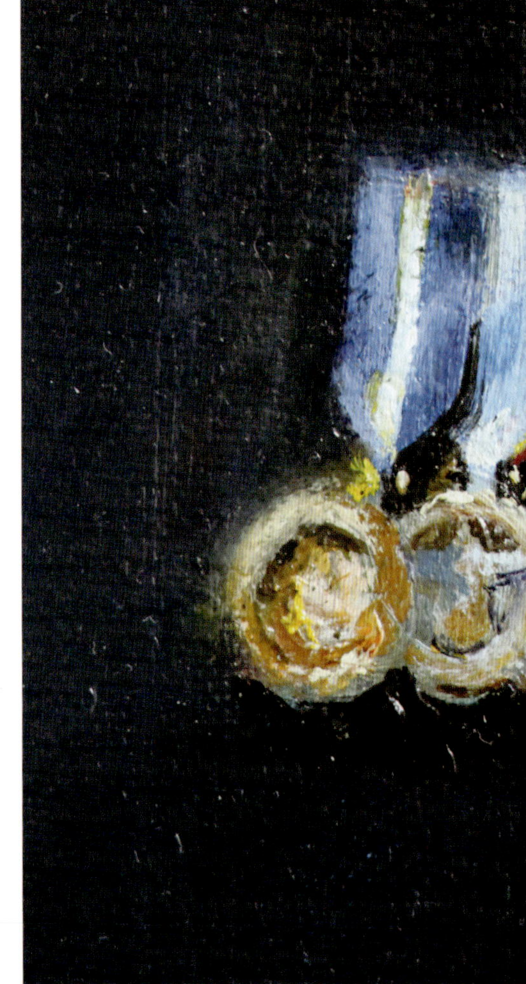

best way to collect perfect photographic data. However, the resultant painting may take on a perfectly finished, but slightly stilted, manner.

Those artists with decades of experience working from life have a better chance to not become a slave to the photograph. They understand the pitfalls, the distortion, the captured frozen moment in the snapped shot, and they know how to compensate for all of that. Artists new to this creative process may find it too tempting to copy every nuance, every fine distinction the camera detects—a dangerous scheme.

Consider working only from life in the beginning. Or at least be involved in weekly life-drawing sessions to keep your skills sharp. Concert pianists do scales to warm up. Opera singers continue to work with coaches and free their voices with warm-up vocalization. Ballet dancers go to class daily to stay limber. Artists' skills are no different. We need to work daily.

Make your choice: Learn all about photography and carry a photographic studio with you for the perfect photographic portrait, or gain a reasonable working knowledge of an all-purpose, handheld camera that can take great photos as you move around the subject's environment collecting essential data. Blend the two. Do what works best for you.

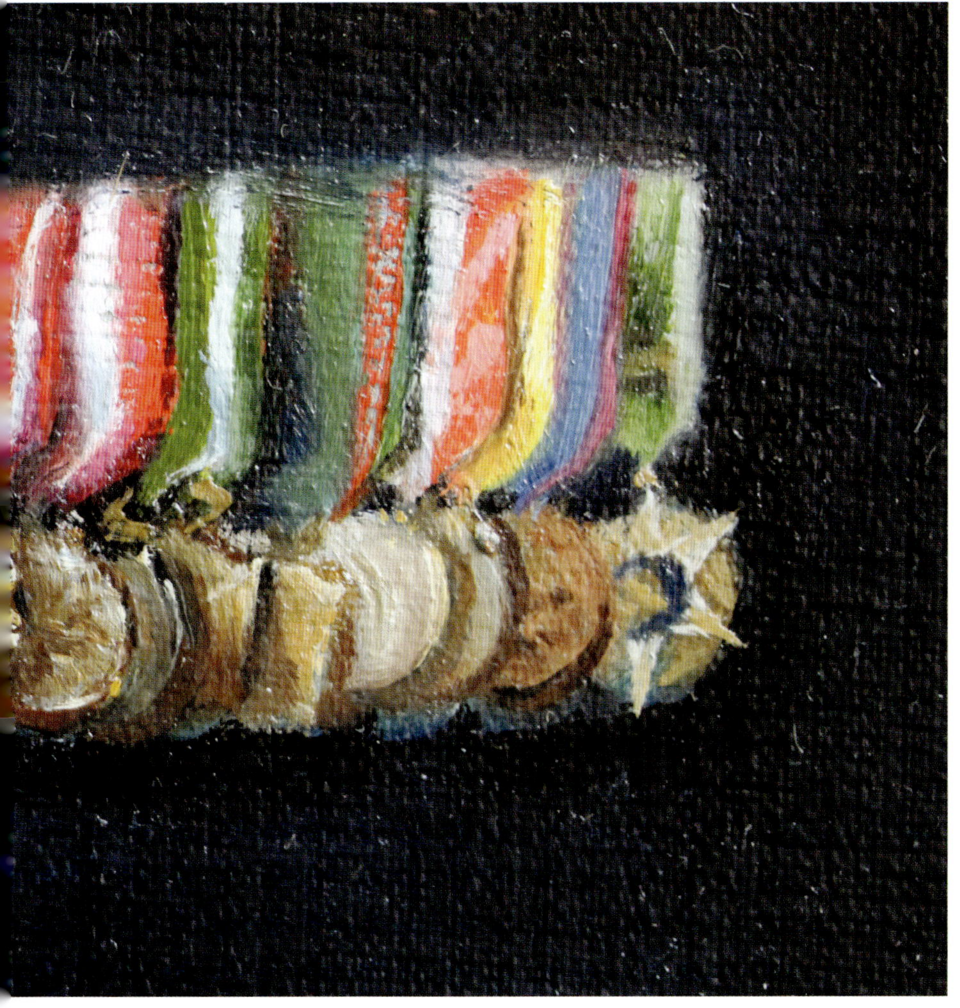

Dealing With Details

To prevent rushing exacting details such as the military medals, request to have the uniform or other complicated clothing in the studio on a model's stand so enough time can be taken to render the items as carefully as desired. If that's not possible, take the best photographs you can.

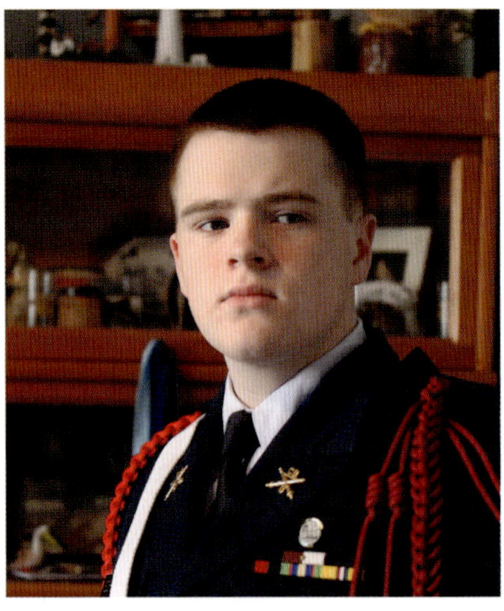

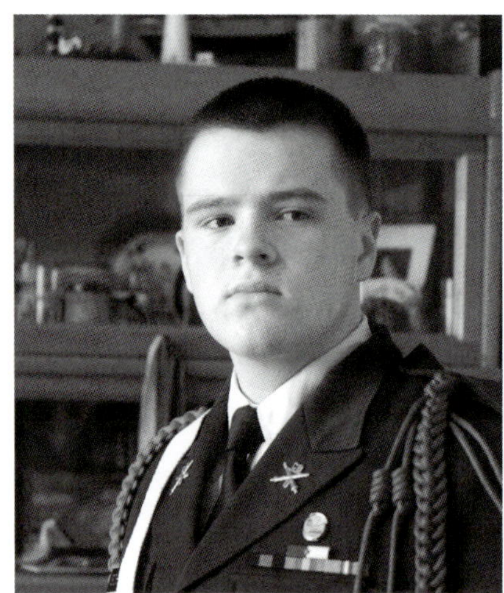

Monochromatic Textures

Really study the black-and-white image. Notice how much more closely related the textures and objects of different colors are. Might you have painted two objects too different if you had not seen it this way?

Working with people in their own spaces instead of the light-controlled painting studio creates constant challenges for the portrait painter. Often the location is so much of the story of the painting, any assistance in data collection is valued.

Digital has changed the way we use photography. Its greatest asset is the obvious ability to shoot and immediately see what was captured.

It's particularly useful when working with large outdoor sculptures or at locations that have finicky weather. Constantly active children and their pets pose different challenges. Props that are too large or too valuable to move to the studio for a later sitting also need to be photographed. Also, military uniforms with their intricate insignias, ribbons, braid and exacting details; wedding dresses; debutante gowns or any clothing with complicated designs, beading or lace are more easily painted from life in the studio or by using macro close-up photography.

Digital photography manipulated on the computer screen can help us strengthen our drawing and observation skills. Here are a few helpful digital tools for the portrait artist.

HOW TO REMOVE COLOR FROM A PHOTO IN ADOBE® PHOTOSHOP® ELEMENTS

1. Open a photo in Photoshop®.
2. Go to Enhance on the toolbar at the top of the screen.
3. Pull down the menu Enhance, and put the cursor on Adjust Color. This will open an additional menu to the side.
4. Find and click on Remove Color. This turns your color photo into a black-and-white photo.

LOCATE AND SIMPLIFY FORM

Among the hardest things to determine when drawing and painting is the value of each area of the drawing. Strong rendering of the values will provide a form that will be solid and have dimension.

Use any means you can to understand and strengthen this light/dark concept. Using digital photography and your computer will give you a unique opportunity to study values. Most software that arrives with new digital cameras or with an affordable, readily available software program like Adobe Photoshop Elements® will help you perform a simple task, starting with changing a color photo into a monochromatic photo.

Make a colorful scene simpler to assimilate by removing all color from the digital image using Photoshop Elements so you can study the image monochromatically.

UNDERSTAND VALUE DIVISIONS

If you are having trouble using a photo for reference, it is likely that the color is confusing you or the value differential is not broad enough on the value scale. Photoshop Elements can assist in dividing a photo into two, three, four or an infinite number of values. Let this help you practice and train your eye to see these variations.

Use this computer technique whenever you are having trouble with drawing from life. This is a valid tool to teach yourself what to look for in life and future photography.

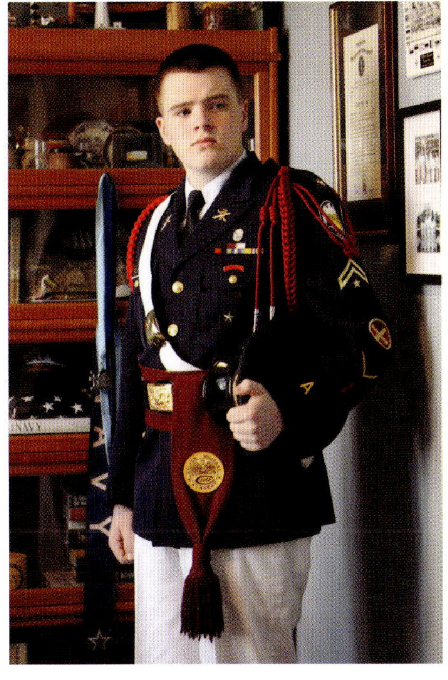

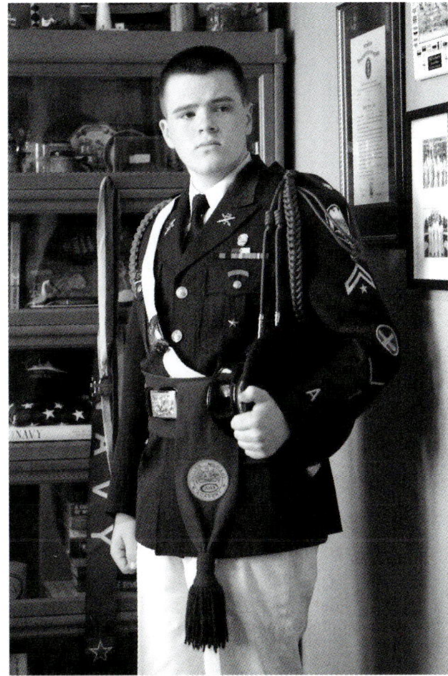

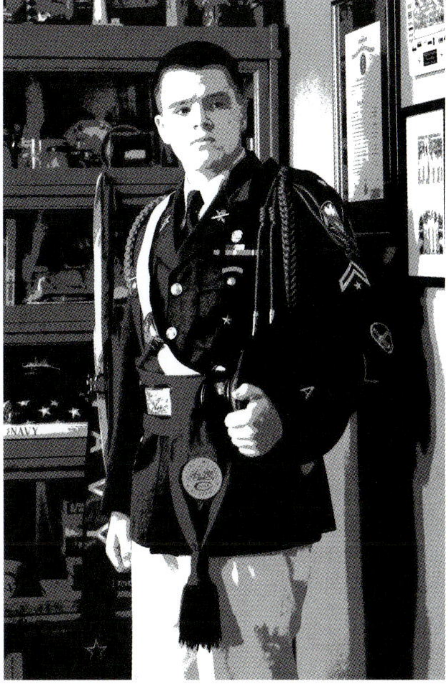

HOW TO POSTERIZE IN ADOBE PHOTOSHOP ELEMENTS

1. Create a black-and-white image, then go back up to the tool bar and go to *Image*.
2. Pull down this menu and find *Adjustments*.
3. Hovering over Adjustments will drop down another menu. On this drop down menu, find and click on *Posterize*.
4. A small, independent window will open offering the opportunity to change levels. A number will appear next to the word *Levels*. This number represents how many values you want to see this photo divided into.
5. Put the number two in the box. This is a two-value division of the photo into only black and white. Study the forms the white and black silhouettes make and note how the light is all connected on the light side and the shadow is all connected on the dark side.
6. Go back to Image. Choose Adjustments. Click on Posterize. Change the number of Levels to three. Now you can see the image in three values: black, white and a middle gray. Often, this is the way you might sketch an image. Using toned paper as your middle value, adding charcoal for the darks and chalk for the lights, you might arrive at a similar flat division of three values.
7. Study this image. Are you surprised at some of the choices the computer made as it had to choose a clearly defined value of light, middle or dark?
8. Now go back to Image. Choose Adjustments. Click on Posterize and change the number of levels to four. The photo develops into a more recognizable series of black, white and two gray values. When we sketch, we add more dimension to the values by virtue of the sketch strokes—light or heavy strokes, feathering strokes, bold strokes, contour strokes, all help to define more dimensions and planes rounding objects from the background to the foreground. But the computer has laid out the four values in flat puzzle pieces. Again, study how these values stay true to the level of light they independently receive.

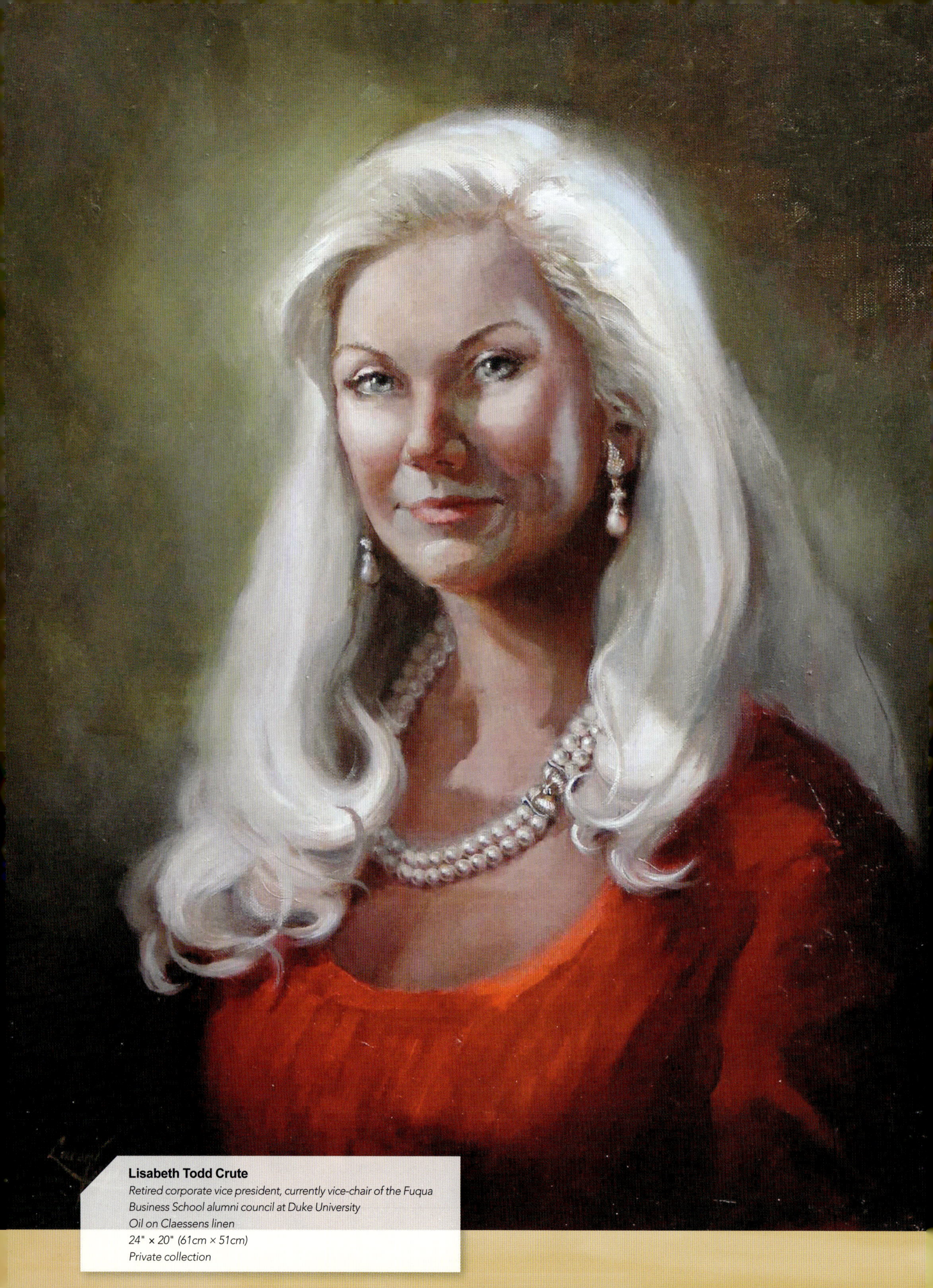

Lisabeth Todd Crute
Retired corporate vice president, currently vice-chair of the Fuqua Business School alumni council at Duke University
Oil on Claessens linen
24" × 20" (61cm × 51cm)
Private collection

CHAPTER 2

CONSTRUCTING THE HEAD & FEATURES

Likeness is achieved by deliberate, careful study. Formulas are great, but nothing replaces the three S's: Stare. Study. Sketch. Long, slow, careful study.

The opportunity to build a painting with beauty, expressive story line, heartfelt emotion, clever color usage and strong design elements is all in your hands. Now to make it also look like the person is the cream! So now the hard work begins.

"I have been impressed with the urgency of doing. Knowing is not enough; we must apply. Being willing is not enough; we must do."
—Leonardo da Vinci

Comfort in Familiarity

When determining how to represent the sitter for a final portrait, there are two things to consider concerning expression: What is the sitter's most typical state of appearance, and can the artist achieve a great likeness from live sittings?

Photographers, when meeting a person for the first, and perhaps only, time to finish a sitting, must make immediate decisions about the sitter. The artist has the luxury of meeting the sitter multiple times, and in that collection of visits, the gained familiarity provides a comfort level of accumulated knowledge of the sitter, her appearance, her attitude and her personality.

THINK LIKE A SCULPTOR

If only every painter could experience a great sculpting class, their progress in conquering the three-dimensional knowledge of the head would be vastly hastened. Begin the study of this section by thinking like a sculptor creating and manipulating the form with hands in the round. Think in planes. With closed eyes to grasp the concept, prepare to paint by going through these mental images:

- Beginning with a large mass, imagine carving away everything that doesn't relate to the large shape of the head.
- Carve into this head/skull shape the largest planes where the form sits in the shadow, making certain that the cavities of the eye sockets, the nostrils, the ears and the corners of the mouth are deep enough to maintain the shadow and describe the most general of shapes.
- Imagine chipping away at the smaller planes that create movement of the form in the midtones. This will clarify and explain the smaller changes of direction.
- Refine the final touches that help to activate chosen highlights—as in the eyes—and it is done!

GOLDEN RULE

Classic beauty can be defined and gauged by nature's perfect mathematical division called the Rule of the Golden Mean, the Golden Ratio or the Fibonacci Sequence (also known as Divine Proportion and calculated as phi). Divisions of segments equal a 1:1.618 ratio. This can be found throughout nature. In the human body, it is seen in the face, every limb and every body part.

BRANCHING OUT

When studying, carefully consider each time something appears, is bent, is divided, turns or moves. One head, two arms, two legs; each of those divided into three (upper arm, lower arm, hand and upper leg, lower leg, foot), and five fingers on each hand with five toes on each foot. It's rather like a tree; the visible part starts with a single strong trunk and divides into additional divisions as it rises.

A PAINTER'S PROCESS

As a painter, the placement of paint should be applied as broadly as if the shapes were created by a sculptor.

- Work from the general and large shapes starting with massing in dark shadows.
- Allow the darks to all connect on the dark side of the form.
- Follow by developing the mid-values. With more care in direction and placement of their values, turn and move them in and out of the form.
- Refine the small details to complete the picture with final touches that continue to reinforce the direction of light.
- Drop in the highlights and it is done!

Note the correlation between the two mediums. Paint like a sculptor: from the general to the specific and from the grand overview down to the details. This will make a successful painting.

Working with the simplest of shapes, the following lessons will simplify the complexities of the head and features. Divide the face into simple geometric forms, and the many undulating surfaces and total topography will become easier to handle, to recognize and to paint.

THE EYES

The eyes are the single most important feature in the painting. The more correct the eyes appear, the more correct the balance of the face. Keep them soft, clear, wet and expressive. Take more time to resolve the character in the eyes, and the reward will be that the painting is recognized by family, friends and colleagues to be unquestionably the intended person.

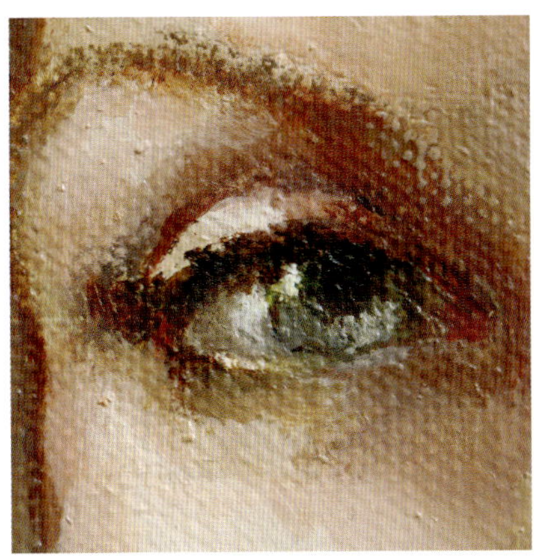

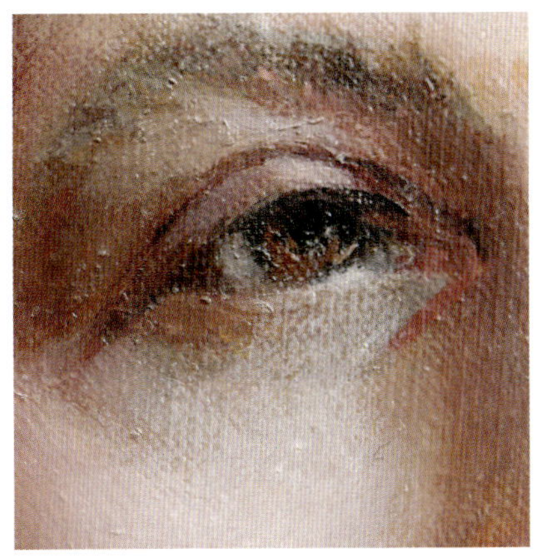

Allow the Eye the Focus It Deserves

Notice the techniques used to seat the eyeball deeply enough into the socket in both of these samples. The female on the left displays a soft roundness to the brow bone on the upper eye socket and a soft transition from the lower eye socket into the upper cheek (zygomatic) bone. The man's eye has a less pronounced brow bone while the whole of both the upper and lower eyelid area sits more evenly on the surface and not so deeply into the socket. Compare, too, her delicate eyebrow and fuller lash area to his naturally full eyebrow and thinner eyelash.

LOOK INTO THE EYES

The eye is one of the few places in the head where a hard edge is preferred. The viewer's eye seeks out hard edges to focus on. Place a hard edge and a prominent dark-to-black value in the pupil. Follow with a firm, dark edge in the upper lash area touching the pupil to provide a high contrast with the upper lid and the nearby sclera (white of the eye). Use this hard edge and high contrast to bring the viewer's focus to the eyes in the portrait, just as people look into each other's eyes when greeted in real life.

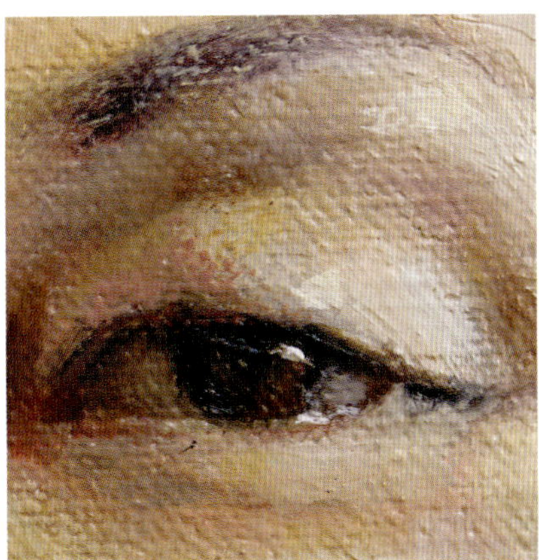

The Asian Eye

The lovely Asian eye addresses an eyelid structure that sits with more fullness on the surface of the eye socket. Yet, note how the clear definition of a strong socket structure remains apparent.

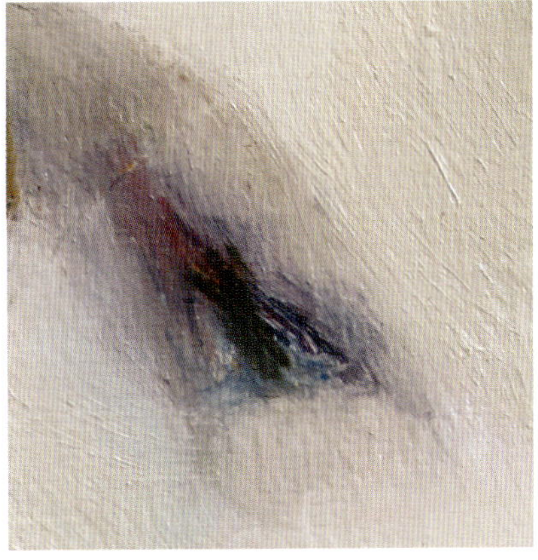

The Eye in Profile

When painting the eye from the front, the artist concentrates on the bull's-eye effect of the pupil surrounded by the cornea surrounded by the sclera. This is a circle within a circle on a ball covered by lids (triangles) and all seated into a round-cornered square—the eye socket. The profile view is an ellipse in a triangle.

CONSTRUCTING THE EYE, FRONT VIEW

MATERIALS LIST

- Ampersand Gessobord, toned to middle gray
- Flake White Replacement
- Yellow Ochre
- Cadmium Red
- Burnt Sienna
- Alizarin Crimson
- Cobalt Blue
- Ivory Black

In a badly painted portrait, eyes often look as though they have been applied flatly on the surface of the face. Learn the construction of the eye and its depth of placement down into the eye socket, and you will achieve a beautiful, wet, lively eye with minimal trouble. Each step of this construction of the eye will be simplified by using geometric shapes.

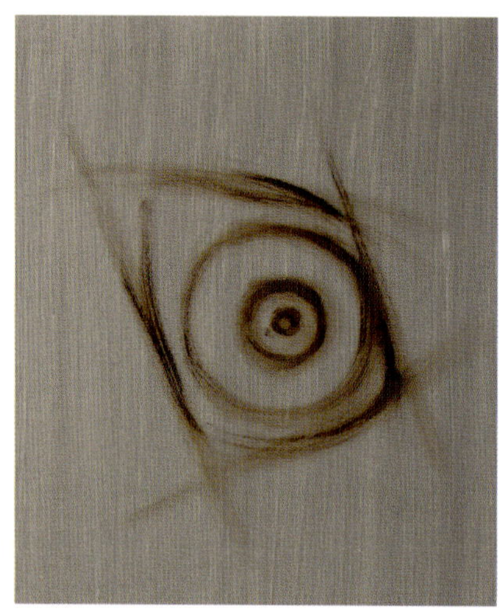

1 ESTABLISH THE BLUEPRINT

Place a rectangle to build the eye socket on the board or canvas with a relatively dry brush. Use Burnt Sienna and Ivory Black to make a color similar to Burnt Umber. The color at this dry-sketch stage establishes the footprint where we will build the flat planes. Inside the rectangle, paint a circle for the eyeball. In the center of this circle place two concentric circles that look like a bull's-eye target.

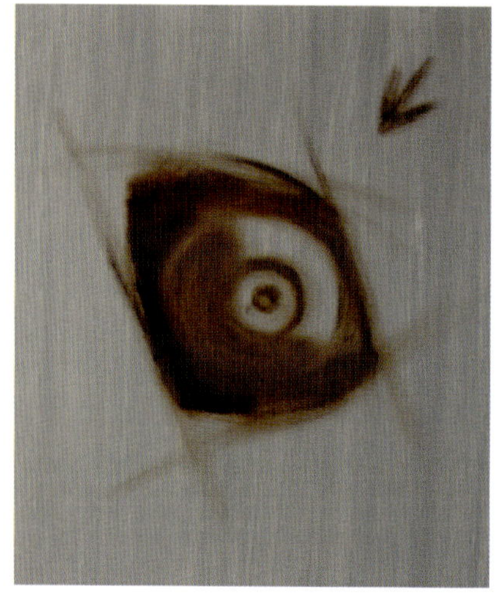

2 ADD DARKS

Place a small arrow as a constant reminder of the direction of light (it will be painted over later). Use Burnt Sienna and Ivory Black as a very thin, dark mixture to drybrush inside the eye socket and on the shadow side of the eyeball, being mindful of the direction of light (arrow direction).

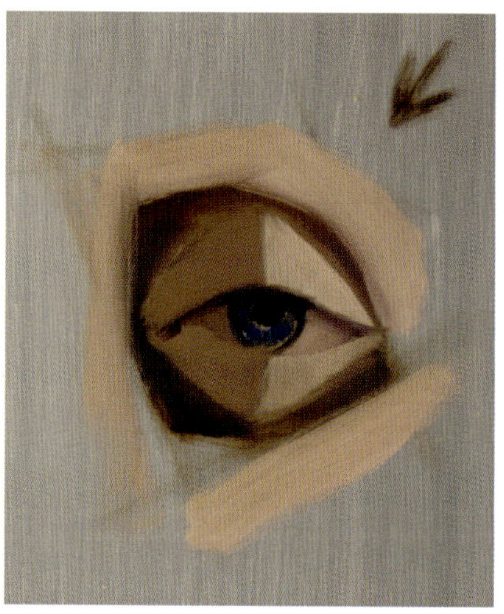

3 PLACE MIDDLE VALUES

Fill the pupil with Ivory Black. Place a thin mixture of Cobalt Blue with a touch of Ivory Black in the iris, outer circle and colored part of the eye.

To simplify laying in the upper and lower lids, continue to use geometric shapes. Mix Yellow Ochre and Alizarin Crimson into the previous dark mixture and add a little White. Place a triangle of this middle-value skintone mixture on the shadow side of the eye on the upper and lower lids. Lighten the mixture with white and place two triangles on the upper and lower lids on the light side.

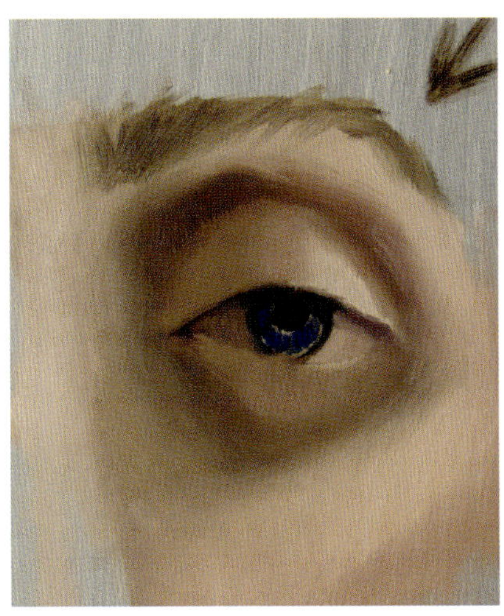

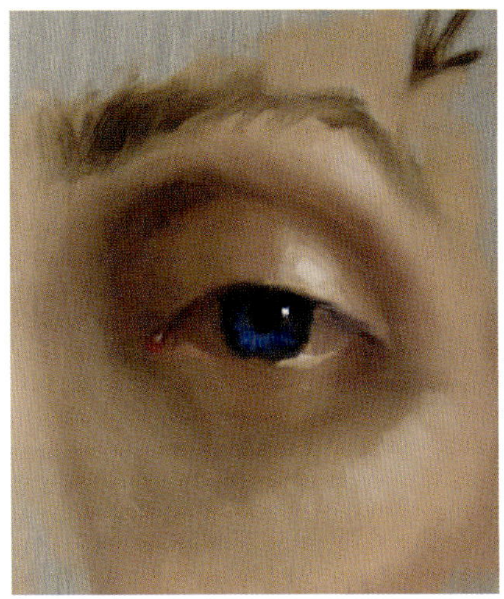

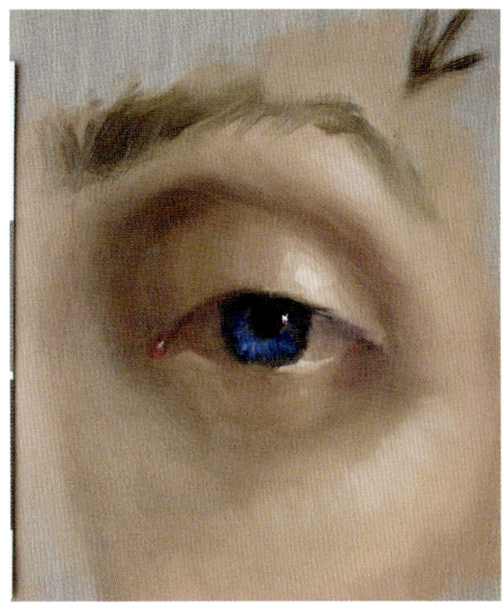

4 BLEND SKIN AND ADD EYEBROWS

Add Yellow Ochre, Alizarin Crimson, a touch of Ivory Black and white to the medium-value mixture on the palette to create a more realistic skin tone in light. Add new planes to areas around the eye, including forehead, cheekbone and eye socket.

Add the eyebrow with Ivory Black, Burnt Sienna and Yellow Ochre. Use brisk strokes up and outward to "grow" the eyebrows.

Blend and soften areas into one another so that the transitions between the shadow, middle and light areas connect. Add warmth to the inner and outer corners of the eye with Alizarin Crimson and Cadmium Red at the tear duct.

Soften the depth of the darkest shadows by lightly feathering your brush over the areas with mid-value skin color. Make certain there is a change in value to represent the shadow that the thickness of the eyelid casts on the eyeball.

5 ADD HIGHLIGHTS

Add highlights to the brow bone, the upper lid, the lower lid and the cheekbone to strengthen the direction of light on the surface of the face. The only place on the entire portrait where you should use pure white is a catchlight in the eye at the edge of the iris and pupil. Add a touch of white to represent moisture on the lower lid where the iris meets it. Direction of light may also create a highlight on the tear duct. Soften, feather out edges and assess your progress.

Reduce the depth of shadow in the socket to make this eye not look too tired. Adjust highlights in small increments, blending along the brow bone and really rounding out the bone from the shadow depths. Do the same for the zygomatic bone—the high cheekbone under the eye, blending outward and upward.

6 MAKE IT MOIST

Moisture in the eye will bring it to life. Add the catchlight in the eye at the edge of the muscle of the cornea and pupil—where the color of the eye meets the open hole of the pupil. Add a touch of light on the edge of the lower lid where the color of the iris and the sclera (white of the eye) meet as they touch the lower lid. A reduced-value highlight is sometimes needed on the ball of the tear duct as well.

UNIVERSAL CLOCK FACE

Think of the eye as a clock face. The illustration shows the light entering the eye at the catchlight at two o'clock. The light travels through the translucent cornea and lands on the cornea at seven o'clock. Notice how this opens up the eye and makes it seem more alive. On life-sized head and shoulder paintings, this will be more noticeable than in smaller images where the painted head may only measure 2" to 4" (5cm to 10cm) high.

THE EYE IN PROFILE

MATERIALS		
Ampersand Gessobord, toned to middle gray	Yellow Ochre	Alizarin Crimson
Flake White Replacement	Cadmium Red	Cobalt Blue
	Burnt Sienna	Ivory Black

The single biggest mistake when painting or drawing a profile is the placement of the eye. The ball of the eye sits so well into the socket on the skull that it is completely protected by the ring of bone that surrounds it.

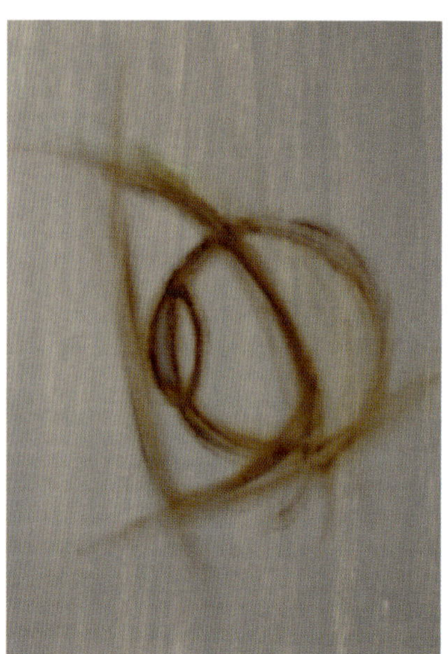

1 **DETERMINE PLACEMENT**
First, place the dark triangle to serve as the eye socket. Place the eyeball deep into the socket. Compare the line drawing with the skull.

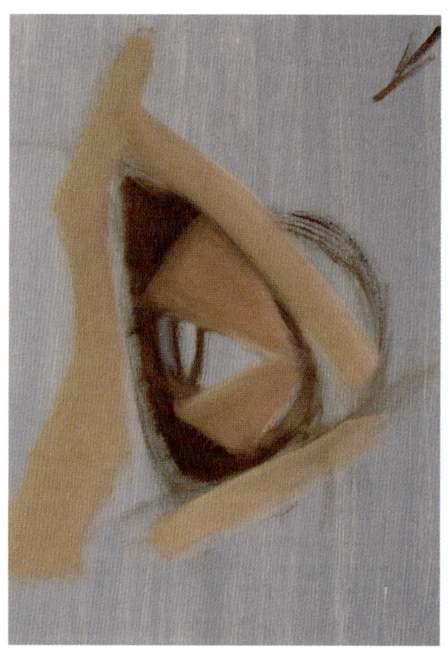

2 **ADD SHADOWS**
Starting with the darkest value of skin-shadow mixture, fill the visible eye socket. Place with middle-value skin mixture on the surrounding bone area and the eyelids.

The eyeball is surrounded by a ring of bone.

The entire socket sits back from the nasal bone.

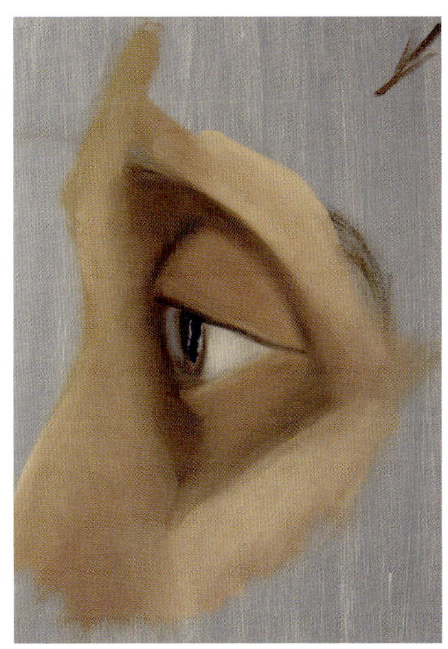

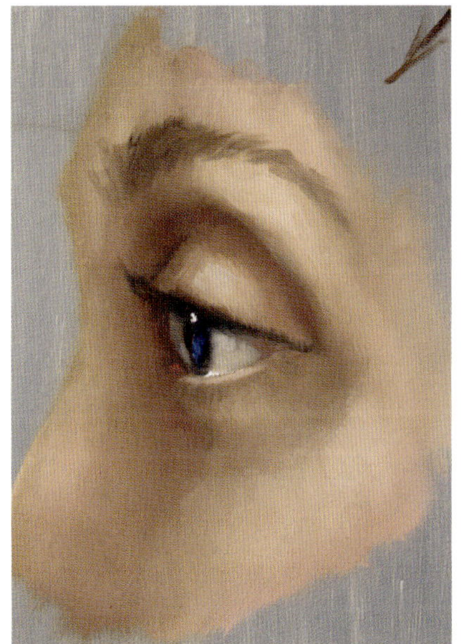

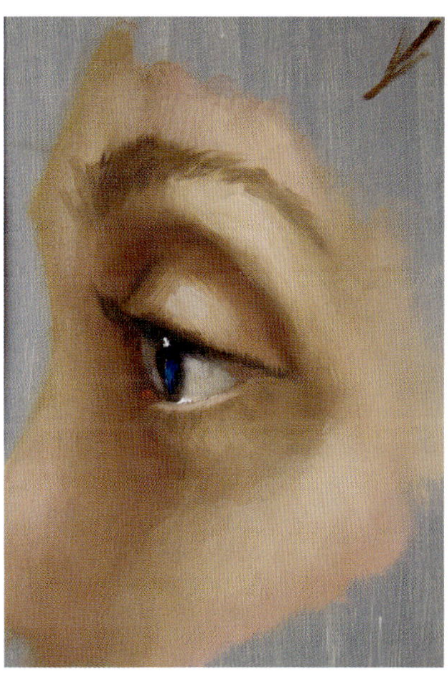

3 ADD SKIN AND BROW

Add additional skin to the brow, the bridge of the nose, the glabella and the cheekbone. Place the pupil as an ellipse in the eye and place the dark color of the iris. Place the sclera (white of the eye) with some skin tone with added white and a small touch of black.

4 ADD HIGHLIGHTS

Lighten with local skin tone all the areas that might be touched by light, using the arrow as a directional indication of the light source. Add eyebrow hair and indicate eyelashes. Add lighter area of the iris. Using white, place a catchlight or highlight at the upper part of the eye between the pupil and the iris. Also add a catchlight at the junction of the sclera, the iris and the lower eyelid to give the impression of moisture.

5 COMPLETE THE PICTURE

Finish with the highest key light of skin tone to reinforce the direction of light on the skin at the brow bone, on the eyelid, on the cheekbone and on the bridge of the nose.

THE NOSE

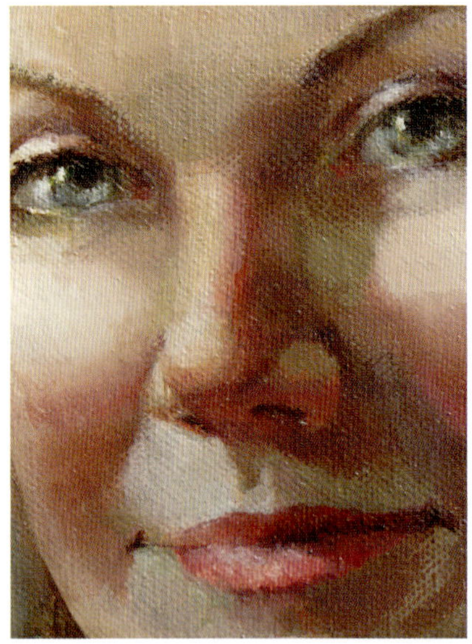

FIND SIZE RELATIONSHIPS TO KEEP PROPORTION

All body parts correlate to other body parts. In designing the nose, note the size of the person's thumb. They will be approximately the same size/length. However, keep in mind that the nose gets larger and longer with age.

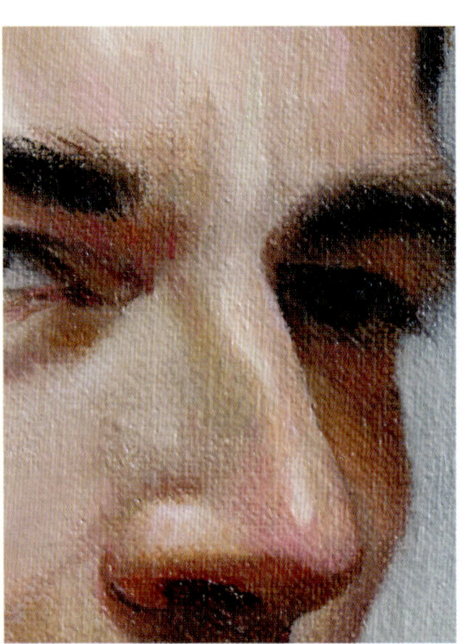

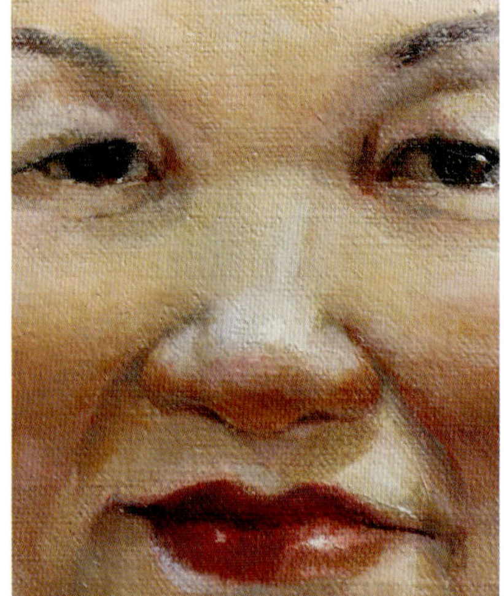

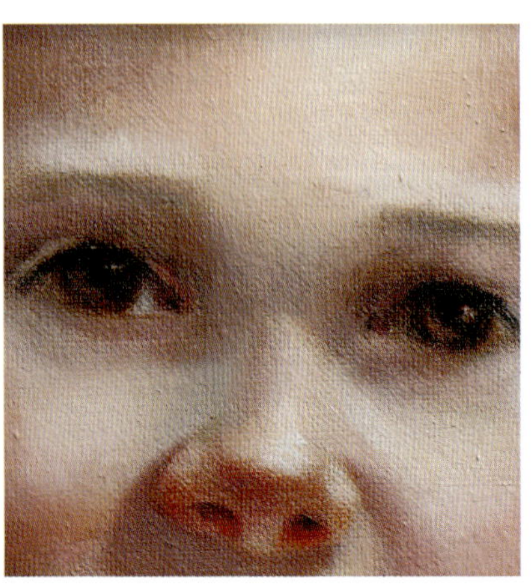

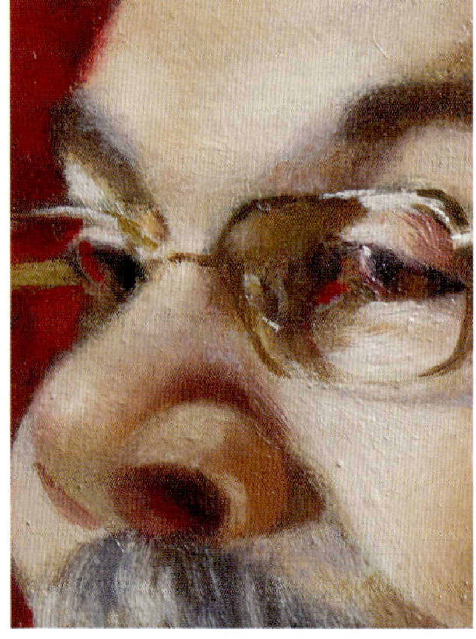

The nose is certainly the most prominent feature to carry information about ethnicity, age and family resemblance. The keys to painting the nose are dimension, direction of planes, believable projection outward from the face and color temperature to push and pull the structure in and out of the picture plane.

THE NOSTRILS

As with all other things relating to painting great faces, practice is the only way to begin to fully understand this structure. Here are a few key ideas to keep in mind while constructing the nose:

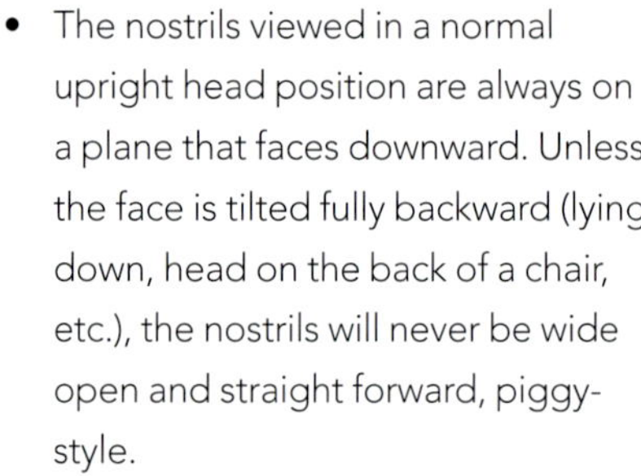

- The nostrils viewed in a normal upright head position are always on a plane that faces downward. Unless the face is tilted fully backward (lying down, head on the back of a chair, etc.), the nostrils will never be wide open and straight forward, piggy-style.

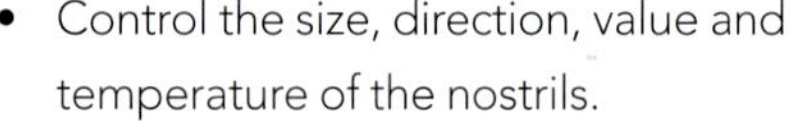

- Control the size, direction, value and temperature of the nostrils.

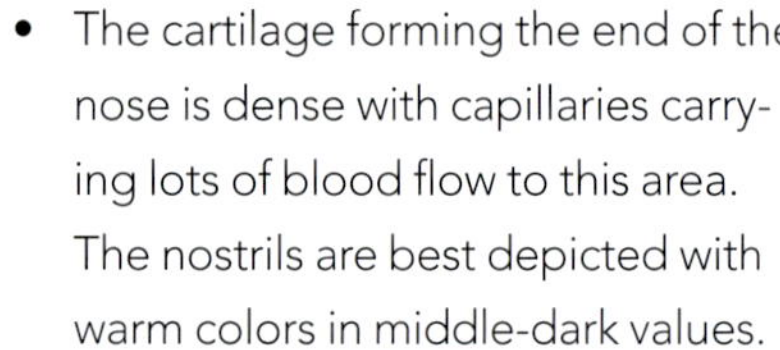

- The cartilage forming the end of the nose is dense with capillaries carrying lots of blood flow to this area. The nostrils are best depicted with warm colors in middle-dark values.

Light and Shadow Define the Structure
The light on these noses from these various paintings provides strong clues to gender, age, race and the direction of light on the face.

CONSTRUCT THE NOSE

Using medical illustration techniques, the nose can be understood through its skin, muscle, membranes, cartilage, bone layers, etc. But there may be an easier way for the painter to build this construction without attending a pre-med anatomy class. Remember middle school geometry study and shapes? Use a series of triangles and rhomboids to simplify the nose. (Note: There is a muscle in the back attached to the scapula named a rhomboid. Not *that* rhomboid, but the four-sided geometric shape.)

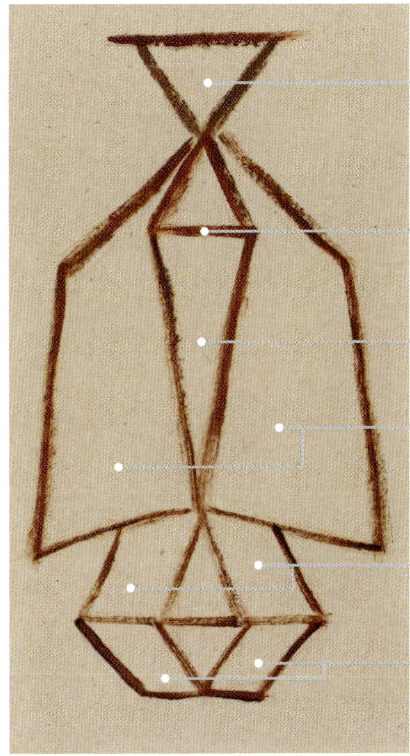

The glabella between the two eyebrows is a downward-pointing triangle.

The rhinion (the point on the upper nose where the nasal bone stops and the cartilage begins) often has a noticeable bump that can be felt and very easily seen on many people.

The ridge of the nose is often the dividing point between light and shadow.

The sloping skin from the ridge attaches to the cheek area.

The end, or the ball of the nose, can be drawn with a triangle in the center of two rhomboids representing the wings or nostril areas.

The bottom of the nose, the shelf that projects outward, mirrors the shapes representing the area above it.

HOW IT WORKS

By connecting a series of these shapes to one another, a general explanation of what to look for becomes apparent: planes are facing up toward the light or down away from the light.

- Triangles shaded are facing downward away from the light.
- Clear triangles are facing upward and being bathed in light.
- Rhomboids appear in the wings or nostrils and also connect the nose to the face.

Light source

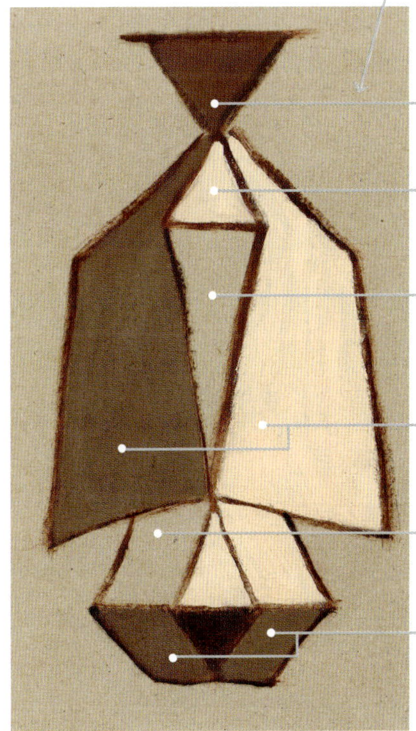

The glabella between the eyebrows turns slightly downward and requires some shadow.

The top of the nasal bone is facing upward toward the light.

The ridge divides the light and shadow.

The sloping area away from the light requires a shadow, and the sloping area closer to the light source requires light.

The area on the shadow side faces upward and receives a middle tone. The center and side facing the light both receive light.

The underside of the nose faces downward, is shadowed away from the light and sometimes is hit with reflected light.

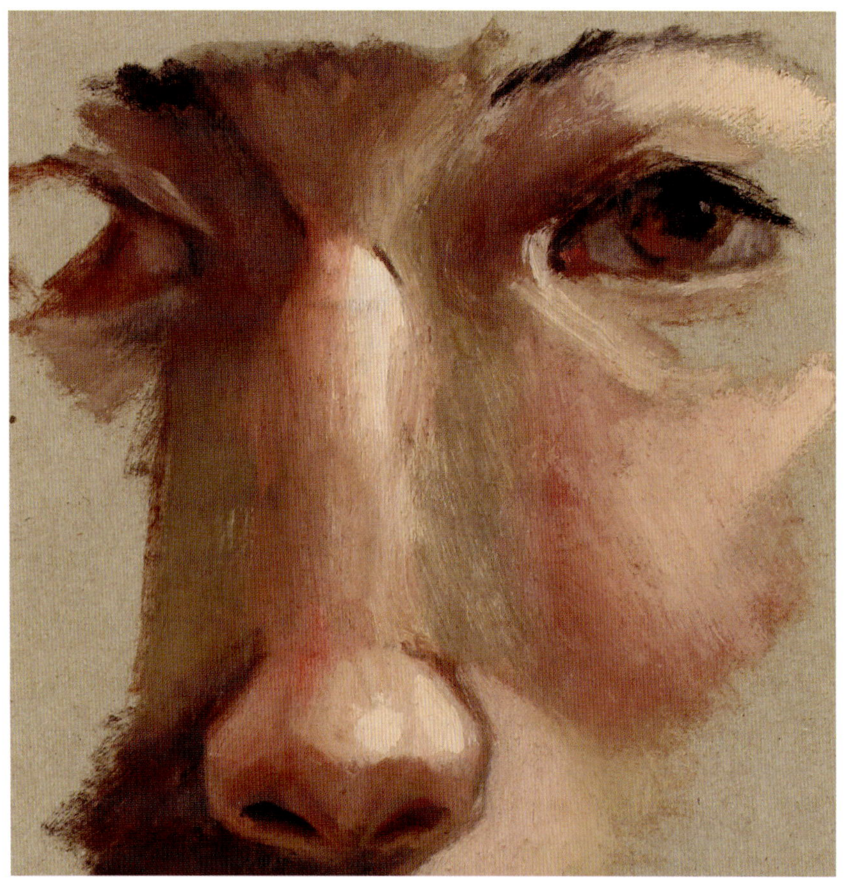

Warm and Cool Tones to Mold the Nose

Allow color temperature to help push and pull the topography of the nose and cheeks in and out of the picture plane. Even in this very quick oil sketch, the viewer should be able to clearly distinguish the hills and valleys of the nose and cheek area thanks to temperature changes. Warms advance from the flat plane and imply movement forward or outward toward the viewer. Cool tones recede, falling away from the viewer.

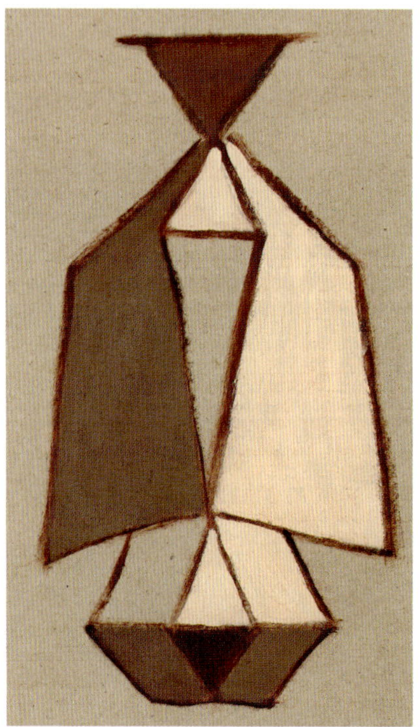

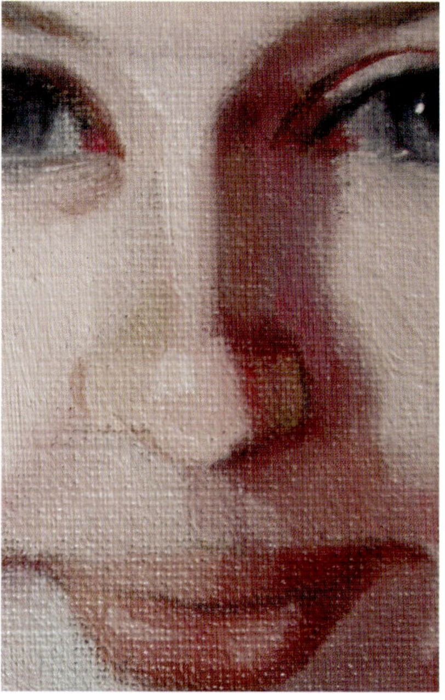

Begin With Simple Geometric Shapes

Begin with general knowledge of construction, and change what is needed according to the individual. Here, the shelf that projects forward from the face at the bottom of the nose has no nostrils visible due to the slight downturn of the head. Stare, study and sketch what you see, not what you have been told or what you think you see.

BUMP ON THE NOSE

The *osseocartilaginous junction* is where the light touches the bump on the bridge of the nose—every nose. This is a very important spot to define the character of the nose and, occasionally, even the person's ethnicity and heritage.

To break down this word, *osseo* = bone, *cartilaginous* = cartilage and, of course, a junction is a meeting point.

THE NOSE IN PROFILE

It will always be easier to paint and draw the nose from profile as there are only a few planes and directional lines to handle. See how simple this construction is from the diagram.

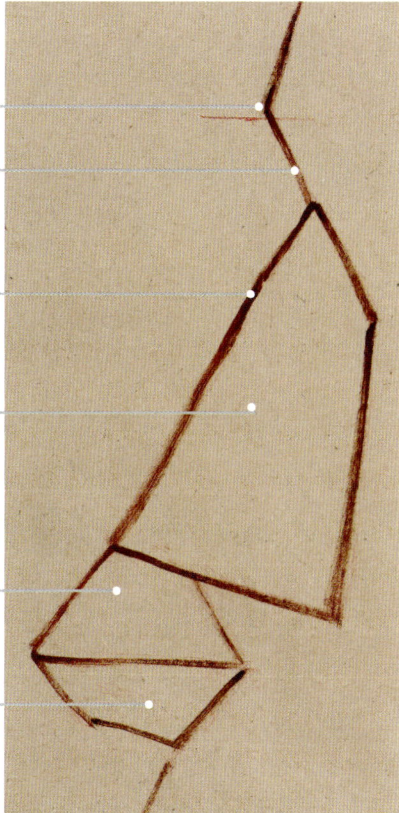

The forehead or frontal bone turns direction at the glabella above the nose.

The glabella turns slightly downward away from the light.

The rhinion is where the nasal bone stops and the cartilage begins.

The side of the nose slopes from the ridge to the cheek.

The upper part of the ball or wing of the nose faces upward toward the light.

The underside turns away from the light in shadow.

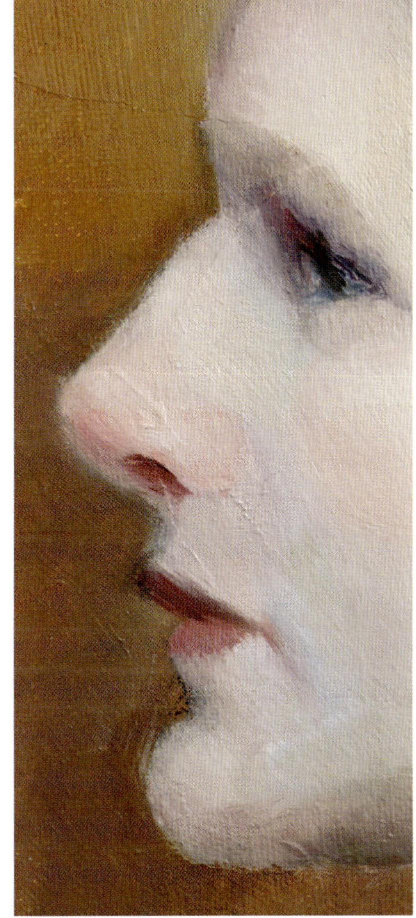

The Upturned Nose

Notice the direction of the shelf or the underside of the nose where the nostrils are in the diagram. Now notice how this direction was actually changed in the painting for the unique nose on this model. It takes only a minor change in direction of a line, plane or color to hit a likeness straight on or lose it completely.

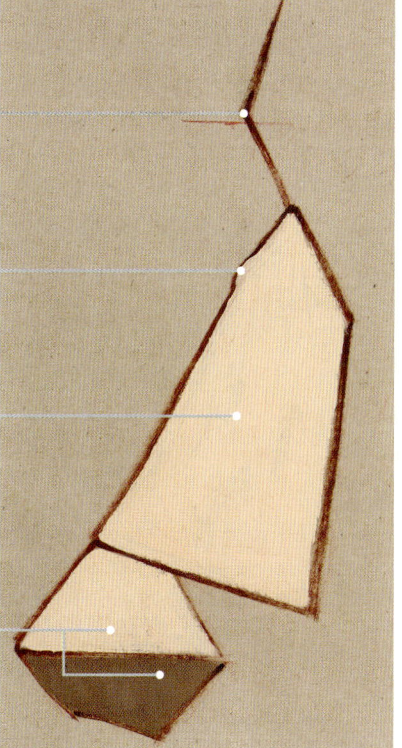

The sharpness or roundness of this particular part of the ridge of the brow can harden a face and its expression. Note a somewhat more distinct change of direction on men's faces at this point than on women's.

There is a catch of light at the rhinion in most lighting situations.

The sloping side of the nose often needs to be cooled to move it back into the face as it attaches to the cheek.

The entire area at the end of the nose, both at the top in the light and the underside away from the light, have a decidedly warmer temperature due to the concentration of blood vessels.

THE MOUTH

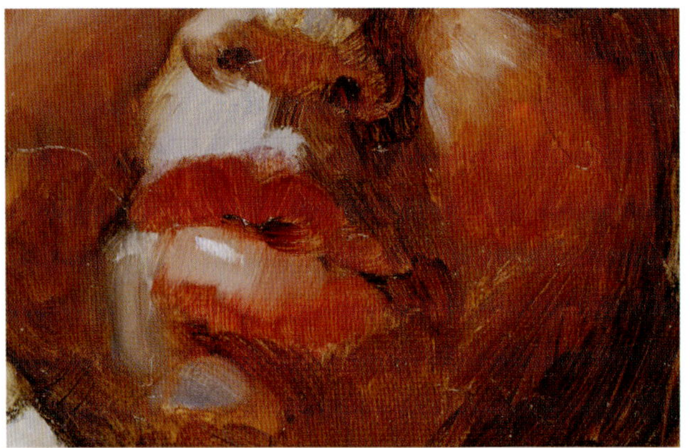

The Natural Mouth

Artists who work solely from photos sometimes forget that children and many adults tend to mug for the camera and smile because it is expected. The natural mouth is easier to paint at the sitting. When relaxed, the closed mouth is very expressive and lovely.

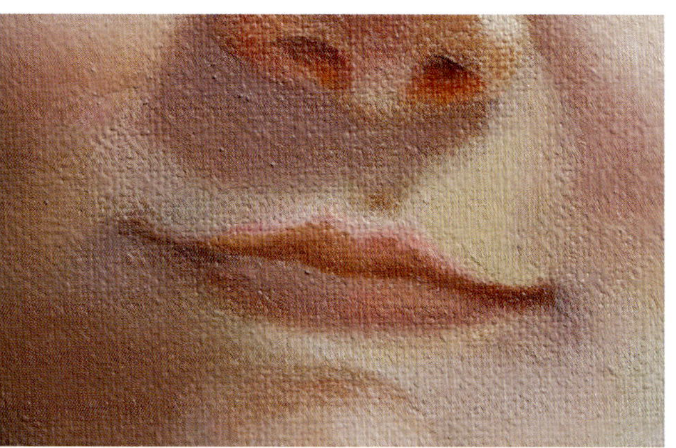

Children's Mouths

Yes, even children, who are the busiest models on the planet, will have their quiet moments while you sketch or paint away. Try letting them draw as the painting progresses, share a story with them, or better yet, let them share a favorite story or event with you. These will surely evolve into facial expressions that will be priceless, enthusiastic and memorable.

The mouth has been a most problematic feature for artists. Many painters know John Singer Sargent's statement, "A portrait is a painting of a person in which there is a little something wrong with the mouth." But don't be intimidated. It is only difficult until you have studied it completely as an abstract form. See only the shape of the light and the shape of the shadow. The form will then appear.

It is difficult at best to depict the mouth in a comfortably relaxed state. The model could become more tense or uncomfortable as they sit for long periods. To avoid a tense model, or worse, a sleeping model, the artist may engage them in conversation.

MUSCLES THAT NEVER REST

With twenty-six muscles surrounding the mouth, it appears to always be in motion with changing expressions. Even at rest, people tend to move their lips if only to lick them when dry, purse them in deep thought or try to maintain an expected expression... especially when a camera is in sight. Unfortunately, the camera may find the most unnatural of mouth expressions. The harder a person tries to hold a posed smile, the tighter and less natural it becomes.

THE NATURAL MOUTH

The artist who has the opportunity to spend time with the subject may observe their natural expression while conversing and sketching. This will happen as meetings become more relaxed over the development of the painting. It sometimes comes together over time as a collective knowledge of the relaxed face.

THE MOUTHS OF BABES

Even when not speaking, people tend to react to stimuli with their mouths subconsciously. Observe as a person sits quietly and watches television, reads a book, waits in a waiting room or at an airport. Even a sleeping baby moves his mouth and tongue often while dreaming that he is still nursing. What could be cuter than that little poochy, kiss-mouth thing that happens?

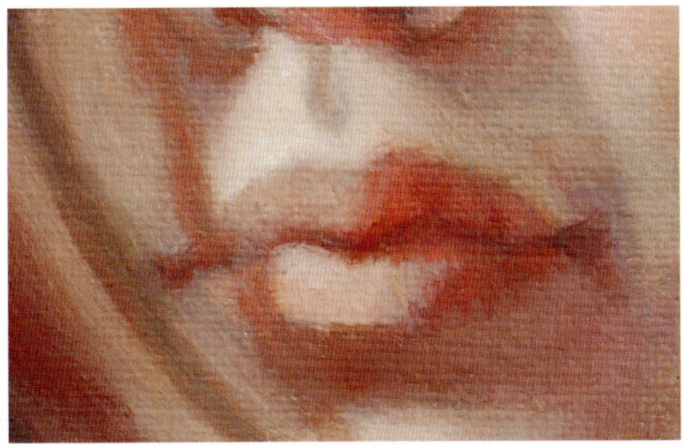

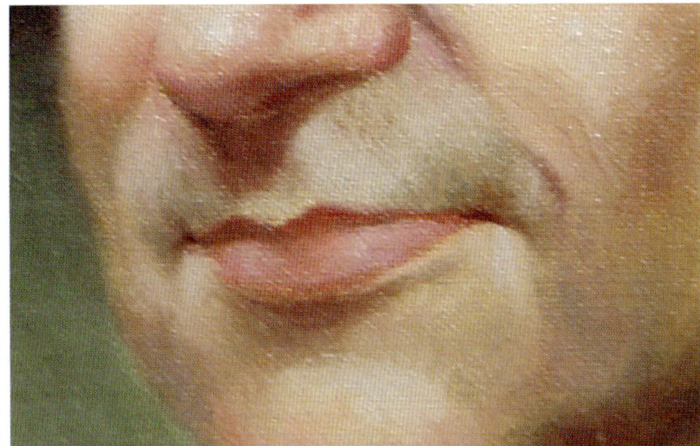

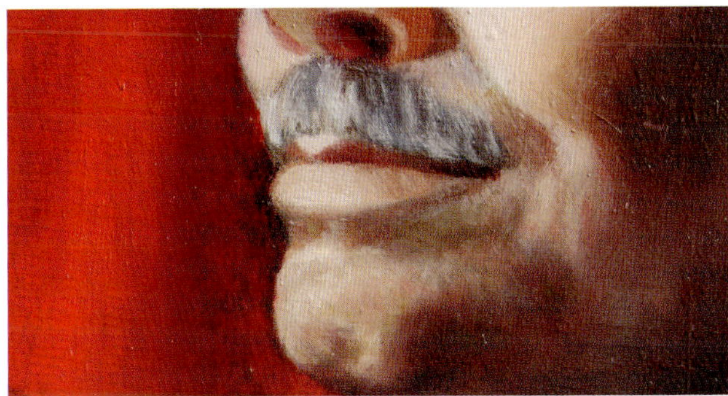

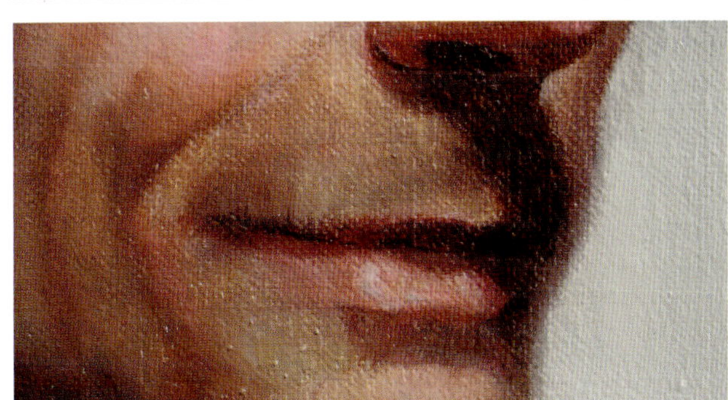

Light and Shadow Planes Set the Lips
Breaking up the top lip into planes that either face or turn away from the light, you will find four shapes. The bottom lip can be divided in half horizontally. The bottom half of that lip turns into shadow.

The Cast Shadow From the Lower Lip
The fullness of the lip determines the amount of the cast shadow underneath the structure. The upper half of the lower lip faces into the light and often catches a bit of a higher light on the moisture. That upper half can be divided into four planes that move into and out of the light.

THE SHAPES OF THE MOUTH

Each person has features that fit to their face. Some have very thin lips, others very full, rounded lips. In either case, the bottom lip tends to have more fullness than the upper lip. In a normal, at-rest position, the upper lip is thinner than the lower lip—somewhere between 2 to 3 ratio to a 1 to 2 ratio. The lips both appear thinner when stretched into a wide, closed-mouth smile. It takes slow, careful study and consideration to determine the changes.

THE SMILING MOUTH

Some people never look like themselves without a signature smile or grin, open or closed, crooked or pouty. It is very much a part of who they are, but it has to be natural, not forced. That is the key.

Is an open smile the most typical expression of your subject? If the model is in fact a person who expresses great happiness and a perpetually pleasant outlook, the open smile may work quite well. But beware of the cheesy photo grin.

THE KEY TO THE MOUTH: THE HORSESHOE SHAPE

Artists get hung up on the outer appearance of the lips with little concern for the actual shape the mouth forms inside the skin. Internalizing this concept helps the artist look for lighting issues as the mouth moves from dark into light and then back into middle light. The most important key to drawing and painting the mouth is to remember that the entire area is rather like a horseshoe. Think dentures.

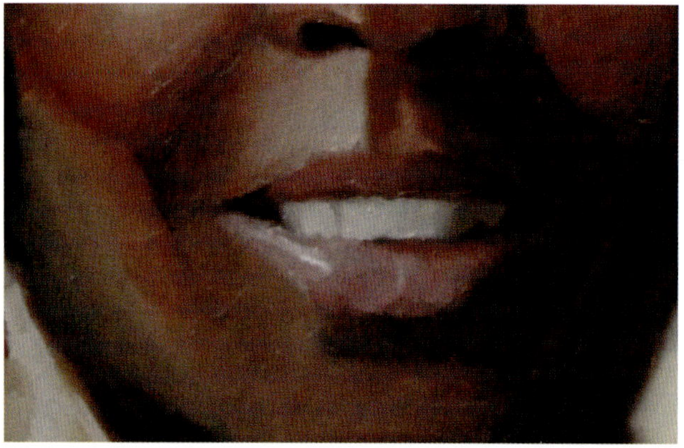

Horseshoe Shape

As the shape of the lower face becomes more familiar to the artist, the smiling mouth becomes easier to paint. One edge or surface of one tooth will have limited direct light on it. Each tooth is in a different lighting value they move around the U-shape. Practice by setting up some dominoes on edge in a horseshoe or U-shape. Put a single, strong light source directed as a light might enter the open mouth. Note the value changes as the teeth move away from the light source.

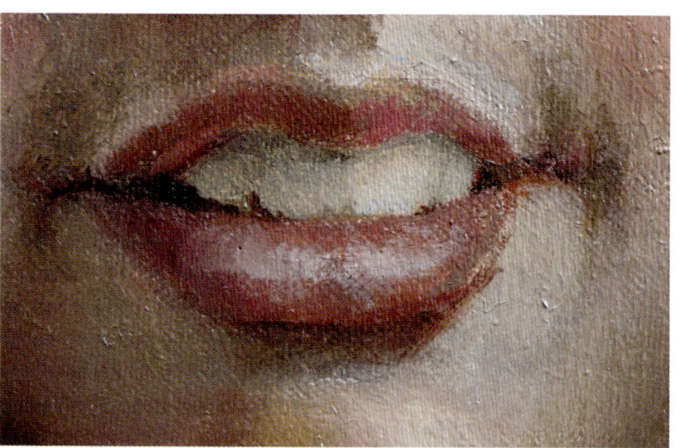

Natural Teeth

The relaxed lips, if not in a broad smile, will expose a few teeth. Though our lexicon includes the phrase "pearly whites" referring to teeth, use caution in mixing tinted whites. A too-white mixture will ruin an otherwise beautiful face. Bring the color and values down to keep them natural.

Picture how the teeth and gums fit deeply into the cheek area on the dark side of the head. Then they curve around so the front teeth are in the light and continue to move around deeply into the back of the mouth on the other side. Be mindful of the direction of the light, and that it is only one light source.

The teeth are never all in the same light or appear to be on the same plane, and therefore flat. Use the experience gained painting still-life setups. This mouth/teeth area will be similar to painting a cup that moves in and out of shadow with cool and warm colors, in and out of the picture plane. Practice painting a plain white porcelain cup.

THE COLORS OF TEETH

Teeth vary from skin-toned, to tints of green, gray, blue, pink, yellow. There is a national craze to whiten teeth to unnatural levels of white. Instead of overdoing the white quality of bleached teeth, back off to a tint that coordinates with the underlying skin tones.

The next time you are in a dental office, ask the technician if you can see the samples of porcelain teeth they use to match patients' teeth for crowns and dentures. It is astounding how many tints there are. When you do this, be sure to take both white and middle gray paper to hold behind the samples to get a true representation of the tints.

RULE OF THE GOLDEN MEAN

The Rule of the Golden Mean applies to all things in nature. In the human face and figure, we can mathematically find the perfect proportion by using phi (the proportion of 1 to 1.6180339). Here, where we are talking about the natural smile, even the proportion of the visible teeth can be calculated with this ratio. The height of the front tooth is 1.618 the size of the width. The large front tooth is 1.618 the size of the tooth next to it and so on. Art and science are inextricably interwoven.

THE MOUTH

Use rhomboids and triangles to divide the upper and lower lips into planes.

THE SIZE AND WIDTH OF THE MOUTH

Using an eye as a form of measurement, the mouth measures from one and a half to two eyes wide. The mouth in a relaxed state, measured from corner to corner, fits directly under the pupils.

To study this, look at a head directly from the front. Draw some plumb lines down from the pupils of the eyes and see how those lines intersect with the corners of the mouth.

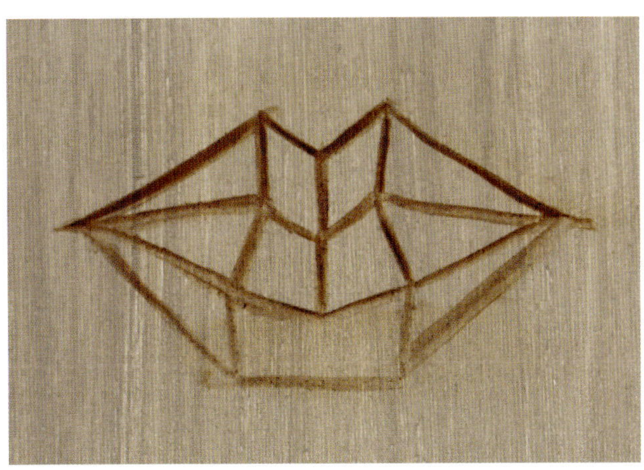

1 DIVIDE INTO SHAPES
The upper lip can be divided into four parts. The lower lip can be divided into four parts facing upward and three parts facing downward.

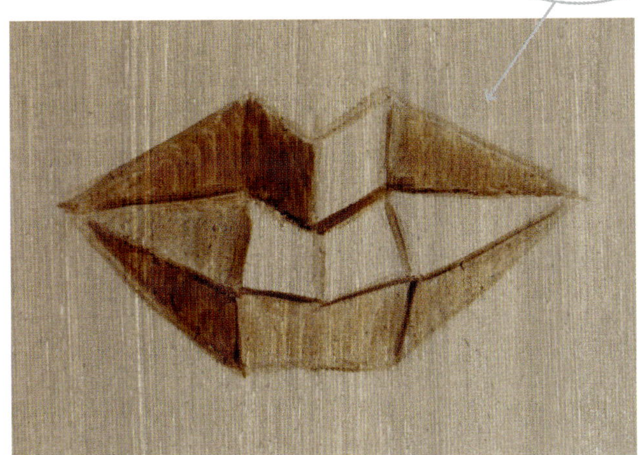

2 IDENTIFY THE LIGHT SOURCE
Keeping the geometric shapes intact, this is a simplification of a female lip construction with soft, rounded forms. Notice the light/shadow patterns from the upper to lower lips. The arrow represents a light source to help make the lips more sculptural and help differentiate the planes that catch the light or are turned into the shadows.

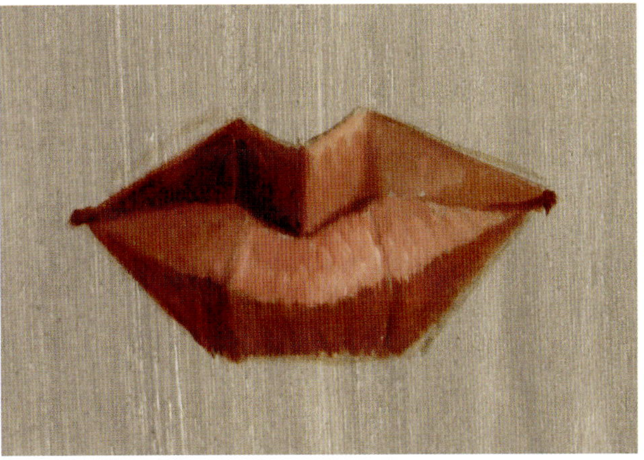

3 ADD COLOR
The structure becomes completely visible as color is added. Now the division of the lower lip is well understood as the light touches the soft and rounded upper portion and the underside remains in shadow.

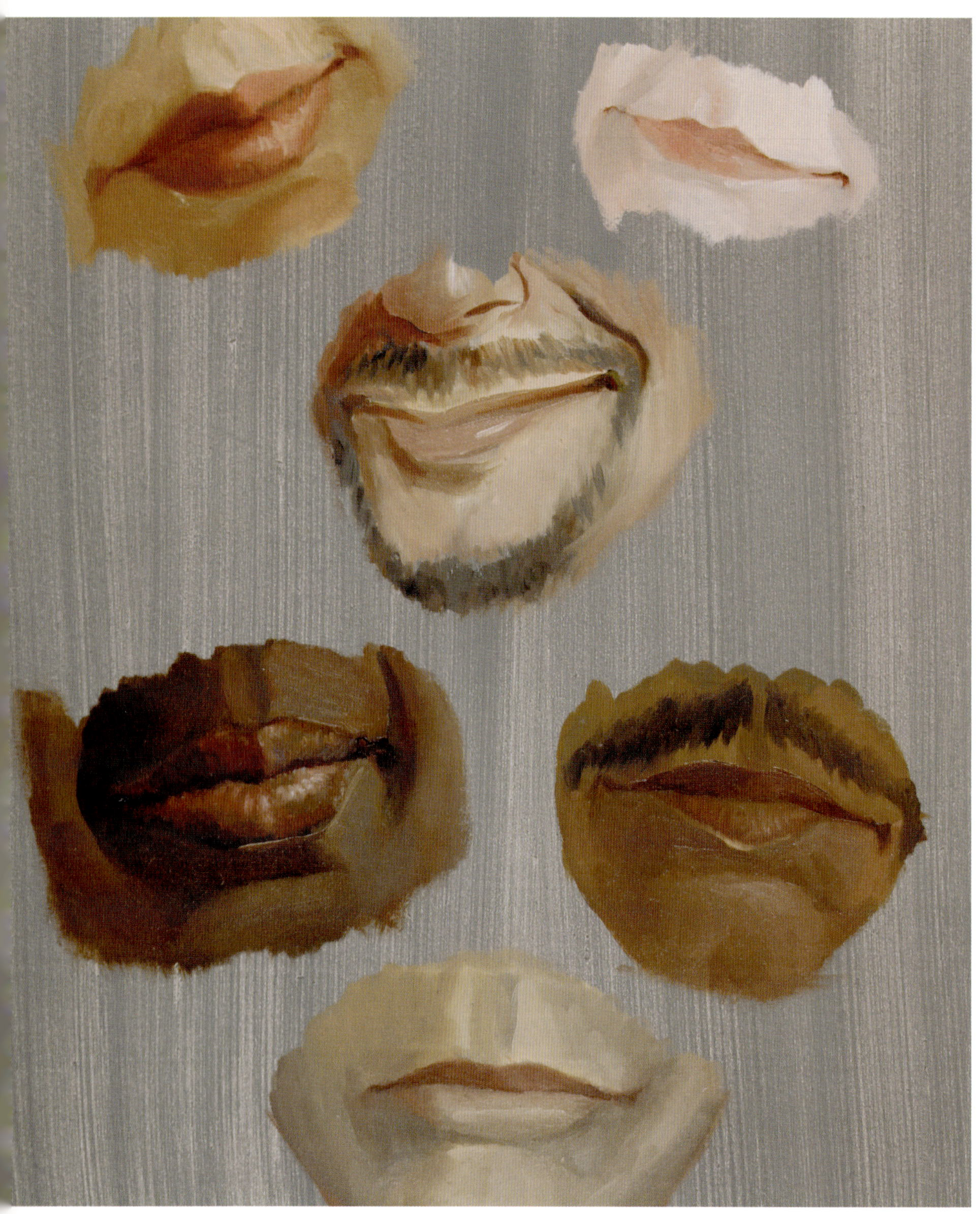

Characteristic Grins

The mouth is among the most challenging of the features because it is nearly always in motion. Find the most pleasant, characteristic expression to finish off the face.

EARS

Ears are one of the features too often ignored or painted badly because artists assume they are too complicated. Long, feminine tresses may permit hiding the ears occasionally, but this will not always be the answer. More than half of your clientele may be people with short, cropped hair and women with updos—and nowhere to hide those pesky ears.

EAR FORM AND COLOR

Ears are formed from cartilage and are full of capillaries that permit blood flow close to the surface of the skin. Therefore, like the tips of fingers, toes and nose, the ears tend to take on a slightly warmer hue than the face or neck.

EARLOBE

The earlobe (lobule) is the only part of the ear structure that has no cartilage. Therefore, the lobe takes on many forms from flat and angular to round and plump. There are people with no earlobes, having the outer rim move down directly into the face with no drop or shape to the lobe. And there are people with full, dangling earlobes.

EAR POSITION ON THE HEAD

The point of attachment of the ear to the head is in alignment with the eyes. Please be very cautious about this placement. Remember how glasses sit on the face with the earpieces resting on this attachment point of the ears.

The cup of the ear can sit quite flat to the head or project outward very noticeably. These ears that protrude outward are sometimes a little disconcerting when on a young boy or a grown man. The artist cannot change their appearance for fear of ruining the overall likeness to the sitter. The direction and tilt or the angle of the head in addition to lighting changes may reduce attention to this feature. But these differences can change the appearance of the sitter dramatically. Be true to the sitter.

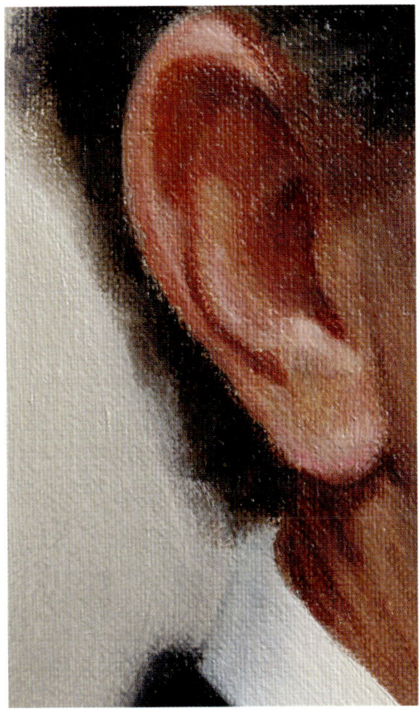

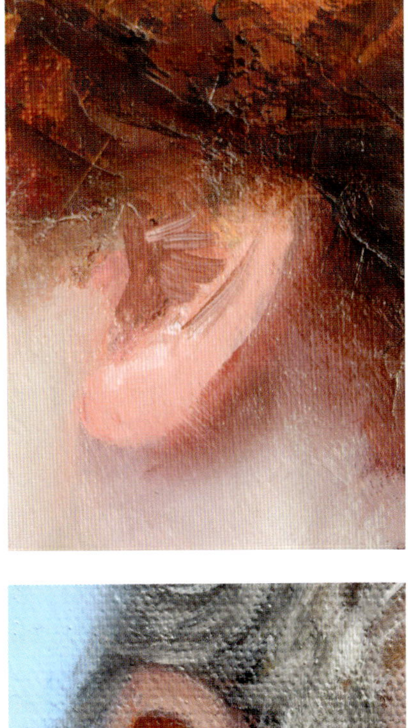

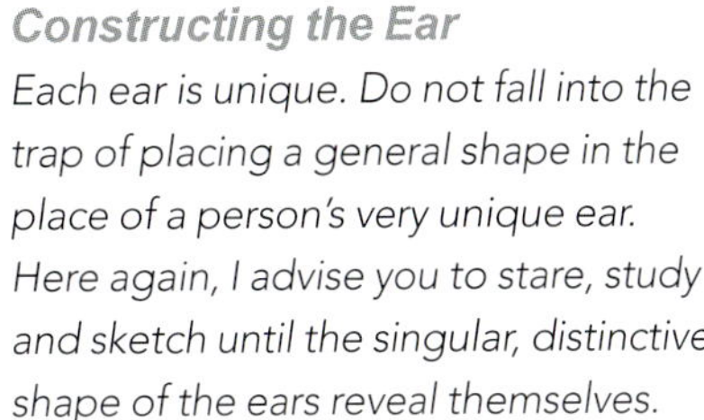

Constructing the Ear

Each ear is unique. Do not fall into the trap of placing a general shape in the place of a person's very unique ear. Here again, I advise you to stare, study and sketch until the singular, distinctive shape of the ears reveal themselves.

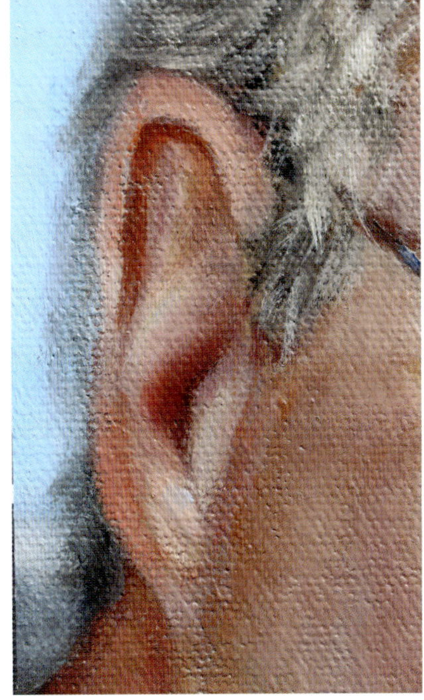

THE EARS INDICATE AGE

The ears are as important as the other features in distinguishing likeness and age. The length of the ear is approximately one-third the length of the head. Ears continue to lengthen with age.

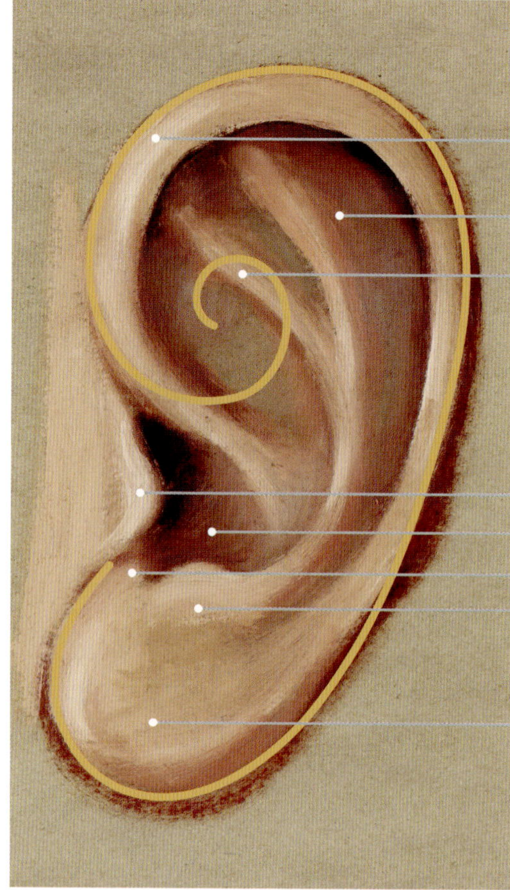

The Parts of the Ear

Again we can go back to the mathematics and Fibonacci. The Rule of the Golden Mean is apparent in the shape and proportions of the ear. Here, the human ear even exhibits the Fibonacci spiral.

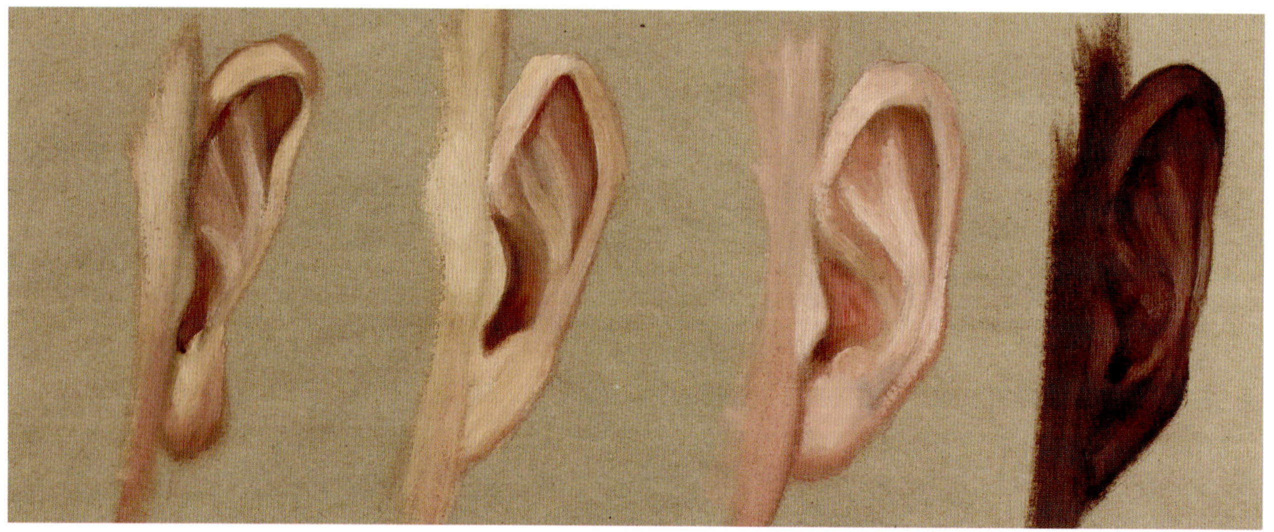

Slight Differences in Ears

Although the ear is universally the same, it is the slight differences that must be discerned. Look at how each of these are generally related in shape and size, but on closer study, the viewer can detect minor shape differences and directional changes in the underlying cartilage that makes up the visible ear.

EAR CONSTRUCTION SIMPLIFIED

Using interlocking circles and a Y-shape gives the artist a simplified approach to the construction of the ear while the head is in profile and the ear is flat on to the viewer.

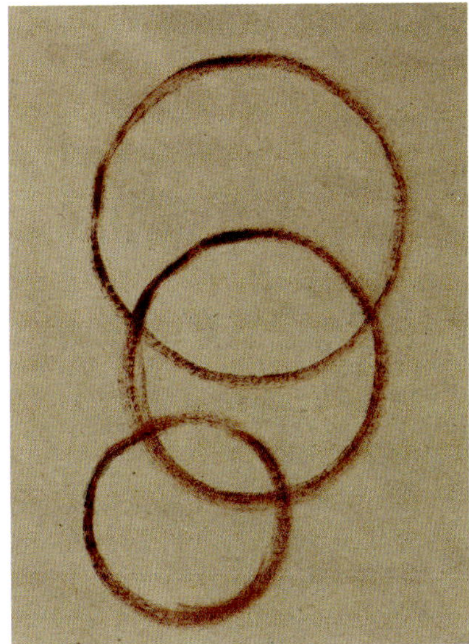

1 **DRAW THREE CIRCLES** *Use interlocking circles of descending size to create the basic blueprint of the ear.*

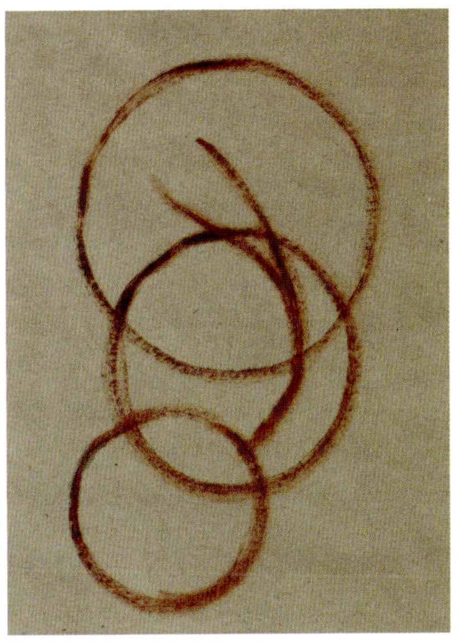

2 **FORM THE ANTIHELIX** *Inside the ear shape is a piece of cartilage shaped like a Y that curves from the inner top area to the opposite side ending near the antitragus.*

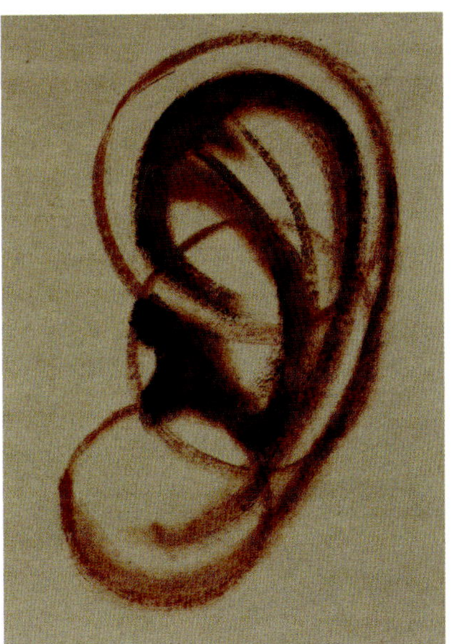

3 **ADD SHADOWS** *Place a shadow deep under the helix wrapping around the ear, a shadow under the antitragus and onto the flat, scooped area, the concha, that enters the ear canal.*

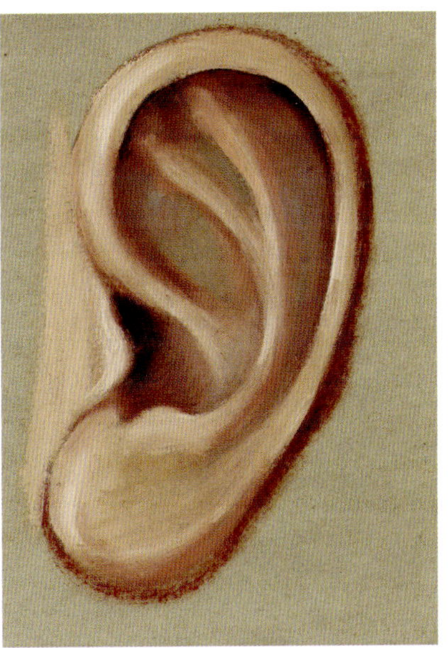

4 **ADD SKIN TONE IN MIDDLE VALUES** *Continue to shape and round each of the areas leading down to the lobule or earlobe. Keep the hue fairly warm throughout the ear as compared to the base color of the face.*

FOUR WAYS TO PROPORTION THE HEAD

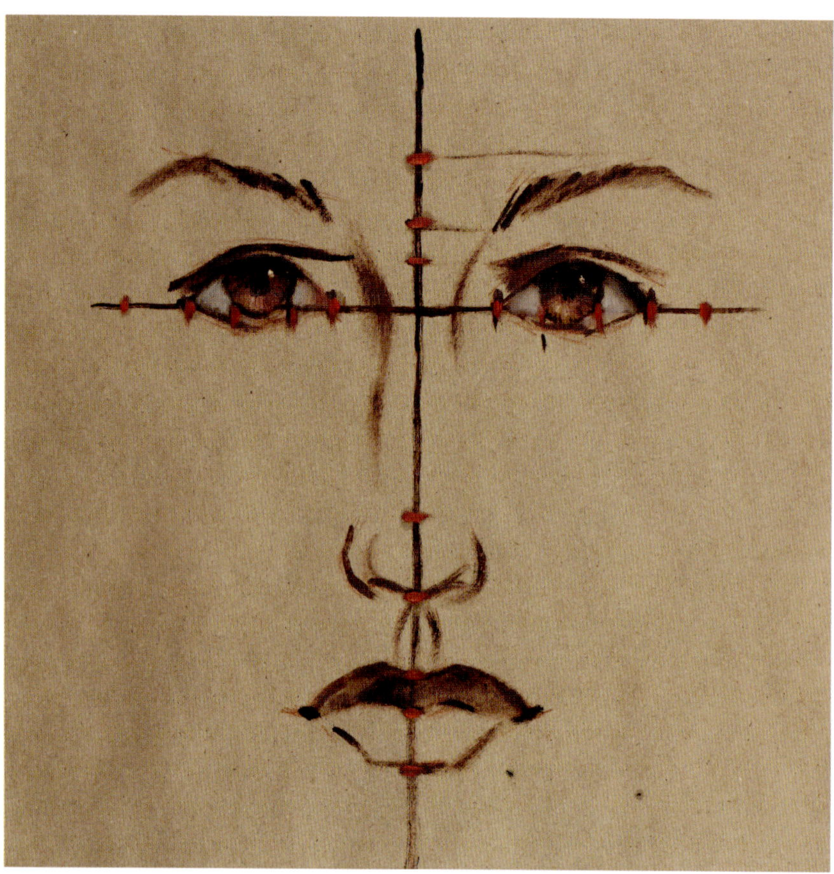

Head as a Kite
This is an easy and exceptionally accurate technique to capture the markers for the features.

As instructors, we can provide some generalities to the human form to encourage your further study. And although formulas and information for classical beauty can be written, sometimes the most beautiful people are those with vastly different or irregular features. Their images follow no norm, no classic pattern. Their beauty comes from within and their portraits may become the most impressive of paintings.

There are four popular methods to place the features on the head: the kite method, the halves method, the thirds method and the fifths method. Few people fit this formulaic method of division, but from this beginning, the artist can learn to see the variances.

PLACE FEATURES AS A KITE

This method is adapted from the Sight-Size Method working from the center point between the eyes at the vertical center of the face and where the nose and the horizontal of the eyes intersect. From this center point, measure outward to the inner corner of the eye, then to the outer corner, finishing with the center of the pupil.

Continue measuring in the opposite direction for the other eye. From the central point between the eyes, note the vertical measurement to the tip of the nose, the bottom of the septum (the cartilage that divides the nostrils), then the upper lip center, the division between the lips and finally the bottom of the lower lip.

Working from the center outward, as in most Sight-Size Methods, provides accurate placement and shape of the skull around the features.

DIVIDE THE HEAD IN HALVES

Divide a 9" head (23cm) in half from the top of the head to the bottom of the chin and place the eyes at that middle

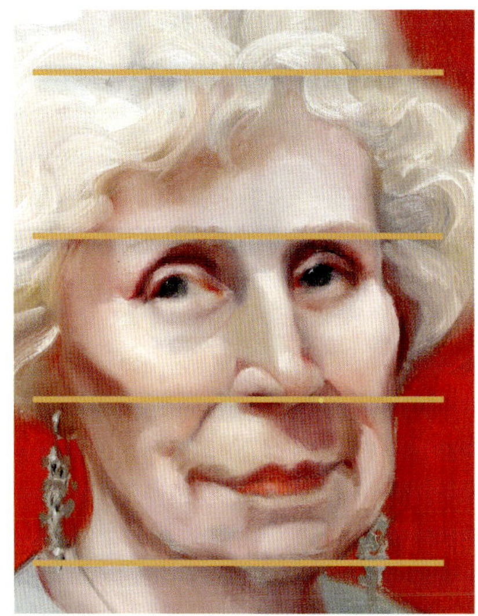

Dividing the Head in Thirds
When the face is divided into thirds, it helps to remember the zones of color. In the upper third, the skin is close to the bone with little fatty tissue beneath and appears slightly more golden. The second third has the highest concentration of blood vessels around the eyes, nose and cheeks, and is slightly more red throughout. The bottom third around the mouth and jawline has a slightly cooler appearance. This is especially noticeable in men where the beard helps to deepen that cool effect.

Veronica Samuel
Artist, painter, jeweler
Oil study on toned Ampersand Gessobord
20" × 16" (51cm × 41cm)

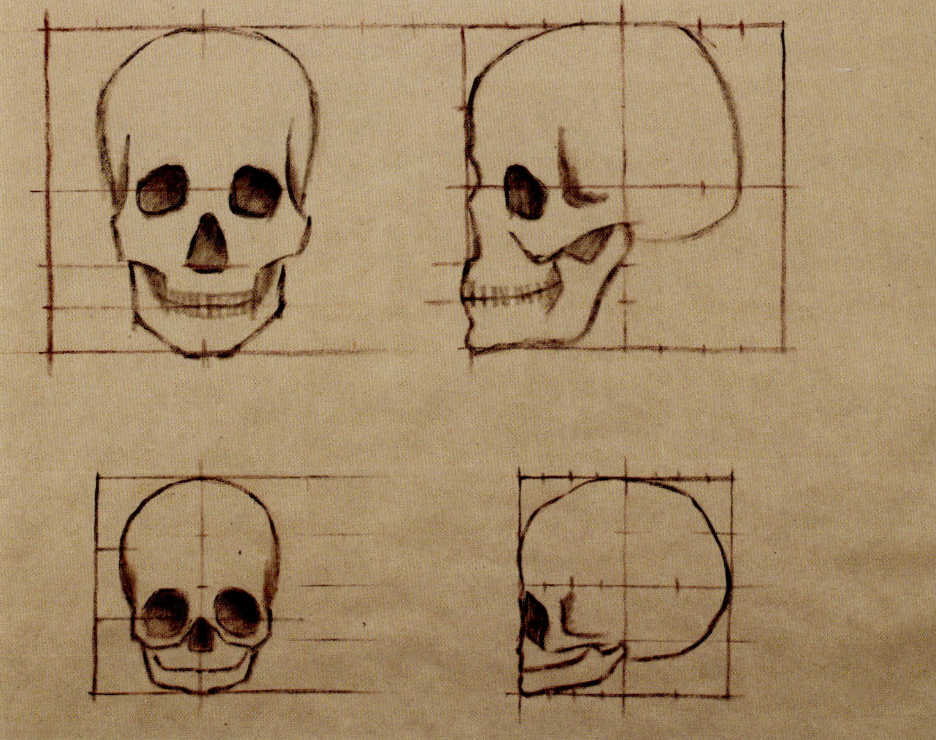

Divide the Head in Halves
Directly compare the 9" (23cm) adult skull to the one-year-old baby's skull. The one-year-old skull is approximately 6" (15cm) high, 4" (10cm) wide, 6" (15cm) deep. The eye sockets sit two-thirds of the way down, and all of the features fit onto the lower third of the skull. Notice that the eye sockets are almost exactly the same size in the adult and baby.

point. The pupils sit approximately 2.5" (6cm) apart. Dividing the distance from the eyes to the chin in half again marks the bottom of the nose. Dividing the distance from the bottom of the nose to the chin determines the placement of the bottom of the lower lip.

An adult male head is decidedly more angular than a woman's. The skull can be seen as more angular or sharp while the woman's skull has smoother, curved transitions.

Using the head as a length of measurement, the head in profile is approximately seven-eighths wide, and from the front is approximately two-thirds wide.

DIVIDE THE HEAD IN THIRDS

Used very often by artists and described in the writings of Leonardo da Vinci, the head divided in thirds will measure:

- one-third down from the hairline to the eyebrows
- one-third down from the eyebrows to the bottom of the nose
- one-third down from the bottom of the nose to the bottom of the chin

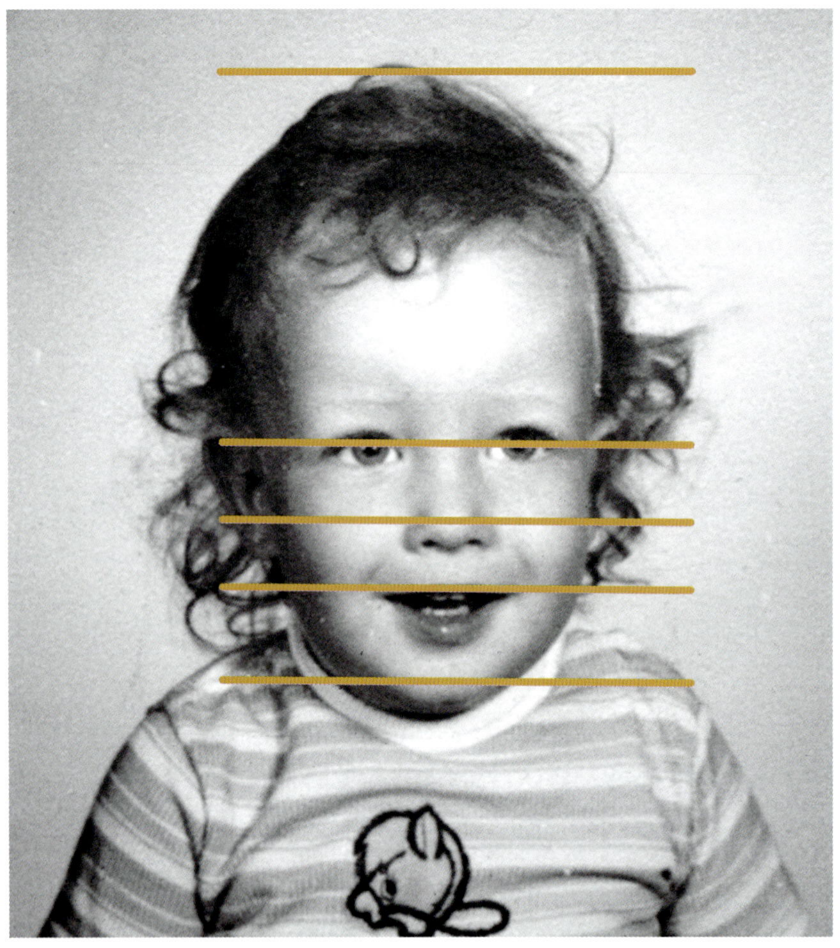

Drawing Proportions Change With an Open Mouth
On this photo of a child with an open mouth smile, the head is first divided into thirds. The lower third is now divided into thirds again. This open mouth smile can change the lower proportions as the jaw moves downward.

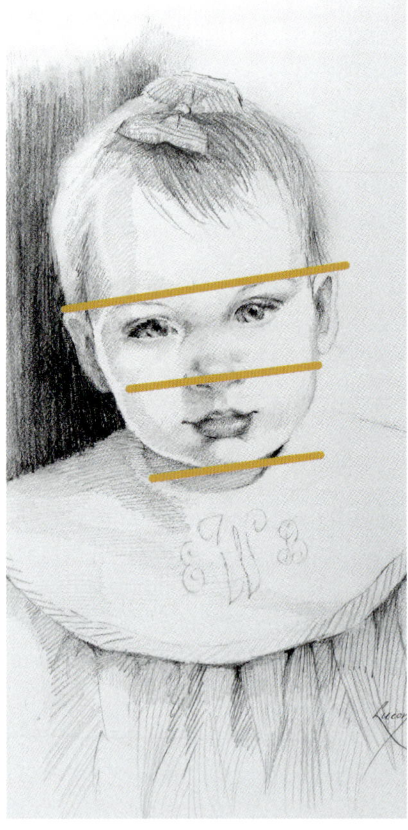

Divide a Child's Head in Thirds
This drawing of Baird shows all of the features in the lower part of the head. Walt Disney made a fortune imbuing his characters with child-like proportions: large eyes, tiny nose and tiny mouth all in the lower two-thirds.

THE THIRDS METHOD AND CHILDREN

For very young children, newborns to about three years old, notice the distinctly different proportions of the head while the cranium is considerably larger than the diminutive features of the face. Measuring from the top of the head to the chin, mark three equal sections. The eyes will be located on the one-third mark. The lower third of the face can be divided in half to locate the bottom of the nose. Dividing the balance in half locates the division between the lips.

Other things you may notice while sketching young children are that the eyes appear to be slightly farther apart, lashes appear longer and eyebrows are much sparser. The irises are nearly adult size even at the youngest ages, so the open eye is nearly filled with color showing little of the scelera or whites of the eyes.

Babies' noses have very little definition to the bridge. The cheek across the bridge of the nose to the next cheek appears to be nearly flat. The septum is flatter in babies, making the bottom of the nose straighter across from wing to wing than in older people. While chins are tinier, less noticeable and tend to recede, the apples of the cheeks are rounder.

DIVIDING THE HEAD IN FIFTHS

Another formula to divide the head is using a compass and dividing lines into fifths. Use interwoven circles to give a very accurate gauge. This method always appeals to the inner engineer/mathematician in workshops.

The face is approximately five equal eyes wide. The nose is usually the width of one eye. The distance from the bottom of the lower lip to the chin is one eye long. The distance from the corner of the mouth to the jaw is one eye wide.

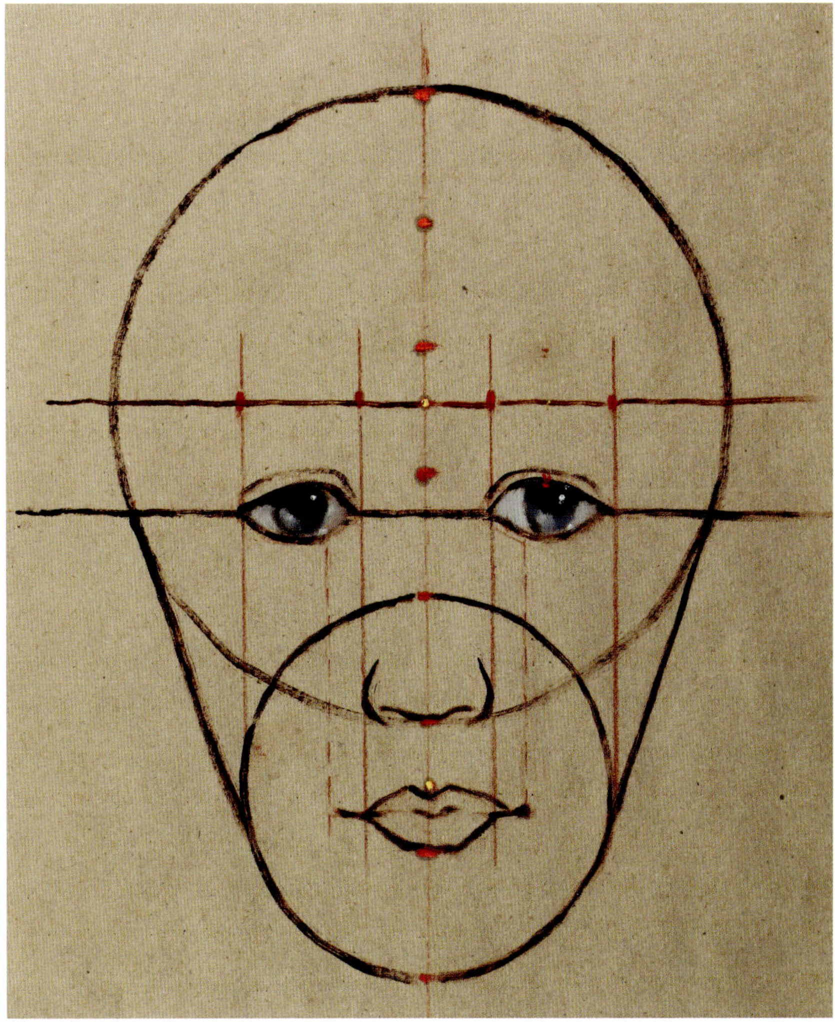

Dividing the Head in Fifths

Careful consideration and study of this method gives the artist a strong basic understanding of the proportions, but do not let it hinder the inevitable need for variants required for each individual.

1. For a 10" (25cm) head, draw a 7" (18cm) circle. Bisect through the center horizontally. Divide this line into 5 equal spaces.

2. Add a vertical line through the center (intersect the yellow dot) extending beyond the bottom of the circle.

3. Divide the vertical line into 5 equal spaces inside the circle, and add two more equally-spaced marks below the circle.

4. Draw two vertical lines down from the horizontal line that bisects the circle at the first mark. Create a new circle that starts at the fourth mark from the top and moves out to the two vertical lines that have just been drawn downward. This circle is 3 marks wide.

5. Draw two straight lines at points on horizontal line from the outside of the upper circle to the lower circle.

6. Draw a horizontal line inside the upper circle parallel to the first horizontal line. This is the line where the eyes will sit between the second and fourth vertical sections.

7. The bottom of the larger circle is the placement for the bottom of the nose.

8. Between the lower mark on the vertical line in the lower circle and the yellow dot (exact center of the lower circle) is the placement of the mouth.

9. Please note that the end result is much like beginning with an oval and using the dividing-in-halves method.

SCULPT WITH PAINT

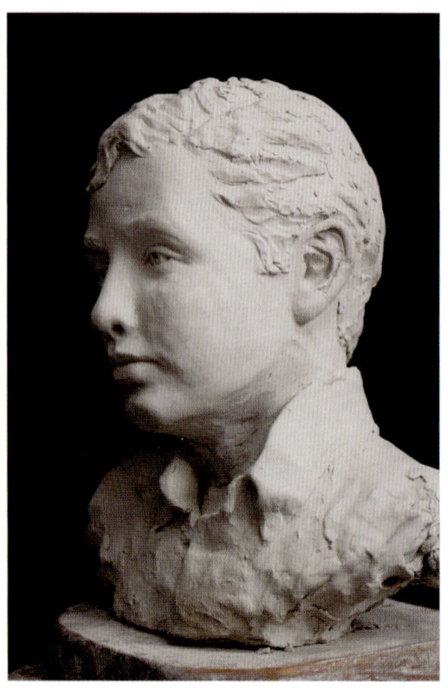
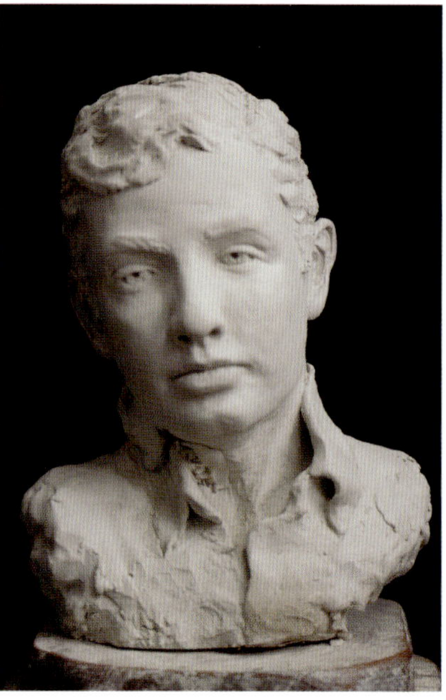
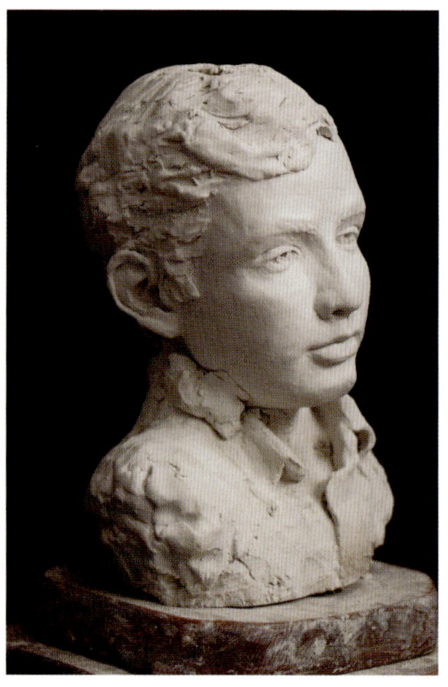

The Three-Dimensional Head
Consider this unfinished clay sculpture as another version of sketching. Note how far back from the front of the face the ear sits in the two three-quarter views.

Be aware of proportions, but don't be hampered by grids, maps or too many rules. Feel the face with your eyes. Let your mind translate the movement in and out of the topography of the face as if you were touching it with your fingers and forming it in clay.

Look at this unfinished clay head. The benefit of studying sculpture is that complication of color has been removed. If we were to draw or paint this form monochromatically, we could easily study the planes. Imagine touching the shapes of the face as you draw or paint. Feel the shapes. Use thumbs to flatten the glabella, dig out the sockets of the eyes, build back in the eyes and lids, build up the bridge of the nose and move from the ridge of the nose down to the cheeks. Flare in the wings of the nostrils, place the septum and the philtrum as they round onto the lips, indent the corners of the mouth, curve into the chin, and take care not to make the zygomatic bone too high or sharp in this young boy.

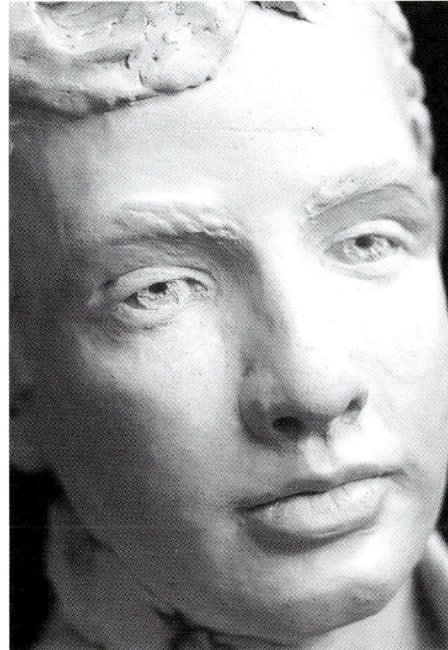

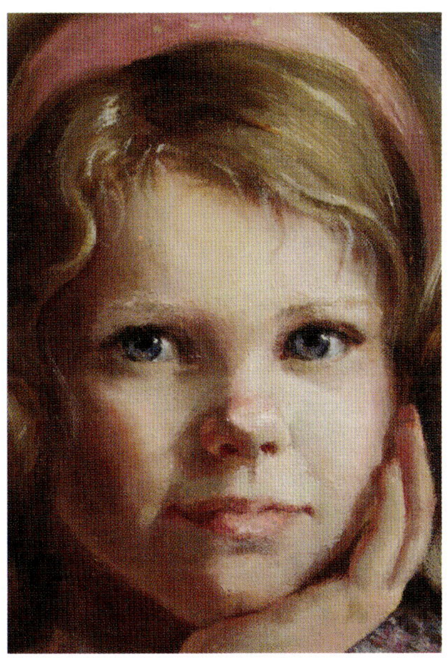

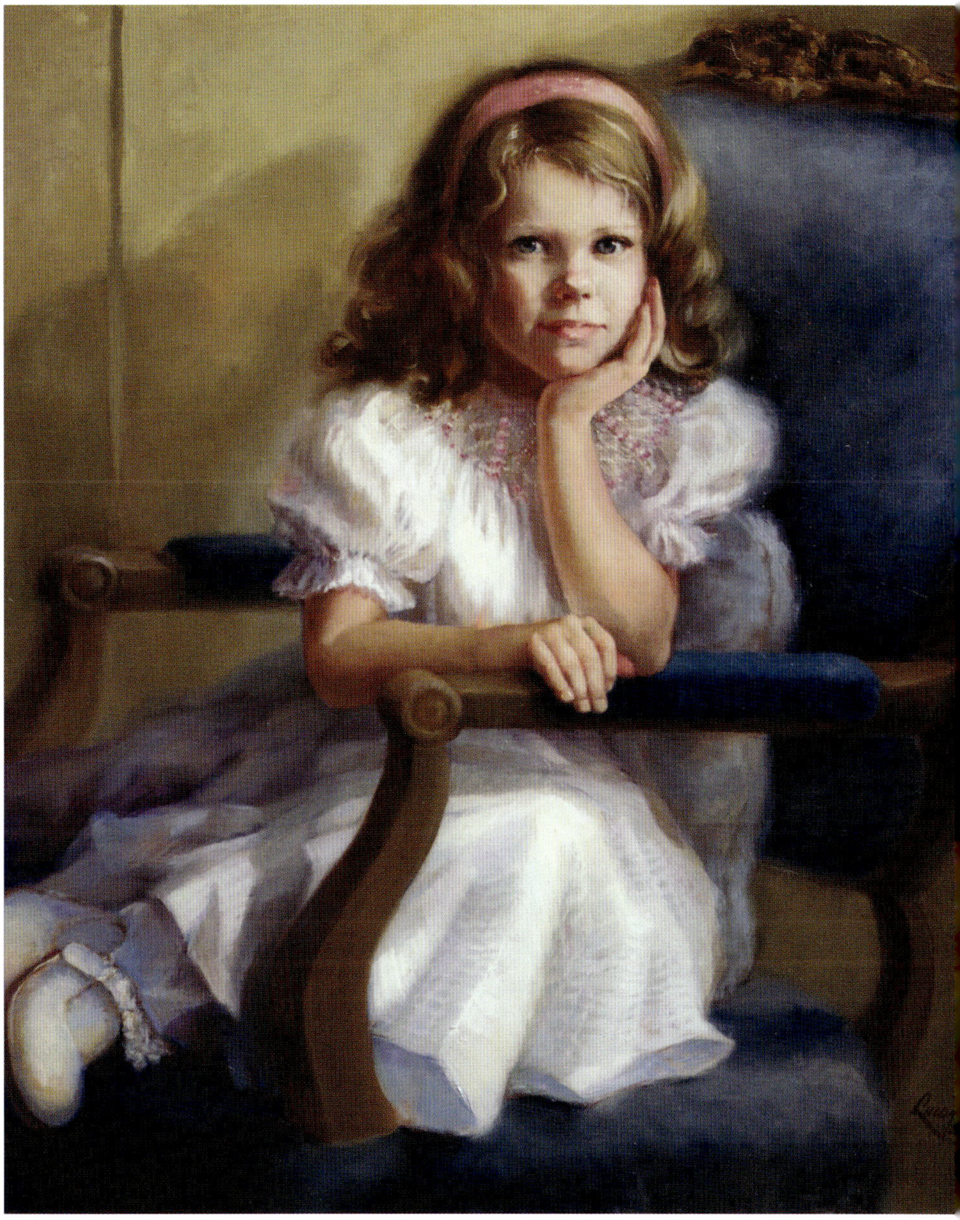

Comparing Sculpture, Painting and Life

Look at the firm, soft and lost edges in the sculpture and in the paintings. To create the illusion of a life-like child's head in paint, the artist must see and feel the three-dimensional shape in her mind. Look at the firm edge of the shadow on the upper cheek where the light travels across the face to the edge of the cheekbone. Compare it to the softer edge and relaxed muscles on the rounded lower cheek into the mouth area. It is the same, from the sculpture to the painting to life.

Haley Stoltz
Oil on Claessens linen
36" × 30" (92cm × 76cm)
Private collection

UNDERSTAND WHAT'S UNDERNEATH

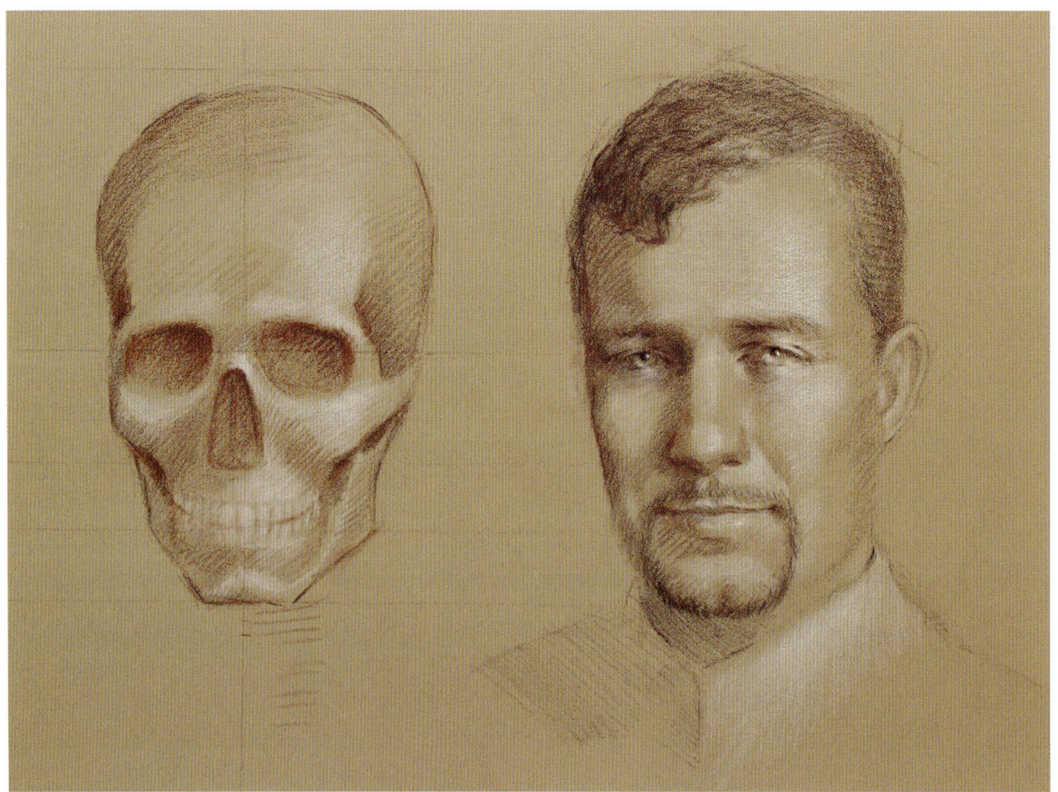

The Foundation of the Face: The Skull Within
This demonstration with the face about 1 to 2 degrees off center is a perfect example of what should be going through the artist's mind while drawing the face. Think and feel the skull in the mind while observing and recording the outer layer.

Al and Skull, a Monochromatic Study
Charcoal and chalk on Ampersand Pastelbord—sand tone
16" × 20" (41cm × 51cm)
Private collection

My paintings were described once as "having enough solid structure that we can see she painted the skeleton first, muscle and skin appropriately and layered with the clothing and hair." Although it is unnecessary to carry each of these layers to complete finish, in reality all of those things should be in your consciousness as you are observing and studying the person you are portraying.

As your drawing of an individual progresses, keep the skull in mind. Be cognizant of the nasal bone, bone structure around the eyes and the zygomatic bone as it moves from above the ear canal downward toward the tip of the cartilage of the nose. The dip in the temple area, the crease under the lower lip and the rounding out into the chin are all very specific cranial features. Determine how this person's features are unique—a little higher, a little lower, straighter, rounder. Take the time to study. Draw all the time.

Once the anatomy becomes second nature, work moves more quickly. It is the same with materials of different mediums. There are idiosyncrasies that become expected as the material or the process becomes more familiar. Spend more time going to life drawing or simply collecting "found" people in everyday life.

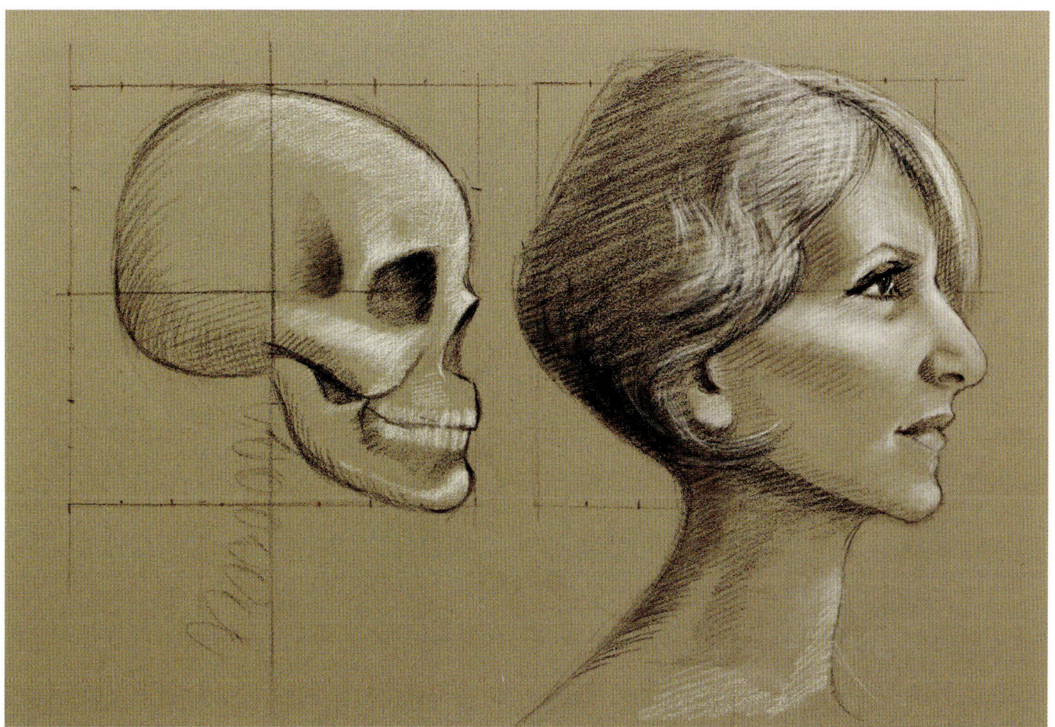

The Skull Under Hair

When working on women, try to structure the head as if the hair were not confusing the proportions. Essentially, look through the hair. This side-by-side drawing of the head with the skull should help you understand not only where, but how much, hair is covering the skull.

Squint while looking at this sketch. Is the skull apparent through the skin?

The Outer Layer as it Relates to the Skull

As the face takes shape, do not lose the basic foundation of the construction beneath the skin. Look at both of these carefully. Can you feel what is underneath? Compare the examples on these two pages. Go from the drawn face to one of the skulls and your own soft skin to feel the bone beneath. Compare the point where each plane changes. Be certain we can feel the eye socket. Make the nose project outward. Give the lips softness as they lie over the underlying teeth.

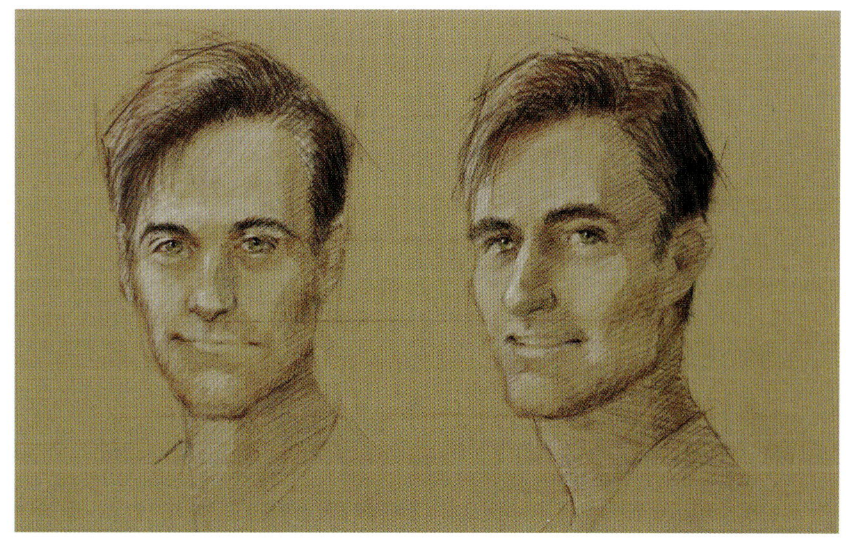

Kevin Blume
Charcoal/pastel study on Ampersand Pastelbord—sand tone
16" × 20" (41cm × 51cm)

TRAIN YOURSELF WITH SKETCHING

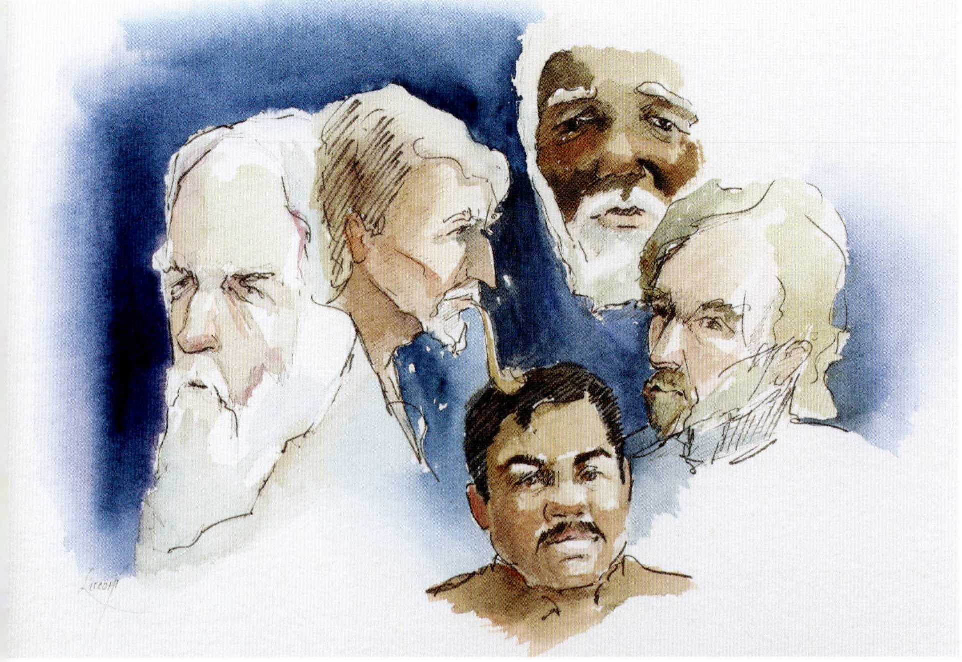

The Constant—The Sketchbook
These ink sketches at the airport were later washed with watercolor from a pocket watercolor set while sitting at the food court. There is no reason not to be collecting great faces everywhere every day.

Men—Logan Airport Study
Faber-Castell waterproof ink pen and watercolor on Kilimanjaro
9" × 12" (23cm × 31cm)

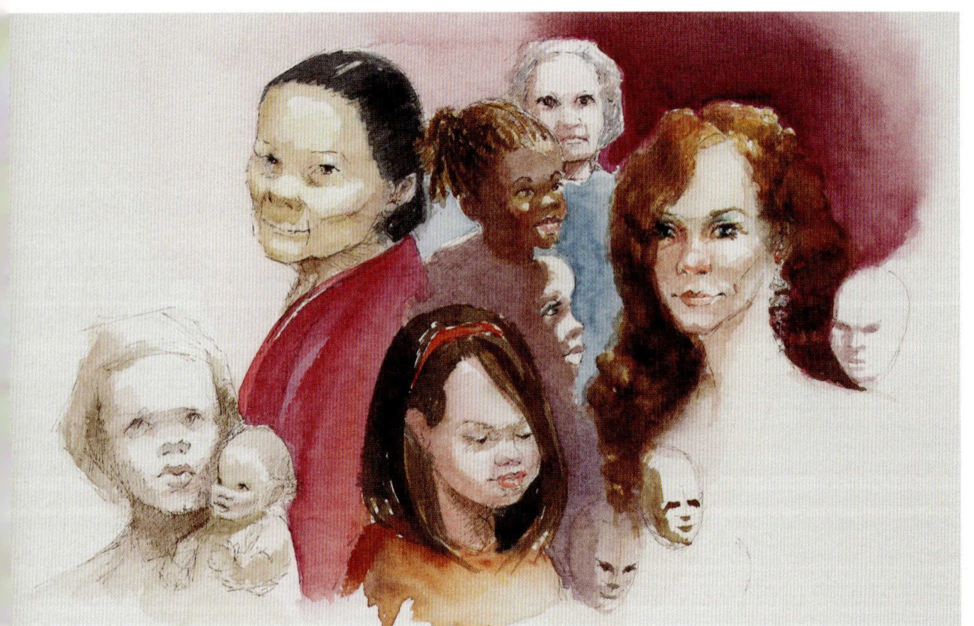

Women—Burbank Airport Study
Faber-Castell waterproof ink pen and watercolor on Kilimanjaro
9" × 12" (23cm × 31cm)

Always keep a sketchbook at hand full of "found" people. Watch the masses at schools, shopping centers, stations, airports, beaches, anywhere people are plentiful. Draw in ink. Think and act quickly. Do some memory drawing and painting. Catch what you can in the moment, and add color later. Working in ink encourages quick, concise decisions of position, length, direction and weight.

HAIR

Hair is easily painted when the artist concentrates on the overall impression the hair gives instead of the individual strands. In the dark passages, keep the paint thin and transparent. In the middle values, bring sufficient paint to the canvas with your brush and move with broad strokes along the contours of the hair. Determine the unique texture and, with soft edges, dance along the particular rhythm of the movement. Add highlights according to the temperature of the light falling on the mass. Keep everything soft until the end. If shinier highlights or lighter notes are needed, go back in with a soft brush and paint to emphasize the light's point of contact with the hair.

ALLA PRIMA

Alla prima is an Italian term meaning "at the first," or the first time. Artists who paint in this manner mix the paint in the correct value, hue and temperature and put it down in the correct spot in one brilliant stroke…and then leave it alone. The resulting, slightly more opaque paint always looks fresh and spontaneous. Amazing!

HAIR EDGES

Edges are the nemesis of well-painted hair. We have all seen the painting with the beautifully painted face and the cheap toupee-looking hair to cap it off. It is because of edges. Nothing will kill the painting faster than painting rigid, solid-looking, sharp-edged hair.

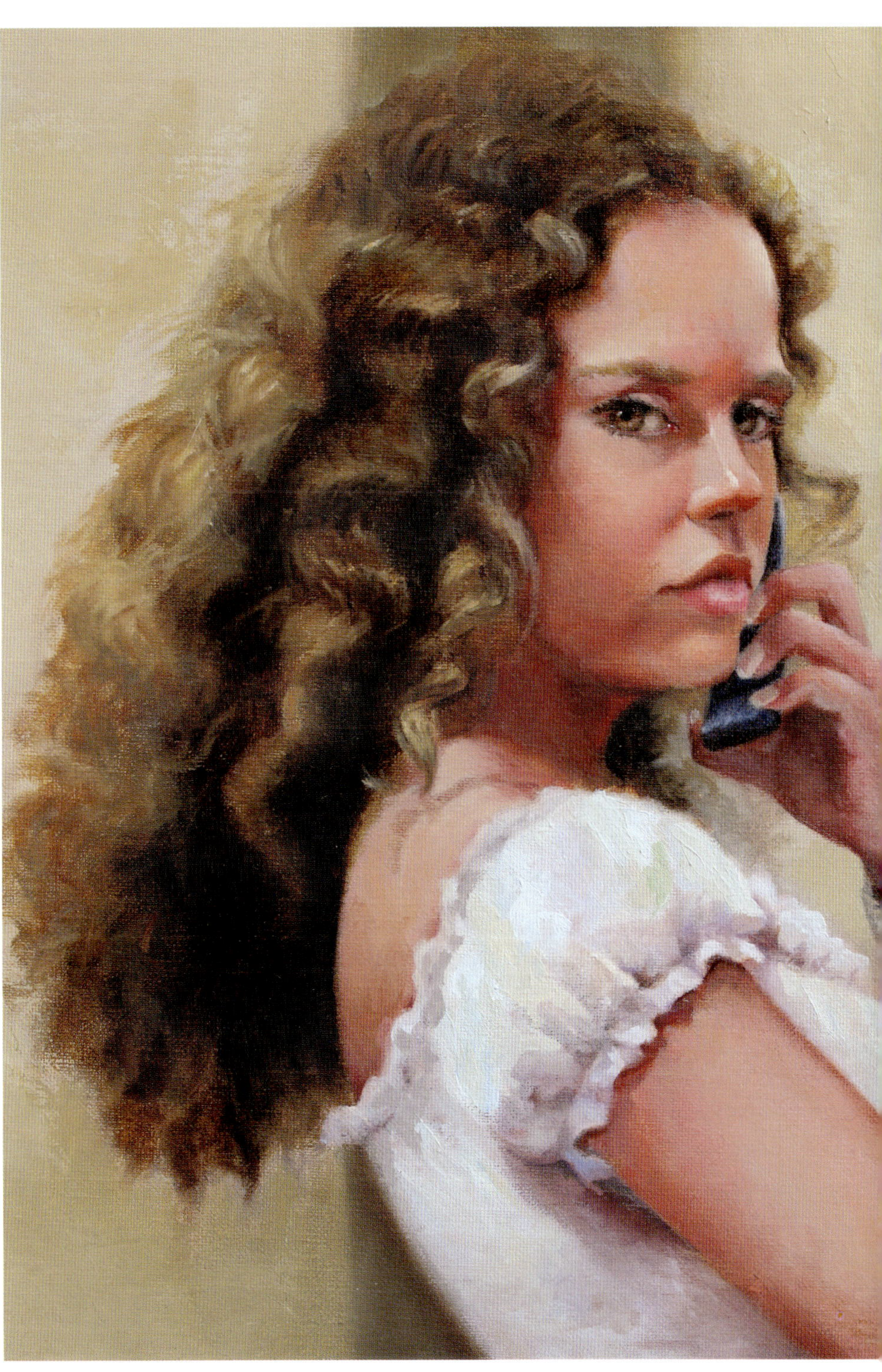

The Texture of Hair

When painting great faces, the artist must consider all the surrounding textures of clothing and hair with the same amount of care. The texture of this Italian girl's hair is undeniably soft, thick and wavy.

Atteggiamento (Attitude)
Oil on linen (detail)
42" × 30" (107cm × 76cm)
Private collection

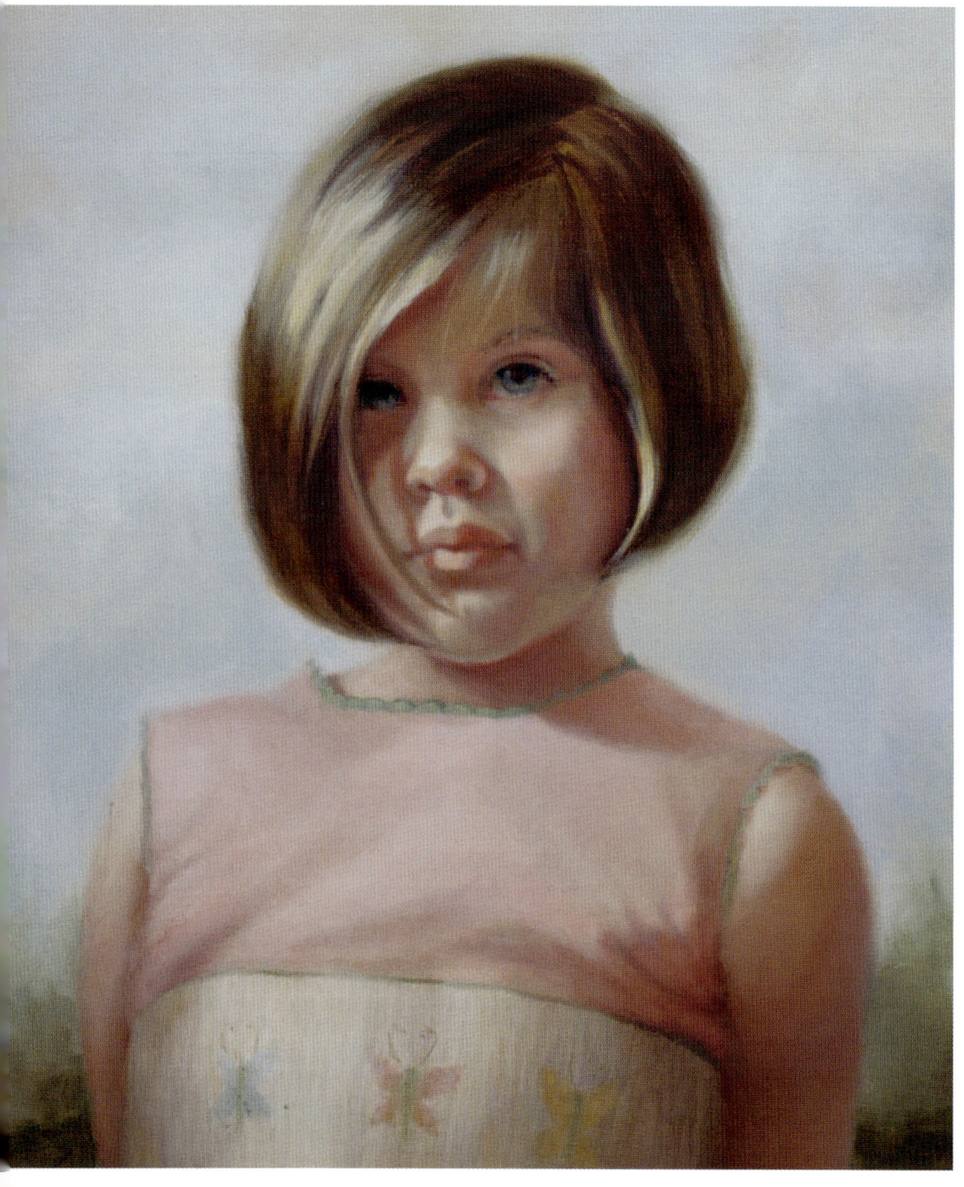

GLAZING

Glazing is a method of using a medium-to-thin oil color to nearly transparent quality and applying multiple layers to achieve the desired value, hue and temperature. Imagine placing multiple layers of stained glass one on top of the other to create an altogether different color. The light shining through these layers and bouncing back out creates a magical effect of depth.

The Hairstyle
Hairstyles and clothing in women often remove the timeless quality to a modern painting more than in paintings of men or children. These items seem to clearly stamp the decade on the image. With this child, however, the silky smooth hair is cut in a no fuss style that will defy time.

Ellie Pegrem
Oil on Claessens linen (detail)
36" × 42" (92cm × 107cm)
Private collection

The very best way to combat this is to keep all of the paint moist and receptive. This is the goal of *alla prima* artists. Those who work in carefully constructed layers or glazes must find ways to keep both the hair and any object it falls across wet so the colors may be feathered together and kept soft edged. These artists sneak up on the finish, but with equally satisfying results.

HAIR TEXTURES

The texture can dictate everything about the style, the ethnicity and the attitude of the person. We know with all the hair products today, anything can be done. Study the effect that light and shadow have on the follicles. With the deft handling of a good still-life artist, consider the appearance of thick, heavy-hanging hair, light wispy child's hair, smooth curls, crinkly waves. They are all a challenge best handled as a still life. No matter what sketches, remember to keep edges soft.

HAIRSTYLE

Recommend that the subject handle her hair for the portrait as she would any other day. If it is an informal portrait, anything they do with their hair on

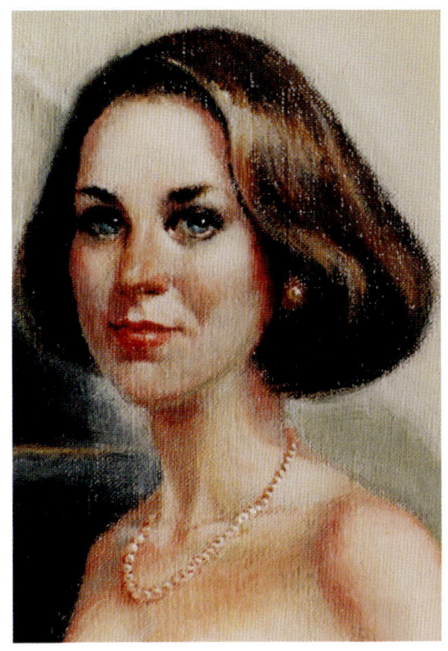

Brunette Hair
The striking beauty of the brunette here is only enhanced by her green/blue eyes. This detail is from a 48" x 36" (122cm x 92cm) full length painting of Anna in her debutante gown with a grand curved staircase leading upward behind her. The very dark warm colors in her hair framed her face beautifully in this otherwise pastel-filled canvas.

Anna White
Oil on Claessens linen
48" × 36" (122cm × 92cm)
Private collection

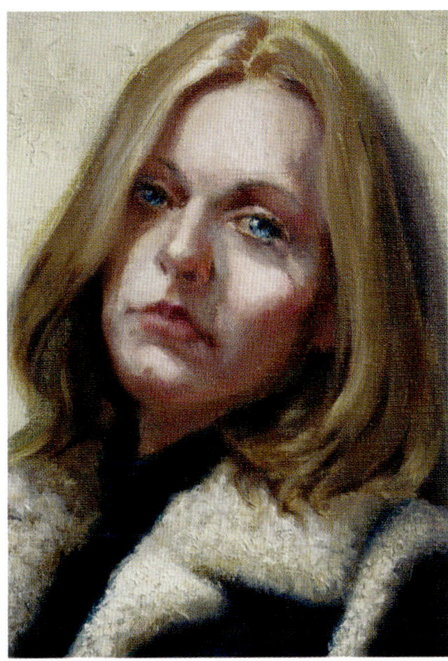

Blonde Hair
The blonde here is closer to a strawberry blonde. Pale skin and clear blue eyes made a striking image. The hair color was painted using an adaptation of the blonde and redhead charts in chapter three.

Katherine Sweeney
Oil on linen (detail)
42" × 30" (109cm × 78cm)
Private collection

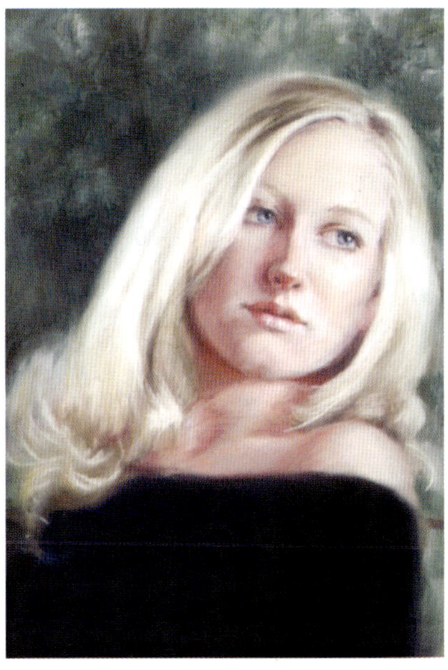

Golden Hair
Pay attention to the lack of yellow in the hair. It is a variety of soft mossy greens, neutral yellows and earthy gray-browns.

Abby Morris
Pastel on foam-mounted Kitty Wallis (detail)
32" × 40" (81cm × 102cm)
Private collection

a daily basis will be fine. If the portrait is more formal, certainly an updo may be just the ticket. But have her refrain from going to a stylist and becoming someone she is not for the day. This is going to be a lasting tribute to her. The people who will see the portrait need to trust that this is how she really looked. Encourage her to represent her natural self.

HAIR COLOR

Suggestions for color mixtures are covered in charts included in chapter three. They are by no means the only combinations of colors to mix. They are simply suggested as a place to start.

Hair color in paintings by new artists is often too saturated with color straight from the tube. Hair, like skin, is subtle and needs quieter colors and desaturation of bright pigments. Natural hair nearly always needs a touch of a complementary hue to tone it down. For instance, think of adding a touch of Sap Green to a redhead to take the edge off the bright set of tube colors.

MEN'S HAIR

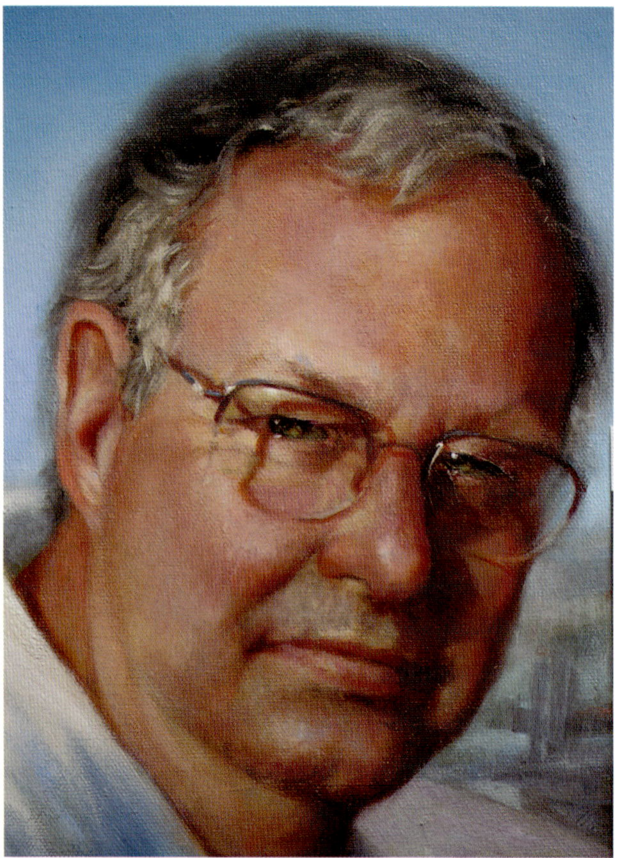

The Changing Hairline

Use three brushes with hair color, skin-in-shadow color, skin-in-light color. Alternate among them to pull those lost and firm edges of hair-into-skin with great ease. Follow up with a few strokes of light in the hair. But don't overdo. Finish with a fan brush to knock off any remaining edges.

Son of a Fisherman
Oil on Claessens linen (detail)
40" × 30" (102cm × 76cm)
Private collection

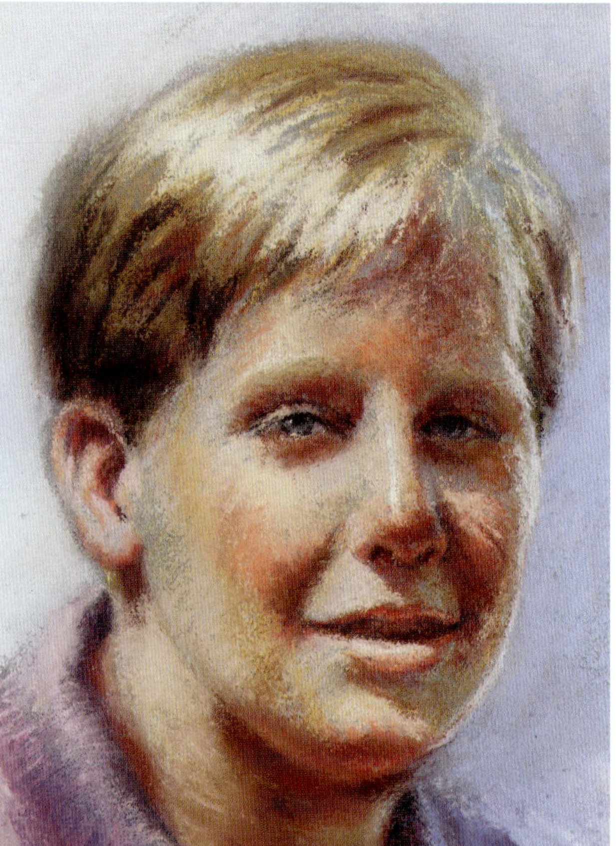

Boy's Hair

The boy had just finished practice when he came for a sitting. Natural and slightly shaggy, he was the perfect image of the active twelve-year-old. Using a variety of gray-brown to golden pastel sticks, and keeping in mind the five elements of light and shadow, we proceeded to work outdoors where he was most at home.

Peter After Tennis Practice
Pastel on studio-made granular board (detail)
30"× 24" (102cm ×61cm)
Private collection

The most beautiful of images exhibit great, natural hair. The secret is lost edges. The softer the transition between skin and hair the better, and this is never more important than when painting men. The variety of hairlines with varying degrees of baldness and thinning hair, moustaches, beards, bushy or thin eyebrows and sideburns offer the greatest of challenges.

A TECHNIQUE FOR NATURAL HAIRLINES

If you're going to err in one direction or another when painting hair, err to being too soft with edges rather than too rigid. This will always provide a stronger painting in the end. Too harsh a division between the skin and hair will create a bad-toupee effect at the hairline and a theatrical, glued-on-the-face look to a moustache or beard. The key to painting disappearing hues and lost edges is to paint with soft sable brushes

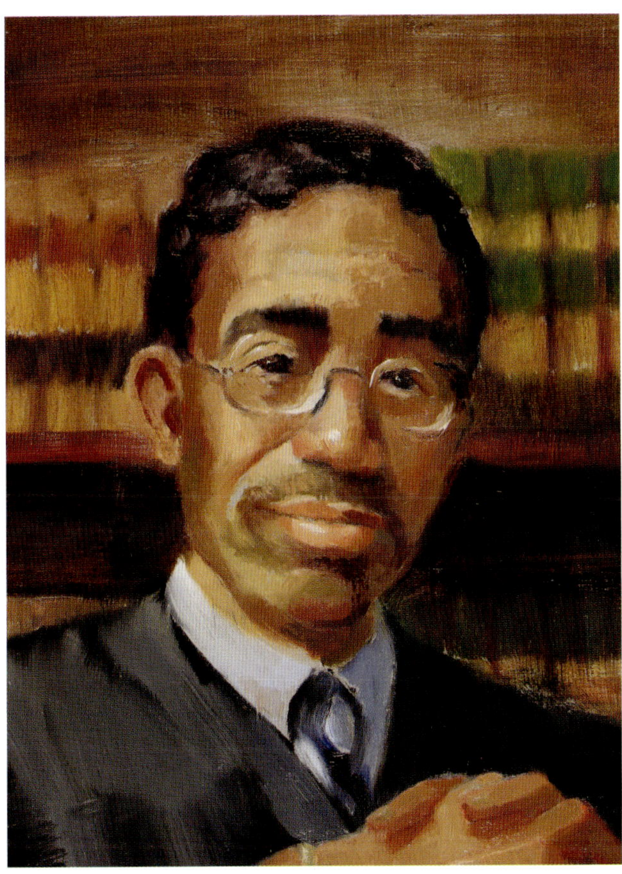

Wavy Hair

Judge Morgan's dark wavy hair and distinguished demeanor reminded me of 1940's movie stars. In the final painting, I was very attentive to the lost and found edges of the curve of the hair on the skin.

Michael R. Morgan
Superior Court judge, state of North Carolina
Preliminary oil study on Ampersand Gessobord (detail)
16" × 20" (41cm × 51cm)
Private collection

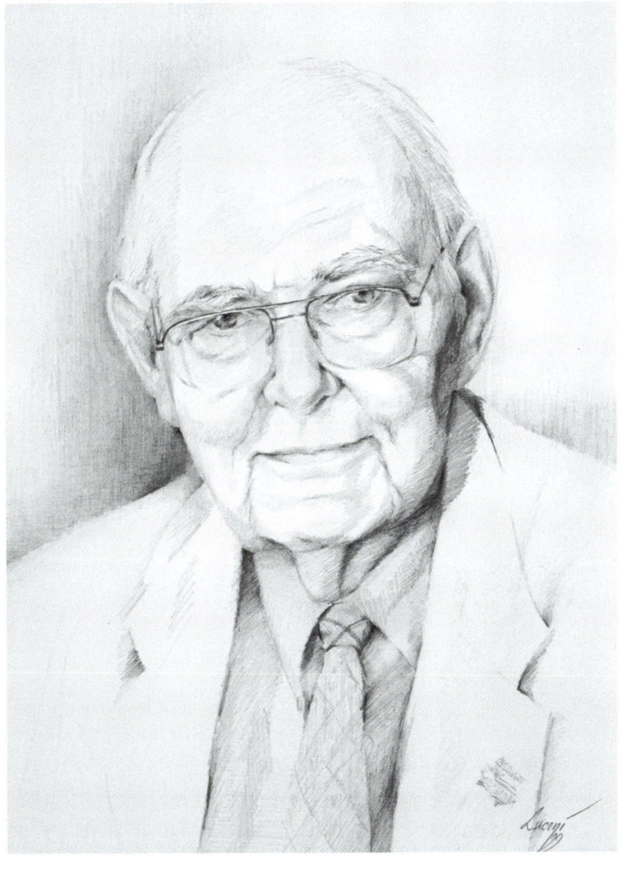

The Balding Gentleman

This preliminary sketch for a retirement portrait for the North Carolina Department of Agriculture commissioner shows an elegant and believable combination of structure and receding hairline.

James Graham
Commissioner, North Carolina Department of Agriculture
Preliminary graphite study on bristol for full-length state retirement portrait
14" × 11" (36cm × 28cm)
Private collection
Permission of the state of North Carolina Department of Agriculture

and keep the paint very malleable and receptive to movement. Try using two brushes—one with the skin tone, one with some of the hair tone—and alternate frequently between the two to achieve a realistic appearance of the hair growing from the skin.

BALDNESS OR RECEDING HAIR

Just as we often speak about putting women in their best light, which will enhance their most beautiful features and minimize their occasional flaws, men's lighting is critical as well. This is especially important in the case of the older, balding gentleman. Make certain that the lighting is suitable and avoids too sharp a highlight in an unflattering way on the head. Maintain the focus on the strength of the features and the face. Continue as in any portrait so that the first feature people see is the eyes.

FACIAL HAIR

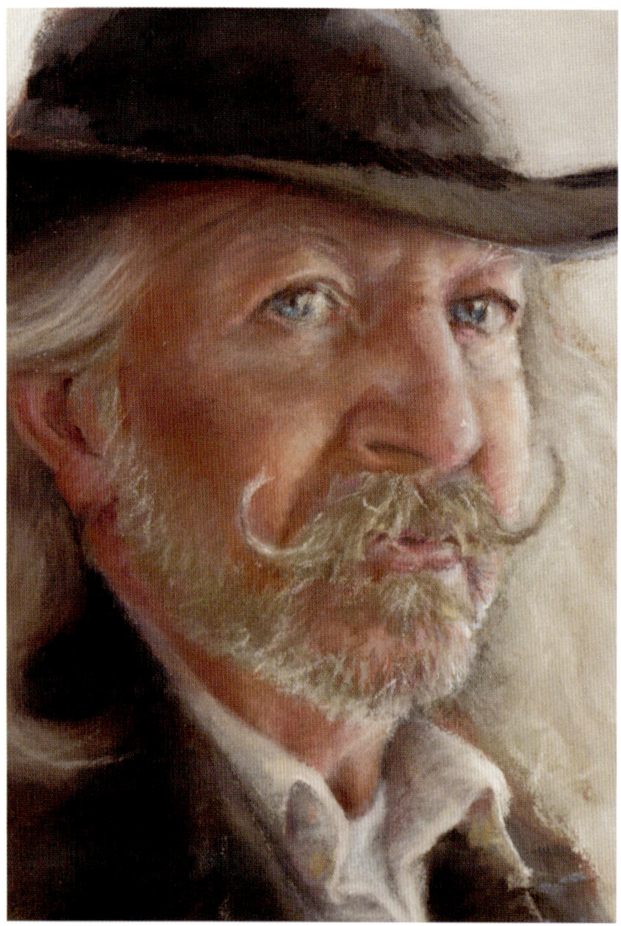

The Unique Moustache

Robert is a veteran and a mountain man from Maggie Valley in the Blue Ridge Mountains. A gifted artist, yes, he really does have a true handlebar moustache.

Robert Case
Pastel on Ampersand Pastelbord (detail)
20" × 16" (51cm × 41cm)
Private collection

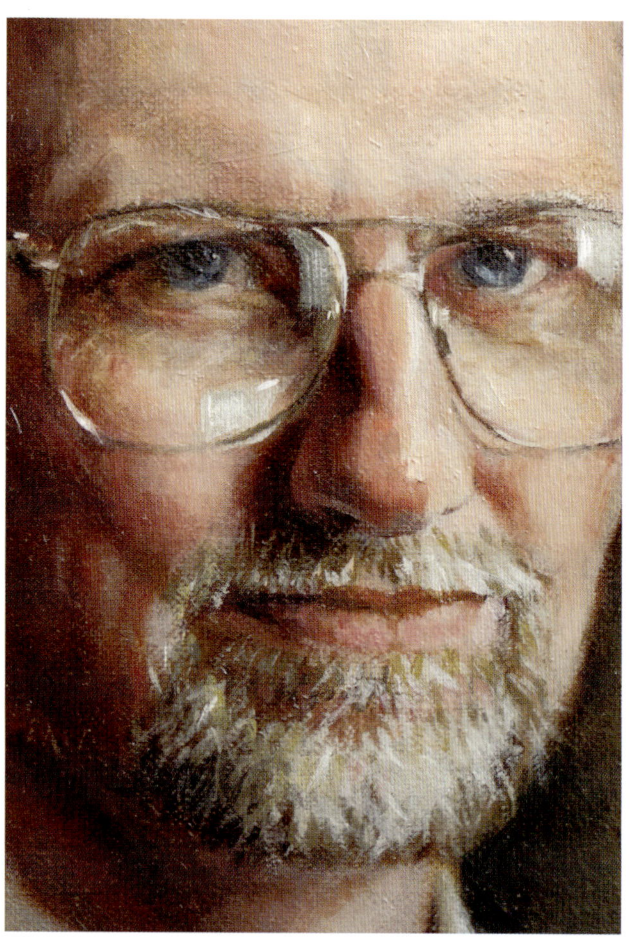

The Trimmed Goatee

This detail of Dr. Soroos offers a great example of a well-shaped moustache/beard combination on a strong Scandinavian-American face.

Dr. Marvin Soroos
Oil on Claessens linen (detail)
40" × 30" (102cm × 79cm)

So many gentlemen are wearing beards and moustaches today. Just as with hairstyles, if the right style of facial hair is chosen, it can be a smashing look. When painting the hair of the face, notice that it is often a slightly different color than the hair of the head. In younger men, the beard can go slightly redder and tends to show a bit of white long before the hair of the head. Nevertheless, pay close attention to the manner in which the upper line of the beard is trimmed and experiment with the fullness of the moustache. Here are some particularly wonderful examples of looks that are unique and handsome.

EYEBROWS

Eyebrows are exceptionally important for likeness and expression. From big, shaggy, unruly eyebrows to those that are wispy and barely there, the trick is to keep the edges extremely soft and loose.

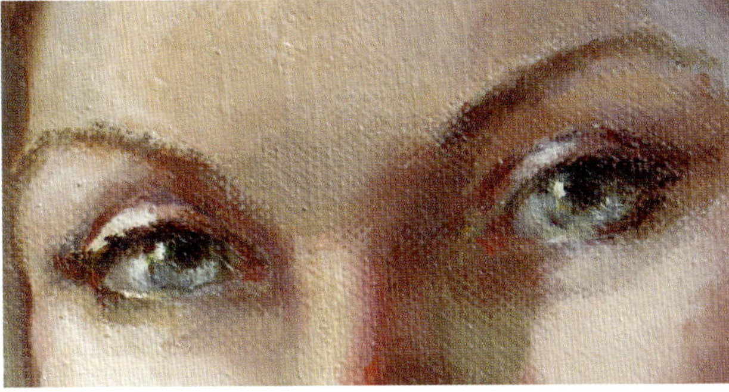

The Perfect Eyebrow

A beautiful brow needs to travel from between the eyes up and over the pronounced upper eye socket bone and disappear to a wisp at the outer end. Lost edges are the key to the softness. Take care to make the eyebrow color neither too dark nor too light. The eyebrows frame the eye like a good frame surrounds a painting—to present but never upstage it.

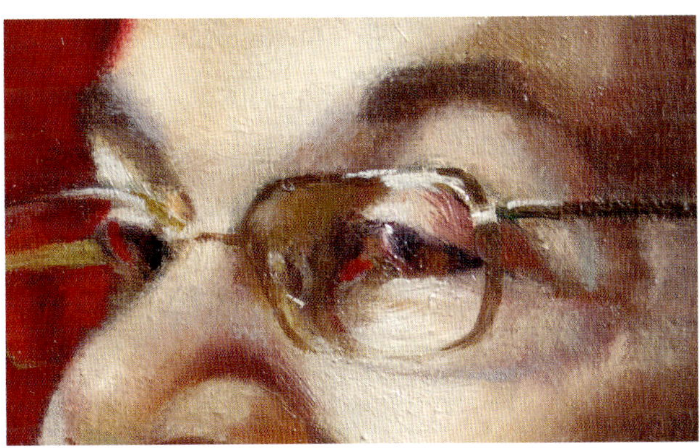

The Soft, Expressive Eyebrow

When working on honey- or darker-colored skin tones, use a thin layer of color marking the path of the eyebrow with one value darker than the skin. When placing the darker brow into the wet paint, it becomes easy to shape and soften at the same time.

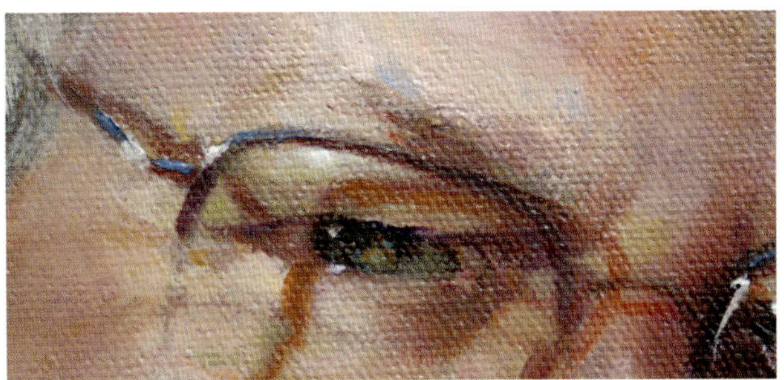

The Sparse Eyebrow

Note how the two-brush technique was used to great advantage in this eyebrow, where mostly skin is showing through fine, sparse hair.

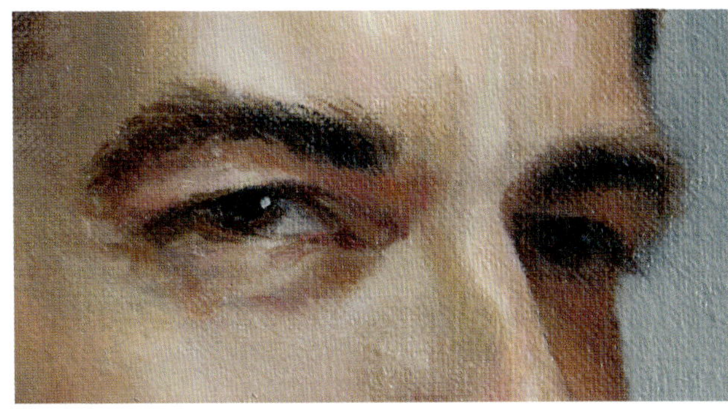

The Full Eyebrow

This man had much fuller eyebrows, but the edges both above and below the hair of the brow were softened repeatedly with skin tone to prevent a glued-on look.

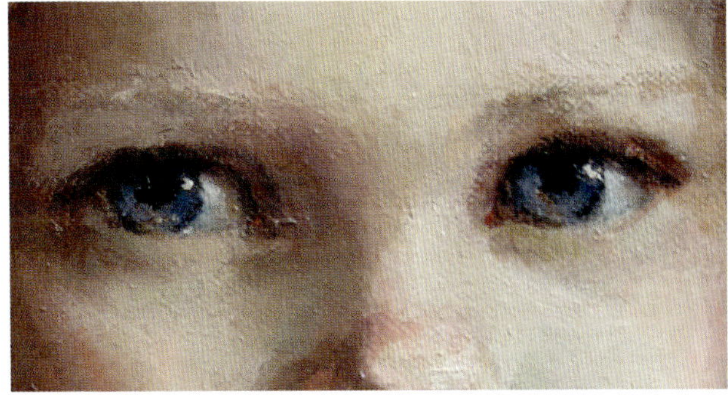

The Small Child's Eyebrow

The wispy, nearly invisible eyebrow on a blonde child still needs to have a feeling of placement and structure. The trick is to paint the hair very closely related in value to the skin, keeping the bottom edge of the brow a fraction of a value darker. It will give the impression of silky volume and still be barely there.

HANDS: AN EXTENSION OF EXPRESSION

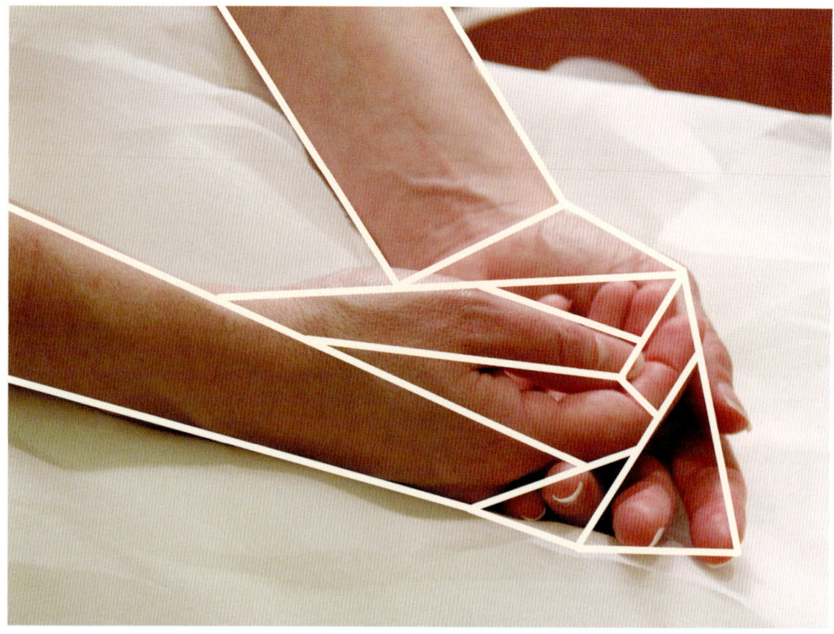

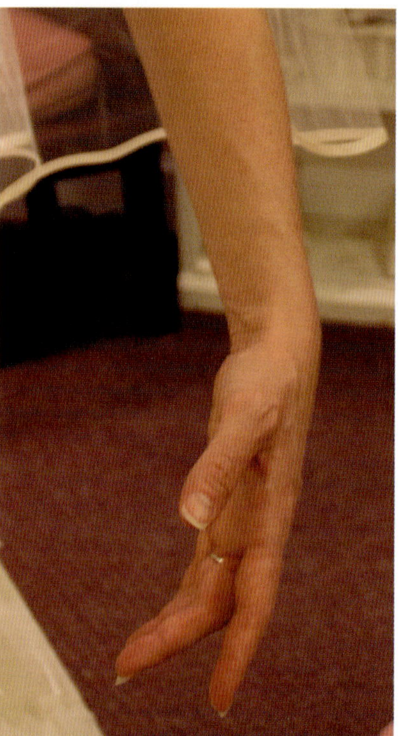

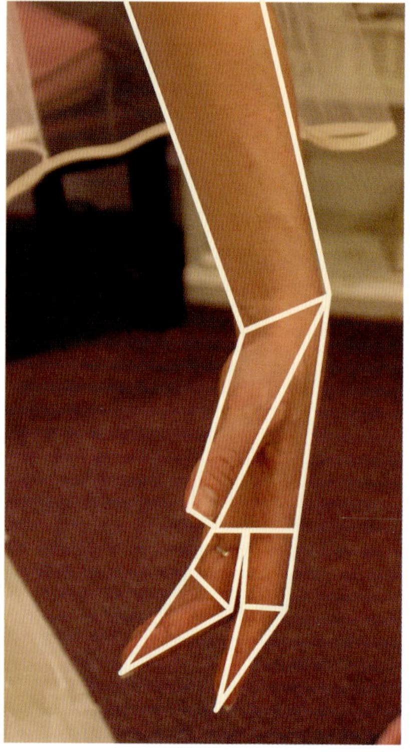

Graceful Renaissance Hands
This is a perfect example of the natural beauty people exhibit when unposed. In preparing for a bridal portrait in pastel, this Washington, D.C. bride multitasked by sitting for our preliminary graphite sketch while at a gown fitting. Luckily, the mom's camera was nearby when the bride twisted to see what the seamstress was doing to the train. Look at that amazing Renaissance hand!

It is common for buyers and collectors to choose their portrait artists not by how the artist has painted the face, but by the hands. An artist who has mastered the anatomy of the hands and other body parts can surely create rhythm and expression on the face.

PAINTING HANDS

There are no combinations of hand, wrist, fingers that cannot be broken down into geometric shapes to simplify what appears to be complicated. Break down into triangles, squares and rhomboids. Or if it is easier for you to see in curvilinear shapes, try circles, ellipses and cones. Look for the rhythm and line of movement from the shoulder through the elbow, to the wrist and out the fingertips.

Because of their many parts, angles, joints, directions and their nearly constant exposure, the hands are among the most challenging aspects of the portrait. It would be nearly impossible to paint hands in the same exact position twice as portraits are created over time. People use their hands to show emotion, punctuate statements, gently caress a child, cling to a loved one, gesture toward a cherished object.

During a planning sitting, the artist must choose to sketch the moment when the hands are exactly at their most useful in the design of the composition. Confronting the complexity of the single hand alone is worth the undertaking, but consider multiple hands interacting between mother and child or siblings. There is a challenge worth achieving.

FEMALE HANDS AT DIFFERENT AGES

The hands are another example of the Golden Mean in nature giving perfect dimension and proportions mathematically to their design. Although the back of the hand is fairly bony and angular at each of the joints, the interior of the hand is soft and padded with muscle. The back of the hand or the open palm can be drawn or blocked in with a square at any age. Although knuckles tend to enlarge with age (and possibly a touch of arthritis), they begin in infancy appearing as dimples on hands with baby fat.

NOTES TO STUDY THE HANDS

- The hand, if placed with the heel of the palm at the bottom edge of the chin, will touch the hairline with the longest finger.
- In that position, the second knuckle on the longest finger will meet the eye.
- Knuckles create an arc across the four fingers. They are not in a straight line.
- Fingers can only move and bend in one direction. But the thumb can bend and rotate, giving it a much wider range of motion.

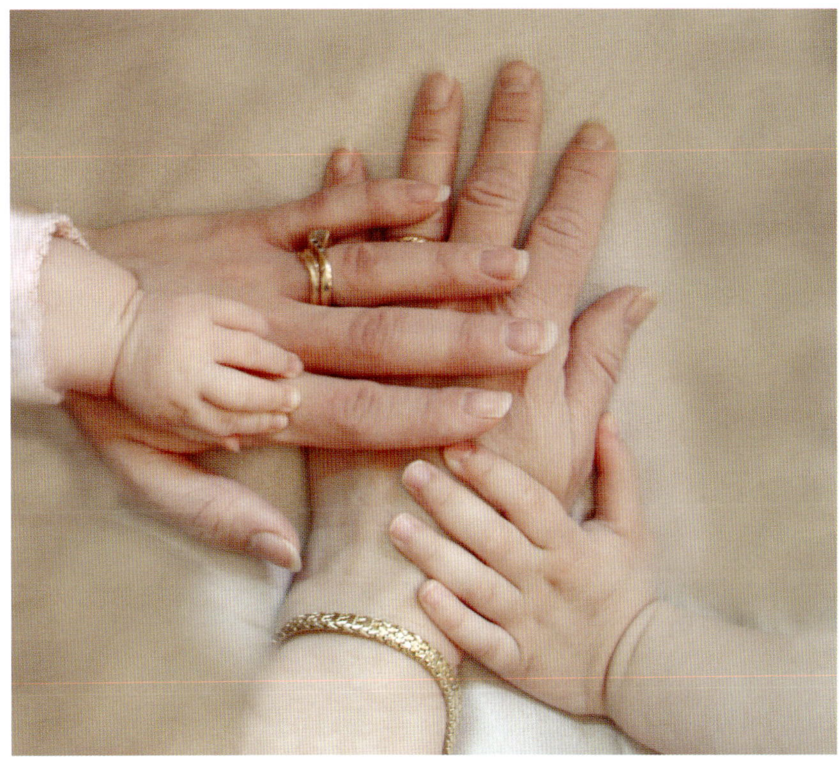

Multi-Generational Hands

Look how the dimples on the back of the girls' hands turn into knuckles on the adult hands. See how the young adult hand differs from the older adult. Study the texture of skin and also the changes in the finger knuckles and shape of the fingers as they age.

Anatomy of the Hand

There are 27 bones in the hand, with eight in the wrist. The fingers have three moving joints, while the thumb only has two.

Use any one of the smallest segments or (distal phalanges) at the tip of the finger as a unit of measure. The next segment (intermediate phalanges) will be 1.618 times longer. The third segment (proximal phalanges) will again be 1.618 times longer. And the bones in the palm of the hand (metacarpals) will be 1.618 times longer.

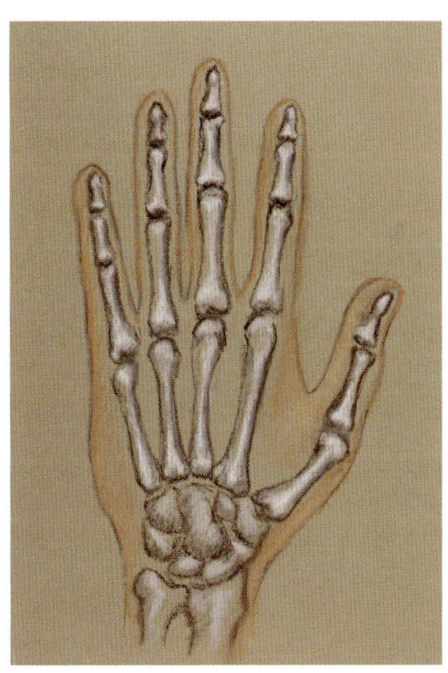

Hand Skeleton Study

Pastel on Ampersand Pastelbord—sand tone
10" × 8" (25cm × 20cm)

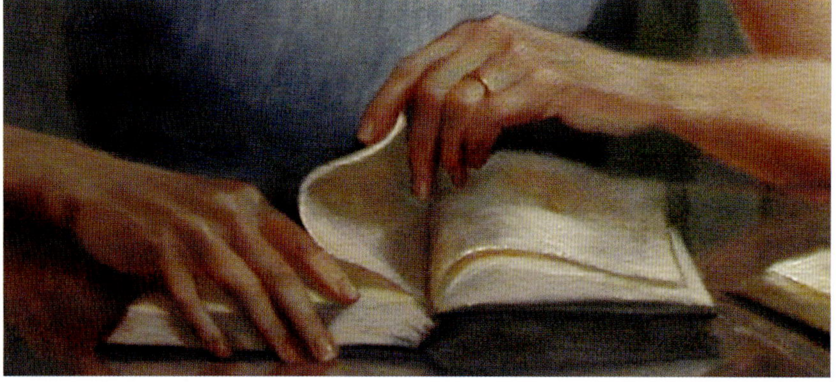

Relaxed Hands With Book

Watch as people move. Find a pleasing design in the natural positions they take. They expect a good likeness, but you must first make a good painting. Choose things that enhance the painting.

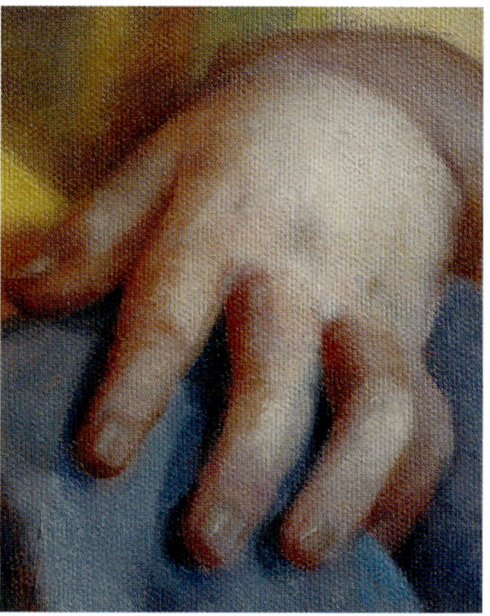

The Child's Hand

Children have the most wonderful way of using and resting their hands. Notice the soft, rhythmic form this hand takes.

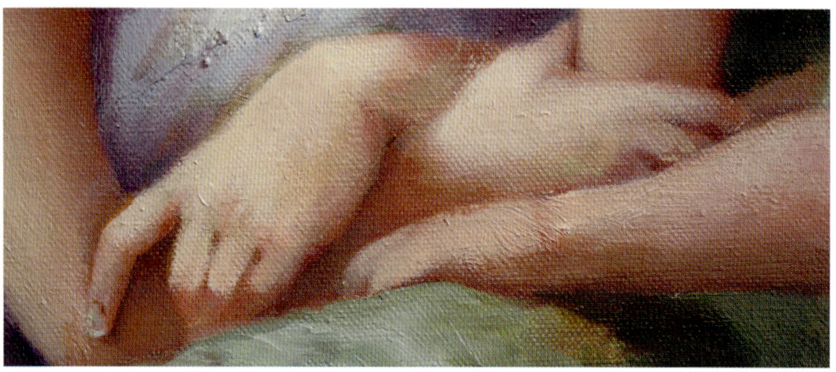

Multiple, Interactive Hands

Do not hesitate to use multiple hands or interactive hands. The designs become a feature of the painting. But please do not try to pose something like this. Just pay attention to the natural movement of your sitters. When something wonderful happens, just ask them to hold it for a moment while you record it in your notes.

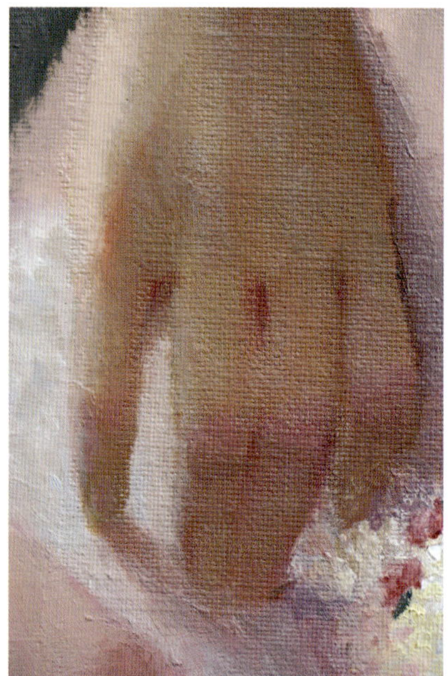

The Dropped Hand

The dropped hand in a truly relaxed pose can be most beautiful. Look for these things and react as they happen. Note how simply the color is applied with that delicate feeling of the fingertips gently touching the pillow.

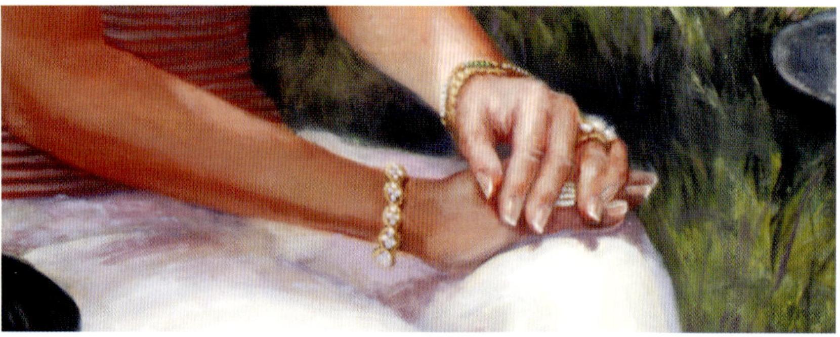

Poised Hands With Jewelry

These gentle hands, decorated with elegant jewelry at a moment of rest, are another reason why the portrait artist needs to be a precise still life artist as well.

MEN'S HANDS

The hand will help to proportion the balance of the figure. A man is, on the average, ten hands high. The best hands in paintings look relaxed and as if they could reach out to the viewer.

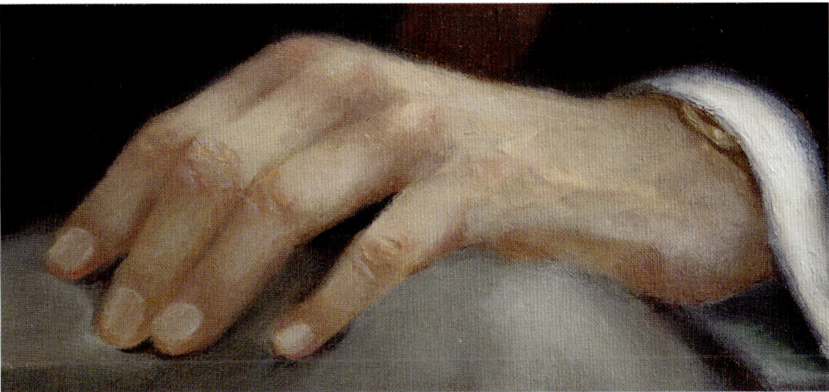

Hand on Knee

The relaxed hand on the knee of a crossed leg is a perfect example of how dividing a complex object into simple geometric shapes can make the task easier. Look at the back and side of the hand as a rectangle. The area of knuckles to first joint of the first three fingers as a square, and all other shapes as rectangles. Look at the fingernails painted with a value lighter and grayer than the skin tone. The indication of shine or a highlight on a couple of them should be done with great subtlety.

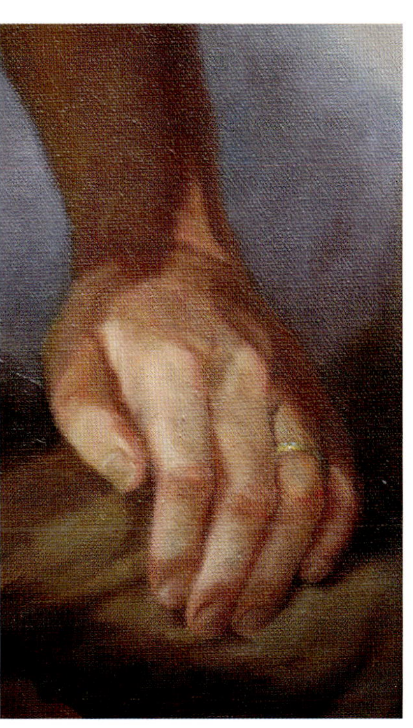

Comfortable Placement

A hand is pressed against a knee as the gentleman leans forward to tell a story. Here, the hand is natural and comfortably placed. The outdoor lighting lays shadows across the wrist, back of the hand and fingers in an interesting pattern.

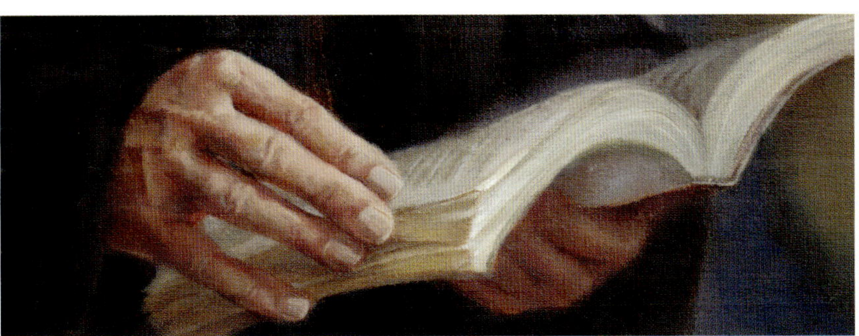

Active Hands

The professor is ready to turn the page. The impending motion is poised at the fingertips.

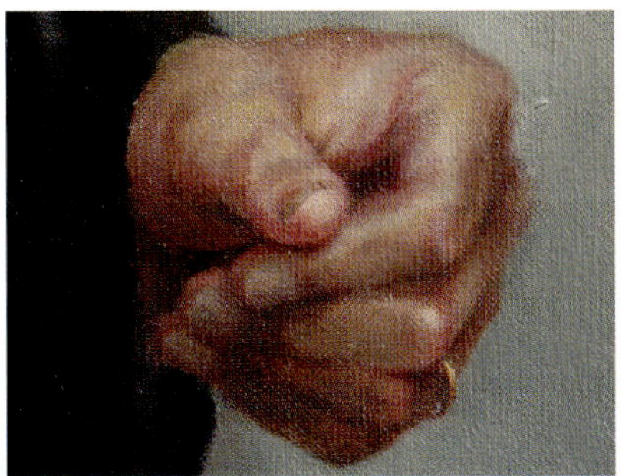

Relaxed Hands

The relaxed hand gesture is part of the debonair attitude of this painting.

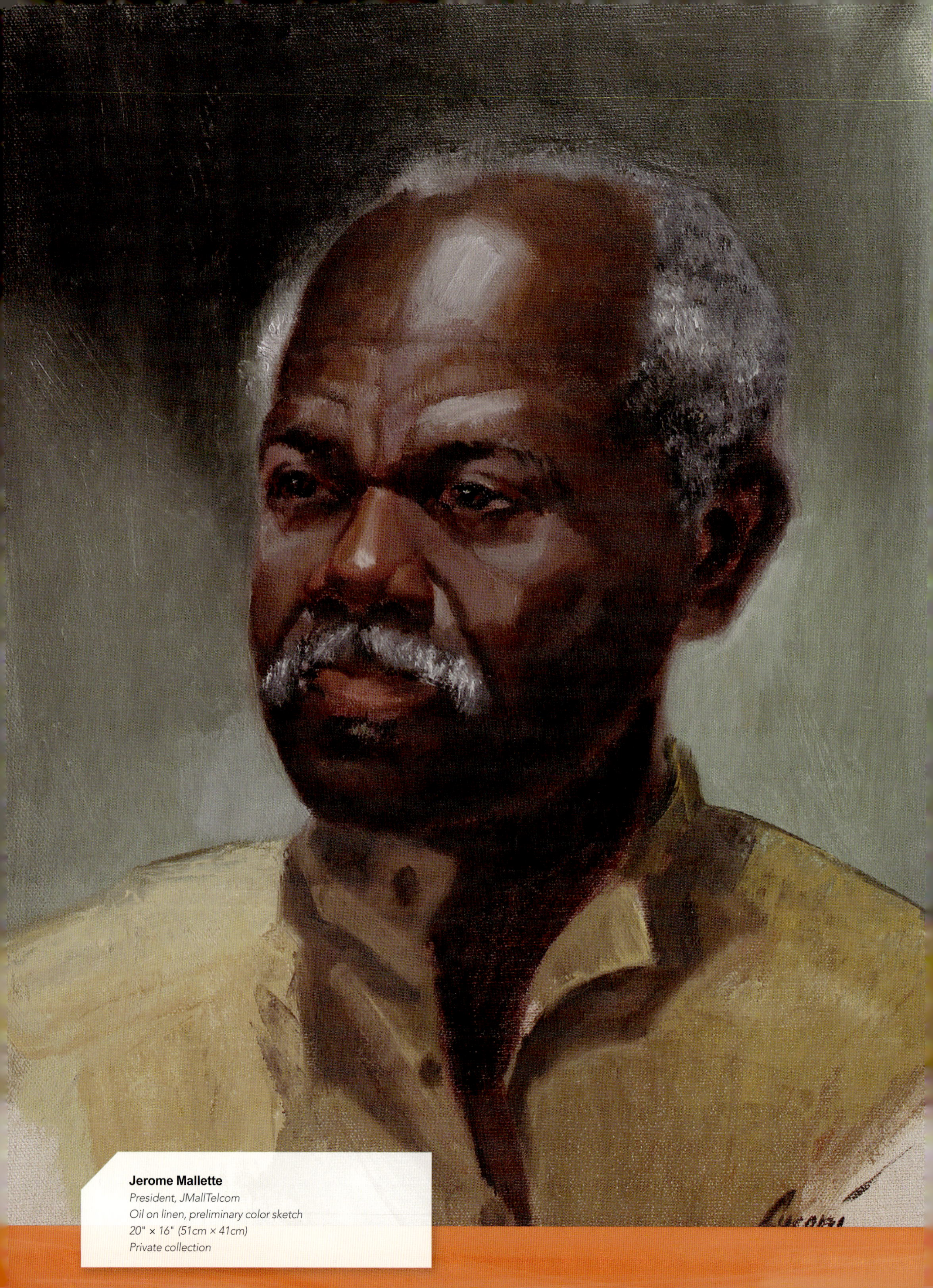

Jerome Mallette
President, JMallTelcom
Oil on linen, preliminary color sketch
20" × 16" (51cm × 41cm)
Private collection

CHAPTER 3

THE COLORS OF PEOPLE: SKIN & HAIR

The skin and hair color charts in this chapter were originally created to encourage portrait- and figure-painting students to dive fearlessly into their work. They help you build confidence and get going. Although no chart or formula can be perfect for multiple portraits, they will help you achieve colors reasonably related to the model or subject being painted and provide a starting point.

We have seven billion people on this planet. It would be impossible to supply a color chart for everyone. There are an infinite number of combinations of colors that could be used for painting people around the world. This is not to say that these charts are the only way to approach mixing skin tones; however, these charts provide a jumping-off point, a simple way to begin with confidence. These ten charts have been among the easiest and most frequently requested by my students.

"When I judge art, I take my painting and put it next to a God-made object like a tree or flower. If it clashes, it is not art."
—Paul Cézanne

The Color of People
Painting skin tones is a long and complex process to study. The dark skin has underlying cool tones enhanced by the cool tones of his graying hair.

COLOR CONSIDERATIONS

Never settle for a color mixture that you know is wrong. Slow down and think about the process. If you put something down on the canvas in haste, the balance of precious painting time may be spent going back to correct (and correct and correct) that passage. And then it may never be exactly right. It is better to abandon the mixture and begin again.

Plan your work and work your plan. Think about color, tint, hue, temperature, value and placement ahead of time. If necessary, test the mixture before it is added to the canvas by keeping a scrap of similarly toned canvas next to the workspace. Test it on the painting if it can be easily removed. If wrong, remove it and try again. The hair and color mixtures offered in this chapter will provide a place to begin.

A BASE OF COLOR

All human skin is a general combination of the three primaries, with a red-yellow mixture base. All ethnicities can rely on a red-yellow with a cool added to the mixture, offering vast differentials in value and temperature. Our challenge is to stare, study and sketch a solution in color.

NEUTRALS

After mixing as suggested in the color charts that follow, neutrals may be the answer to the subtlety and delicacy the artist desires. Colors in nature have great subtlety. Although paintings with brilliant saturated color can be exciting, there is much to be said for neutral-based, organic-feeling paintings. Really intense and saturated colors in attempts to paint the face or figure are rarely successful. Knowing how to achieve neutrals will benefit the painting greatly.

Go paint the landscape. Those who rush will see only a mass of green. Those who take their time to stare and study will begin to notice the darkest greens verging on blues in the cedar and fir trees, the grayer green in the oak, the yellow green in the birches. The variations continue to each variety and tree, and in each temperature of lighting as it changes throughout the day.

People are the same. The colors are mixed from the same pigments with the slightest of variations.

MIXTURES AS STARTING POINTS

As mixtures are created on the palette, leave a little of the original color. Drag some out of this mixture to make an adjustment. Make your change and leave a little in a puddle. Drag some out, make a change and continue. As the painting continues, there may be a need for one of the minutely different variations created in an earlier changed mixture.

COLOR TEMPERATURE

Cool colors recede and warm colors advance. This is true in all painting. Every mixed color other than the primaries can be nudged toward cooler or warmer. This can be one of your most valuable tools to build lively and dimensional figures and faces on your flat ground.

In natural space, aerial perspective and atmospheric perspective are affected by the air through which the artist views an image. In a field of flowers on a dewy morning, the *plein air* painter views the distant flowers through heavy mist and humidity. Those distant flowers are the same color as the ones nearby. But to paint those distant flowers on the flat canvas, the temperature of the flowers' hue must be cooler than those in the foreground to deceive the viewer. Cooling the distant flowers while warming those in the foreground encourages the viewer to believe that there is distance and dimension across a painted field of flowers. So too must the portrait painter push and pull the features of the face into and out of the flat surface of the canvas though the relative distance is only a few inches instead of feet or yards or miles. The theory is the same: Warm advances, cool recedes.

COLOR IN SHADOWS

Colors in shadows maintain the same identity as the local color. But the intensity is reduced more in the shadow than in the light. The most intense color appears at the shadow line—that edge defining the turn of the form from the plane in light to the plane in shadow.

Everything is relative. The colors, values and sharpness of the shadow edges relate to the distance, quality and temperature of the light source. The color is directly related to the value.

HOW TO USE THE COLOR CHARTS

What follows in this chapter are some basic formulas for painting various skin tones and hair. These are by no means the only way to approach the subject. Begin with these ideas and continue to experiment to create thousands of variances that will be observed from person to person. Above all, have fun with it.

CHART NAME

Each chart begins with an identifying ethnicity, hair color or description that may fit the category of the person being painted. Their colors may closely resemble the choices of mixtures on this chart or be somewhat related to these mixtures. Again, keep in mind that this is an inexact science, but still will be useful during early choices of color mixtures. Hold a chart up to your subject and determine which one suits them best.

COLORS NEEDED

Preceding each chart is a list of the pigments needed to make the color mixtures on the chart. The oil colors listed can also be used by acrylic painters and watercolorists.

WHAT THE COLUMNS MEAN

The colors, which have been hand mixed and applied to the left and middle columns of each chart, are the same in both columns. The only difference is that the background is middle gray in the left column and white in the middle column. This shows how the same color mixture responds on a toned canvas vs. an untoned white canvas.

The column to the right lists the actual color mixtures and where they are applied (lips, skin in shadow, hair in light and so on).

The first three colors reading down the chart start with dark and work toward light. This is a combination for a proposed hair color. The first is hair as it may appear in shadow, the second is hair as its own local color, and the third is a possible color of the hair in white light. Plus (+) and minus (-) signs help indicate an adjustment for more or less of a color. A double plus (++) sign indicates much more (or a lot, if a triple plus); a double minus indicates a very small amount (or just a touch, if a triple minus).

The second section down is the skin color starting from dark to light—first in shadow, second as local color, last as skin in light. Again, reflected colors of nearby objects and clothing are not being considered in this chart.

The last section with one color only is a suggestion for lips (without makeup). Lips begin with the skin-in-shadow mixture and then are supplemented with one or two colors and additional white as listed.

THE COLOR STUDY

The charts used in this chapter were developed for my students who were primarily working in oil. My pastel students begin with the color reference chart at the back of the book, giving them a quick translation of the colors, and then they box the clusters and related family of colors for each of the ten charts for future use. Acrylic artists may use the charts directly, but note that as the acrylic color dries and darkens, some things can be done utilitzing the translucency or opacity of the tubed colors. Watercolorists will find that the colors listed can be used with a tempered, somewhat less saturated quality to the finish, which is perhaps not as bright as their normal work. Using a touch of Chinese White or gouache can provide additional options to control skin and hair color.

Finally, keep in mind that reflected light or the color of the source light—warm or cool—is not addressed in these charts.

BRUNETTE

COLORS NEEDED:

- Flake White Replacement
- Yellow Ochre
- Cadmium Red Light
- Burnt Sienna
- Cobalt Blue
- Ivory Black

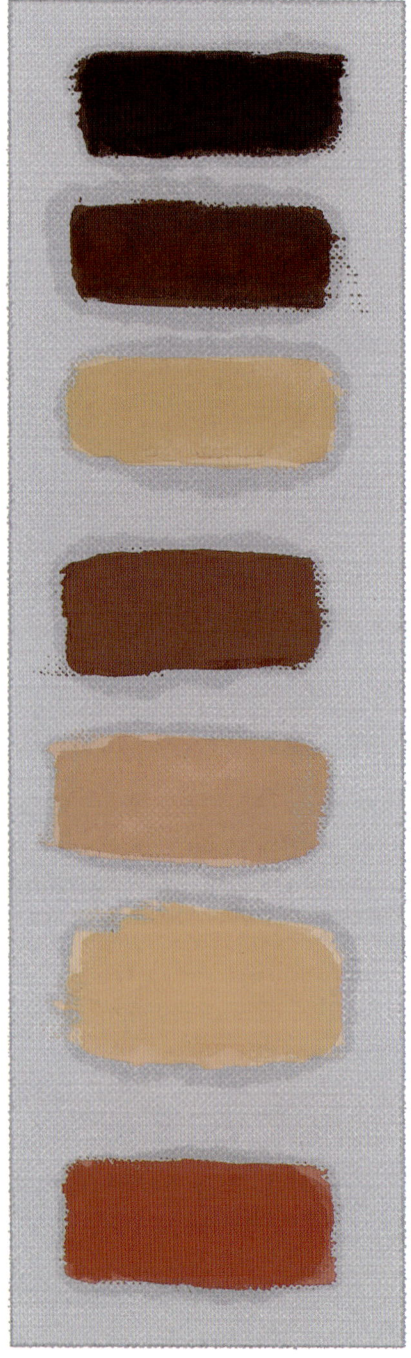

Hair in Shadow:
Yellow Ochre, Burnt Sienna, Ivory Black

Hair in Light:
+Yellow Ochre, Burnt Sienna, -Ivory Black

Hair Highlights:
Yellow Ochre, Burnt Sienna, Ivory Black, +Flake White Replacement

Skin in Shadow:
Yellow Ochre, Cadmium Red Light, +Cobalt Blue, -Flake White Replacement

Skin Local Color:
Yellow Ochre, Cadmium Red Light, +Cobalt Blue, -Flake White Replacement

Skin Highlight:
Yellow Ochre, Cadmium Red Light, -Cobalt Blue, ++Flake White Replacement

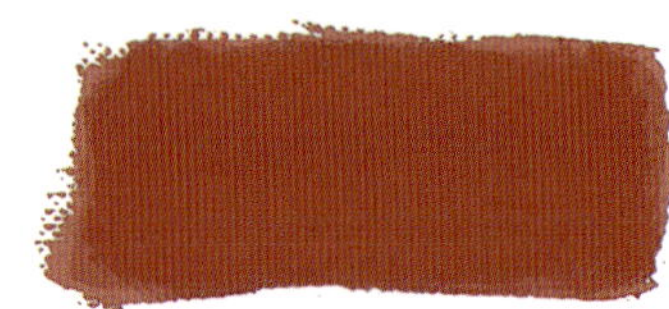

Lips:
Skin-in-shadow mixture, Cadmium Red Light, -Flake White Replacement

Skin (Local Color)

Mix Yellow Ochre and Cadmium Red Light. Add Cobalt Blue to neutralize and Flake White Replacement. A child's skin tones will often be higher key than an adult's that has been affected by the elements for years. Adjust mixture as needed.

Highlights in Hair

Hair highlights depend on the source light and the tendency of the individual's hair. In the light, brunette hair can tend toward redhead, blonde or a more neutral, slightly cool appearance.

Hair in Shadow

Mix Yellow Ochre and Burnt Sienna. Use Ivory Black in the mixture as if it were a blue. It will desaturate the mixture, keeping it from being too garish. Study the depth of color for this individual and adjust Burnt Sienna and Ivory Black as needed.

Skin in Shadow

Mix Yellow Ochre and Cadmium Red Light. Add Cobalt Blue to neutralize. Add Flake White Replacement to lighten and lightly gray the mixture. Continue to desaturate as needed after studying how the clothing and surroundings affect the skin in shadow.

Lips

Start with the skin-in-shadow mixture and add Cadmium Red Light and Flake White Replacement. Keep lips desaturated, unless a lipstick effect is desired.

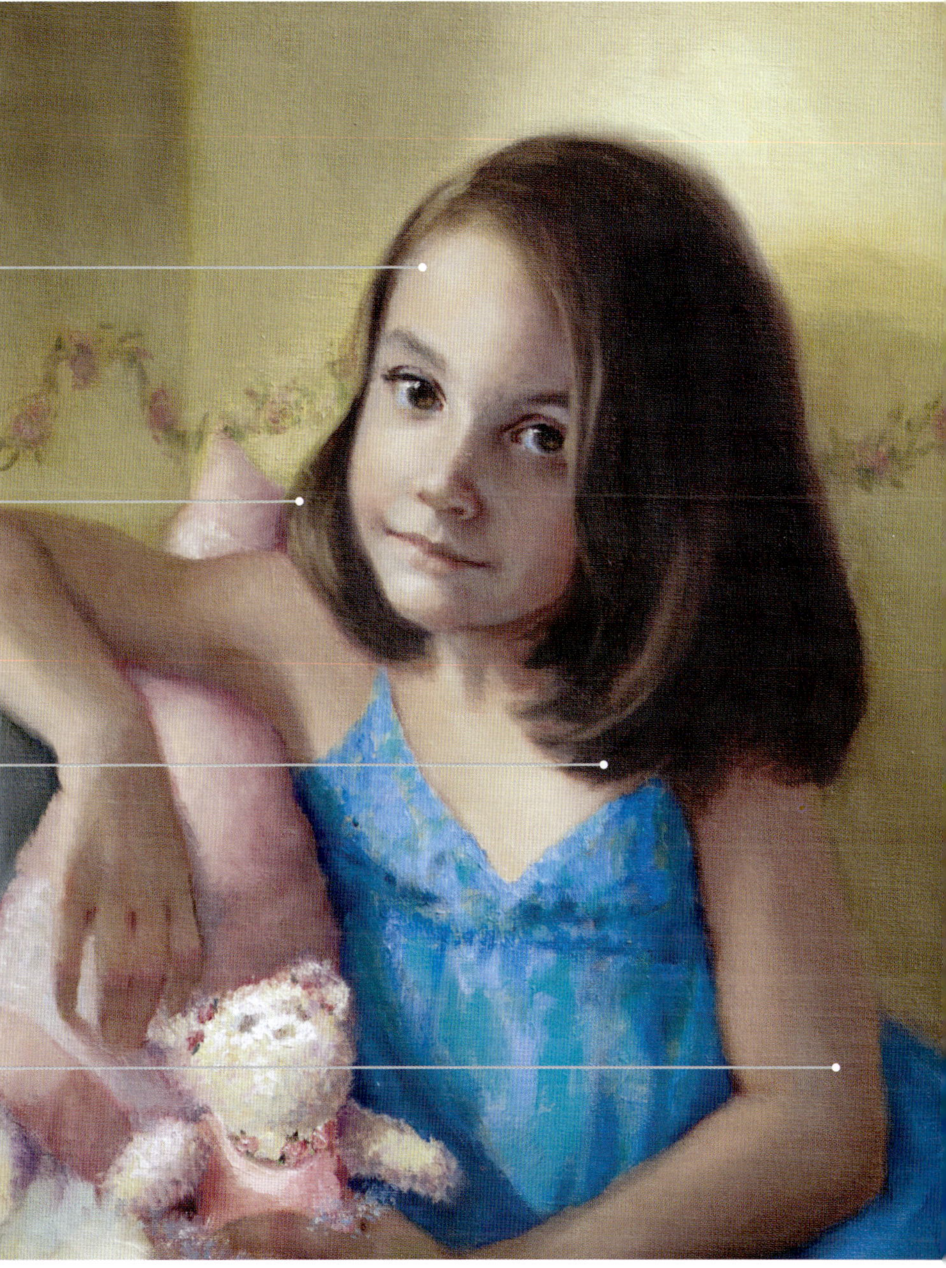

Color Surrounding Color

Lighting, clothing and surroundings will dramatically change any color mixture considered for the skin tones in the painting. If this young girl had worn a pink dress, the skin tones would have needed a different approach. When the background bounces color into the skin and hair, the artist must try to depict the color as closely as possible. Variation is the only constant in painting.

LC
Oil on Fredrix archival linen board
20" × 16" (51cm × 41cm)
Private collection

REDHEAD

COLORS NEEDED:

- Flake White Replacement
- Cadmium Yellow Medium
- Yellow Ochre
- Cadmium Red Light
- Burnt Sienna
- Ivory Black

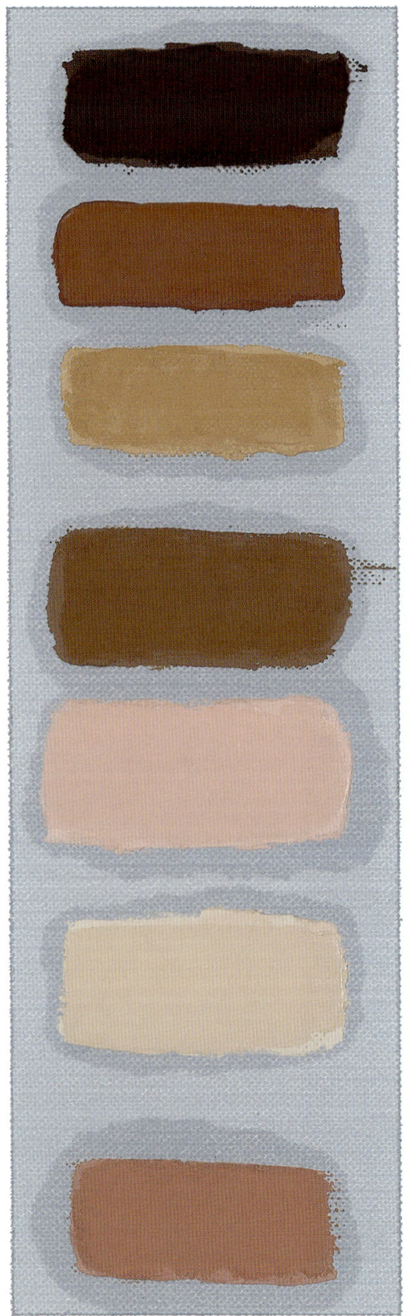

Hair in Shadow:
Cadmium Red Light, Yellow Ochre, +Burnt Sienna , --Ivory Black

Hair in Light:
Cadmium Red Light, Yellow Ochre, ++Burnt Sienna

Hair Highlights:
Cadmium Red Light, ++Yellow Ochre, Burnt Sienna , Flake White Replacement

Skin in Shadow:
Cadmium Red Light, Yellow Ochre, Ivory Black, -Flake White Replacement

Skin Local Color:
Cadmium Red Light, Cadmium Yellow Medium , -Ivory Black, +Flake White Replacement

Skin Highlight:
Cadmium Red Light, Cadmium Yellow Medium , --Ivory Black, ++Flake White Replacement

Lips:
Skin-in-shadow mixture, ++Cadmium Red Light, White

Hair in Shadow

Natural redheads can vary from light strawberry blonde to rich, dark chestnut colors. In all cases, the artist relies on Burnt Sienna in the base mixture, using the pigment as an orange when it is mixed with other pigments. Build the brick-like colors with Cadmium Red Light, Yellow Ochre and Burnt Sienna and neutralize with Ivory Black.

Hair in Light and Highlight

Mix Cadmium Red Light, Yellow Ochre and Burnt Sienna. Flake White Replacement lightens and neutralizes as the white cools the mixture. Depending on ambient light, a touch of Sap Green or Ivory Black might be needed.

Skin (Local Color)

Mix Cadmium Red Light and Cadmium Yellow Medium. Neutralize this powerful mixture with Ivory Black. Add Flake White Replacement until the necessary value is reached. Redheads have what is often referred to as "peaches and cream" skin, which may require even the shadows to be a higher key than expected.

Skin in Shadow

This high-key shadow is Flake White Replacement to cool Cadmium Red Light and Yellow Ochre with Ivory Black and Flake White Replacement.

Lips

Start with the previously mixed skin-in-shadow mixture and add touches of Cadmium Red Light and Flake White Replacement.

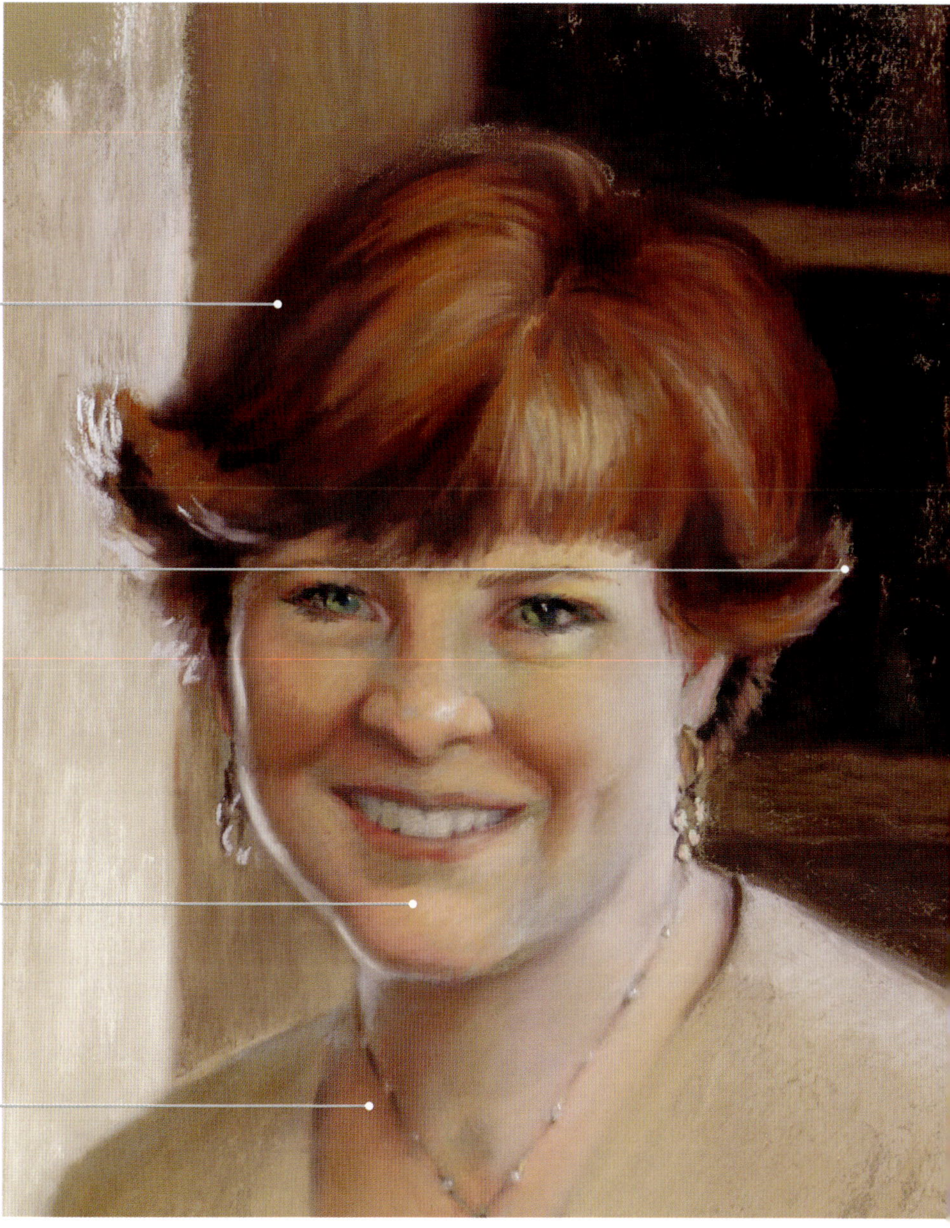

The Hardest Tone: Pale Skin

The overuse of any white will result in a chalky, grayed-out finish. Rely on the pigments and their temperature tendencies in mixture, learn what they can do and experiment to create the perfect tint. The Cobalt Blue notes were feathered over the side planes of the nose, the jaw line/ mandible area and the neck where the cool temperature turns the planes away from the viewer.

Kim Oliver Schneider

Executive director of gynecology and obstetrics, University of North Carolina hospital, Chapel Hill, NC
Pastel on Ampersand Pastelbord—sand tone
20" × 16" (51cm × 41cm)
Private collection

BLUE BLOOD/PORCELAIN

COLORS NEEDED:

- Flake White Replacement
- Yellow Ochre
- Alizarin Crimson
- Cobalt Blue
- Ivory Black
- Ultramarine Blue (optional)

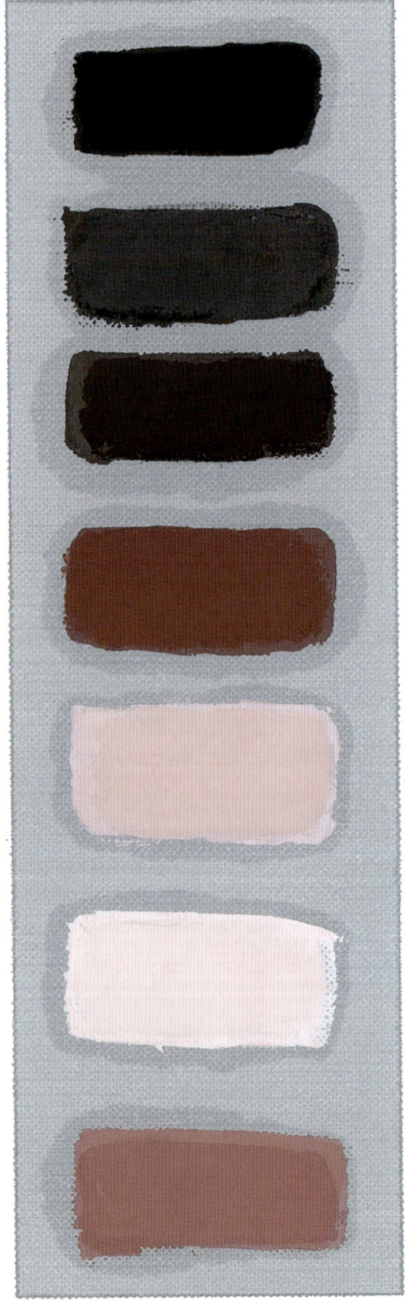

Hair in Shadow:
Ivory Black, Alizarin Crimson, Cobalt Blue

Hair in Light:
-Ivory Black, +Alizarin Crimson, Cobalt Blue, -Yellow Ochre

Hair Highlights:
Ivory Black, Alizarin Crimson, Cobalt Blue, +Yellow Ochre

Skin in Shadow:
Alizarin Crimson, -Yellow Ochre, Ivory Black, -Flake White Replacement

Skin Local Color:
Alizarin Crimson, -Yellow Ochre, Ivory Black, +Flake White Replacement

Skin Highlight:
Alizarin Crimson, Yellow Ochre, --Ivory Black, +Flake White Replacement

Lips:
Skin-in-shadow mixture, Alizarin Crimson, Cobalt Blue, +Flake White Replacement

Hair in Light and Highlight

Here the Ivory Black, Cobalt Blue, Alizarin Crimson and a touch of Yellow Ochre have been modified with Flake White Replacement to address the very cool light entering the office window overlooking the Capitol Building.

Hair in Shadow

Mix Ivory Black with Alizarin Crimson and Cobalt Blue to achieve a rich dark so typical of this skin/hair combination.

Skin in Highlight

Begin this mixture by putting Flake White Replacement on the palette first. Mix into this pile a touch each of Alizarin Crimson and Yellow Ochre to tint the pile. Add in an even smaller amount of Ivory Black. Mix thoroughly. Depending on the subject, a minute amount of Cobalt Blue or Ultramarine Blue may be needed to deliver the results expected.

Lips

Begin with the skin-in-shadow mixture of Alizarin Crimson, Yellow Ochre, Ivory Black and Flake White Replacement. Add to this a small amount of Alizarin Crimson, Cobalt Blue and Flake White Replacement.

Women with this skin tone sometimes use a brighter lipstick to brighten their faces and pale skin. Make a clear, artistic decision whether that saturated color will help or hurt the portrait.

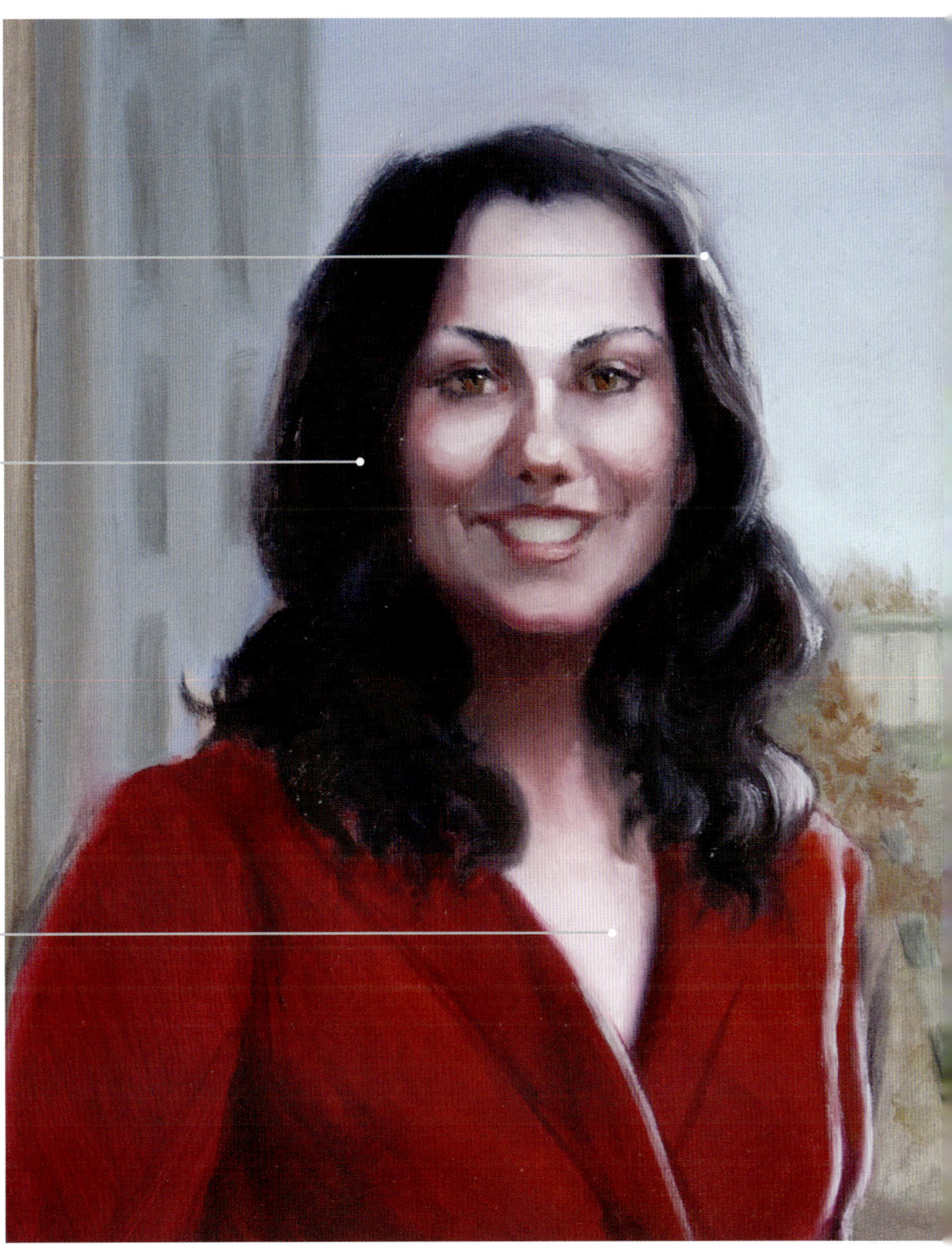

Use Temperature to Mold Features

Among the most difficult to render is blue blood or porcelain skin. This is the lovely, transparent quality of pale, white, elegant skin tones that generations of art students have studied for centuries from traditional, academy-trained artists. The trick for success is to allow the temperatures of cool and warm tints of white to mold and sculpt the head instead of relying solely on values.

Anna Smith
Attorney, Raleigh, NC
Oil study on Ampersand Pastelbord (detail)
20" × 16" (51cm × 41cm)
Private collection

BLONDE

COLORS NEEDED:

- Flake White Replacement
- Yellow Ochre
- Cadmium Red Light
- Alizarin Crimson
- Burnt Sienna
- Sap Green
- Ivory Black

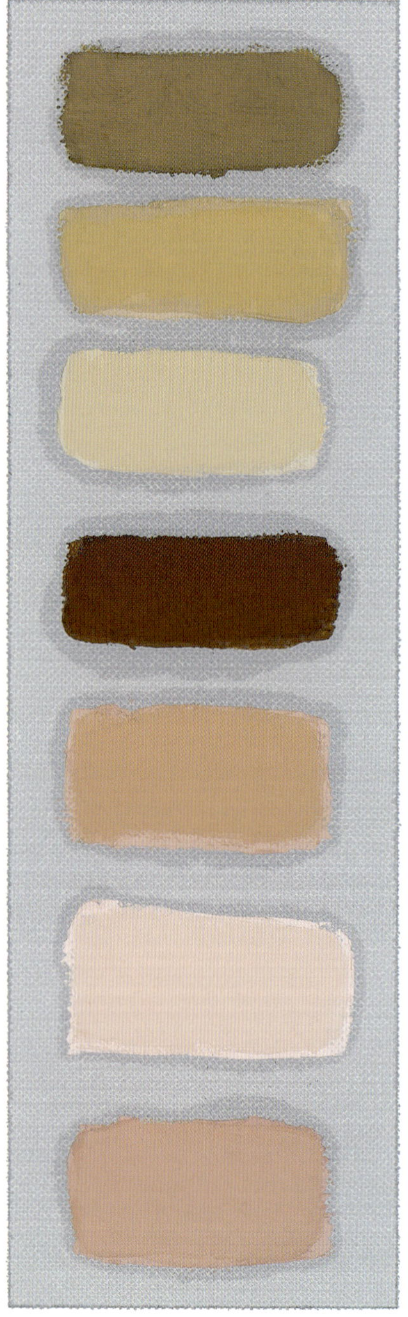

Hair in Shadow:
Ivory Black, Yellow Ochre, -Flake White Replacement

Hair in Light:
-Ivory Black, Yellow Ochre, Flake White Replacement

Hair Highlights:
--Ivory Black, Yellow Ochre, +Flake White Replacement

Skin in Shadow:
Yellow Ochre, Burnt Sienna, Sap Green, -Flake White Replacement (--Cadmium Red Light if needed)

Skin Local Color:
Yellow Ochre, Burnt Sienna, -Sap Green, +Flake White Replacement (--Cadmium Red Light if needed)

Skin Highlight:
Yellow Ochre, Cadmium Red Light, --Sap Green, ++Flake White Replacement

Lips:
Skin-in-shadow mixture, Alizarin Crimson, Yellow Ochre, +Flake White Replacement

Hair in Light and Highlight

Few people attempt a primarily green mixture when preparing paint for hair. But a most natural blonde hair will be created with a mixture of Ivory Black, Yellow Ochre and Flake White Replacement. Black should be thought of as blue when mixing.

Skin (Local Color)

Yellow Ochre, Burnt Sienna, Sap Green (to neutralize the orange in the Burnt Sienna) and Flake White Replacement work well for the base blonde color. Add a little Cadmium Red Light to the mix as you approach the central area including the nose/cheek/eyes.

Warmth in skin is most apparent where the shadow and light meet.

Skin in Shadow

Yellow Ochre, Burnt Sienna with Sap Green to neutralize, a little Cadmium Red Light and very little Flake White Replacement (only if necessary) will produce a great blonde skin shadow. The shadow is lighter in areas where the cool shirt bounces color back into the skin of the neck, cheek and hair.

Lips

Start with the skin-in-shadow mixture and add Alizarin Crimson, Yellow Ochre and Flake White Replacement. Keep men's lips less saturated.

General Notes

Blondes' colors are all generally higher key. Keep the shadows in the hair, skin and clothing closely related.

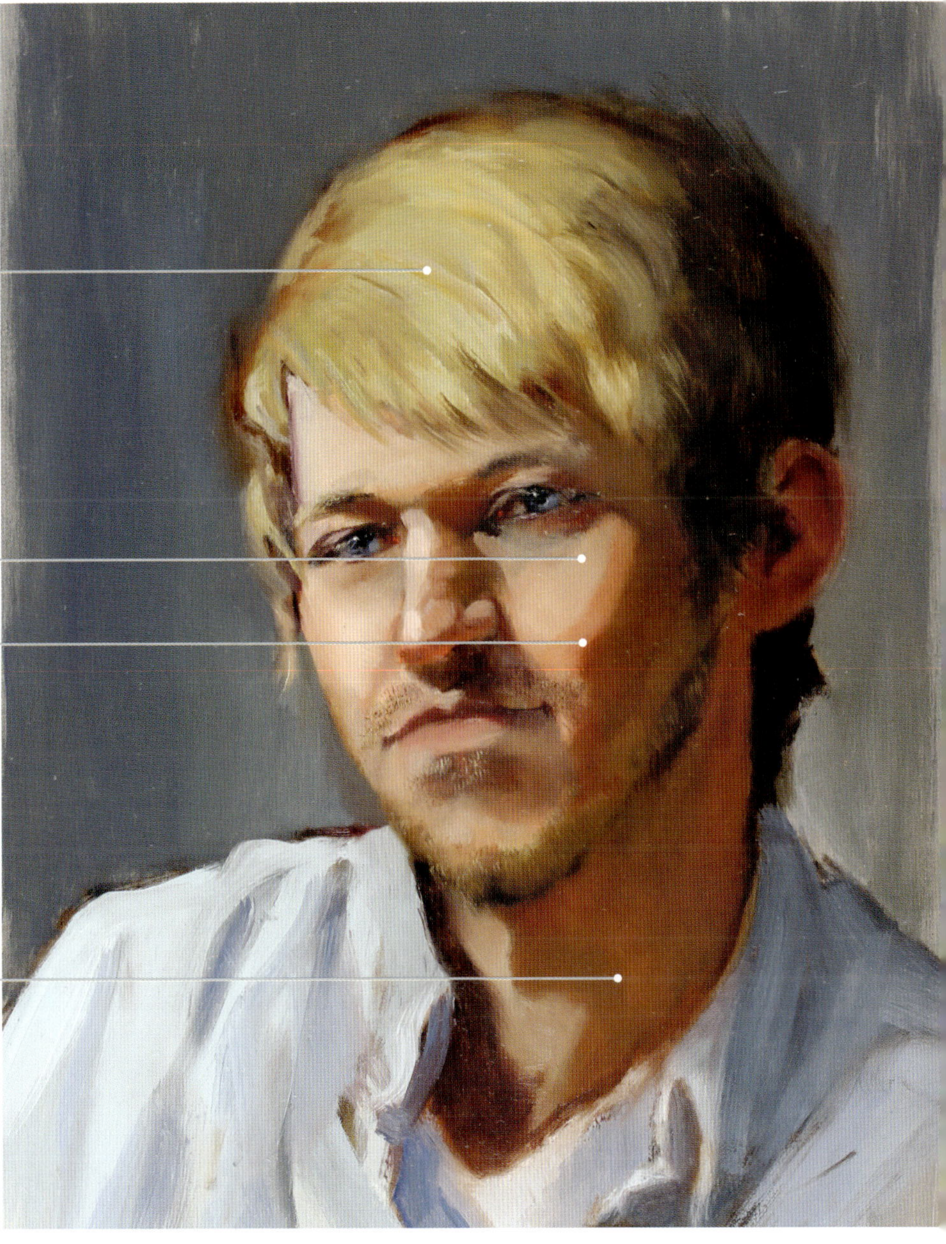

Orange/Peach and Blue Make Gray

When working with blondes, the color of clothing and the surroundings can really overwhelm some models. The soft peachy/pink skin tones can go completely dead if too many complementary colors bounce into the light of the skin. This means that although little blonde girls may look adorable in that blue/green floral dress with ruffles, be careful that the bounced color does not gray out the skin.

Justin Leitner
Oil study on Ampersand Gessobord
20" × 16" (51cm × 41cm)
Private collection

HISPANIC/LATINO

COLORS NEEDED:

- Flake White Replacement
- Yellow Ochre
- Cadmium Red Light
- Alizarin Crimson
- Burnt Sienna
- Sap Green
- Ivory Black
- Cadmium Yellow Medium or Light (optional)
- Raw Sienna (optional)

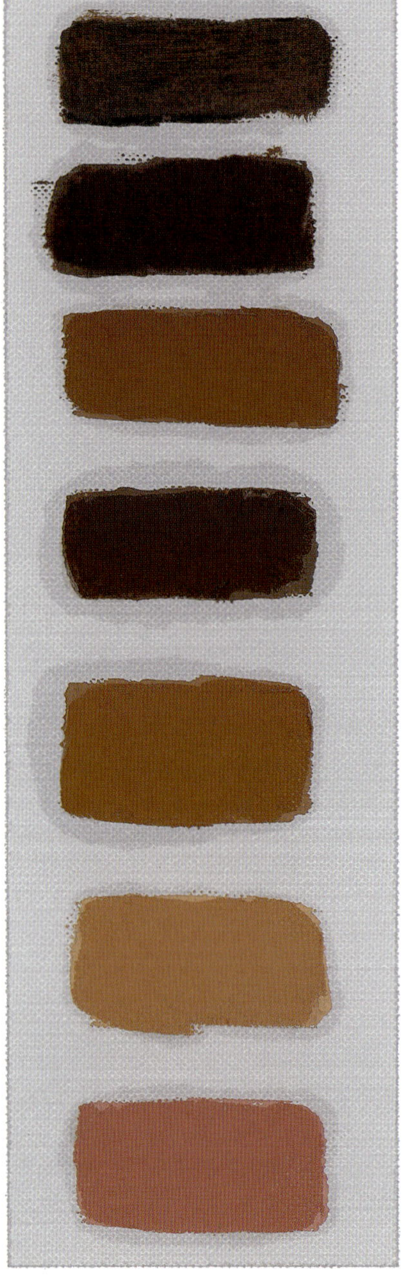

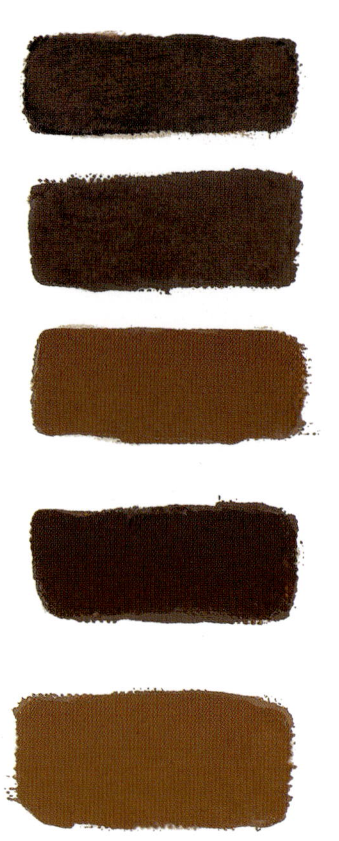

Hair in Shadow:
Ivory Black, Burnt Sienna

Hair in Light:
-Ivory Black, Burnt Sienna, Yellow Ochre, -Sap Green

Hair Highlights:
--Ivory Black, Burnt Sienna, +Yellow Ochre, --Flake White Replacement

Skin in Shadow:
Yellow Ochre, Burnt Sienna, +Sap Green
(or Cadmium Red Light, Cadmium Yellow, ++Sap Green, --Flake White Replacement

Skin Local Color:
Yellow Ochre, Burnt Sienna, -Sap Green, +White
(or Cadmium Red Light, Cadmium Yellow, Sap Green, +Flake White Replacement)

Skin Highlight:
Yellow Ochre, Burnt Sienna, -Sap Green, ++Flake White Replacement
(or Cadmium Red Light, Cadmium Yellow, Sap Green, ++Flake White Replacement)

Lips:
Skin-in-shadow mixture, Alizarin Crimson, Yellow Ochre, Flake White Replacement

To Lighten Dark Hair

Hair will be rich and dark using only Ivory Black and Burnt Sienna for the shadows. However, the rich color will gray out if white is added to lighten. Therefore, for middle values add Yellow Ochre and possibly a touch of Sap Green to lighten.

Skin (Local Color)

Start with Yellow Ochre and Burnt Sienna. Add Sap Green to neutralize the orange in the Burnt Sienna. If the undertone appears more green-based, try a mixture of Cadmium Red Light, Cadmium Yellow Medium, Sap Green and Flake White Replacement.

Place the warmth in the complexion at the junction of the light and the shadow.

Skin in Shadow

After building the shadow mixture with Yellow Ochre, Burnt Sienna and Sap Green, adjust the combination with attention to the surrounding colors and atmosphere bouncing into the skin.

Note that the temperature of the reflected light is the same as the clothing.

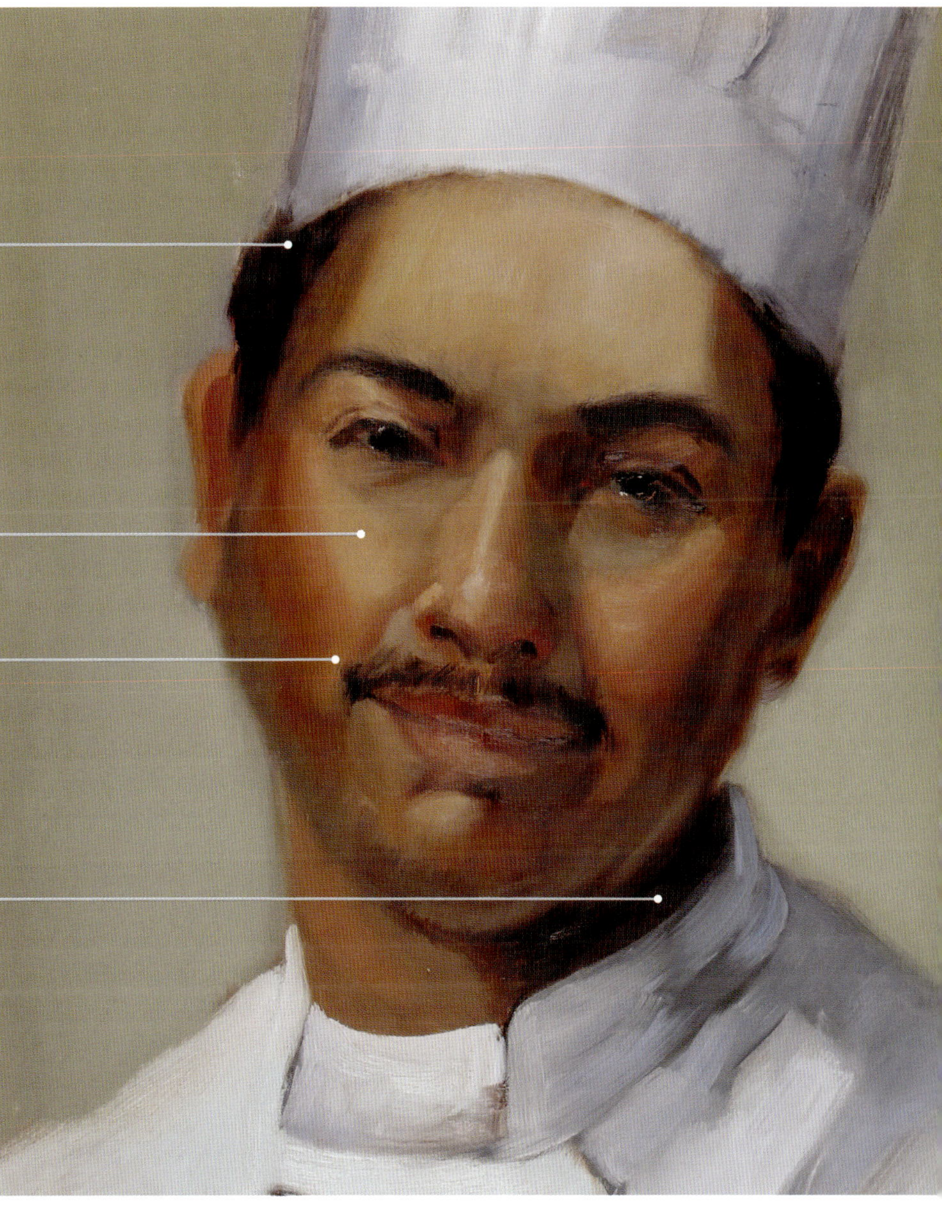

Use True Pigment to Lighten Mixtures

Hispanic and Latino skin has a wonderful richness. To lighten rich, dark mixtures, use a palette knife to keep mixtures pure and clean. Also, use a lighter version of a pure pigment instead of instantly using white to lighten. White, with its bluish undertones, tends to gray out a very warm skin-tone mixture. Try lightening a mixture by adding Raw Sienna, Cadmium Red Light, Yellow Ochre or Cadmium Yellow Medium or Light.

Mario the Chef
Oil study on Ampersand Gessobord
20" × 16" (51cm × 41cm)
Private collection

BLACK, WARM TONES

COLORS NEEDED:

- Flake White Replacement
- Cadmium Red Light
- Alizarin Crimson
- Burnt Sienna
- Cobalt Blue
- Sap Green
- Ivory Black
- Yellow Ochre

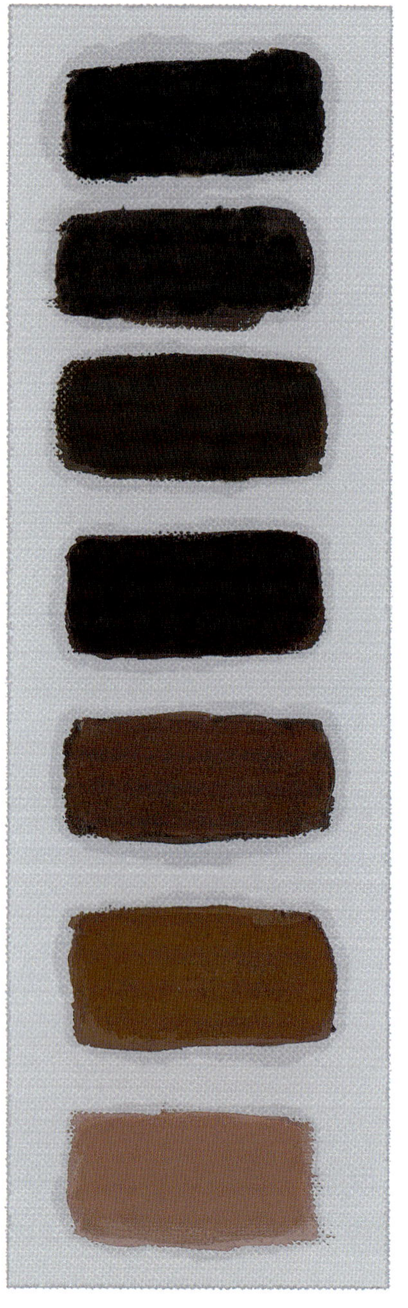

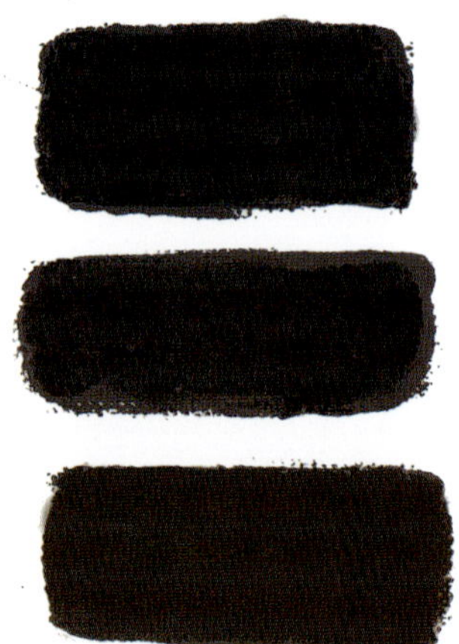

Hair in Shadow:
Ivory Black, Burnt Sienna, Cobalt Blue

Hair in Light:
-Ivory Black, +Burnt Sienna, Cobalt Blue

Hair Highlights:
--Ivory Black, Burnt Sienna, +Yellow Ochre, --Flake White Replacement

Skin in Shadow:
Burnt Sienna, Cobalt Blue, -Ivory Black (-Cadmium Red Light if needed)

Skin Local Color:
+Burnt Sienna, Cobalt Blue, --Ivory Black, Cadmium Red Light (lighten with Yellow Ochre or Flake White Replacement)

Skin Highlight:
+Burnt Sienna, +Cadmium Red Light, Yellow Ochre, --Cobalt Blue, --Ivory Black, --Flake White Replacement

Lips:
Skin-in-shadow mixture, Alizarin Crimson, Flake White Replacement, ---Yellow Ochre

Hair Highlight

The addition of gray notes in this subject's hair requires the addition of more Yellow Ochre and Flake White Replacement to the Ivory Black and Burnt Sienna.

Skin in Light

Add three touches of cool with Cobalt Blue, Ivory Black and Flake White Replacement to three warms—Burnt Sienna, Cadmium Red Light and Yellow Ochre. Adjust the temperature of the final mixture according to the lighting.

Skin (Local Color)

Burnt Sienna, Cobalt Blue, a touch of Ivory Black and Cadmium Red Light will create a base mixture. Add Yellow Ochre or a touch of Flake White Replacement to warm or cool while lightening.

Skin in Shadow

Use Burnt Sienna, Cobalt Blue and a touch of Ivory Black. Add Cadmium Red Light if needed.

Hair in Shadow

The temperature of the surrounding lighting can change the base mixture of Ivory Black, Burnt Sienna and Cobalt Blue by relying more on the warm element or the cool element.

Lips

To the skin-in-shadow mixture, add a touch of cool Alizarin Crimson, Yellow Ochre and Flake White Replacement.

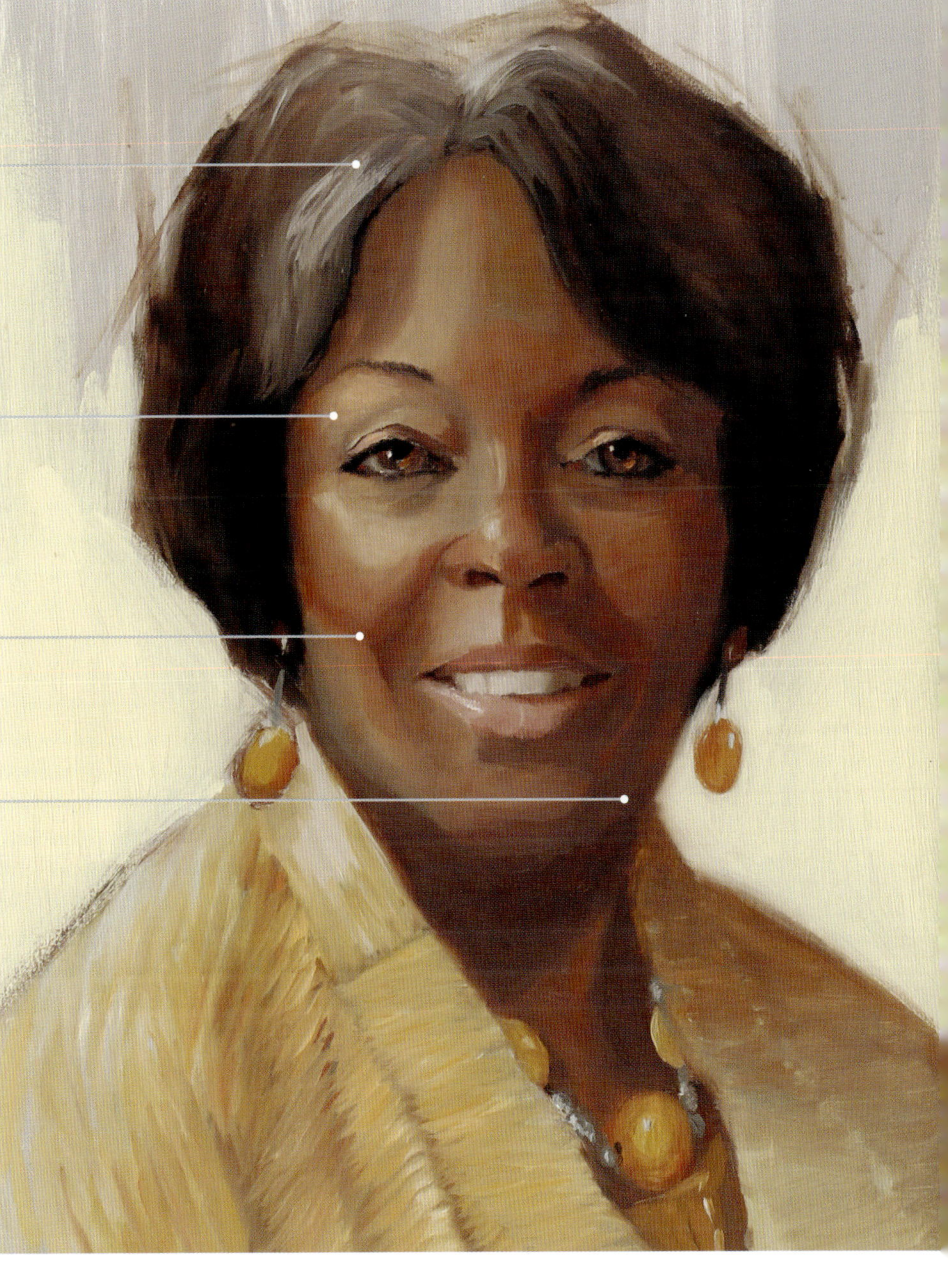

The Value of the Preliminary Color Study

This dynamic study was especially effective because of the wonderful gold clothing and amber jewelry. All of the warms in the skin, the clothing and the eyes play off one another beautifully. A successful attempt to plan the larger portrait, this study implies that this limited palette in a full portrait could be stunning.

Dr. Irma McClaurin
Anthropologist, writer and former president of Shaw University
Oil study on Ampersand Gessobord
20" × 16" (51cm × 41cm)
Private collection

BLACK, COOL TONES

COLORS NEEDED:

- Flake White Replacement
- Yellow Ochre
- Cadmium Red Light
- Alizarin Crimson
- Burnt Sienna
- Cobalt Blue or Ultramarine Blue
- Ivory Black

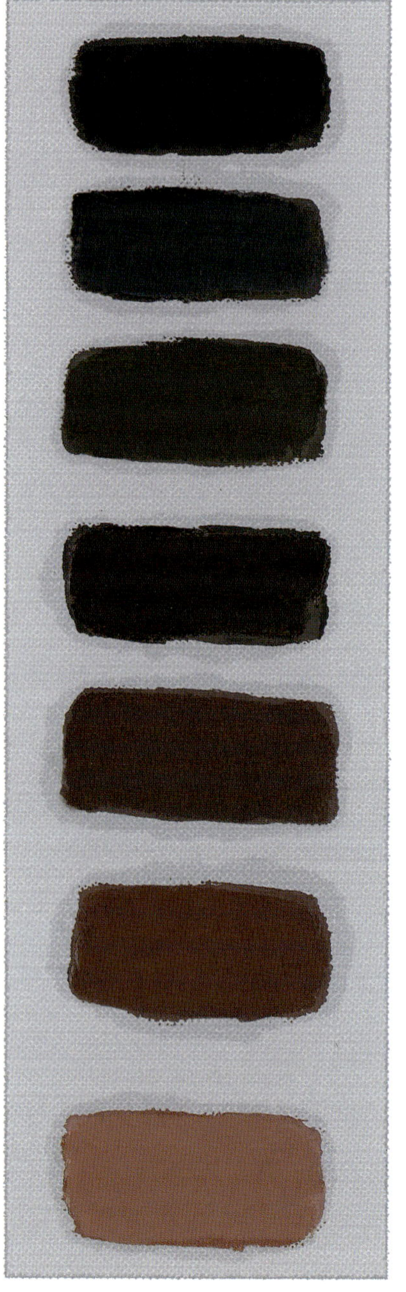

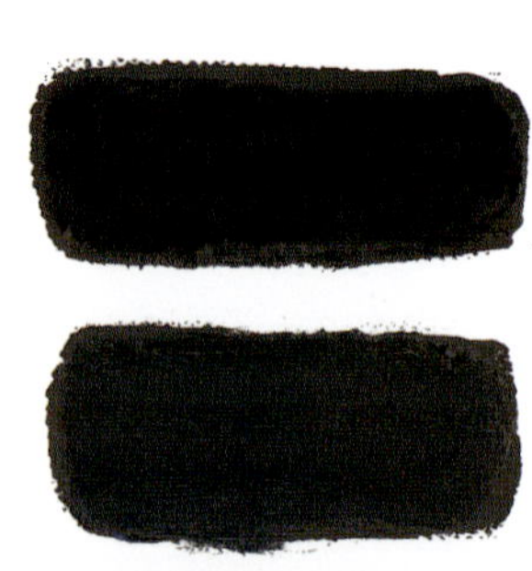

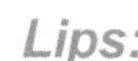

Hair in Shadow:
Ivory Black, Burnt Sienna, Cobalt Blue/Ultramarine Blue

Hair in Light:
-Ivory Black, +Burnt Sienna, Cobalt Blue/Ultramarine Blue

Hair Highlights:
-Ivory Black, Burnt Sienna, Cobalt Blue/Ultramarine Blue, -Yellow Ochre

Skin in Shadow:
Burnt Sienna, Cobalt Blue/Ultramarine Blue, -Ivory Black (Alizarin Crimson if needed)

Skin Local Color:
+Burnt Sienna, Cobalt Blue/Ultramarine Blue, Alizarin Crimson, --Ivory Black (lighten with Yellow Ochre or Flake White Replacement)

Skin Highlight:
+Burnt Sienna, Alizarin Crimson, Yellow Ochre, --Cobalt Blue, --Ivory Black, --Flake White Replacement

Lips:
Skin-in-shadow mixture, Alizarin Crimson, Flake White Replacement, ---Yellow Ochre

Skin (Local Color)

For this head study with predominantly cool underlying skin tones, mix Burnt Sienna with Cobalt Blue, Alizarin Crimson and a small amount of Ivory Black. If necessary, add Yellow Ochre or Flake White Replacement to lighten slightly.

Skin Highlight

The coolest light is skin-highlight mixture with Flake White Replacement and a touch of Cobalt Blue.

Reflected Light

This will be a different color with a change of clothing and a different direction of light.

Skin in Shadow

Use Burnt Sienna, Cobalt Blue and a touch of Ivory Black to neutralize the orange in the Burnt Sienna. If the underlying cool tone needs it, add a little Ultramarine Blue to the base dark. Use a touch of Alizarin Crimson if needed, depending on the brand of paint being used.

Lips

Start with the skin-in-shadow mixture and add Alizarin Crimson, a cool red. Add the smallest amount of Flake White Replacement and Yellow Ochre. Vary values from shadow into light.

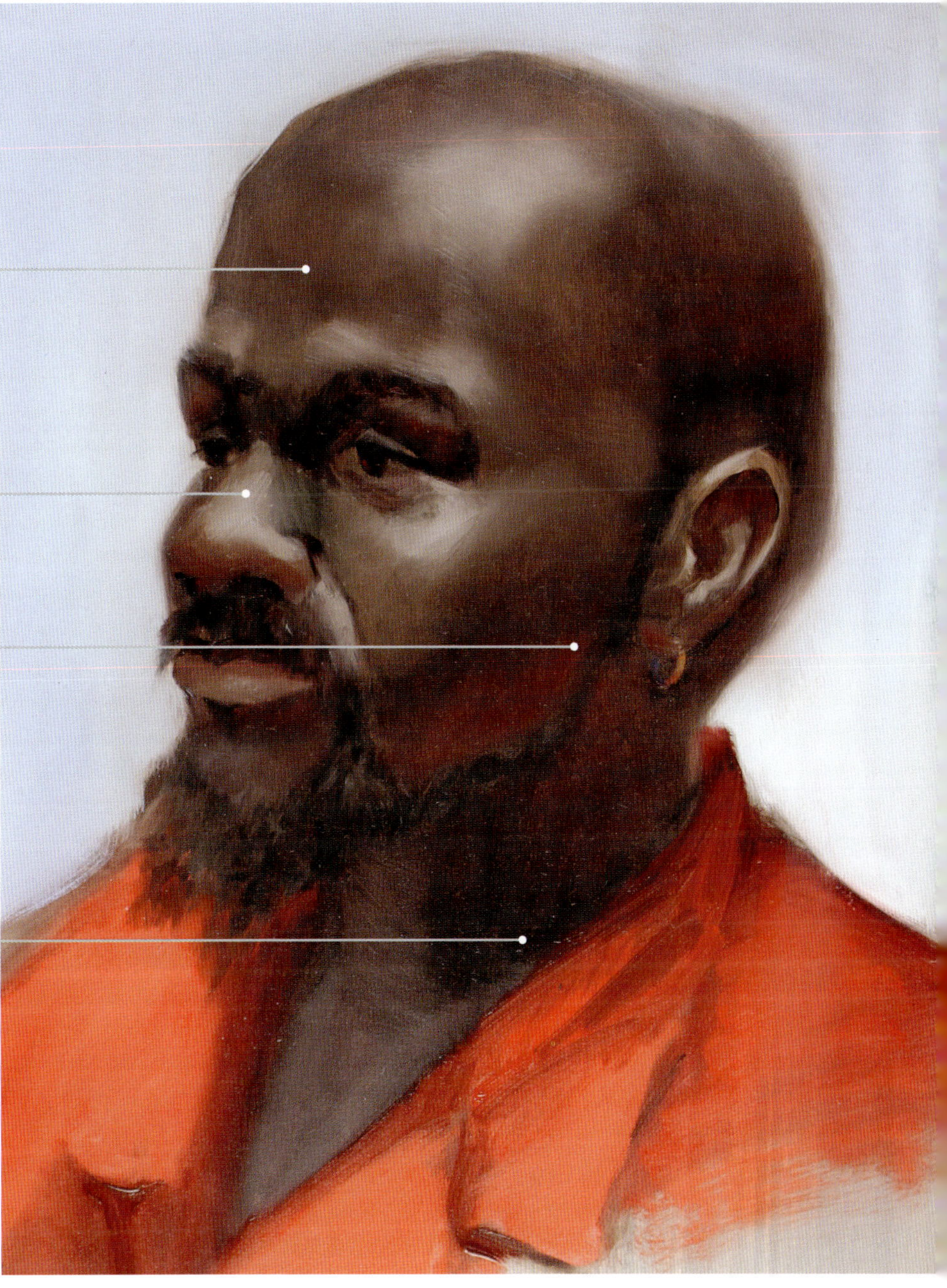

Play Cool Against Warm

Notice the rich darks behind the head, under the chin and on the neck. The skin tones would be almost too cool if they had been totally surrounded by cool darks. Instead, with the clothing to lighten and warm the image, the cool/warm patterns play beautifully off of one another.

Acuma
Oil study on Ampersand Gessobord
20" × 16" (51cm × 41cm)
Private collection

EAST ASIAN

COLORS NEEDED:

- Flake White Replacement
- Cadmium Yellow
- Yellow Ochre
- Cadmium Red Light
- Alizarin Crimson
- Ultramarine Blue
- Sap Green
- Ivory Black

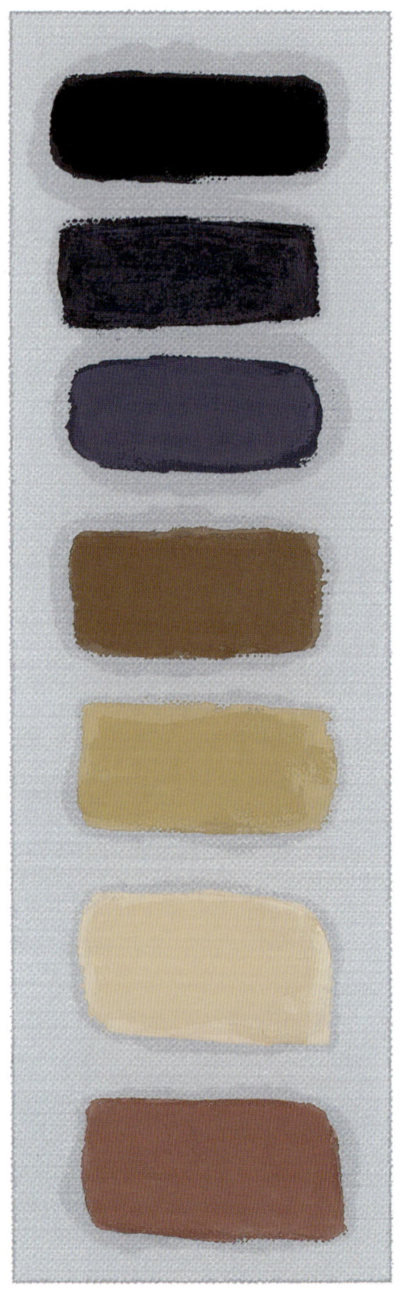

Hair in Shadow:
Ivory Black, Ultramarine Blue

Hair in Light:
-Ivory Black, -Ultramarine Blue, Alizarin Crimson

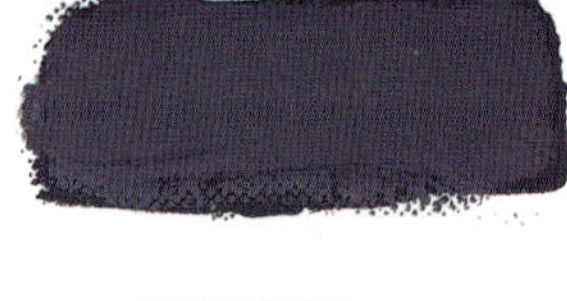

Hair Highlights:
--Ivory Black, Ultramarine Blue, ---Alizarin Crimson, --Yellow Ochre

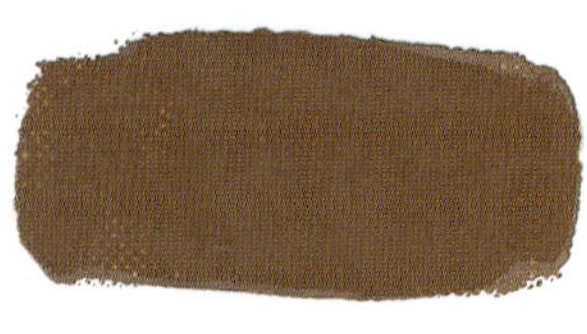

Skin in Shadow:
Yellow Ochre, Cadmium Red Light, Ivory Black, -Flake White Replacement (or choose Alizarin Crimson, Sap Green, Yellow Ochre)

Skin Local Color:
Yellow Ochre, Cadmium Red Light, -Ivory Black, Flake White Replacement

Skin Highlight:
Yellow Ochre, Cadmium Red Light, Ivory Black, ---Cadmium Yellow, +Flake White Replacement

Lips:
Skin-in-shadow mixture, Alizarin Crimson, Yellow Ochre, Flake White Replacement (---Cadmium Red Light if needed)

Hair in Shadow

Mix Ivory Black and Ultramarine Blue for rich, cool undertones for the hair.

For hair in the cool reflective light on the opposite side, add more Ultramarine Blue and Flake White Replacement.

In warm light, warm and lighten hair with the smallest amount of Alizarin Crimson and Yellow Ochre.

Skin (Local Color)

Use Yellow Ochre, Cadmium Red Light and Ivory Black. Think of Ivory Black as a Blue in mixture. It will react with the Yellow Ochre to make a desaturated green, which is then warmed with the Cadmium Red Light. Adding Flake White Replacement modifies the value and maintains a relatively cool mixture.

Skin in Shadow

Depending on the subject, use Yellow Ochre, Cadmium Red Light, Ivory Black and a touch of Flake White Replacement. If the skin tone requires a richer, darker mixture, add Yellow Ochre to an Alizarin Crimson/Sap Green mixture.

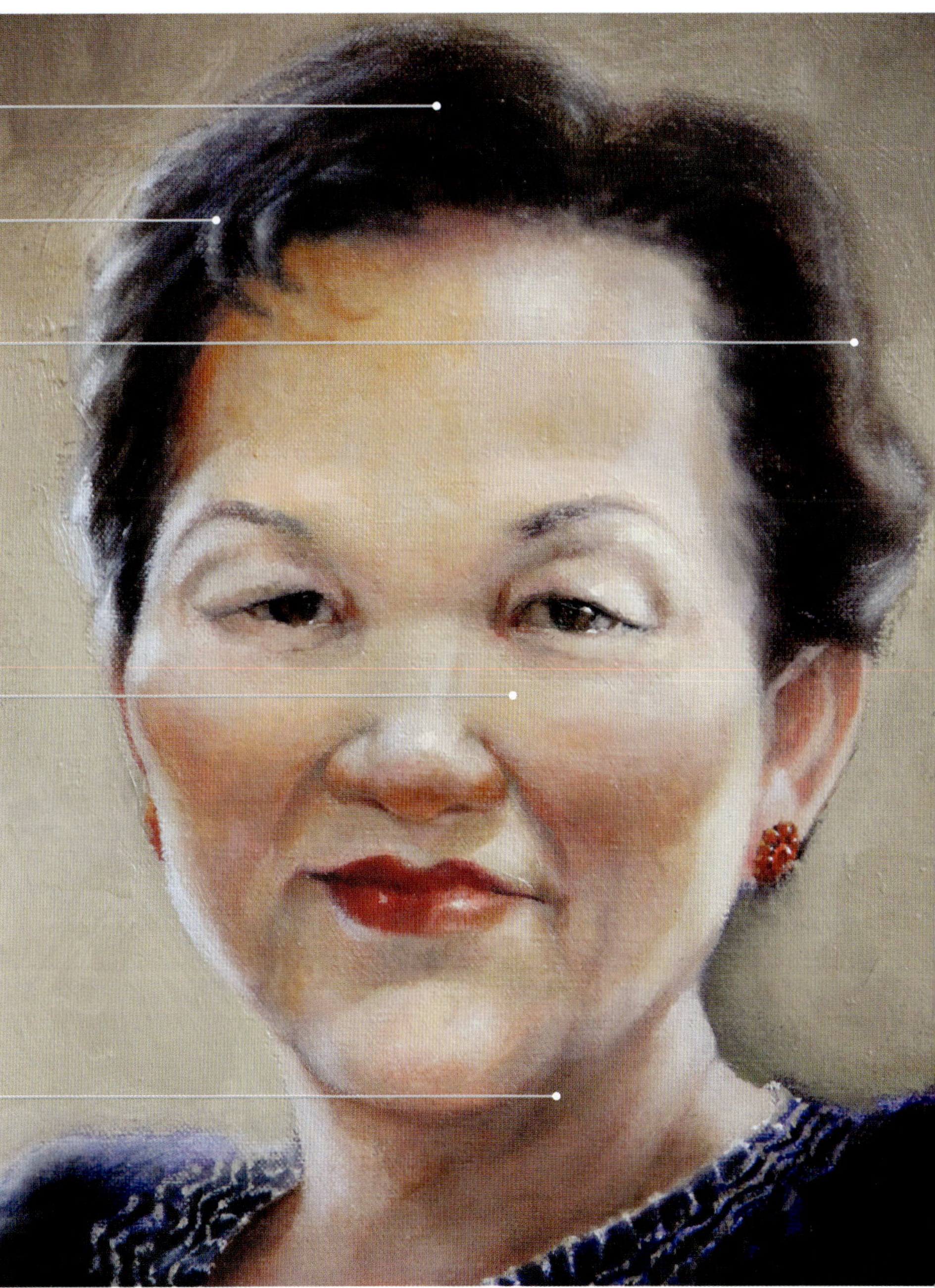

A Key Light for Added Dimension

Experiment with lighting in creative ways. Challenge an otherwise simple, straightforward head-and-shoulders design to be more interesting by using a second, cool key light from the side. With a front-on pose, this can help to define the structure and give a more sculptured effect.

Leong
Oil on Claessens linen
24" × 20" (61cm × 51cm)
Private collection

NATIVE AMERICAN

COLORS NEEDED:

- Flake White Replacement
- Cadmium Yellow
- Yellow Ochre
- Cadmium Red Light
- Alizarin Crimson
- Ultramarine Blue
- Sap Green
- Ivory Black

Hair in Shadow:
Ivory Black, Ultramarine Blue, Burnt Sienna

Hair in Light:
Ivory Black, -Ultramarine Blue, Burnt Sienna, --Sap Green

Hair Highlights:
Hair-in-light mixture, Burnt Sienna, -Sap Green, -Flake White Replacement

Skin in Shadow:
Alizarin Crimson, Burnt Sienna , Sap Green, --Yellow Ochre

Skin (Local Color):
Alizarin Crimson, Burnt Sienna , Yellow Ochre, Sap Green, Flake White Replacement

Skin Highlight:
Skin (local color) mixture, Burnt Sienna , -Sap Green, +Flake White Replacement

Lips:
Skin-in-shadow mixture, +Alizarin Crimson, Yellow Ochre, White

Skin (Local Color)

Begin with Alizarin Crimson, Burnt Sienna and Yellow Ochre. Add the cools of Sap Green and Flake White Replacement. Varying the degree of cool and warm will help to push and pull the planes in and out over the topography of the face.

Daylight is blue. The highlights created by the down lighting for this subject reinforce the cool quality of the daylight.

Color becomes intense at the junction of light and shadow.

Skin in Shadow

Rich with a mix of Alizarin Crimson, Burnt Sienna, Sap Green and a slight amount of Yellow Ochre, modify the mix according to the temperature of the light source and bouncing light from clothing and surrounding colors.

Skin Affected by Weather

Although from Arizona, Mr. Velazquez is an expert on the art and culture of the Inuit Tribes in the high Arctic. He spoke of the harsh conditions in traveling to these locales and working with the tribes. The weather takes a toll on the skin and the body. For people exposed to the elements, keep the color real.

Lips

Start with the skin-in-shadow mixture and add Alizarin Crimson, Yellow Ochre and Flake White Replacement. Keep the lips an earthy color.

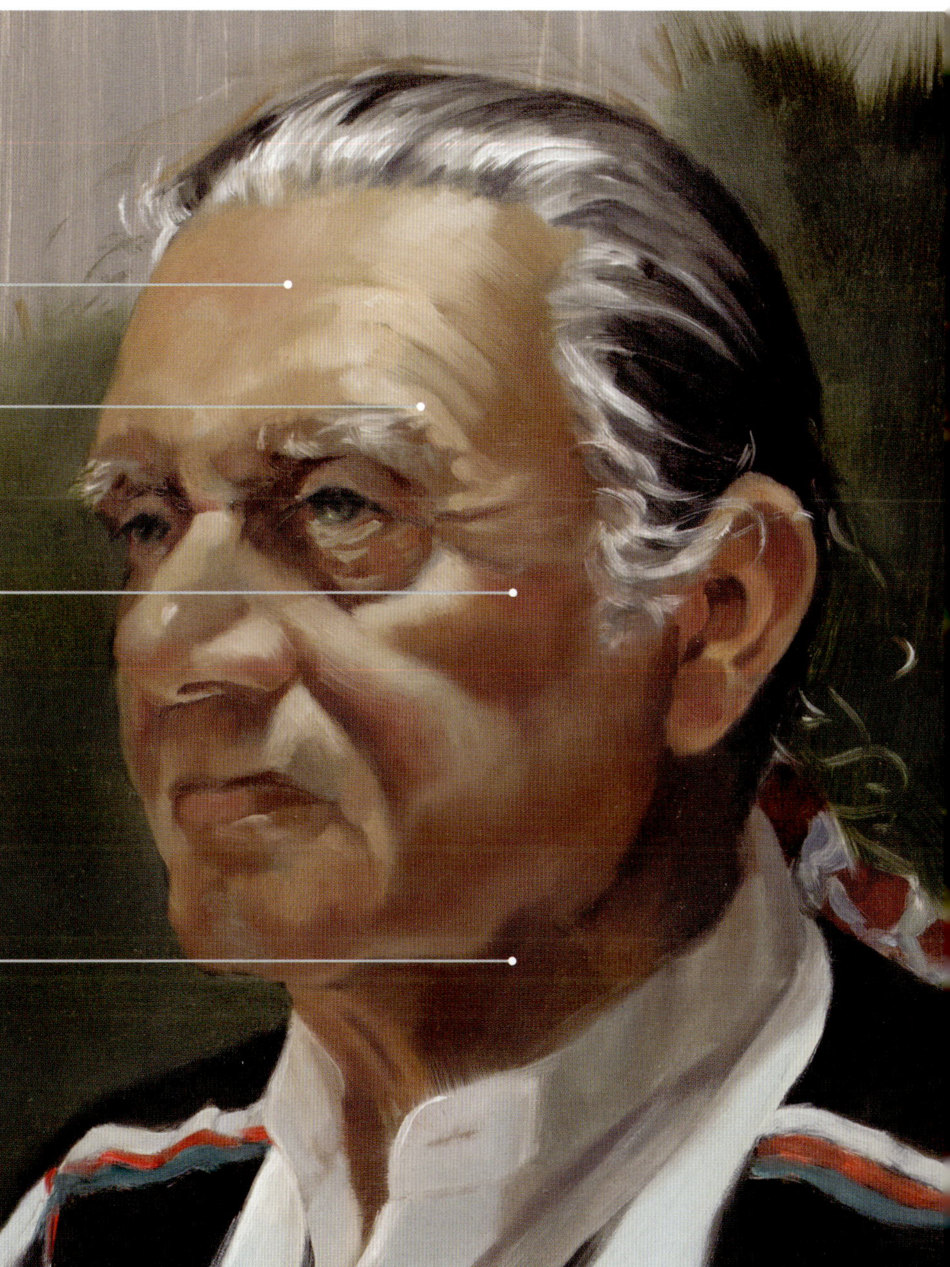

Hair

Start with cool Ivory Black and Ultramarine Blue with Burnt Sienna. The cool light from the sky dominates. Adding different amounts of Flake White Replacement and a touch of Sap Green helps to vary the gray hair.

Carlos Velazquez

Otomi Indian, mechanical engineer and former director of the Dept. of Natural Resources and Environmental Affairs of the Southern Cherokee Nation
Oil study on Ampersand Gessobord
20" × 16" (51cm × 41cm)
Private collection

INDIAN (CONTINENTAL)

COLORS NEEDED:

- Flake White Replacement
- Raw Sienna
- Burnt Sienna
- Alizarin Crimson
- Ultramarine Blue
- Ivory Black

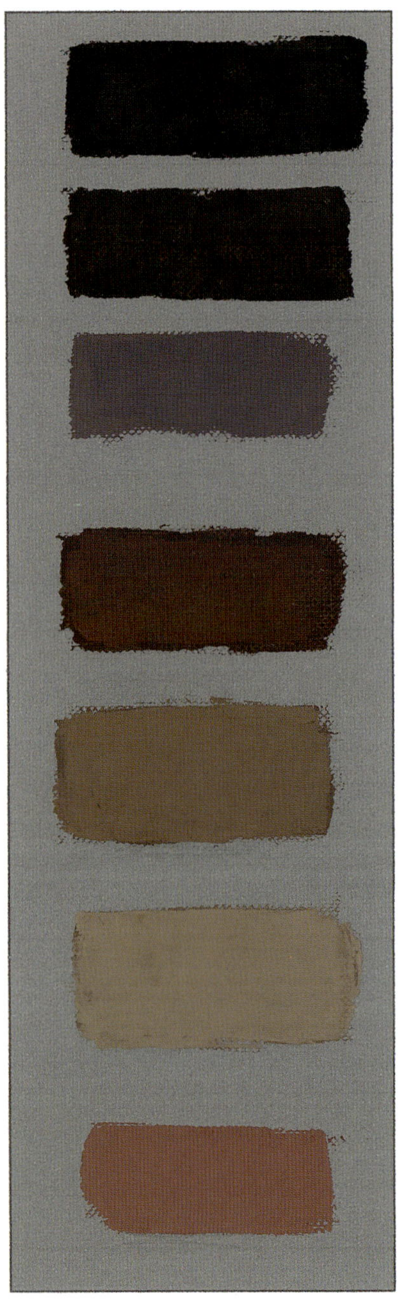

Hair in Shadow:
Ivory Black, Ultramarine Blue, Burnt Sienna

Hair in Light:
Ivory Black, Ultramarine Blue, Burnt Sienna

Hair Highlights:
Ivory Black, Ultramarine Blue, Burnt Sienna, Flake White Replacement

Skin in Shadow:
Raw Sienna, Burnt Sienna, Ivory Black

Skin (Local Color):
Raw Sienna, Ultramarine Blue, Ivory Black, Flake White Replacement

Skin Highlight:
Raw Sienna, Ivory Black, Flake White Replacement

Lips:
Skin-in-shadow mixture, Alizarin Crimson, -Raw Sienna, Flake White Replacement

Skin (Local Color)

Mix with Raw Sienna, Ultramarine Blue, a small amount of Ivory Black, and a small amount of Flake White Replacement. This color will have an ashen quality to it, giving it a recognizable grayed value and tone.

Skin in Light

Start with Raw Sienna, a small amount of Ivory Black and Flake White Replacement. Adjust according to ambient light and surrounding colors.

Skin in Shadow

Raw Sienna (a gold), with Burnt Sienna (an orange) and Ivory Black (a blue), will provide a dark neutral. Here it is, more warm due to the surrounding colors.

Hair

Cool undertones are achieved with the use of two blues: Ultramarine Blue and Ivory Black. To this, add a little Burnt Sienna (think of this as the orange in the mixture). Add Flake White Replacement where the sun touches the dark hair.

Lips

Take the skin-in-shadow mixture and add Alizarin Crimson, Raw Sienna and Flake White Replacement. Remember to mix three values to shape the lips in and out of the light.

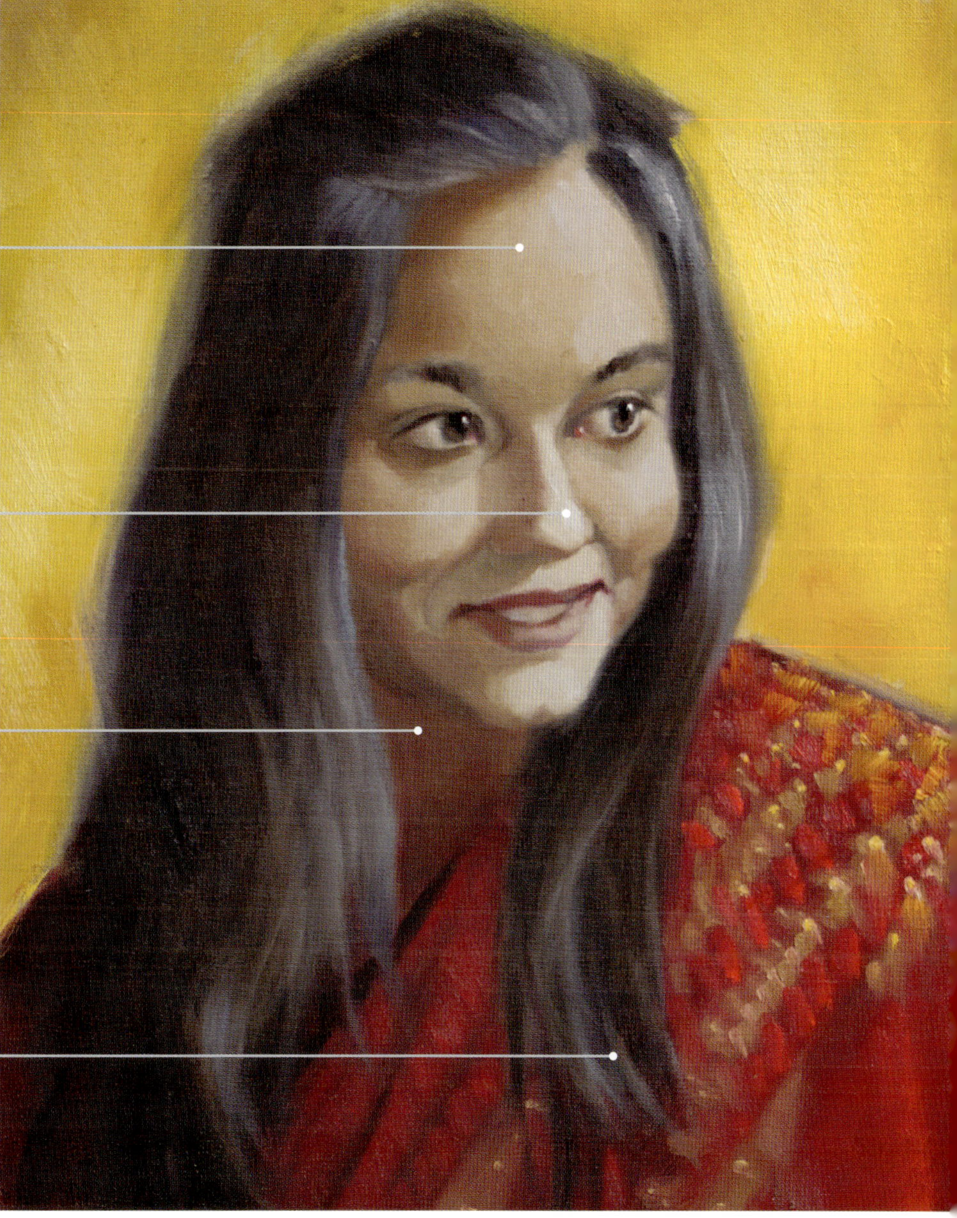

Keep Costume Secondary to Face

This is a wonderful opportunity to paint Indian clothing with brilliant, heavily saturated color—and a perfect time to ask the sitter if they mind having photos done to record the clothing and jewelry. It will often take more time to render the complexity of the color designs and woven material than the face and figure. Don't forget the sketch work.

Vinita Jain
Wife, mother, artist
Oil study on Ampersand Gessobord
20" × 16" (51cm × 41cm)
Private collection

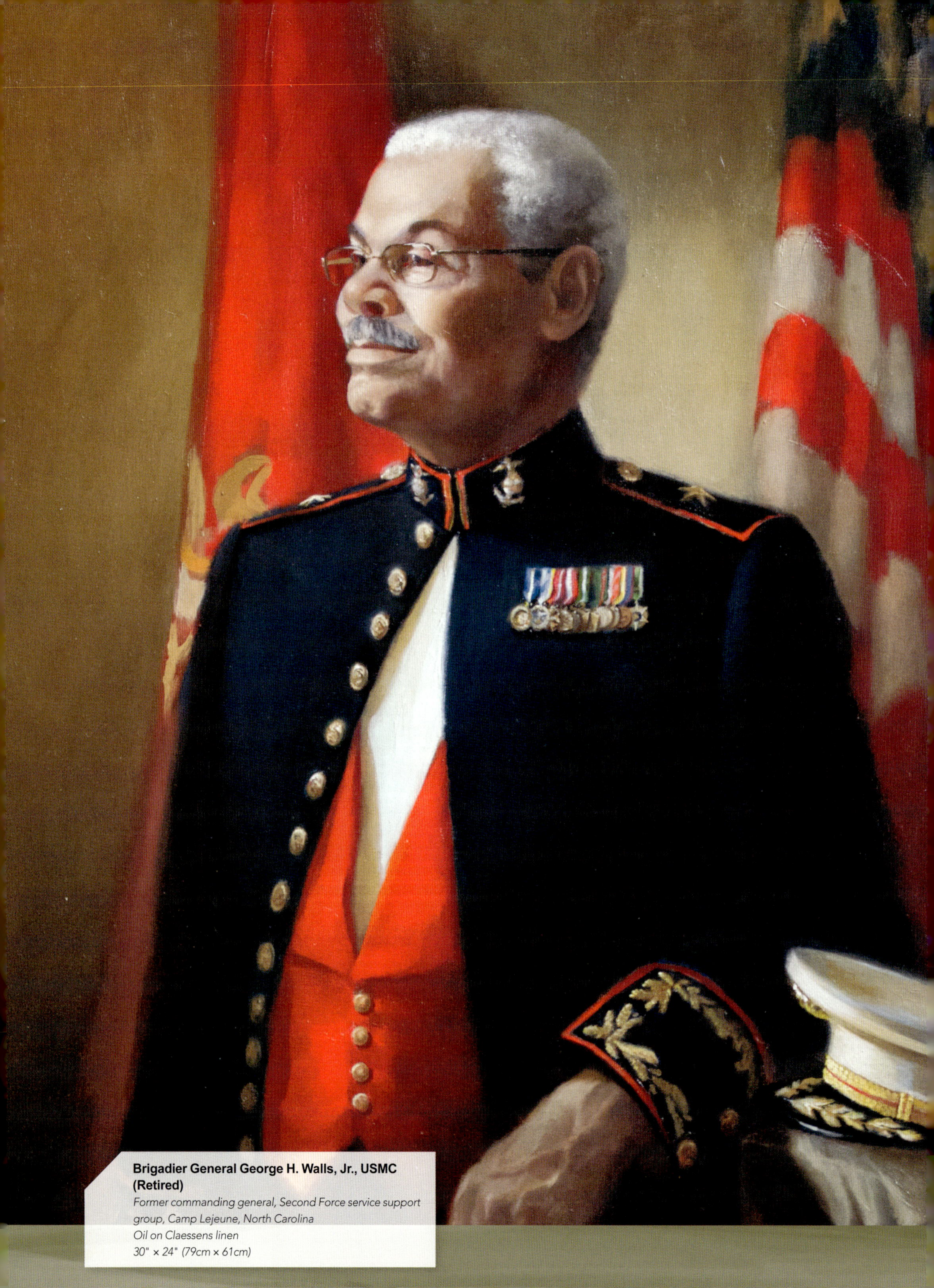

Brigadier General George H. Walls, Jr., USMC (Retired)
Former commanding general, Second Force service support group, Camp Lejeune, North Carolina
Oil on Claessens linen
30" × 24" (79cm × 61cm)

CHAPTER 4

DESIGN DECISIONS

Every work of art deserves careful consideration and planning. Each person's story is complex, multifaceted—convoluted sometimes. It is up to you to make sense of it and record it for the viewer in a well-balanced, clearly understood, wordless narrative of their life at the moment they have chosen. Too large a task? Break it down. Take time to digest the elements. Clarify the key factors and make them carry the story. Remember that once the painting is out of your hands, it is unlikely that your portrait subject will mount a disclaimer by the artist next to the canvas saying, "What I really meant to do was...What I really meant to say was...What I really meant to show was..."

Do it. Say it. Show it. Create the painting as it was meant to be created before it leaves the studio.

"If the artist's will is not strong, he will see all kinds of unessential things."
—Robert Henri

The Story is the Core of Design
Brigadier General George Walls and I worked on several portraits. He was the third black officer to achieve the rank of General in the U.S. Marine Corps. But instead of creating the portrait at Camp LeJuene, he chose to do the sittings at the Naval ROTC building at the University of North Carolina in Chapel Hill, one of several North Carolina universities where he had been a professor of naval science.

BUILDING THE PORTRAIT WITHIN THE SUBJECT'S WORLD

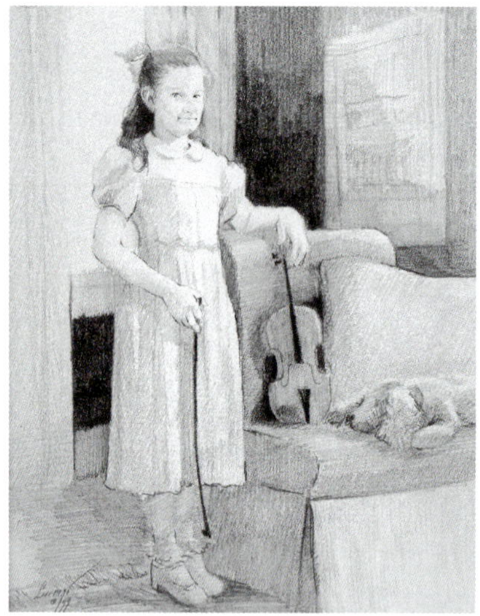

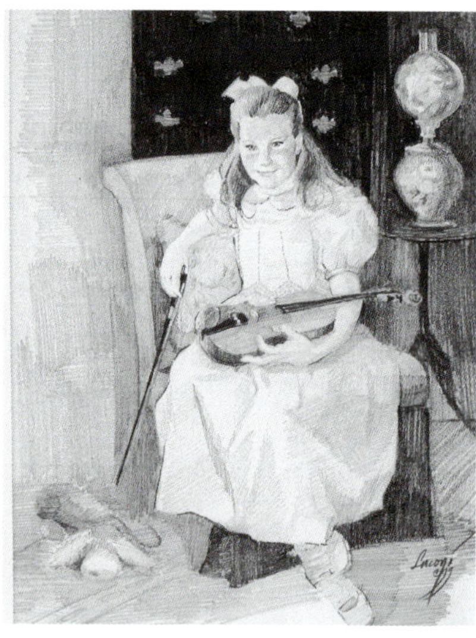

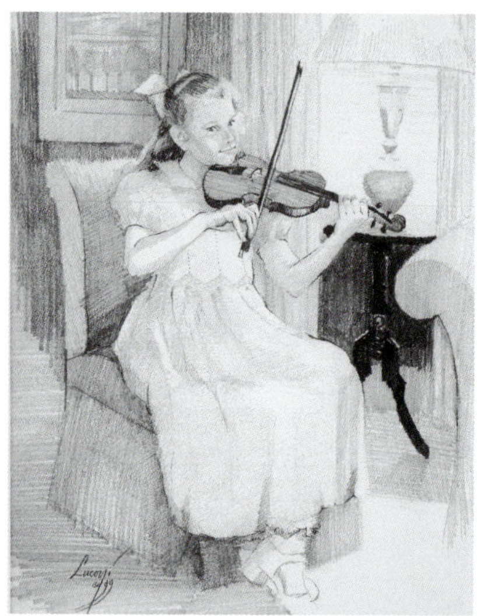

Familiar Environments
The young lady in these sketches possessed many abilities, but she had a particular affinity for the violin. Though other sketches were done, these, in different parts of the house where she spent most of her time, were the favorites. The lamp was her great-grandmother's—a lovely way to carry a piece of family history into the painting, which will someday be viewed by her own great-grandchildren.

Catherine Lee Rentz Wilkerson
Preliminary graphite sketches on bristol
14" × 11" (36cm × 28cm)

Portrait artists must be vigilant in their study of the world around their subjects, not only cognizant of their faces and figures, but of the subjects' environments. The person, place and objects must interrelate in a natural and universal image that can speak without language barriers to anyone anywhere on the planet.

Individual expression resonates with the viewer. The power of the portrait is that it mixes symbolism and elements of psychology in the representation.

Working with multiple sketches permits both the artist and the subject, who may or may not have an artistic flair, to come to an agreement on the ideas that will satisfy both the telling of the tale and the artistic basics of design and composition. Is this a lot of work? Yes.

If necessary, consider it practice. Each time the image is worked, the more you understand and recognize about the subject. But artists must do the work to reach any level of competency or success. There are no shortcuts.

Portraits may include all types of people with complex lives: CEOs, doctors, attorneys, judges, scholars, political figures, performers, military officers, debutantes, children and families. When you hire models, you have the prerogative to create any story desired by use of clothing, props and lighting. But when doing commissioned work, you are new to your subject's story.

Clients are individual and unique, and they each have individual and unique stories to tell. Don't fall into a trap of comfortable patterns, colors and compositions over and over again because they become easy to crank out. Your challenge is to create a new and visually stimulating story with each new portrait, with each new person.

GET TO KNOW THE SITTER

To learn about the sitters, build many sketches at the first sitting. As they chat, sketch. Move to different settings—from boardroom to entry lobby, music room to garden, desk to window. Observe pattern, movement, lighting and so on. Women may change clothing and hairstyles, men may try

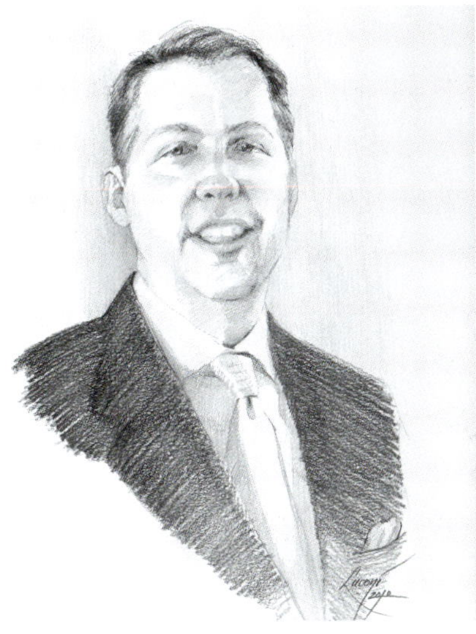

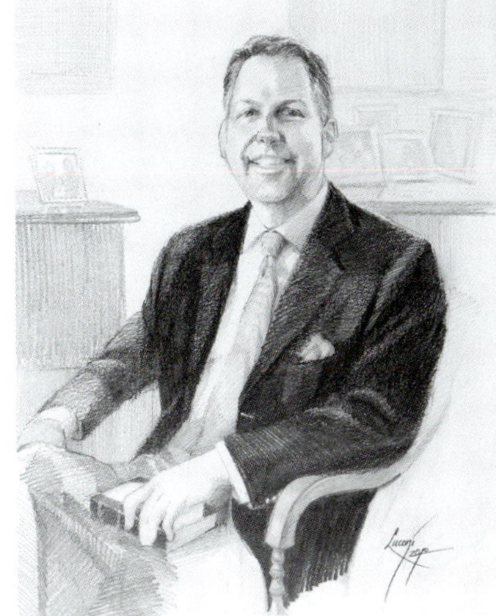

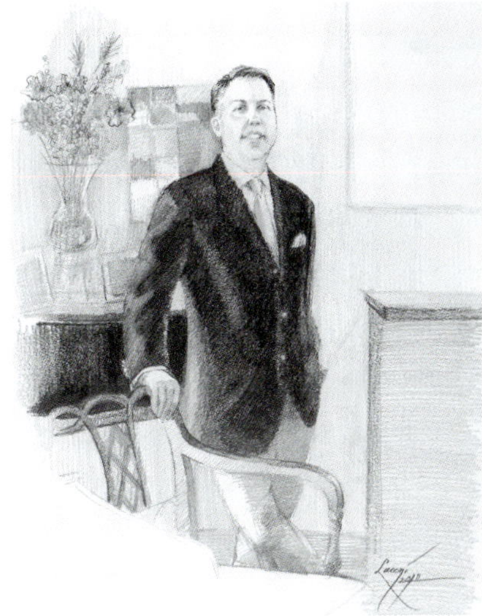

Planning Ahead With Sketches

These five sketches served multiple purposes as the design was to be chosen. First, notice that each of these is a different planning point for the painting: head and shoulders; a half body with hands; three-quarter length standing, and full-length figures, one standing and one seated.

B. Grant Yarber
Retired CEO andpPresident of Capital Bank, business owner/entrepreneur
Preliminary graphite sketches on bristol board
14" × 11" (36cm × 28cm)

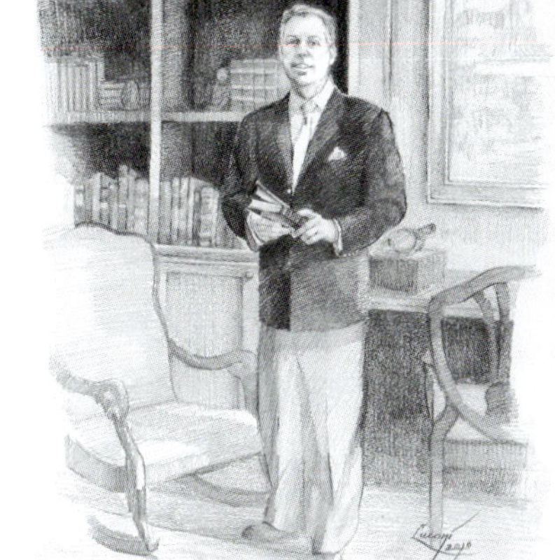

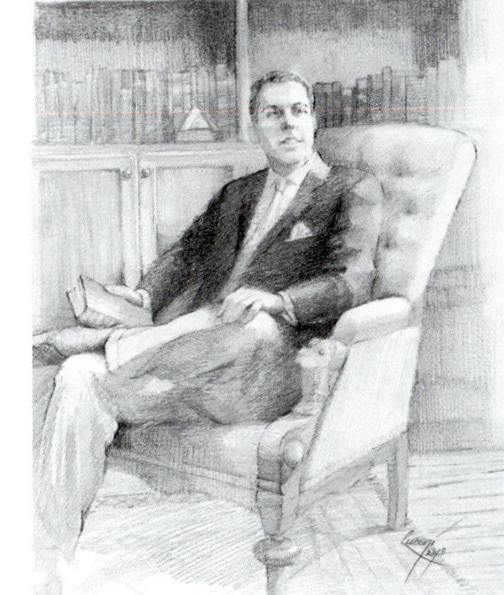

suit vs. shirt and tie vs. casual clothing, all in an attempt to feel most like themselves.

To bring the subjects into the design process and involve them in how they would like to be portrayed, gather a great amount of reference material. Should photography be used? Yes, use photography for anything that cannot be taken to the studio to paint. This may include jewelry, detail on furnishings, beading on gowns, upholstery patterns, a chair hand carved in Europe by the sitter's great-grandfather, the collectible book on the desk, grandmother's silver service or an industry award to a CEO.

Use the allotted time to relax the sitters, observe the surroundings that they interact with each day and find the core of their visual story.

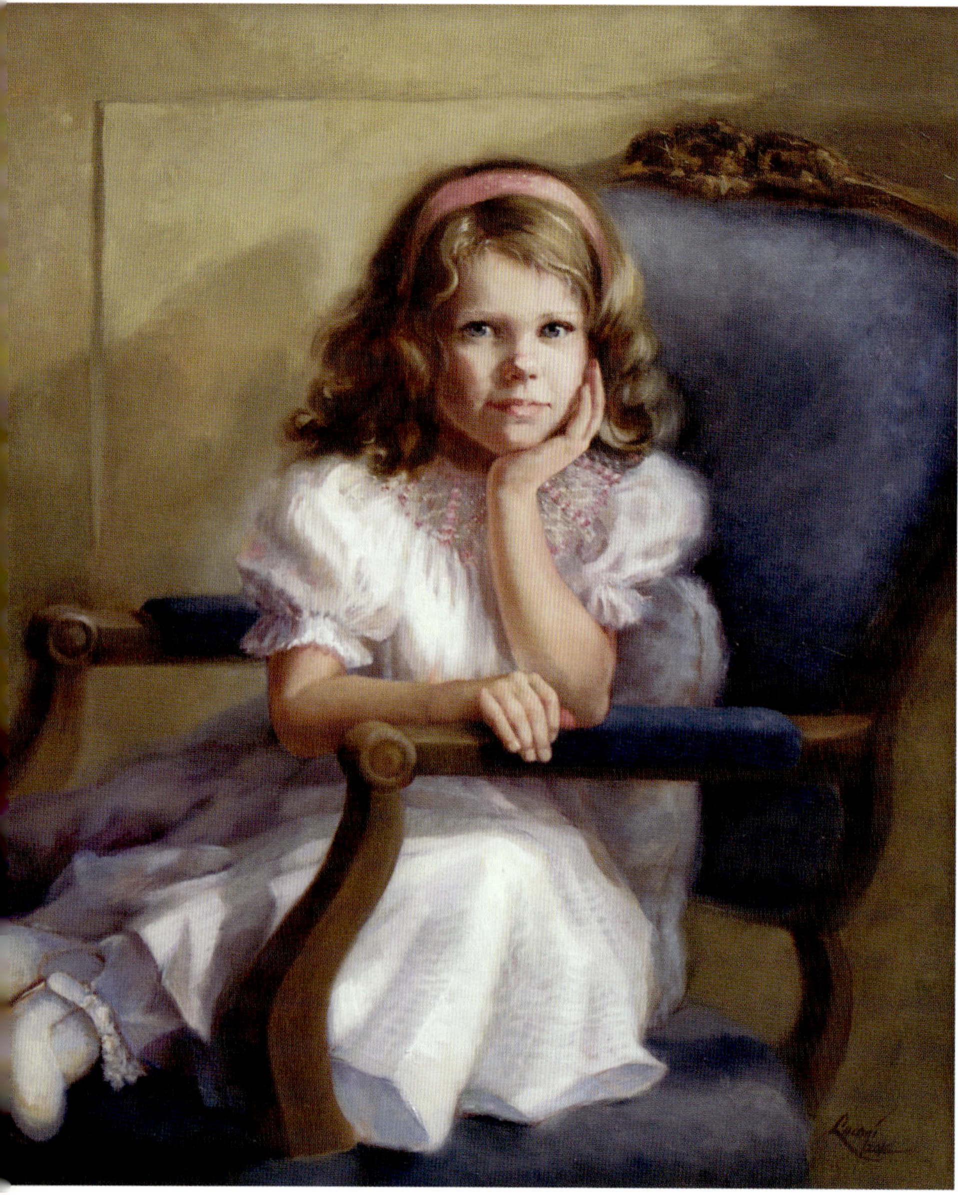

Relating to the Subject
During our sketching session, Haley shared with me the story from Annie, *which she had just seen on stage. All of her sketches displayed different emotions as she acted out some scenes and we sang a few of the songs. But this one was truly Haley—wistful, dreamy and sweet.*

Haley Chastain Stoltz
Oil on Claessens linen
36" × 30" (91cm × 79cm)

Every portrait artist has the opportunity to tell someone's story. The paintings are not simply about recording a great face. We can rely on an expert photograph for that. Instead, we should gather enough information about the person to tell so much more—about her body language, who she is, what her lifestyle is, how she works or plays, what activates her, what motivates her, how she interacts with other people and the world around her.

The artist has the prerogative to set a stage that will best tell the story artistically. But the backdrop, surroundings and props must never overwhelm and, above all, must be true to the sitter. Collectively, it still must be her reality. Final images will never look as though they go together if you add elements simply for the sake of color, placement or balance. Every element must have a psychological or emotional relationship to the subject. Only then will this be an accurate representation.

It is important to collect all the information you can to build a cohesive design. Often the sitter will regale the artist with dozens of life experiences that could certainly be catalysts for a great illustration. But sometimes he will want to include dozens of objects that have no place in a timeless painting. Guide him and edit the things he shares, keeping in mind that less is more. Simplicity is far more appealing than a busy clutter of meaningful but unnecessary objects.

After listening to the stories, guide the sitter to include those things that may be most appealing in the painting. If they are also things the artist enjoys painting as still life or landscape, all the better. Don't forget that the process of painting still has to be exciting and fun for the artist. The painting will be a much more creative and beautiful finished product if your heart is in it.

Over time, artists tend to find their niche with subject matter. The watercolorist painting beach scenes, the pastelist specializing in floral arrangements, the acrylic painter who quickly works scenes on location—all have an endless array of stimulating subject matter. But the portrait artist is obliged to develop painting skills to depict the figure, clothing, jewelry, furniture, bookcases, interiors, landscapes, beach scenes, gardens, boardrooms, silver services, china, crystal and anything else the sitter may come up with from stuffed animals to prized thoroughbreds. Therein lies the challenge. The significance will be obvious at the conclusion of the framed and presented artwork.

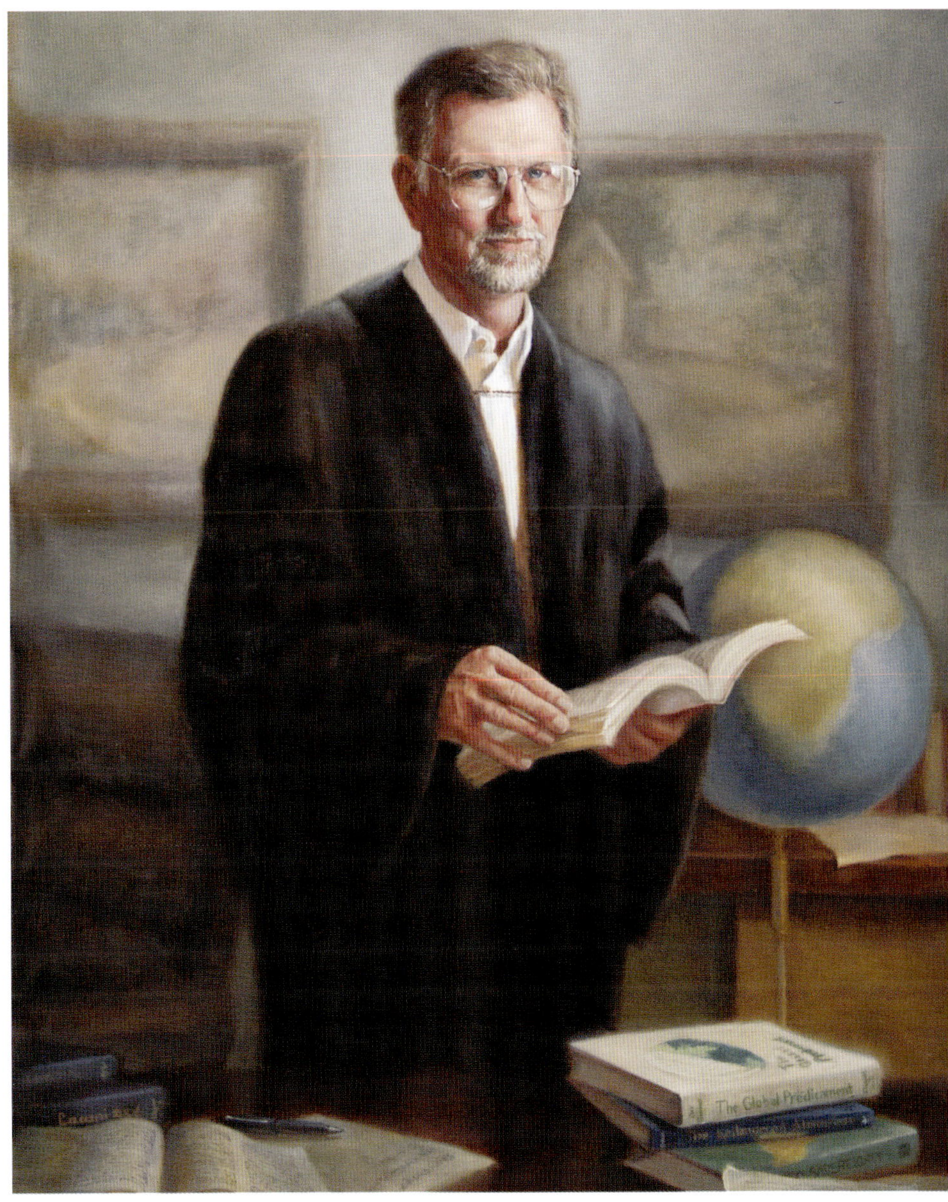

One Image to Describe Multifaceted Man

This professor of international relations and global environmental politics and former department head of political science at NC State University permitted me to paint this portrait in his office. The many books he had authored on the desk, the paintings he had painted of his home state of Montana hanging behind him and the globe representing the constant travel and lecturing he did during his final years before retirement all added up to a fairly complete story of this multifaceted gentleman.

Dr. Marvin Soroos

Retired political science department head, North Carolina State University; author, traveler and artist
Oil on Claessens linen
40" × 30" (102cm × 79cm)

LIGHTING THE SUBJECT

Work in natural light whenever possible. Not everyone has the luxury of a designated room or building for their studio working space. It would be wonderful to be able to control all of the lighting factors and issues all of the time. But in reality, artists are lucky to have a single window or skylight with that cherished bit of natural light. The answer is to augment whatever natural light there may be with additional lighting configurations.

Since the portrait is created on location most of the time, identify the limitations before arriving at the location. When setting up the first sitting appointment, ask pertinent questions about the light, where the rooms are that will be used, what illuminates that space (window, skylight, reflected light from interior hallway, portico overhang, etc.) and what time of day the sitter finds that space most pleasant and appealing. Rule #1: The sitter must be relaxed and comfortable in a natural environment that appeals to him *and* is a part of his real life.

LIGHTING EQUIPMENT

If natural light is not available, using a grouping of two or three lights may become necessary. In the studio, add a track of lights. It offers flexibility of positioning and the opportunity to change the color of the output from each different light if desired. Standing photography lamps can help illuminate the subject, the palette and the easel with even lighting.

Whether in the studio or out on location, a portable set of lights is often necessary, more affordable than ever before and available in all different sizes and travel configurations. Two tungsten halogen Tota-lights by Lowel are extremely portable. These run very hot and must be carefully handled, but the entire system is compact. Two lighting heads, cords and umbrellas to bounce and soften the light effect, gels to change the temperature of the light, collapsible gel frames and stands packed into a case that fits into a suitcase (with plenty of room to spare) weighs about 19 pounds (8.6 kg). Go to the local photo store or go online and directly compare various systems to find a solution from the many options available today.

SETTING THE MOOD

Lighting sets the tone and the mood of a scene. It interprets the place in very different ways. Think about your favorite outdoor place. Imagine sitting there at six AM on a cool October morning. Now experience the same place at eight PM on a warm July evening. The lighting, air quality and general atmosphere are all completely different. Paintings need to make sense, and the viewers need to mentally experience that difference. The painting may begin in one lighting situation, but the temperature and effect probably change when moving the materials back into the studio to complete the work. This is dreadfully confusing and time consuming. Learn to recreate the lighting where and when the workspace demands.

LIGHTING: DIRECTIONAL PLANS

- **Backlighting:** From the rear, creating a rim of lighting around the sitter and objects. The edges of the silhouette will glow.
- **Sidelighting:** One-directional lighting, can often be a more harsh lighting, sending unflattering shadows across the face and figure.
- **Uplighting:** Rather like old-fashioned footlights in the theater. Tends to create a strong and potentially garish effect. This is a wonderful choice for character studies and dramatic effects in costumed models. Consider trying carefully window-lit/bounced light, beach, snow, or water-lit children or people in recreational settings.
- **Rembrandt lighting:** A single source of light flooding the illuminated side and providing a triangular spot of light on the shadow side cheek with mostly dark surrounding.
- **Three-quarter lighting:** Most typically used lighting for portraiture. Originating at a 45-degree angle from above, this light breaks the change in directional planes from the front plane of the face to the side plane. It helps us understand the three-dimensional properties of the head in a clearly defined manner.

CLOTHING SETS FORMAL OR INFORMAL TONE

Make the clothing fit the lifestyle. Encourage the sitters to be as comfortable or as formal as their daily lives require. As far as children go, make the choice to paint who they are today and all that entails, whether it is a ballerina tutu, a cowboy or astronaut costume. They will be this age only once, but they may be painted many times throughout their lifetimes.

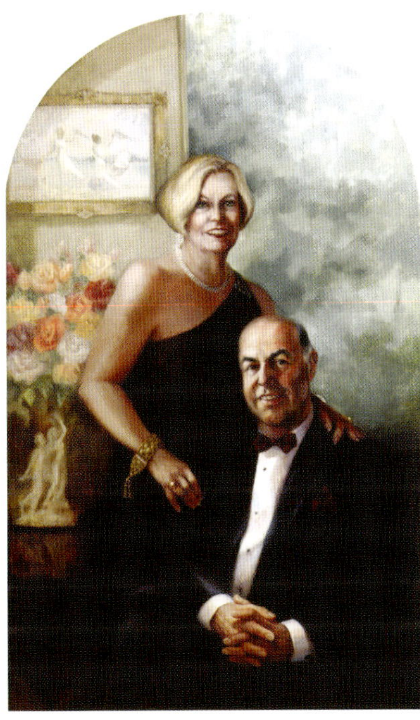

The Formal Pose

This couple enjoyed philanthropic activities in their retirement, and they graced their community by supporting many ventures including the state ballet company and the state symphony orchestra. Their lives involved collecting art, travel, rose gardening and fine, formal events, all of which were depicted in this Palladian-shaped canvas custom created to fit into an architectural detail in their living room.

Mr. and Mrs. Roberg
Oil on Claessens linen
72" × 36" (183cm × 91cm) (Palladian)

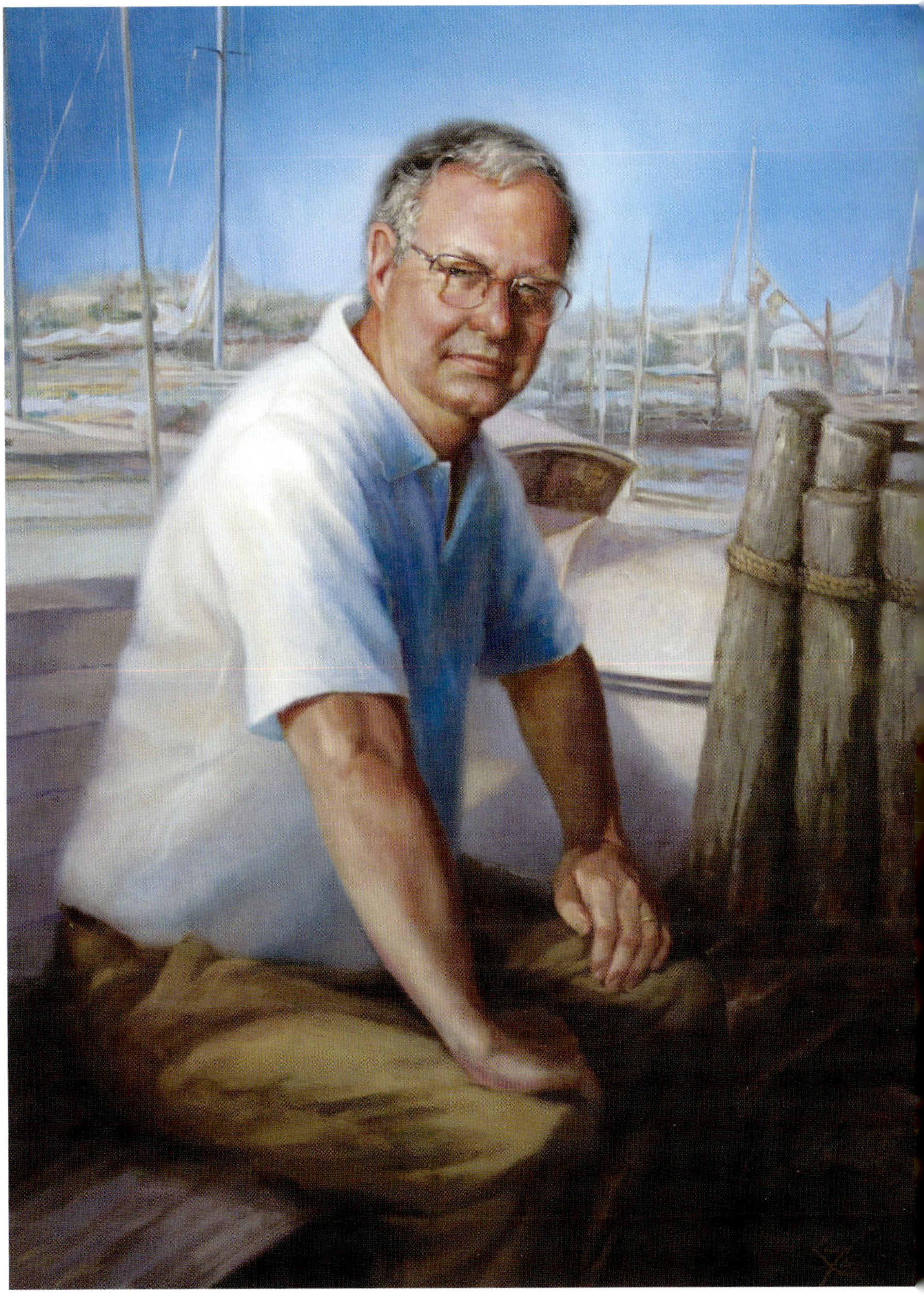

The Informal Pose

I had painted this gentleman at age 40 for his boardroom in a three-piece business suit, seated on a tufted leather chair. At 65, though he had not lived at the beach since his youth, he requested that I paint "the real me, the beach bum." This was where his heart was, and according to his children, this is his storytelling pose.

The Son of a Fisherman
Oil on Claessens linen
40" × 30" (102cm × 77cm)

ACCESSORIES: JEWELRY AND EYEGLASSES

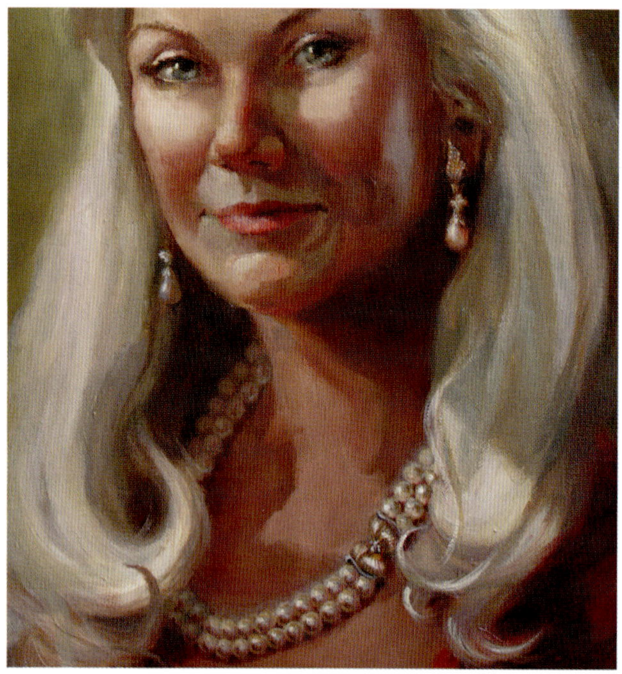

Heirloom Jewelry
This client asked that handling of the jewelry be carefully considered. Her intent was to someday hand down the painting and this exquisite jewelry to her daughter.

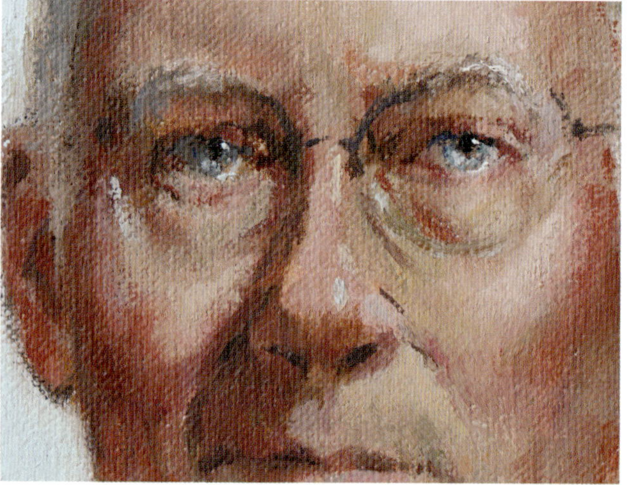

Glasses Float Over the Face
It is very easy to overdo glasses. In this detail, the glasses are evident, if not really there.

The portrait will take on a much more personal connection to the family when realism in jewelry is mastered. The artist is obligated to create a beautiful still life within the boundaries of the portrait.

SMALL WORKS OF ART

These can often be intricate pieces of art made of precious metals and stones that should demand your best attention to detail. This is where some photography can be an enormous help. It is best not to bring clients' jewelry to the studio to study and paint. Use your close-up lens or settings to capture these details, and later use iPhoto, Picasa, Aperture, Lightroom, Elements, Photoshop or other similar programs to play with the image, making it easier to study and paint.

WOMEN'S JEWELRY

Keep in mind that the item requested for inclusion may be an heirloom from three or four generations back, a wedding present from husband to wife decades earlier or a custom-designed anniversary piece. Follow the same principles of building structure and volume painting from dark to light until the jewelry sits in exactly the correct plane and lighting. The jewelry must hang or sit believably on the body, but must never take attention away from the subject of the painting.

MEN'S JEWELRY

Men's jewelry, though usually less of it is worn at a time, often can have a great deal of significance. A lapel pin, a tie clasp, a family coat of arms/signet ring, a graduate school ring, a collectible watch—pocket or wrist—all of these are of great importance to the people who are wearing them. The artist owes it to the sitter, and to the future generations who will view it, to give the small details an appropriate amount of attention in the heirloom painting.

EYEGLASSES

Whether they are to appear on women or men, do less work to achieve a convincing set of glasses. This is another case of practicing still-life paintings to become confident. The glasses must never stop the viewer from looking at the eyes, and they must never clutter the face or bring attention to themselves. Glasses must become a part of the face. Study how parts of the frames disappear into the skin, hair, eyebrows or shadows.

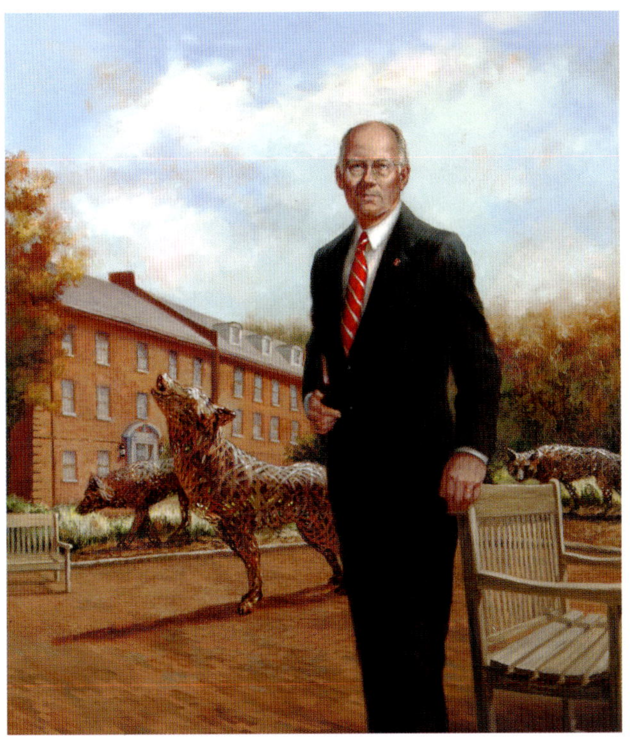

The University Retirement
This official retirement portrait of Chancellor James Oblinger at North Carolina State University is carried by the strong vertical design. Each element—the architecture of the campus building, the brickyard patio, the large bronze sculptures—is an icon of the university and will represent the campus for decades.

Dr. James L. Oblinger
Retired chancellor, North Carolina State University
Oil on Claessens linen
42" × 33" (107cm × 84cm)
Reproduced with permission of the permanent collection, NCSU

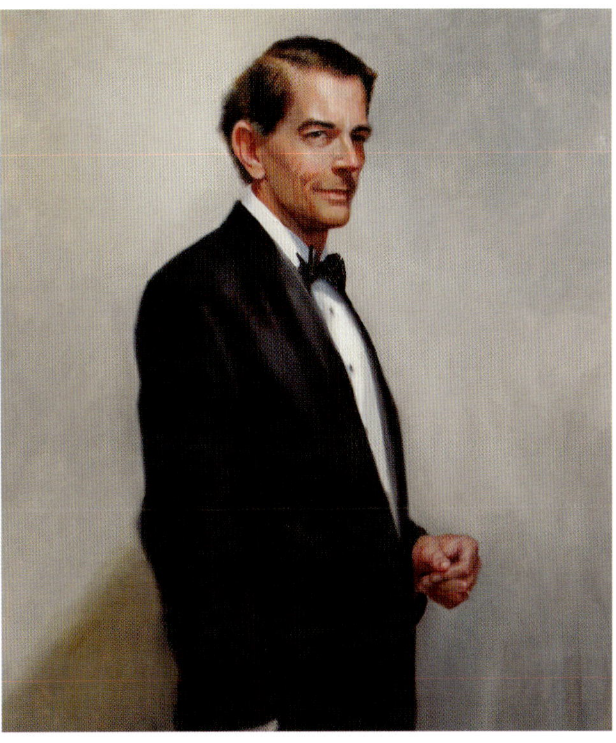

The Timeless Image
Sometimes the draped background is the answer. With clothing that does not necessarily reveal date or season, this elegant gentleman could have posed for this painting in any of many decades. The result is a timeless artwork.

Timeless
Oil on Claessens linen
40" × 30" (102cm × 76cm)

How do you choose what is essential and what is not? Where do you begin? Begin by not simply looking, but by listening. Without prying, ask about things the person is particularly interested in. It may take a little time to find the right combination of topics before reaching that place of relaxing chatter. At that point, observe the changes in body language. Try not to pose people, but instead observe their body language as they relate to their surroundings and the objects they find important. Ask the subject to hold a moment when a good bit of lighting works in concert with a wonderful body/head position in a beautiful background embracing the elements of his life. Capture that.

Work quickly to sketch some shorthand notes of that particular body language or attitude that caught your

PLANNED & UNPLANNED

Keep an open mind during a planned sitting. Often an unexpected location, a stream of light or a particular response from a sitter can propel the design into an entirely different composition. Try it. Experimentation is at the very heart of sketching.

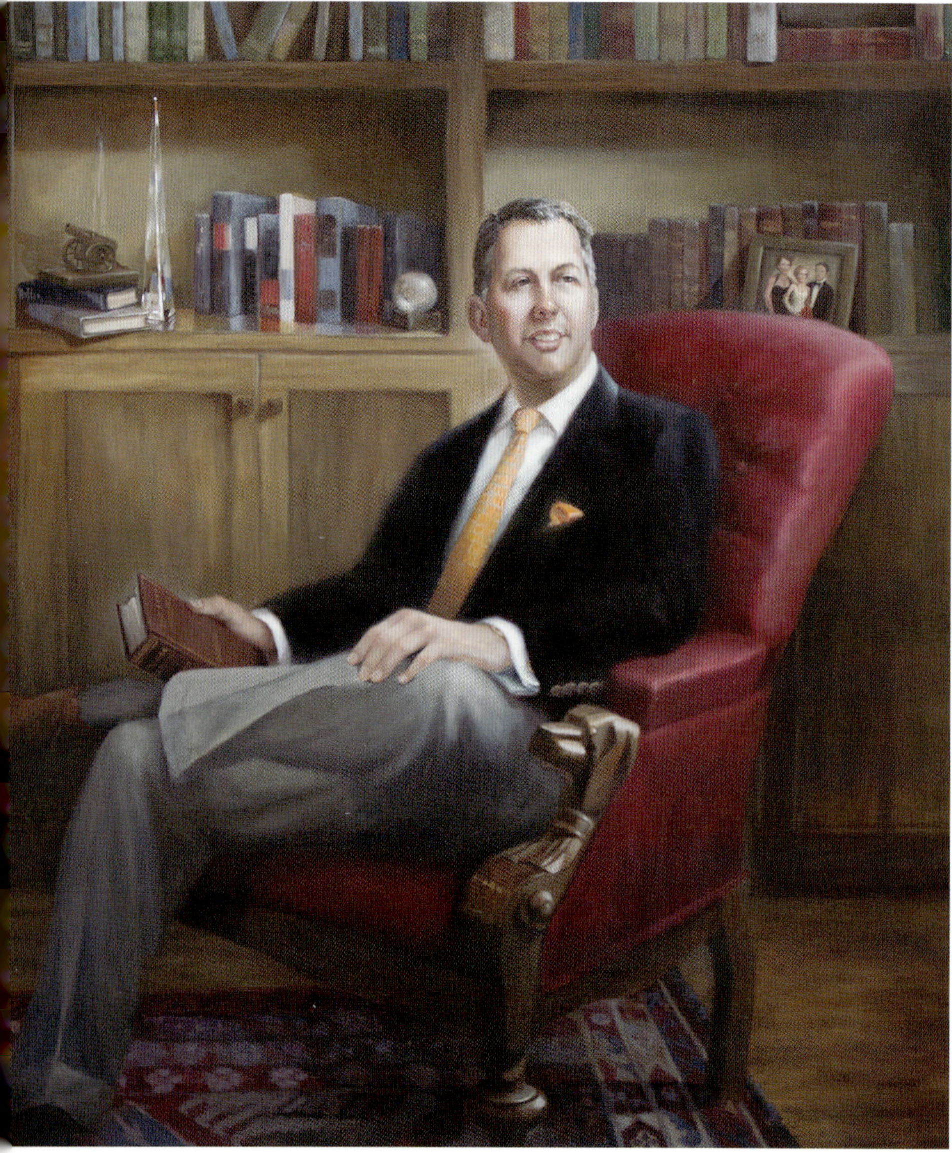

attention. If doing photography, snap off a quick shot (this is where a point-and-shoot may be of more value than a larger, complex camera), put away the camera quickly and move into the sketch seamlessly while diverting the sitter with conversation. Try not to allow him to become too conscious of his position or body attitude. It is that naturalness for which you are striving.

Don't put things in the painting just to fill the space. Let the essential items become obvious. These objects must have substance and meaning. They must speak to the family or corporation. They must augment, verify, enhance and strengthen an already strong story and design, or they will only diminish the painting with clutter.

The Background Tells the Story

The bank president was to be painted at home. Preliminary sketches were started in the living room near a favorite artwork, another near the patio doors by the grand piano, and a few others followed in different locations, but it was not until reaching the private library that he opened up. There, with his collection of first-edition books, a family photo from his daughter's debut, an antique chair from his wife's family, an award from a life-changing business event, were all of the things that represent who he had become: a father, a business leader and a visionary grounded by a strong upbringing.

B. Grant Yarber
Retired CEO and President of Capital Bank, business owner/entrepreneur
Oil on Claessens linen
50" × 40" (127cm × 102cm)

COLOR: SUBTLE VS. SATURATED

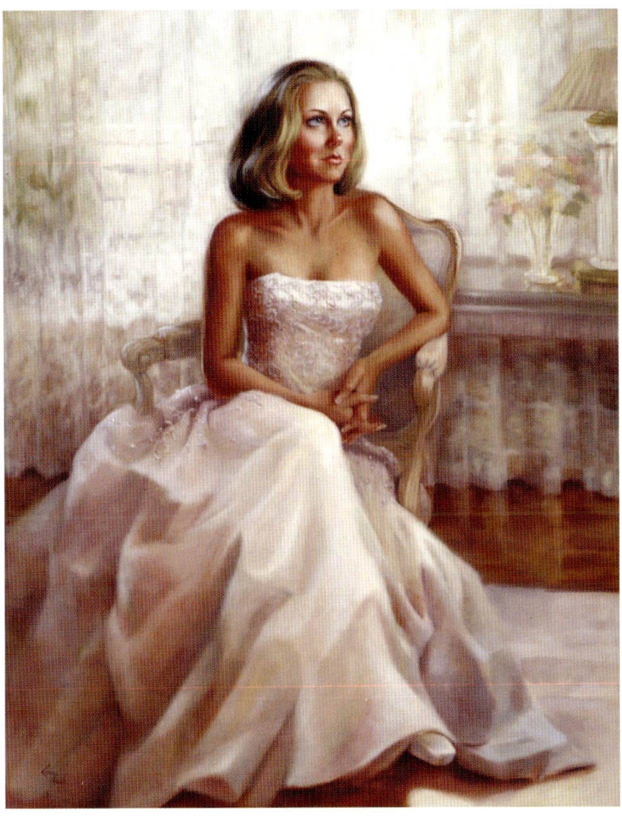

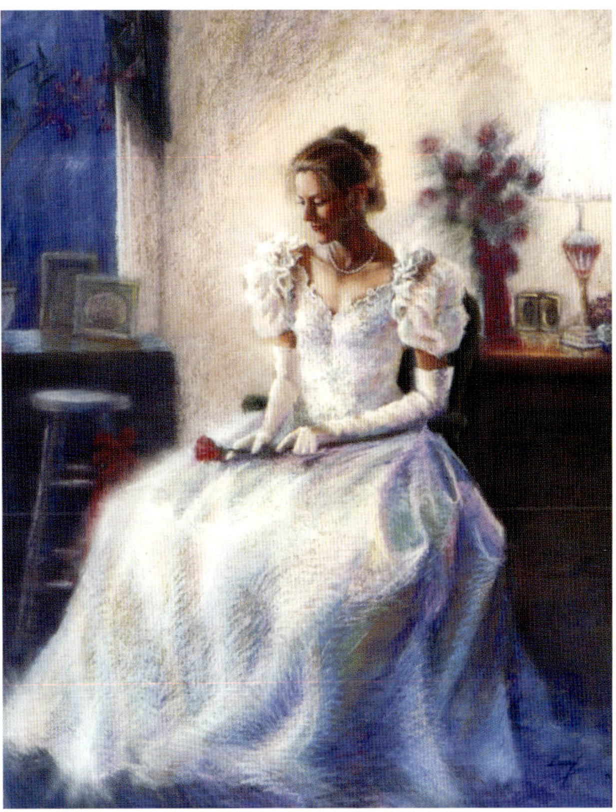

The Quiet Oil

This young woman is surrounded by a soft background. Through the sunlit lace curtains behind her, we can see a lovely patio with an inviting table and chairs. The crystal vase and lamp, roses, warm white carpeting and the crystal and pearl-encrusted bodice on the silk gown all bathe her in a limited palette of colors. The scene is elegant, gentle and serene.

Jaclyn's Debut
Daughter of Mr. and Mrs. White
Oil on Claessens linen
40" × 32" (102cm × 82cm)

The Vivid Pastel

This lovely young debutante had an aura of color and intensity about her that demanded attention. Though she wore a white dress, the opportunity lent itself to splashes of fabulous color that described the white from a distance. Close up, the dress was a myriad of layers of colors, rather like the girl. From a distance she was a quiet, beautiful young woman. But with closer attention, so many layers and facets of her personality emerged.

Katherine's Debut
Daughter of Drs. Brian and Charlotte Sweeney
Pastel on custom pastel board
36" × 30" (91cm × 76cm)

After choosing the pose, composition, story, lighting and attitude of the painting, the artist arrives at one more determining factor—the color. Some say that artists develop a palette and can be recognized by their color usage. But consider these two images of debutantes, one painted in oil and one in pastel. The color palettes were specifically chosen to help to portray more about the individual rather than the artist.

EDGES: SPONTANEOUS SKETCH OR CAREFUL RENDERING?

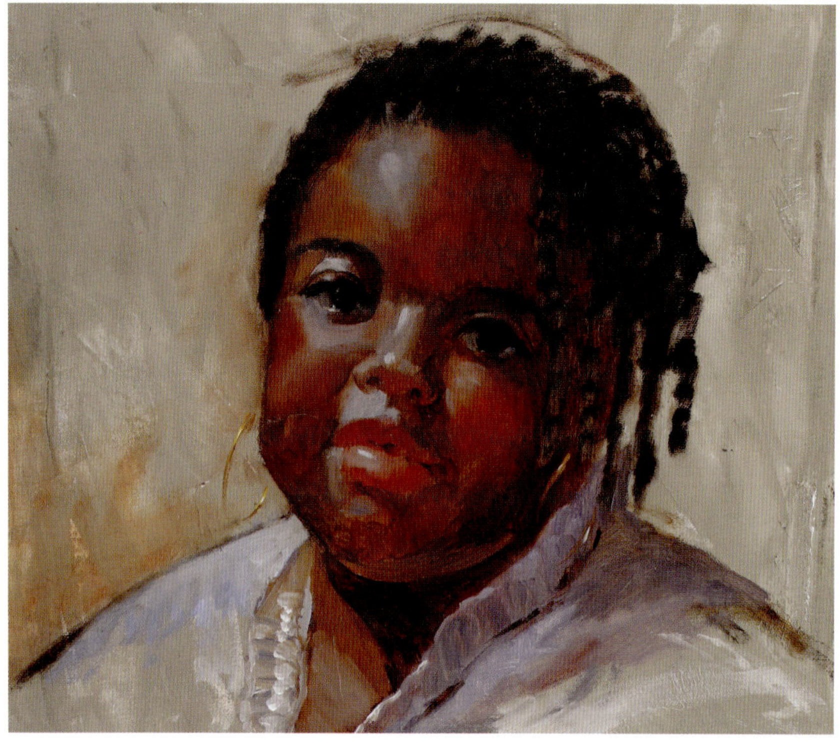

The Alla Prima Quick Sketch
This was completed as a 90-minute quick sketch. The image was simplified with a two-color plan, and large brushes were used to keep the image loose and spontaneous.

Dr. Sharon D. Ware at 12
Oil on linen
16" × 20" (41cm × 51cm)

Your style develops over time. It cannot be forced or planned, similar to a person's individual signature. An artist's signature style will become evident as time passes. Attention to edges, hue, value, chroma, design and approach evolves over time.

Among the important things that wil evolve is the manner in which edges are handled. Large or small, spontaneous painterly images tend to have looser, less-structured edges throughout. Intuitive design and application of paint offers a broader approach that permits a quick response to the subject.

GLAZING TECHNIQUES

Slower paintings created with glazing techniques often are lauded because the resultant painting, which has been carefully layered with translucent, thinned paints, often achieves a high level of realism. Think of this technique as looking through multiple layers of stained glass to reach the desired hue, chroma and value. In this technique, edges can be easily controlled.

ALLA PRIMA AND SOFT EDGES

In the style of alla prima painting, hue, chroma and value are all determined at once. The paint mixture is applied with a skillful stroke, left alone and the artist moves on to the next brushstroke. Often this technique with a more opaque appearance will maintain softer diffused edges as wet paint moves into wet paint.

HARD, FIRM, SOFT AND LOST

Consideration of edges tends to fall into four basic categories: hard, firm, soft and lost.

A *hard edge* can be sharp and often occurs in a place where there is a high contrast in values. For instance, a hard edge could occur where dark hair touches very light skin on the forehead, where very dark lash area touches the highlighted upper lid of the eye, or possibly part of a loose strand of dark drapes down over a cheekbone.

Note that too many hard edges in a painting can be treacherous. The eye tends to naturally seek out a hard edge on which to focus. So if too many hard edges are used throughout the painting, you cannot control where the viewer should look. Use hard edges sparingly.

A *firm edge* in a portrait can help define bony areas. The bridge of the nose and sometimes the highest point of the cheekbone in a particularly angular face have smaller fat deposits so the skin sits closer to the surface of the bone. This stroke gives a strong definition of structure.

A *soft edge* may be better used in a younger, plumper face in the cheek area, and possibly defining the rounded, soft chin or jowl area in older faces. Remember, as the light moves around the softer form and turns into the shadow, you must look for the change in hue and temperature and allow the smoother transition.

A *lost edge* is anywhere the artist completely loses the separation of elements. The viewer is completely unable to distinguish between where an object begins and another one ends. The values are virtually the same and only a minor temperature change may differentiate the two different surfaces. Moving from soft hair into the background, from shadowed skin into clothing, or from overlapping object turning into the plane behind it, the artist has many opportunities to use the lost edge.

Just a bit of advice: It will serve the design well to add a variety of edges. In other words, err in being too soft rather than too hard. Again, our eyes seek out hard edges. If the design is filled with too many unintended hard edges, our eyes will not distinguish where to focus first. If hard edges are limited to the point where you want the focus first, the viewer can begin there and then continue a visual journey through the painting.

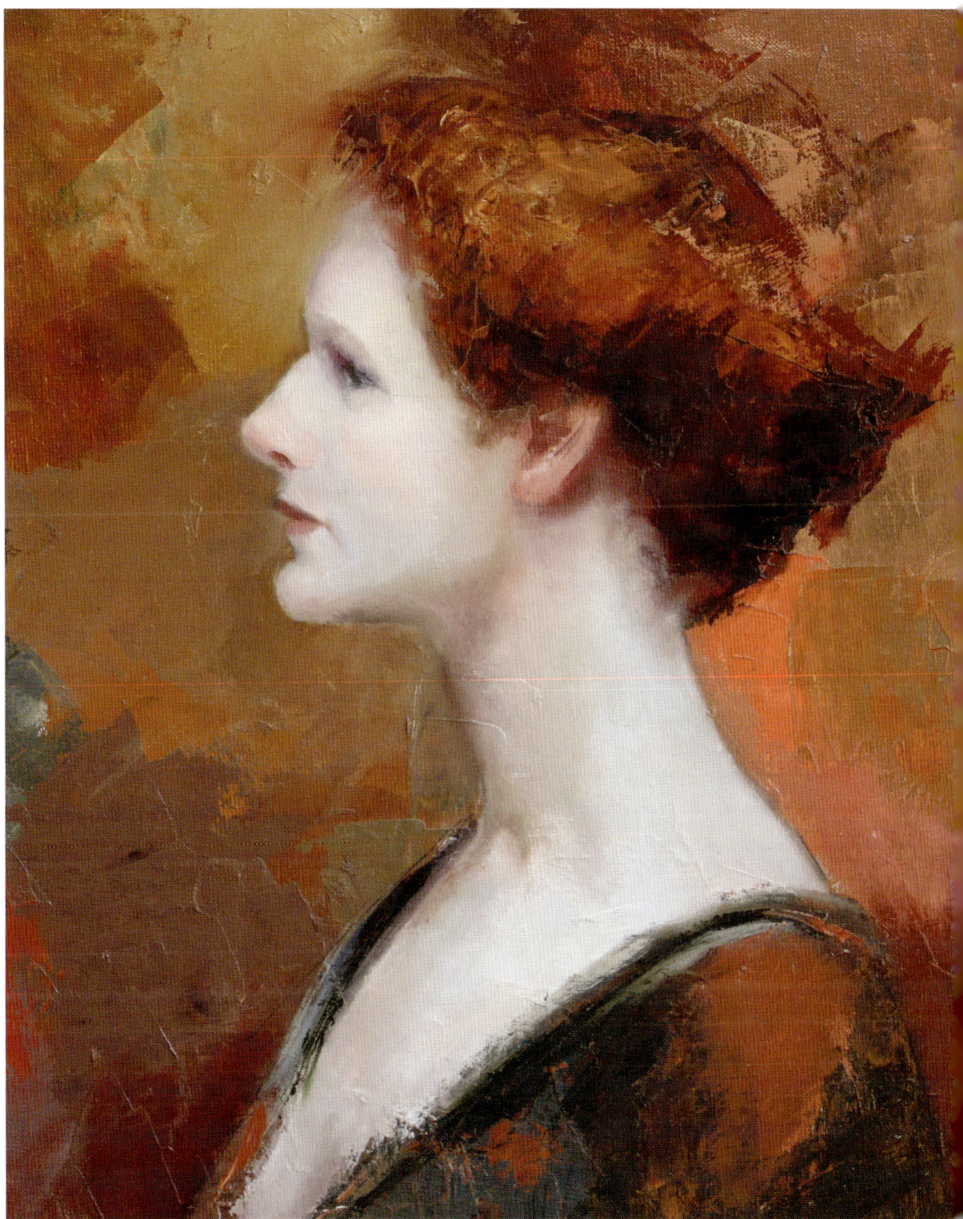

Inspiration and Planning

This painting was carefully planned, even to the edges that would remain firm, sharp and lost. The Japanese Robe *was inspired by two different paintings from a Washington, D.C. museum. A palette knife was used to boldly apply textured color to the background. Flake White Replacement was applied carefully as a silhouette of the skin area before the canvas was put aside to dry for a few days. Soft, sable brushes were then used to mold, push and pull the features, using only tints of temperature changes on the skin instead of relying on value.*

The Japanese Robe
Oil on linen
20" × 16" (51cm × 41cm)

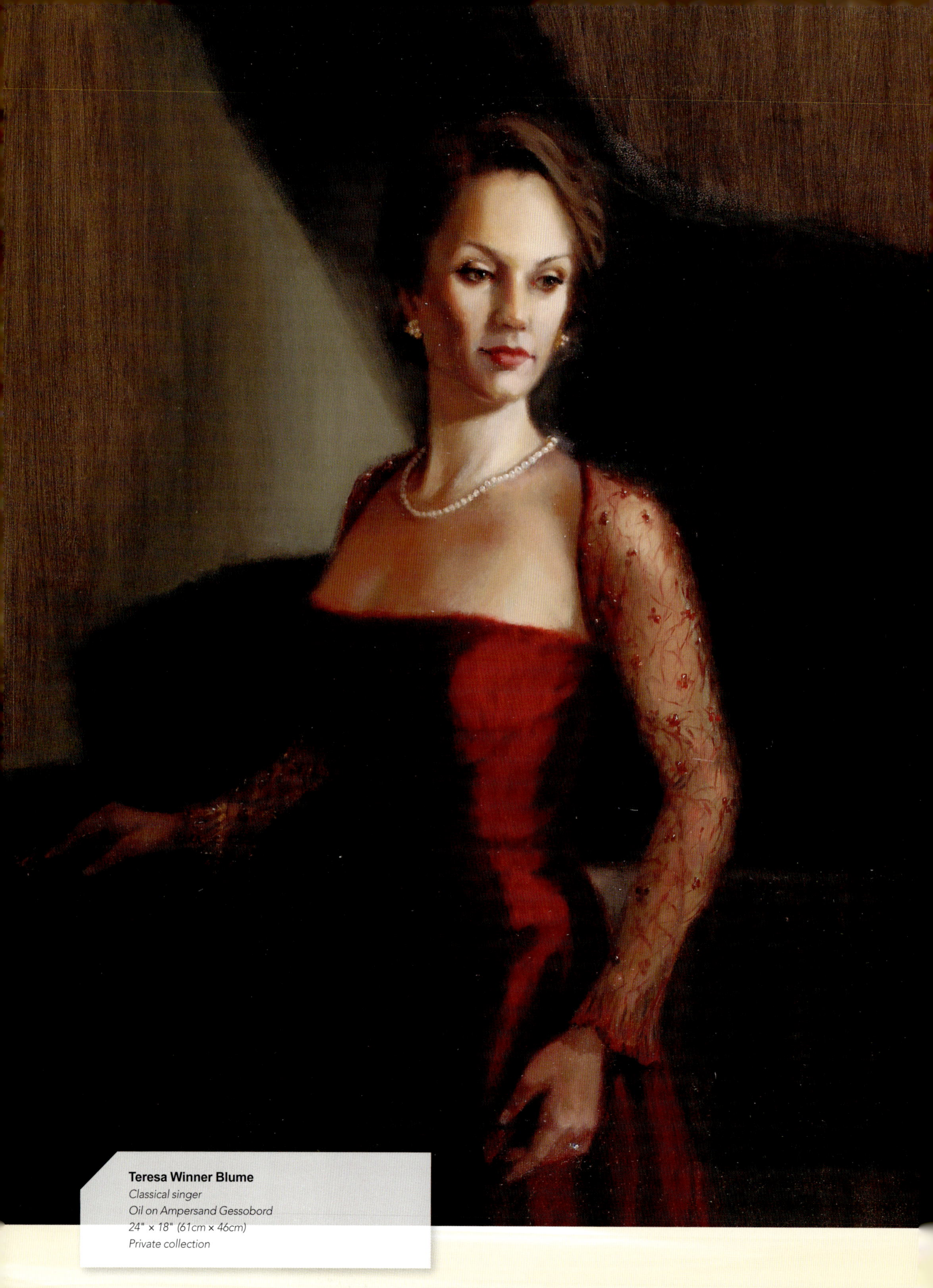

Teresa Winner Blume
Classical singer
Oil on Ampersand Gessobord
24" × 18" (61cm × 46cm)
Private collection

CHAPTER 5

DEMONSTRATIONS

The artist must always create a great painting first. Then it must also be a good portrait. All of the elements of a great painting must be in place and are completely the responsibility of the artist. Consider line, design, balance, composition, color, harmony and story. After these are in place, create the best likeness of face, form and body language that your current skill level permits. The result will be a lasting and timeless representation.

At the beginning of any artistic undertaking, it is appropriate to remember Michelangelo's prayer: "Lord, grant that I may always desire more than I can accomplish." It is most important to continue challenging yourself.

"Every artist dips his brush in his own soul, and paints his own nature into his pictures."

—Henry Ward Beecher

The Dramatic Portrait

The finish is only difficult if you do not begin with a vision of the completed portrait. Artists do tend to get caught up in the process and the sheer joy of painting and sometimes they lose their focus on the finish. It is difficult not to overdo or overwork the canvas.

CLASSICAL SINGER IN OILS

MATERIALS

- 24" × 18" (61cm × 46cm) Gessobord
- Alizarin Crimson
- Burnt Sienna
- Cadmium Red Light
- Cobalt Blue
- Flake White Replacement
- Ivory Black
- Sap Green
- Ultramarine Blue
- Yellow Ochre
- Nos. 1 & 4 filberts
- No. 0 or 1 round
- Mop brush
- Soft fan brush
- Soft hair brush
- Disposable paper palette
- Galkyd Lite
- Graphite pencil
- Large palette
- Photoshop (optional)
- Sketch paper
- Turpentine (or Gamsol)

The woman in this painting is a classical singer. A performance gown was chosen from several. The color and design of the gowns all had different characteristics that provided life and nuances to the music being performed; we wanted this to be true of the painting. The sitting location had an ebony grand piano for the background. A Tota-light by Lowel was used to augment the natural lighting and to add to the stage lighting effect. Sketches and supporting photos were shot, as this was a painting being done 800 miles (1300 km) from the studio.

DO YOUR HOMEWORK

Preliminary phone calls and e-mails helped to determine many of the variables in this painting. Hair up or down, clothing, background and general attitude were all discussed prior to the first meeting.

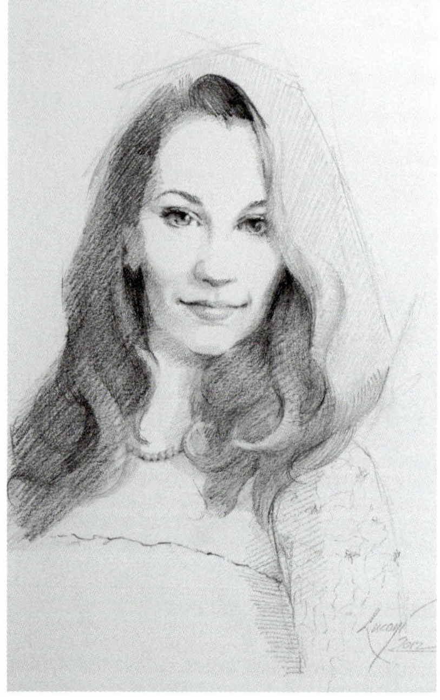

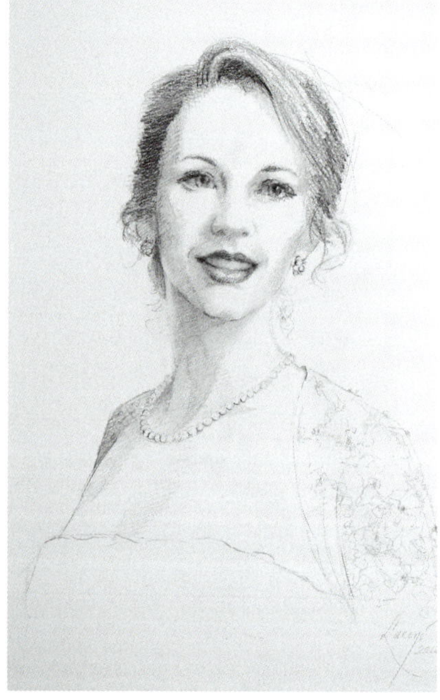

Do A Head Study for Likeness

Begin in person and polish the sketches later in the studio. Hair up? Hair down? Expression? Try as many different things as time permits. Remember, few of the images will be complete at this meeting. Gather the information with the plan to take it away and polish it later. Take the time to edit the images and remove those that will ultimately not make a good composition. Only give choices that will definitely work.

Shoot Supporting Details

Shoot anything that cannot be taken back to the studio: lace, beading, piano, jewelry, etc. Much of the painting will be begun from only the reference material taken back to the studio. Yes, people still do sittings for their paintings. But some are simply unable to offer as many hours as they would enjoy due to their obligations. If you are assured of as many face-to-face hours as needed for the painting, there will be no problem. However, if you will be limited to a set number of sittings or hours, take as much material back with you as you can to make your job easier. Put gowns on dressmaker's forms. Put uniforms on mannequins. Use costume jewelry to begin the pearls in the studio and finish them at the last sitting. Shoot digital details of carved chairs, pianos and other furniture. Be certain that all items are in the same direction of lighting. Do all that can be done while you're at the sitting.

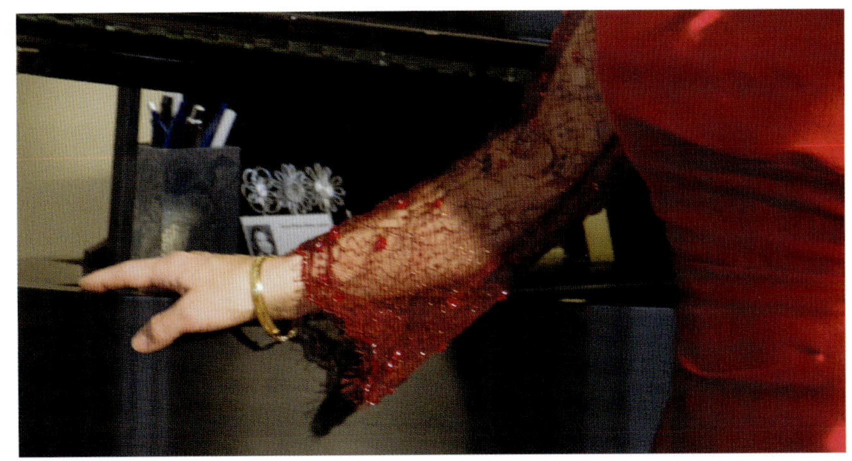

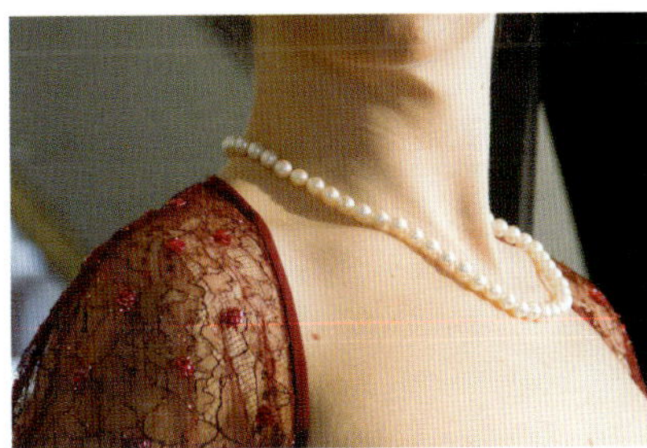

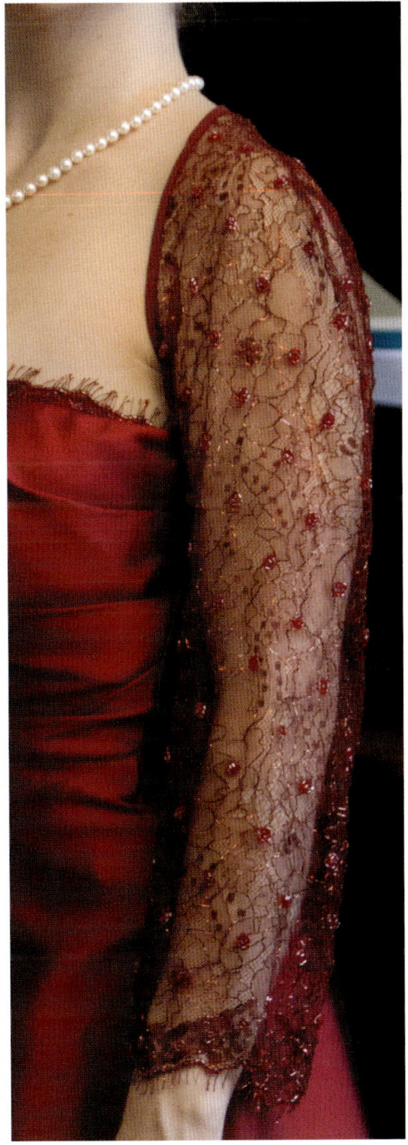

MEDIUM AND SURFACE CHOICES

This portrait was done on an Ampersand Gessobord. The selected graphite sketch of this singer had such a mysterious, ethereal expression and quality to it that it evoked an immediate reaction by people who saw it. The hope is that the painting on board using first bristle and then soft hair brushes will provide a timeless and classical outcome with a hint of an Old Master's blended, soft brush appeal.

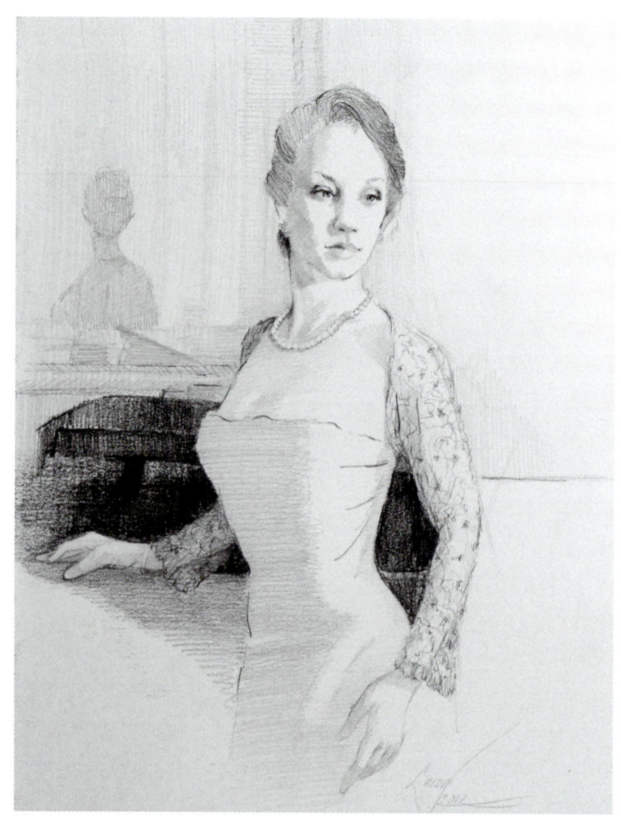

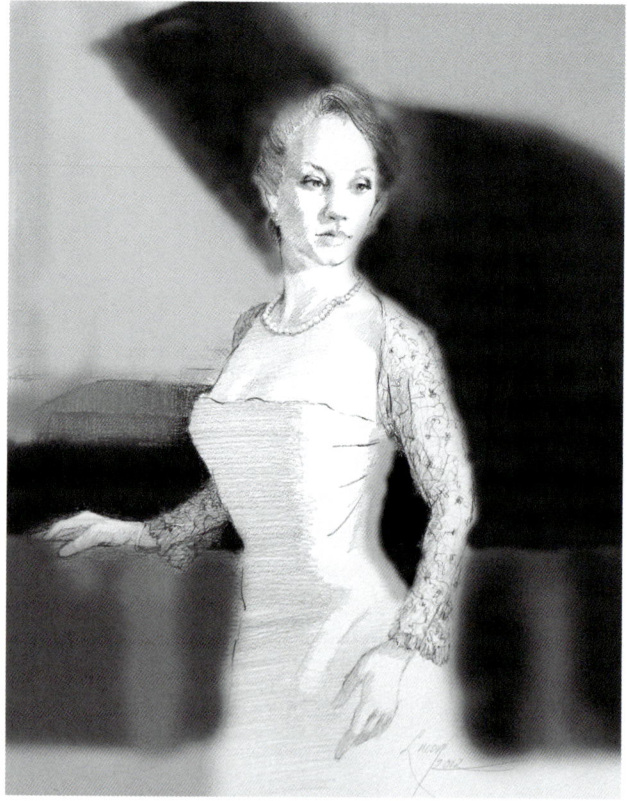

1 CHOOSE YOUR SKETCH AND TRANSFER TO CANVAS

First, choose the image you want to use. Then, if needed, use Photoshop to drop in a different background. Here, the neutral colors in the background and mirror reflection over the short-stick piano lid could be lovely with the brilliant silk gown in cranberry in the foreground. But the long stick on the piano offered a much more dramatic effect and permitted a stronger stage and lighting effect.

Notice that nothing was done to the white of the paper at the singer's face. Because the background was darkened four values, the contrast made the face appear to be even brighter and more strongly lit, which was the desired effect.

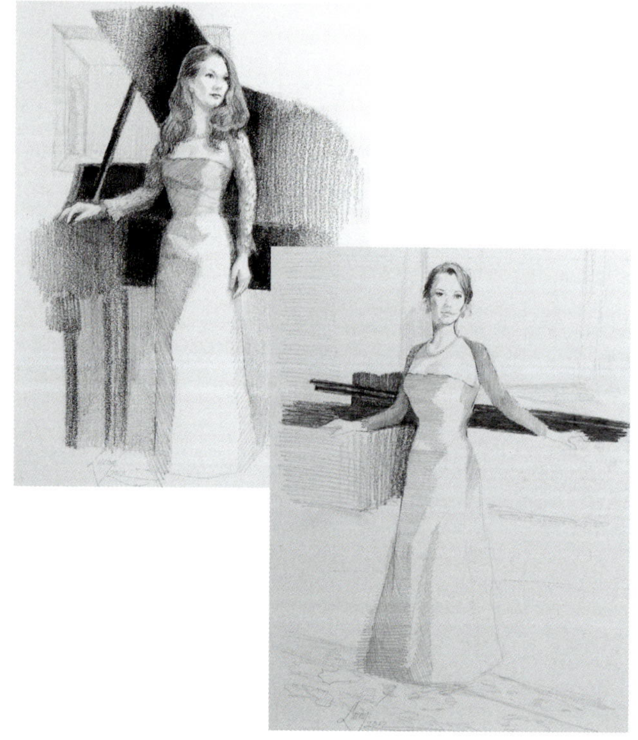

Other options not chosen

A CRAMPED BEGINNING

The first oil line sketch was completely wiped away after realizing that the figure was cramped within the constraints of the space. A rag brought the board back to the toned ground, and another more delicate, quick oil placement sketch was done. Think of the graphite sketch as a blueprint and this oil sketch as a footing or foundation for the painting.

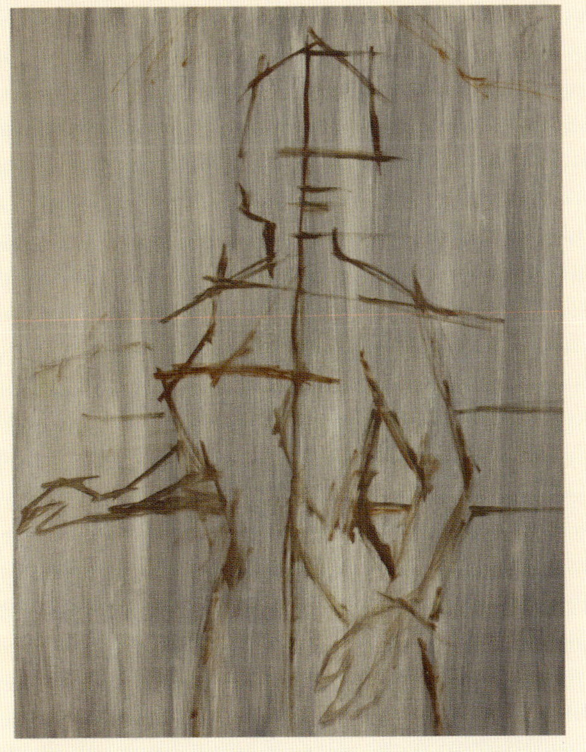

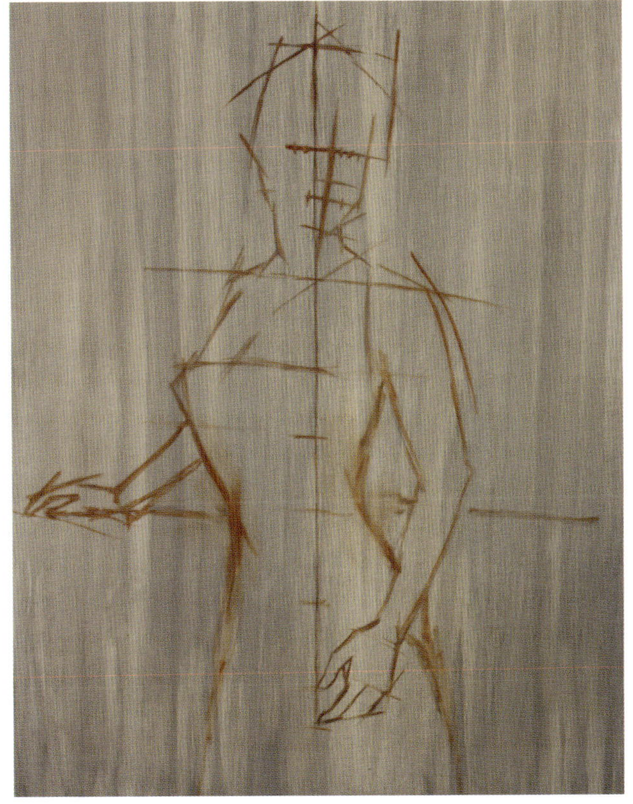

2 WASH IN A TONAL SKETCH

Wash a Gessobord with Yellow Ochre and Ivory Black thinned with turpentine. Dry the board for a week or two so the paint won't lift when applying the next layers of paint. An optional tone for acrylic-primed boards or canvas is to use a water-thinned acrylic paint to tint the ground.

Mix Burnt Sienna and Ivory Black to make a color similar to Burnt Umber. Use a soft hair brush to draw the placement sketch onto the board. Synthetics or sables in round or cat's tongue shapes are particularly flexible and responsive to fluid, calligraphic strokes.

SKETCH QUICKLY AND FREELY

Place the oil line sketch on the canvas in a few, quick strokes, knowing that it can easily be changed. With no investment in time or trouble, changes are more easily accepted. No laborious drawing should be attempted. It will all be covered in paint soon enough. Draw complex drawings on paper. When you approach a canvas—paint.

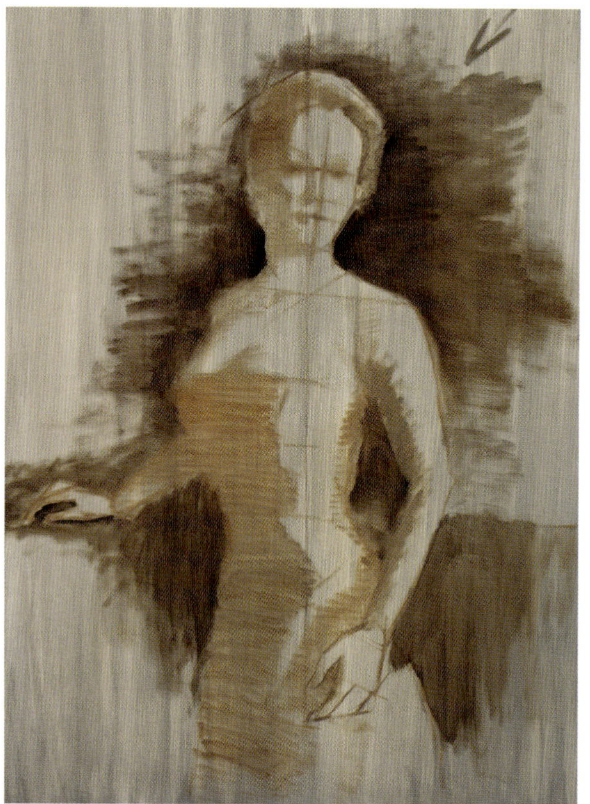

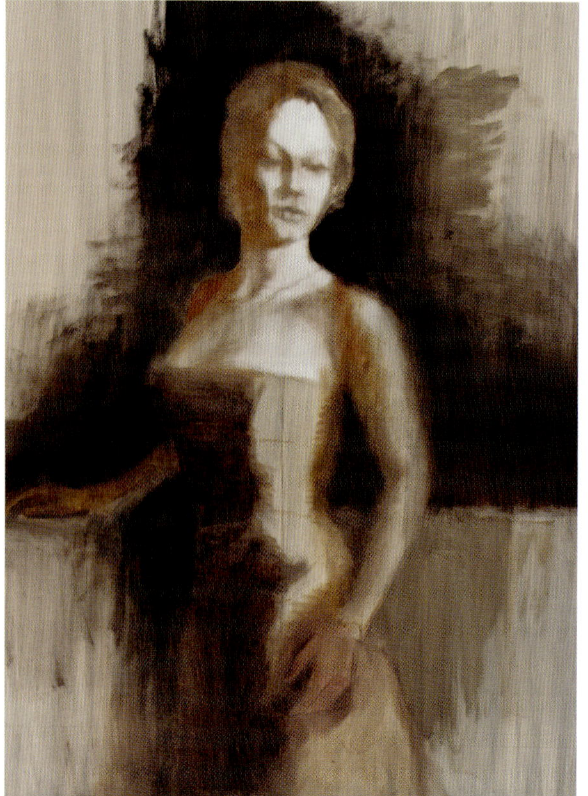

3 DEVELOP THE DARKS

On the toned board with the oil sketch placed, find the shadow line that differentiates the major light and dark planes. Indicate the shadow as it travels down the length of the figure. An arrow places the direction of light. Note that the hair, face and figure have not had additional work done. Only the shadow pattern has been indicated, and the value of the darkness in the background is begun.

LUMINOUS SKIN

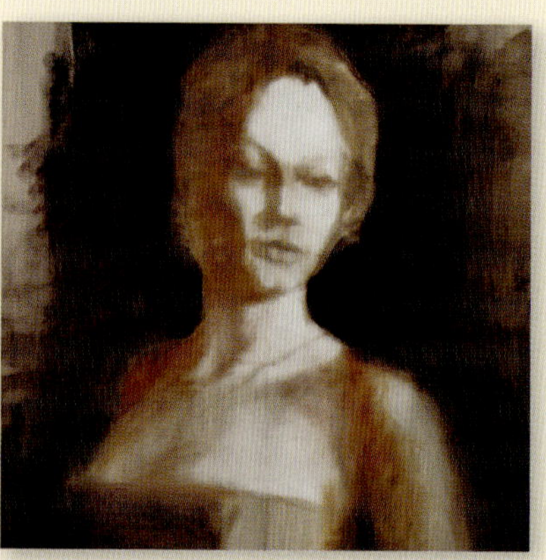

Because the final painting should look as dramatic as possible, the figure should give the impression that a brilliant spotlight is flooding her skin and dress. To boost the strength of the reflective quality in the skin, Flake White Replacement has been thinly applied onto the skin in light strokes with a clean, dry filbert bristle brush. Shadow areas will have no white added.

4 BUILD THE DARKS DARKER

Scrub a thin additional layer of warm dark—a mixture of Alizarin Crimson and Sap Green—into the dress shadow with a clean filbert bristle brush. Then scrub a layer made with Alizarin Crimson, Sap Green and a touch of Ultramarine Blue into the interior of the piano behind her.

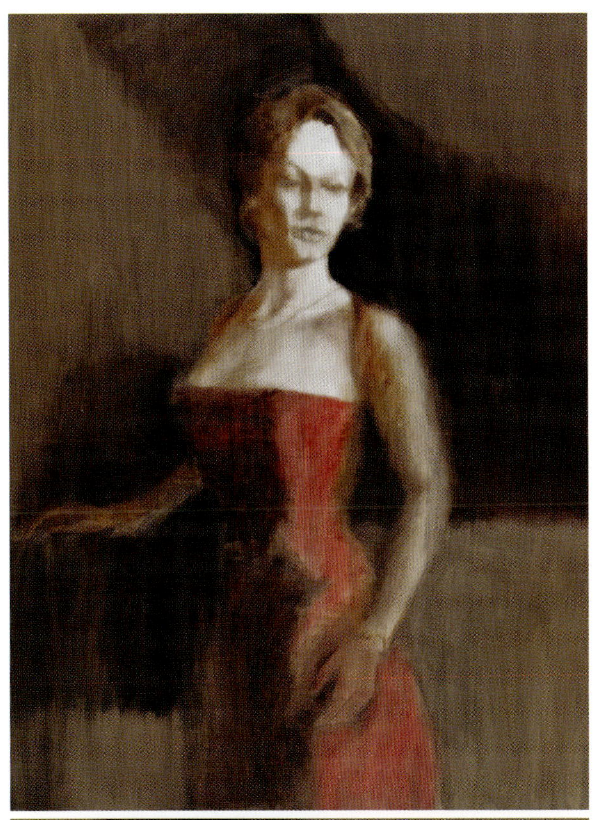

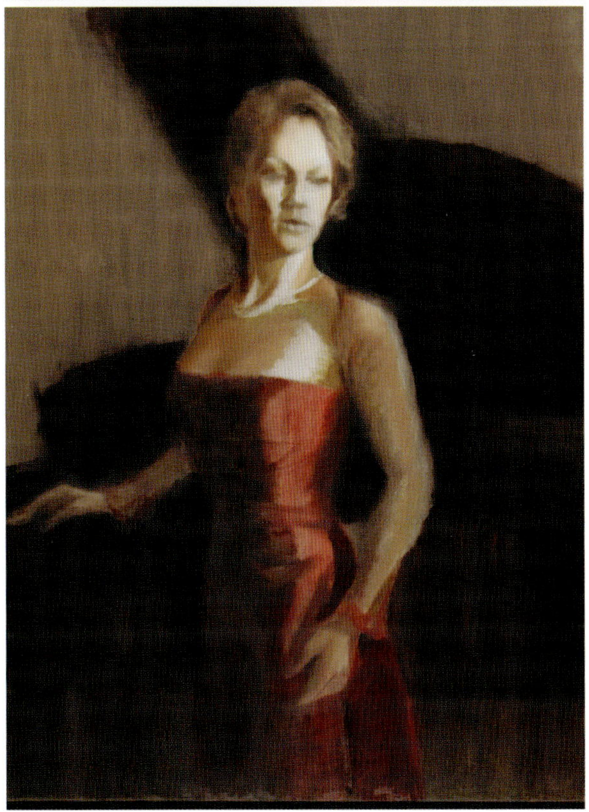

5 DEVELOP THE MIDDLE VALUES

This painting is a very low-key design, so continue the middles at quite a dark value. Very thinly scrub everything into the board. Keep the darks and dark middles very thin to permit them to dry more quickly.

- **Brunette Skin Tone:** *Each of the charts in chapter 3 offers a starting point for skin mixtures. In this case, cool middle values with Cadmium Red Light, Yellow Ochre, Cobalt Blue and Flake White Replacement are mixed with a touch of Sap Green for the chest, neck, shoulder, hands and arms which will have a lace sleeve over them. Since Sap Green also appeared in the dress shadow mixture and the piano mixture, a harmony continues throughout.*

- **The Lights Get Lighter Surrounded by Darks:** *Add Alizarin Crimson to Ultramarine Blue and Sap Green to get a very cool dark. Tuck this mixture into the distant piano hinge area in the interior of the piano at arm/shoulder height to push it back. The curved, closer, elevated edge of the piano is Alizarin Crimson and Sap Green with emphasis on the warmer color to bring it forward. The singer continues to look even brighter.*

THE BEST BRUSH FOR THE JOB

This is not a textural painting. No lumps and bumps to catch light should appear. Therefore, at this stage, use a very soft fan brush to knock down the ridges of paint that catch light. This brush gives great control and can be used in small spaces.

Larger areas benefit from a traditional watercolor brush called a mop. It has the ability to remove ridges, soften edges between values and colors, and really polish the finish. Every time darks are added around the figure, she becomes more luminous. But be certain to use a soft brush to keep her from having hard edges and looking as though she were cut out and glued on like an appliqué.

6 DEEPEN THE MIDDLE VALUES

Paint more Alizarin Crimson and Sap Green into the shadow of the dress. Add Alizarin Crimson, a very transparent color, to the light side of the dress, as this is still a darker middle value in comparison to the skin tones.

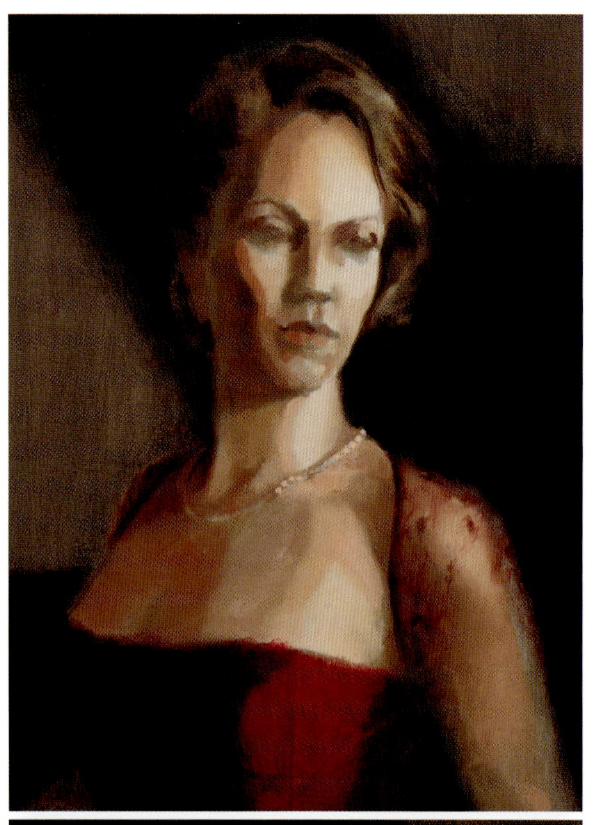

7 BEGINNING THE FINISH

Apply a layer of Alizarin Crimson to the dress in the light using a soft (sable or synthetic) number 4 filbert. Using a very small round, a 0 or 1, add a little Galkyd Lite to thin the same mixture and begin applying thin, calligraphic strokes with a very light touch. Use the same brush to add clusters of beads. Use a number 1 bristle filbert to apply a warm, medium-value mixture of Flake White Replacement tinted with Ivory Black, Yellow Ochre and Alizarin Crimson to make the pearls. With three different values of this mixture, begin on the dark side of the neck and work subsequently lighter as the pearls move into the light.

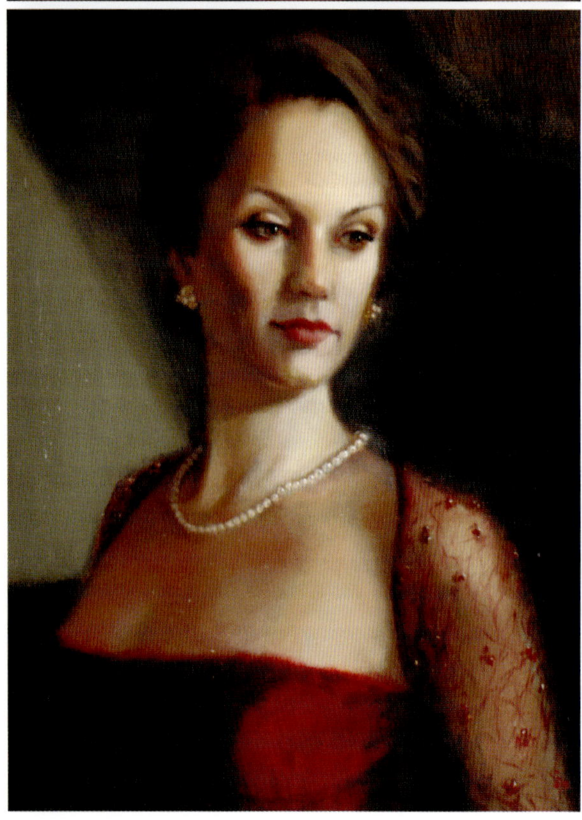

8 DEVELOP THE SKIN VARIANCES IN BRILLIANT LIGHT

First, adapt the the brunette chart 1 mixture with a touch of Sap Green. Stay in the darker skin values. Near the shoulder, change the hues from warm to cool to warm to move the upper body into and out of the picture plane. Do this to mold the shoulder down into the shadow and back out into the light. Use this mixture on the neck and in the cast shadows on the face. Paint the entire shadowed skin in a much higher key to give the effect of strong stage lighting.

Also place a warmer version of the shadow mixture used earlier on the cheek shadow and under the zygomatic bone, brow bone, at the shadow between the eye and nasal bone and on the upper lip.

Place a more saturated version of the skin-in-light mixture all along the forehead, cheek, neck and chest where the light and the shadow meet to help turn the planes. Culture mixture with a tint of white made by adding Yellow Ochre, Cadmium Red Light, a touch of Cobalt Blue and a touch of Sap Green, if needed, to bring the skin fully into the light, as this mixture travels down from the forehead to the bodice of the dress.

9 CLARIFY DETAILS AND CONSIDER EDGES

The painting begins to look finished when fewer things appear to need changes. Soften edges everywhere possible. Look for additional values that need to be lowered or heightened to achieve the intended overall effect. Give the dress an additional layer of Alizarin Crimson—a very transparent color. Add a touch of Cadmium Red Light to enhance a spot or two in the shiny highlight on the dress, but be cautious with this opaque, saturated hue. Do not overdo.

Do not hesitate to give attention to small details, like the gold bracelet under the lace sleeve. Giving just two or three of the beads in various places on the lace a tiny dot of highlight to make them shine can make a painting extraordinary. But be careful not to overdo.

10 STUDY THE FINISH

Set the painting in other rooms to study it in different lighting temperatures and intensities. Often, paintings done in this style will carry very well in dimly lit or candlelit rooms. The skin areas seem to soak up all the ambient light and appear to shine from within.

Have you done your job? Have you used paint properly to wrap lace, silk, pearls and light around an expressive soul?

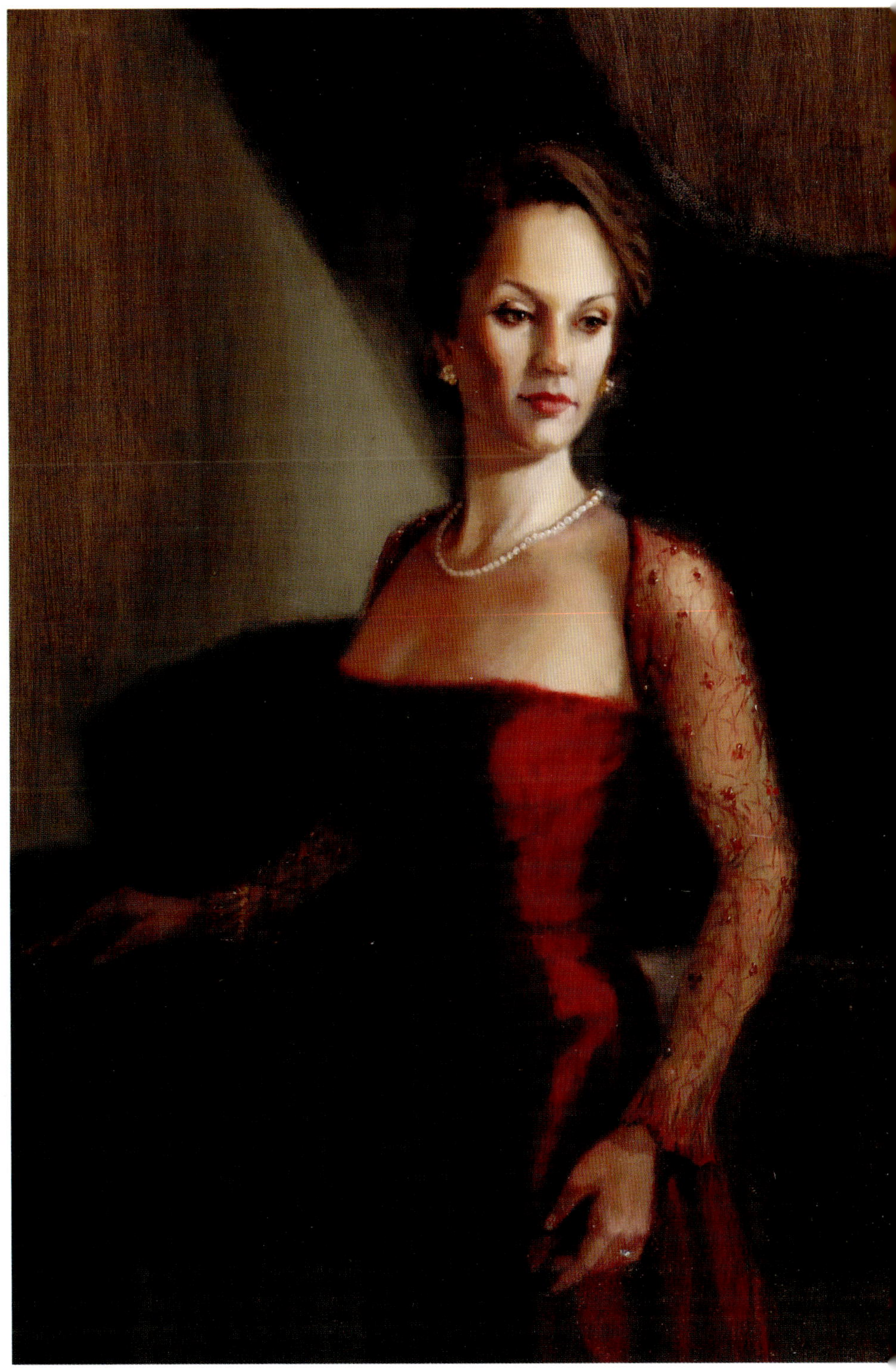

Teresa Winner Blume
Classical singer
Oil on Ampersand Gessobord
24" × 18" (61cm × 46cm)
Private collection

GENTLEMAN OUTDOORS IN OILS

MATERIALS

- 24″ x 20″ (61cm x 51 cm) pastel paper
- 24″ x 20″ (61cm x 51 cm) oil-primed linen canvas
- Alizarin Crimson
- Burnt Sienna
- Cadmium Red Light
- Cadmium Yellow Light
- Cobalt Blue
- Flake White Replacement
- Ivory Black
- Sap Green
- Ultramarine Blue
- Yellow Ochre
- charcoal
- graphite pencil
- palette
- rag
- sketch paper
- tape
- tracing paper
- turpentine (or Gamsol)

PUT YOUR SUBJECT AT EASE

At the first planning meeting, be prepared to put your subject at ease. In many cases, this is the first time that he has worked with a portrait artist. Above all, listen to what he has to say about who he is, how his life transformed him and how he wishes to be perceived in the future. Listen to family and colleagues if the opportunity arises. This often opens up new and interesting avenues as well. Sketch as you converse. The moment he relaxes, you will know it, and then you can really get to work.

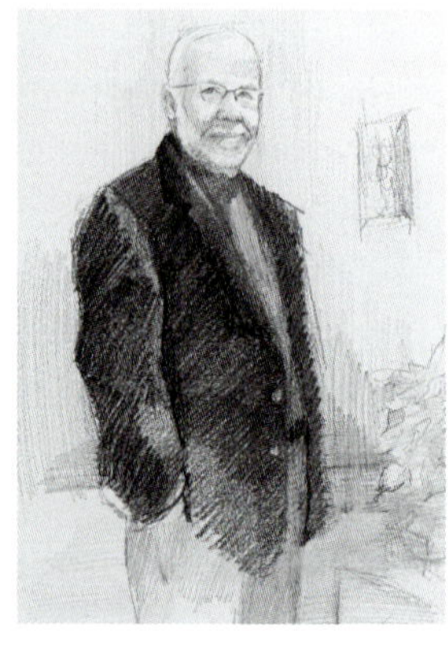

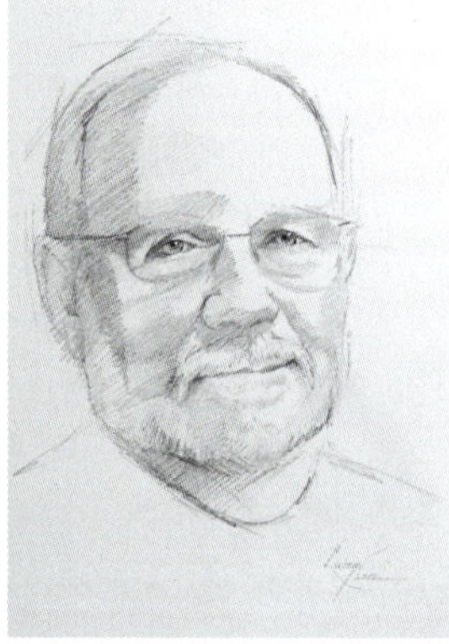

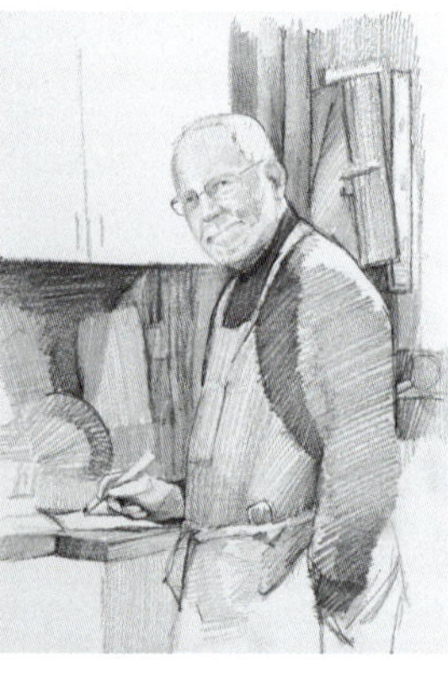

Here are some of the sketches that were collected while visiting with this business leader and community patron. Sketches were done during a visit to his lovely home before he and his wife left for a trip to Italy. We spoke about many things, including their involvement in the regional opera company, their international travels, food, wine and art.

He changed from a comfortable shirt good for relaxing with a book in his library to casual business attire as we moved into the living room and his office, and then to some work clothes as we visited his woodworking shop. It was clear that the formal attire the public sees would not be a part of this portrait. The couple wanted the painting to reflect this very approachable gentleman at home. It was when he donned his favorite traveling hat and we bundled up to go out into the brisk, damp winter landscape that we knew we had found our answer.

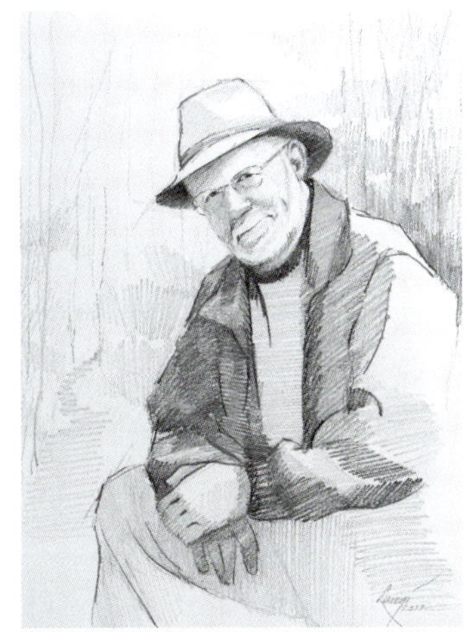

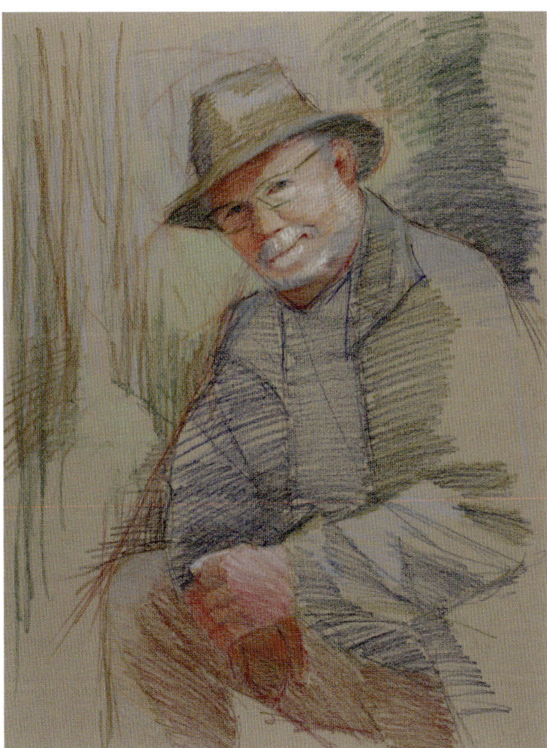

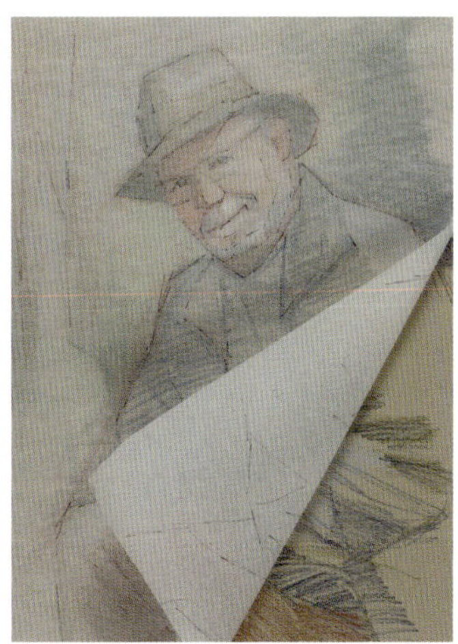

1 CHOOSE THE SKETCH

The sketch becomes the model for this early stage of canvas preparation. Toning the canvas, laying in the image and getting a sense of what you expect from the finished canvas all come together now.

Enlarge the graphite sketch to the size of the 24" × 20" (61cm × 51cm) canvas on a piece of pastel paper. Complete in pastels, using wide, open marks that provide both a general color plan and a blocky version of the painting to size—all of which will require only about 20 minutes. The quick sketch in pastel allows the artist to see how the figure relates to the space in its finished size. This color study plan of cool blues and greens captures the outdoor, forest setting.

Tape tracing paper to the drawing and trace only the pertinent lines of plane changes and any line that may divide light from shadow. Turn this tracing paper over, redraw each of those lines on the back side of the paper with charcoal or pastel. You can now directly transfer the drawing to canvas.

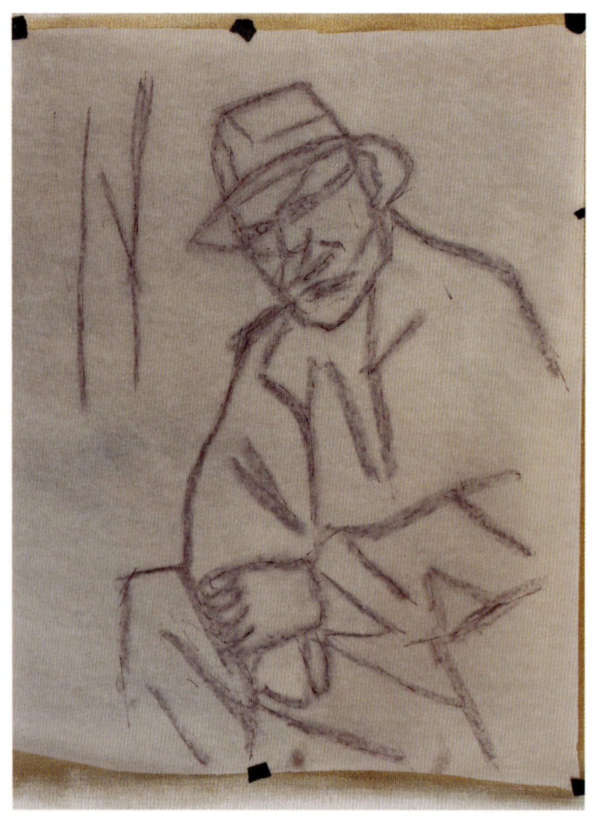

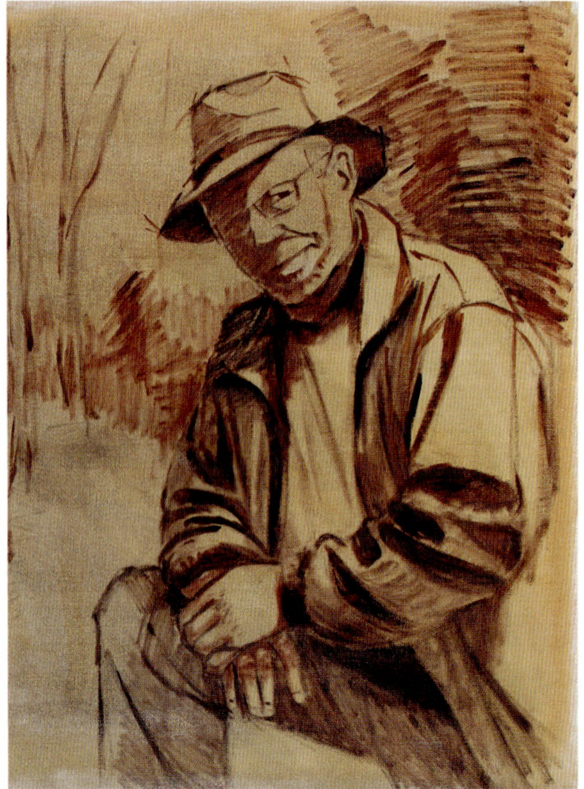

2 DIRECT TRANSFER FROM DRAWING TO CANVAS

Place the canvas on a solid surface and with a rag, rub some Burnt Sienna and Yellow Ochre thinned with turpentine. Tape the tracing paper to the canvas and trace over the drawn lines. This transfers the charcoal to the canvas.

Now strengthen the charcoal lines with some Burnt Sienna and Ivory Black thinned with a little turpentine or Gamsol. Make sure the lines are neither wide nor heavy of hand. Keep these darks extremely thin and transparent. Some lines may change as the sitter moves during subsequent sittings, so do not consider this image completely nailed down. Keep the darks very thin with broad strokes. This way you can fill the canvas and get a feel for the finished work very quickly.

A LITTLE BREATHING ROOM

The canvas used is a medium rough Claessens 66 Linen, which is normally used for landscape painting and broader techniques other than portraits. It was taped unstretched to ½" (1cm) black Gator board. Sometimes, especially in an outdoor portrait, the person needs a little more breathing room. Using unstretched canvas allows freedom of change much like watercolorists do when editing a painting. The extra canvas permits adding or subtracting an inch or two in height or width if the final image demands it. Later in the development of the painting, it can easily be stretched onto wooden stretcher strips once the decisions become obvious.

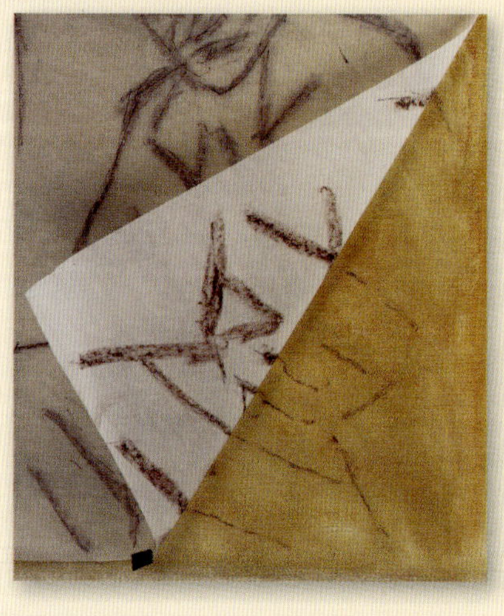

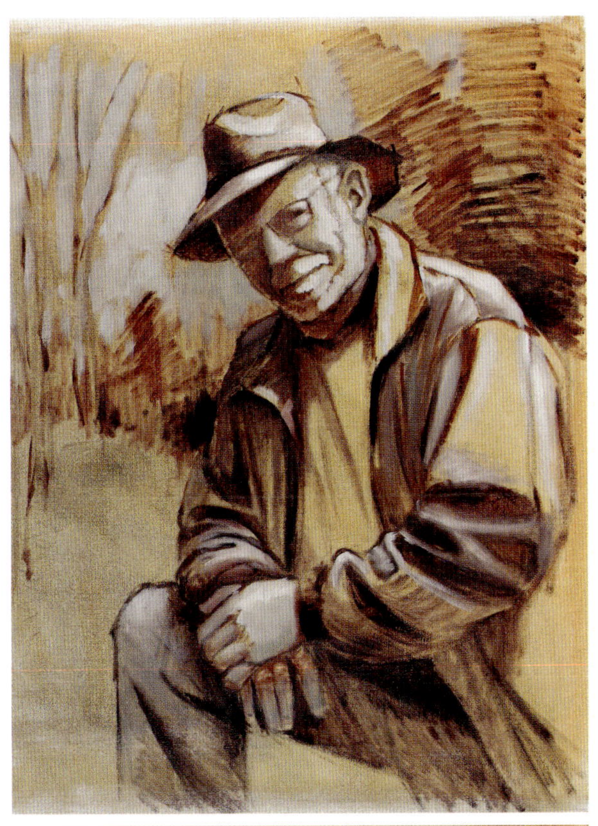

3 DEVELOP THE DARKS

Make the skin as sunlit as possible on an overcast day so he will stand out from the forest background. Place Flake White Replacement thinly on the canvas in the face, hands, sky and areas that are touched by sunlight. This will help to keep those areas brilliant.

Begin to lay in the shadows with thin layers of Ultramarine Blue and Alizarin Crimson in the folds of the jacket. Add a touch of Yellow Ochre and Flake White Replacement to this mixture and begin the dark middle values of the jacket.

SHADOWS AND LIGHT, NOT PAINT-BY-NUMBER

Be cautious not to turn this into a paint-by-number and to only fill appropriate areas developing the figure flatly. Really look at the shadow/light pattern to determine how to turn the figure in and out of the canvas.

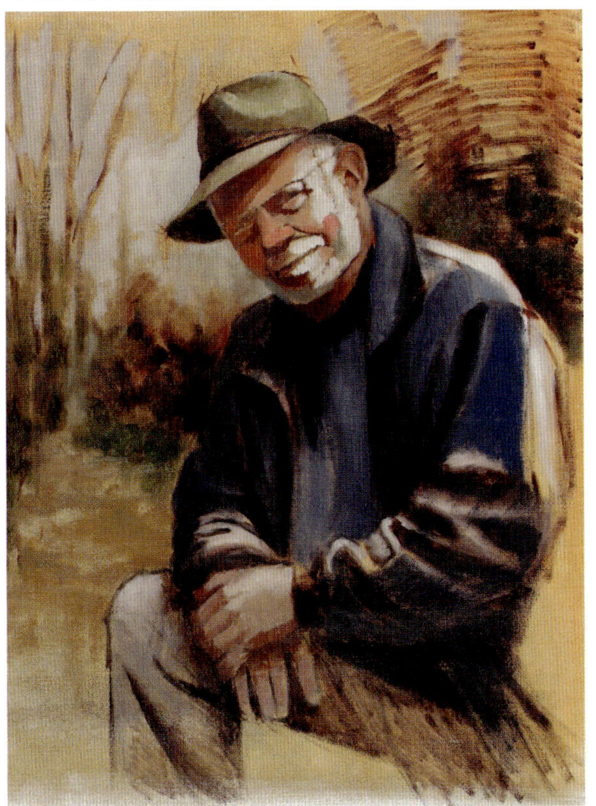

4 ADD COLOR

In the forest over the high shoulder, place a mixture of Sap Green and Alizarin Crimson for the darker areas, and Sap Green and Burnt Sienna near the top. To make the khaki paint, mix Ivory Black, Yellow Ochre, Burnt Sienna and Flake White Replacement. To make the khaki pants, mix Ivory Black, Yellow Ochre, Burnt Sienna and Flake White Replacement.

Because this gentleman was a redhead in his youth, the skin-in-shadow mixture from chart 3 is Cadmium Red Light, Yellow Ochre, Ivory Black and a touch of Flake White Replacement. Mass the shadow under the brim, the eye areas, the cast shadow of the nose, the lips and the chin. Add Flake White Replacement and Yellow Ochre to the mixture for the forehead and nose/cheek area. Add a touch of Sap Green in the mix to paint the dark middle value of hands.

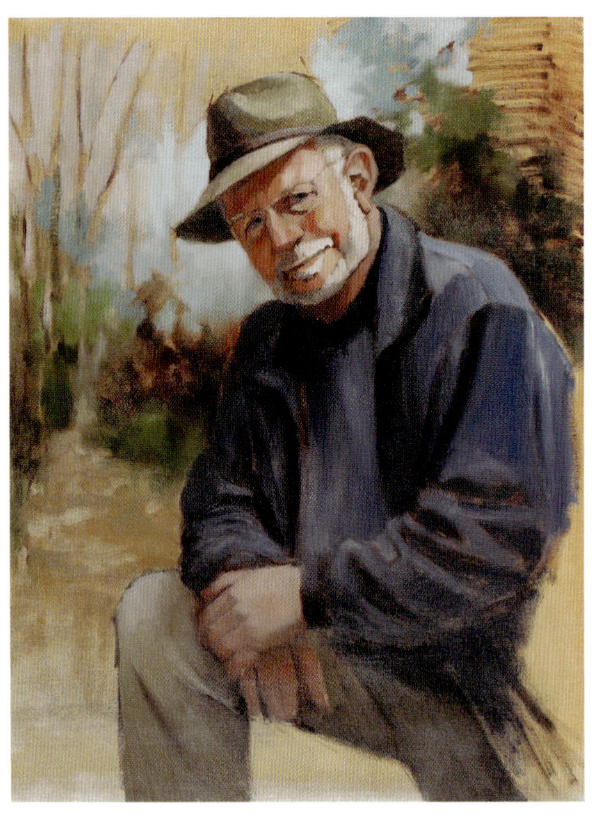

5 DEVELOP THE MIDDLE VALUES

Add subsequently lighter versions of previous mixtures. Give the hat a lighter mixture of Ivory Black, Yellow Ochre, Sap Green, Burnt Sienna and Flake White Replacement on the fold and brim, and the jacket a lighter version of Ivory Black, Ultramarine Blue, a touch of Yellow Ochre and Flake White Replacement. The pants get Ivory Black, Yellow Ochre, Burnt Sienna and Flake White Replacement in the middle shadows with more Yellow Ochre and much more Flake White Replacement in the light on the knee.

Begin the background early-fall greenery with Sap Green, Yellow Ochre and Burnt Sienna. The sky should get Cobalt Blue, a touch of Yellow Ochre and Flake White Replacement with a touch of Ivory Black to neutralize the mixture. The black takes the edge off the blue sky, providing an overcast effect.

Apply the middle and dark values to the sleeve of the jacket thinly. Leave the warmer underpainting that was originally washed onto the canvas clearly showing through. This will give greater depth to the overall color.

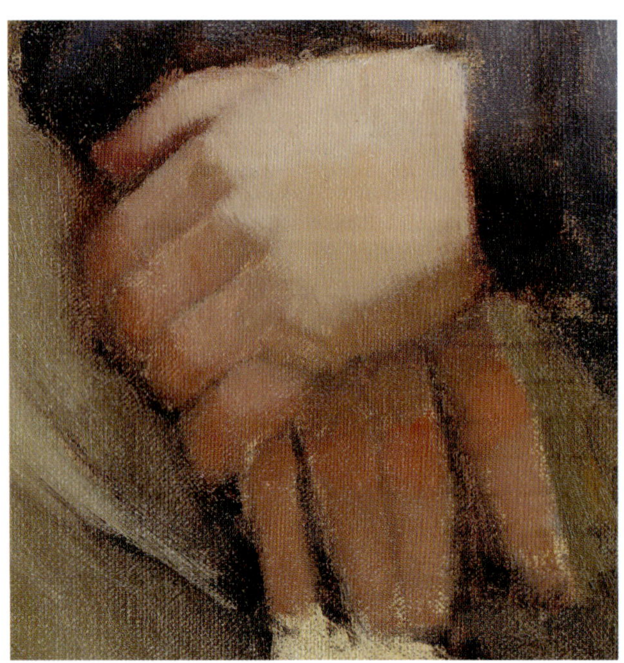

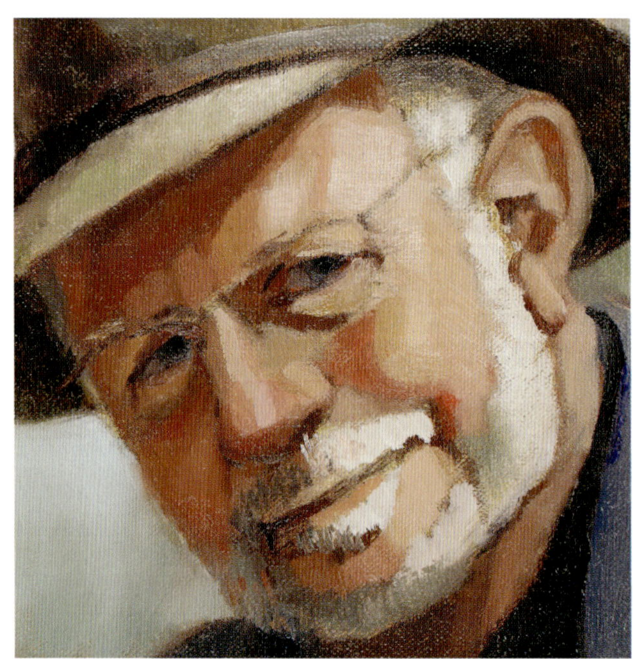

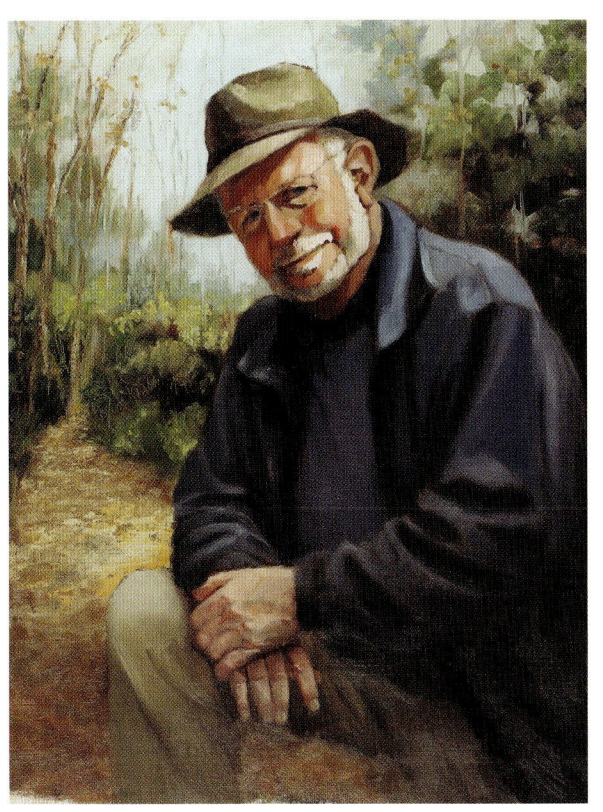

6 DEVELOP THE LIGHTS

Attention to facial features requires that each feature be approached with dark, medium and light to mold the features one at a time. Keep the white of the eyes dark enough to stay in the medium shadows of the face turned toward the light. Retouch the beard, keeping the dark side in a general mixture of Ivory Black, Cobalt Blue, Yellow Ochre and Flake White Replacement. Add more Flake White Replacement and a touch of Burnt Sienna to move the beard from shadow into light.

Lay in the glasses with Burnt Sienna and Ivory Black. Notice how they disappear with a lost edge at both cheeks. The green eyes are enhanced with a touch of Sap Green, Yellow Ochre and Flake White Replacement. Develop the background more fully with additions of fall color mixtures from Sap Green, Cobalt Blue, Burnt Sienna, Yellow Ochre and varying degrees of white. The hands and face are brought up in value with the lightest skin in a highlight mixture of Cadmium Red Light, Cadmium Yellow Light, Ivory Black (to cut the saturation) and Flake White Replacement.

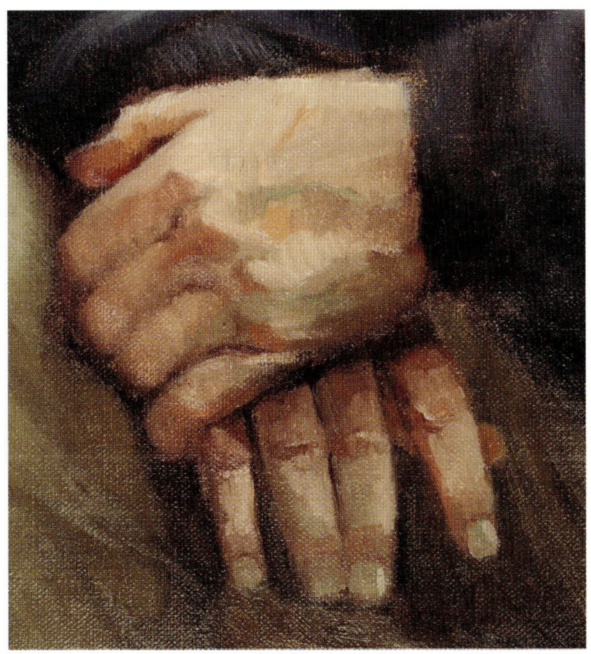

BLOOD FLOW AFFECTS SKIN COLOR

Use a noticeable concentration of warmth on the skin where there are more capillaries to carry blood closer to the surface. This includes the nose, the ears and the fingertips.

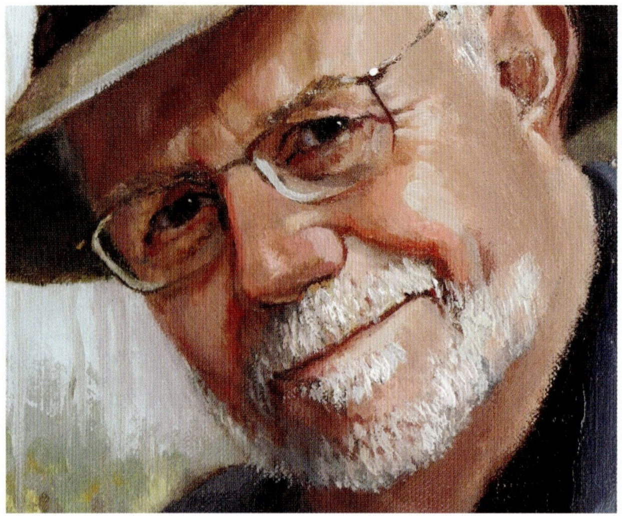

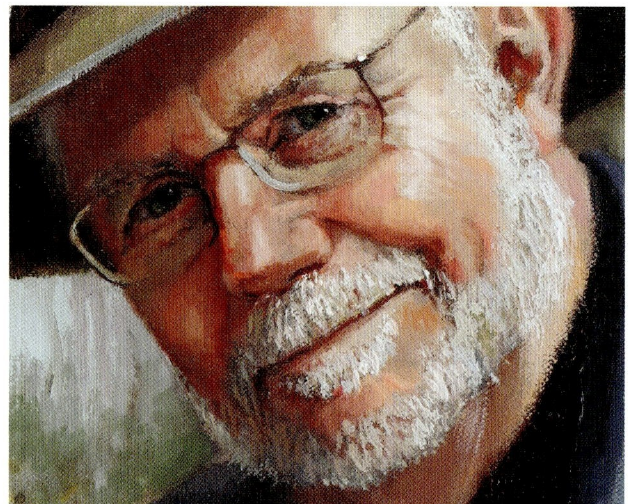

Jaw Correction

To fix an error on the jawline in the light, scrape out the area and add some local color with an addition of Cobalt Blue to push this plane back. This restructures the mandible area and resolves a minor problem with the likeness.

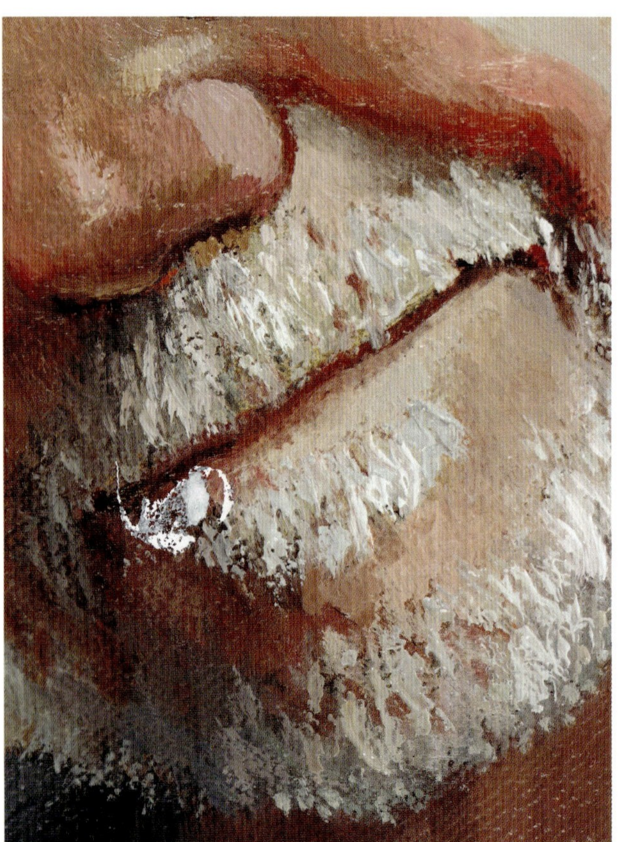

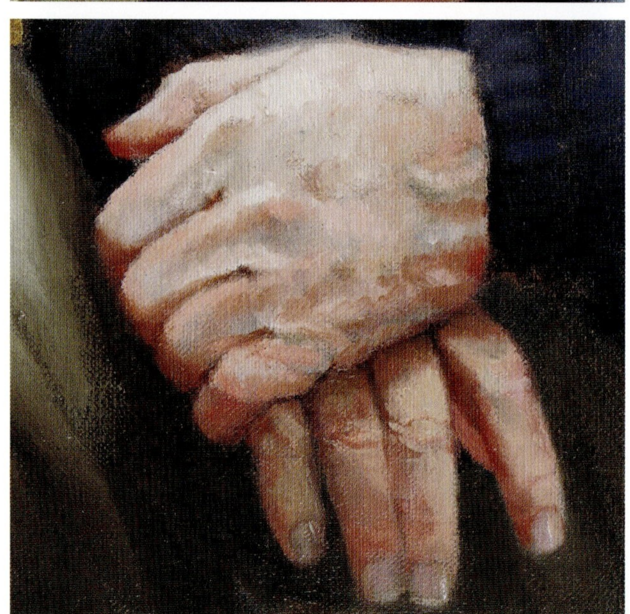

7 CLARIFY DETAILS AND CONSIDER EDGES

At this time, study the painting in different light sources and different rooms. Now get away from it for a period of time. When you come back to it with a clear eye, anything left to be done will reveal itself. Look for things that stand out or catch undesired attention. Soften edges where possible. Clarify a defining hue or value. Feather colors into one another to prevent sharp changes in value or color except where needed.

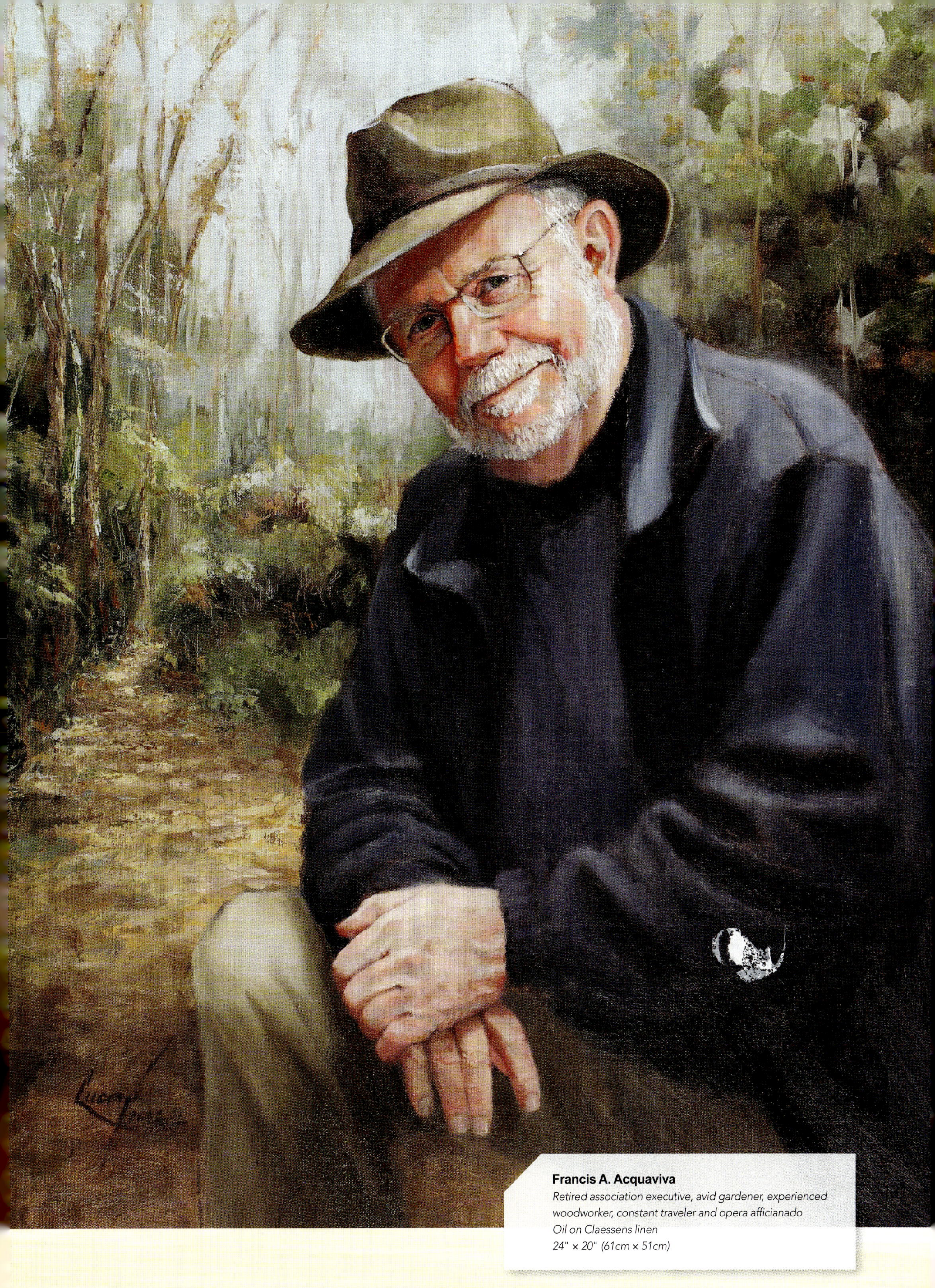

Francis A. Acquaviva
Retired association executive, avid gardener, experienced woodworker, constant traveler and opera afficianado
Oil on Claessens linen
24" × 20" (61cm × 51cm)

SISTERS IN PASTEL

MATERIALS

- 24" × 30" (61cm × 76cm) Ampersand Pastelbord—White
- Sennelier Latour Liquid Fixative for underpainting only
- Faber-Castell and CarbOthello Pastel Pencils in neutral grays, ochres and greens
- Charcoal Pencil
- Holbein Hard Pastels
- Unison Soft Pastels
- Terry Ludwig Soft Pastels particularly the darks
- Sennelier Soft Pastels mid- and high-key ranges

In the phone and e-mail discussions, multiple clothing and background information were suggested by the parents. The working sketches in graphite happened on two different days. Ninety-minute sittings mean working smart and, if things proceed well, the time may be happily extended. When working with children in any combination of sibling and age ranges, it becomes easily apparent when enough is enough.

Plan your work and work your plan. Simplify and collect as much data as possible. Work with only two values of graphite—a 4H for the lightest values and a 4B for touches of dark accents. Add other values to complete the sketches later in the studio. Using a mechanical pencil is another option.

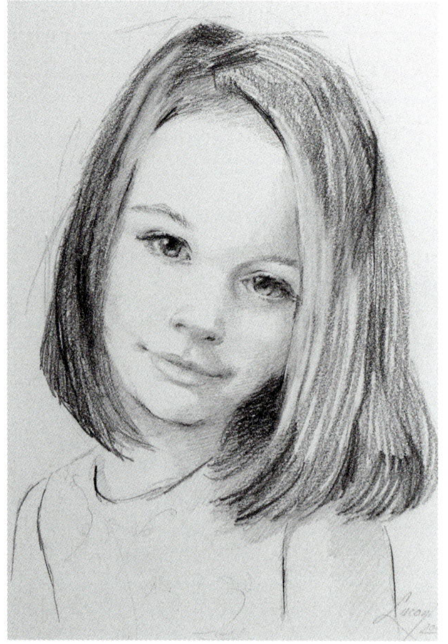

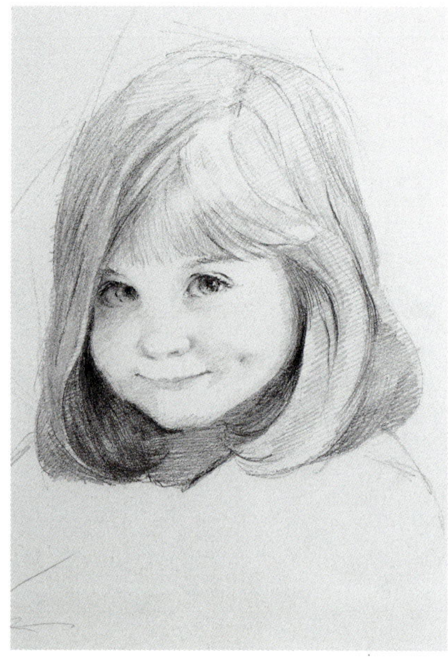

The Head Study for Likeness
While sketching or photographing, jot down notes in the sketchbook about initial impressions and characteristics of personality, coyness, introversion or extroversion, accommodating attitudes, chatty qualities, curiosity and interests. When speaking with children instead of speaking down to them, they open up in the most delightful ways, happily sharing their world, their interests and their amazing ideas. Occasionally, to prevent children from being overly self-conscious and to encourage a more overall relaxed atmosphere, parents may be encouraged to enjoy some quiet, free time alone… perhaps for a cup of tea in a different room.

MEDIUM AND SURFACE CHOICES

The children's portrait is done on Ampersand Pastelbord. This fine granular ground permits an amazing amount of layering to adhere to the surface. By using dark and medium values of hard pastels to begin the work, the tooth of the surface will not fill too quickly. Vigorously adding subsequently lighter and softer pastels as the layers advance mimics the effect of working thin to thick or lean to fat as is done in oil painting.

PHOTOS FOR PROPORTIONS

Photos are shot for the purpose of collecting data that cannot be carried to the studio and for relationships and proportions of body sizes of the children of different ages. This is particularly important if pets are part of the composition. It is too easy to incorrectly proportion a dog or cat if adding them later. A quick shot serves this purpose quite well. No matter what configuration you end up with, you will have that proportional reference to hold onto.

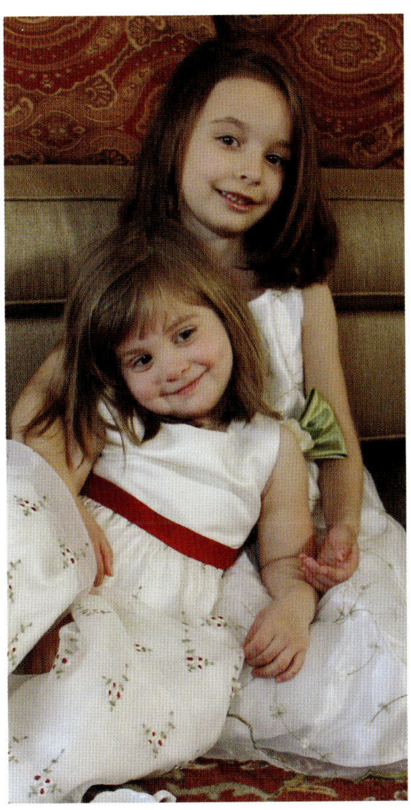

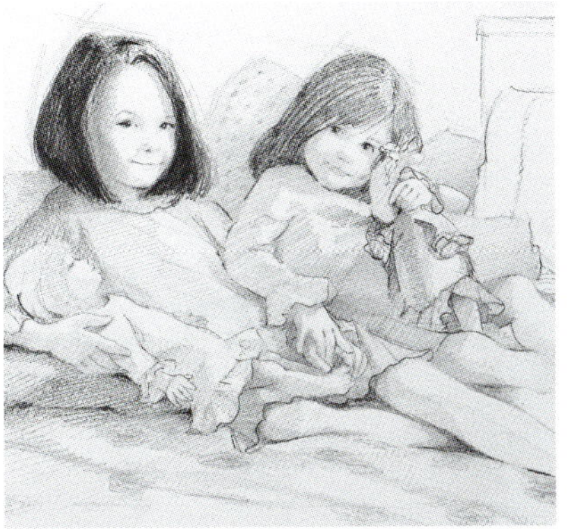

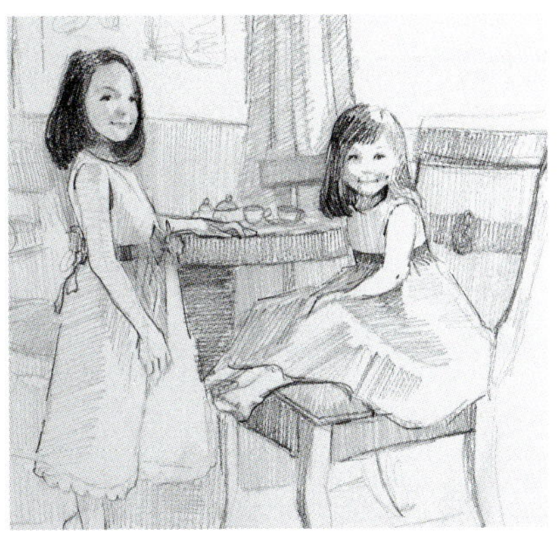

Casual Vs. Formal

My first sketches were of the girls in their party dresses. The unexpected came into play with a few sketches on another day in a corner bedroom filled with tints of color. All four figures—the children and their favorite dolls—were wearing the same nightgowns. Bodies, hands and dolls all interwoven with genuine love and friendship could carry this beautifully into a full-color pastel. Remember to let the emotion and sentiment play as big a part in the completed portrait as the likeness.

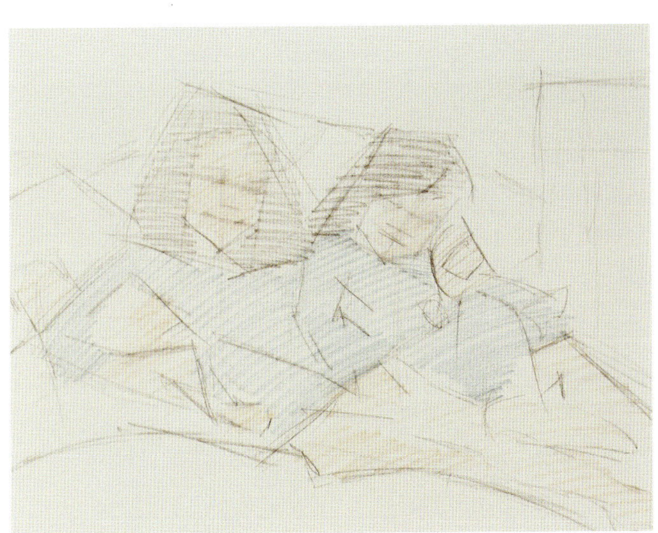

1 THE UNDERPAINTING IN PASTEL

Choose a toned paper or board as a ground for the subsequent painting. Consider whether the temperature of the tone will suit the final image. In this case, will warm undertones enhance the cool tones in the nightgowns and soft skin, or would a cool surface be more suitable?

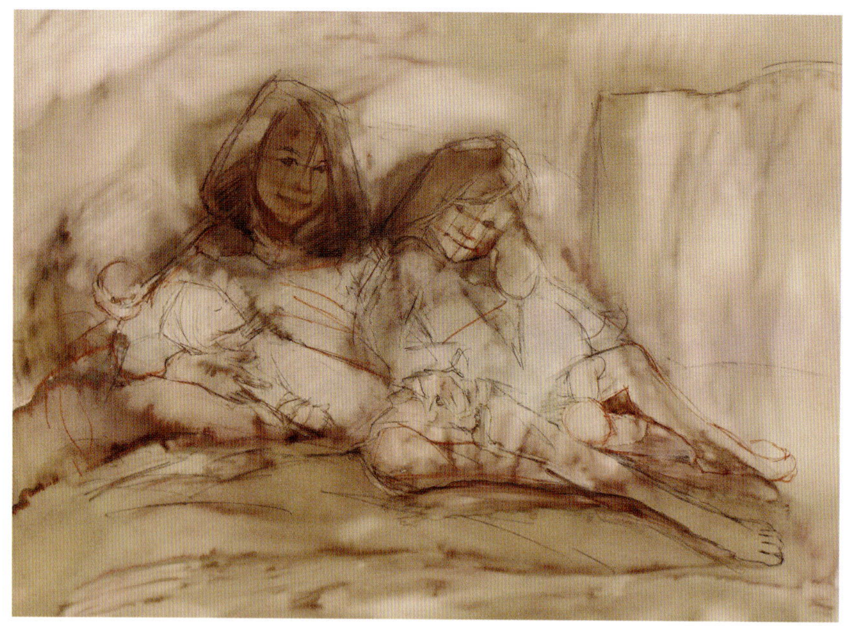

2 WASH IN THE TONAL SKETCH

Pick a single color ground to appear through and under the pastel to provide harmony and consistency. Use it as a foundation over which the colors will be built. This can be done with washes and can be particularly effective when needing to achieve rich darks.

Allow the drawn sketch to show through by applying a wash of warm brown ink in a watercolor technique. Or, using the side of the pastel stick, broadly fill an area that needs to have an underpainting base. Follow over this with a bristle brush and liquid fixative to melt the pastel and spread it as needed.

3 DEVELOP THE DARKS

This is a very high-key painting. However, the children are both brunettes, which will frame their faces nicely and bring attention there. Establish the shadow side of the people, dolls and toys now to stay on track throughout the painting.

Fill darks in the feature areas. Give the hair, clothing and pillows a layer of roughly applied darks in broad, open strokes. Create an optical blending of color by applying subsequent layers of open strokes.

Use the Color Reference Chart for Pastels, Brunette, to see groups or families of colors gathered from multiple brands of pastels. Check the chart and augment those listed with other soft and hard pastels of similar hues. The hair is based on Burnt Umber, Burnt Sienna and grayed Yellow Ochre combinations. The nightgowns are based on Ultramarine and Cobalt Blues. Place some grayed Yellow Ochre dark-middle value on the pillows and wall behind them. A similar grayed dark-middle value travels down the shadow side of the faces as a cooler base to help turn the head. Use hard pastels in Burnt Sienna-based dark-middle shades to start the skin tone and use an Alizarin-based middle-dark on the pillow under the hand of the older child.

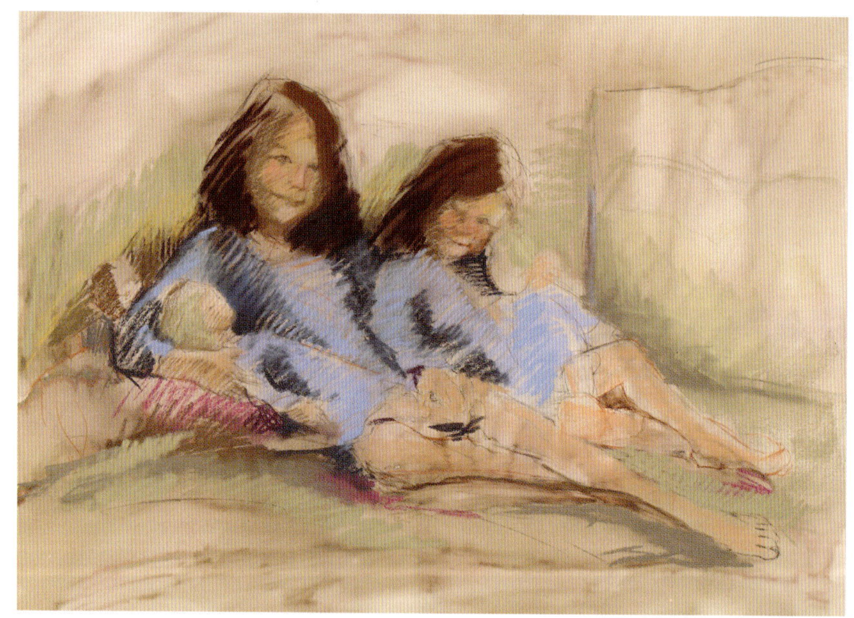

KEEP YOUR BRUSHES SEPARATE

Use a brush that is dedicated to pastel painting. Do not alternate using it among pastel, acrylic and oil painting.

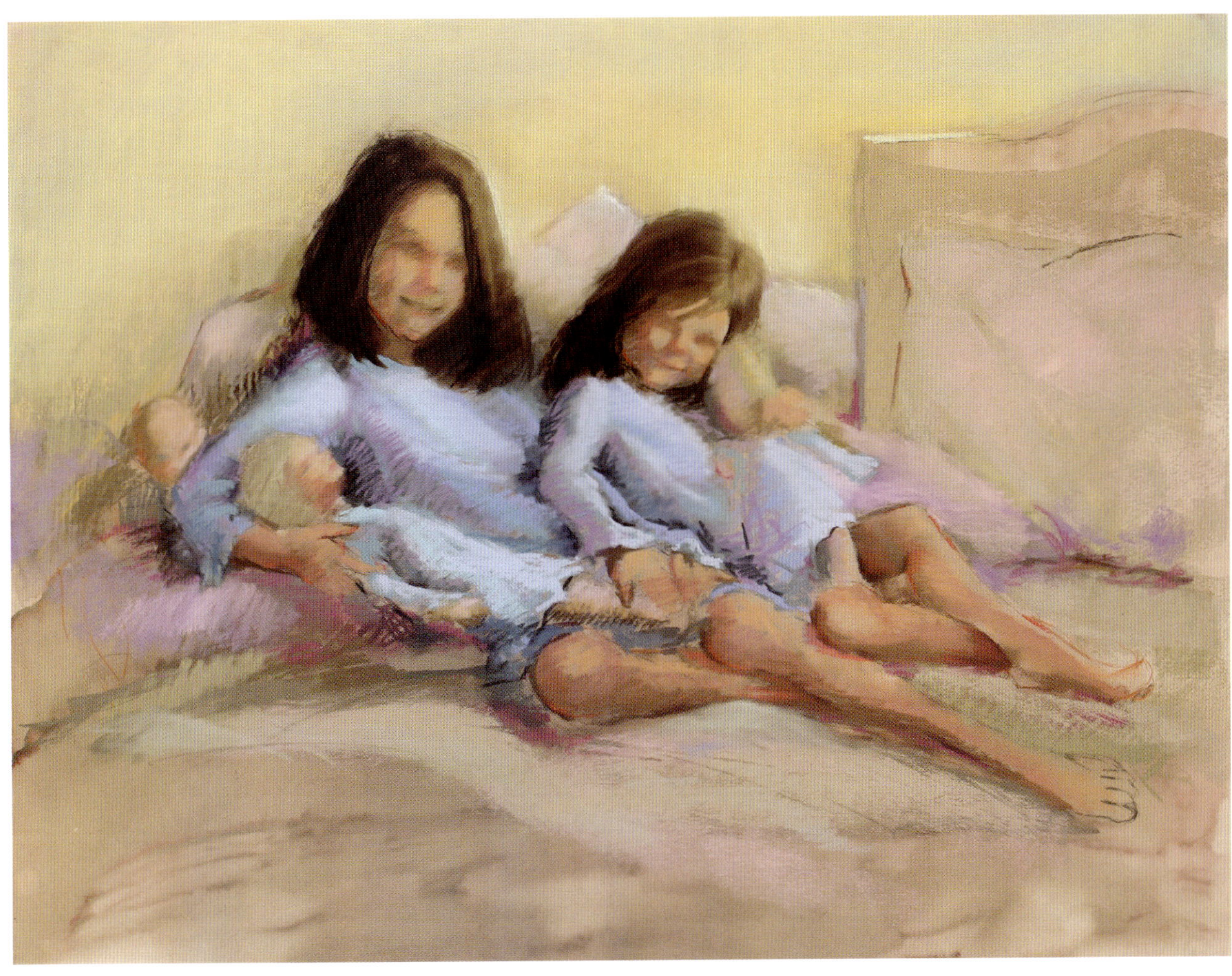

HUE AND VALUE CHOICES FOR MIDDLE VALUES

The bulk of the painting is in middle values. The darks maintain the drama, and the lights provide the sparkle. The high-key values in tints of primary colors will carry the bulk of the story of two delightful little girls who love one another.

The higher value blues are still in the same family of Ultramarine and Cobalt shades. The dark pink areas are all very cool pinks from the Alizarin Crimson family and lavenders that have a decidedly blue undertone. This will help with the transition from the blues in the clothing to the pinks in the bed linens.

4 DEVELOP THE MIDDLES

Build the middle values. Apply color to the entire support. Don't single out one area to take too far into a finished state without considering the other areas at the same time. Each edge affects the neighboring edge, each change of plane in light affects each neighboring plane in shadow, and each hue affects each neighboring hue.

Work over the whole painting at the same time. Let the images appear as if in a fog: vague, but observable. In each following layer of paint, the images become slightly more defined and delineated. Late in the painting, pay close attention to detail.

Do not attempt to detail their features at this stage. However, with the application of some middle darks and middle lights, the head structures become more evident as the shadow line defines the change in planes from the front of the head to the side. Notice how the eye sockets are clearly understood without the detail of eyes and lids.

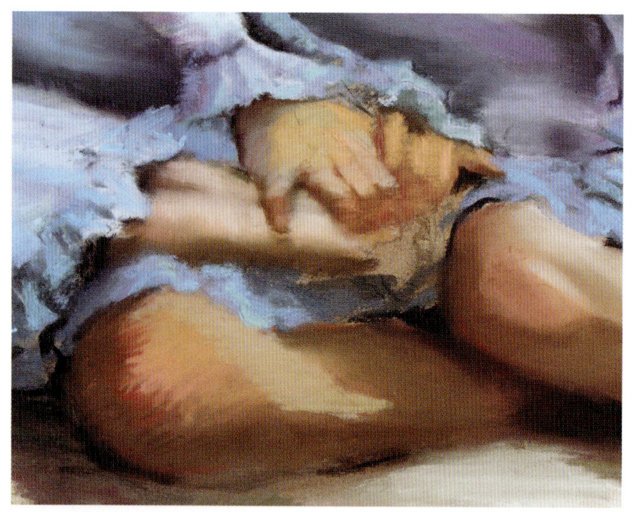

5 DEVELOP THE LIGHTS AND MODEL THE HANDS

Keep the shapes broad. The paint will go on in a different manner as it mingles with the previous layers of paint. The light values now help model the hands and their smaller individual digits. Pay special attention to the anatomy of the knees and kneecaps on the older girl's slim legs. Use the mixing charts for the knees, feet and hands. Follow the pastel color chart for Brunette Skin Highlight. For these two, pull colors from the skin-in-light on the Blonde chart. These colors have a slight green undertone that is beneficial to neutralize some of the highly saturated colors.

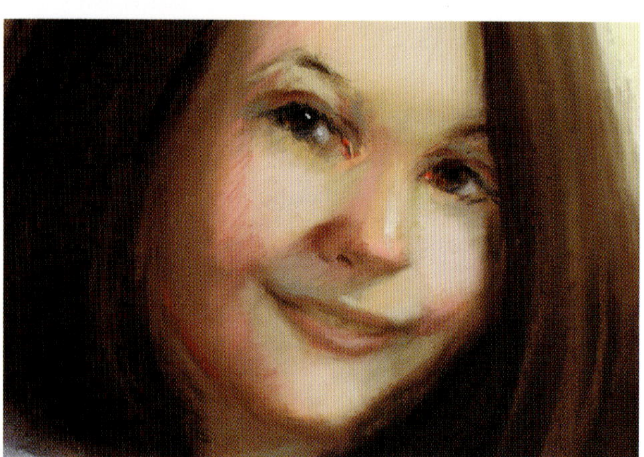

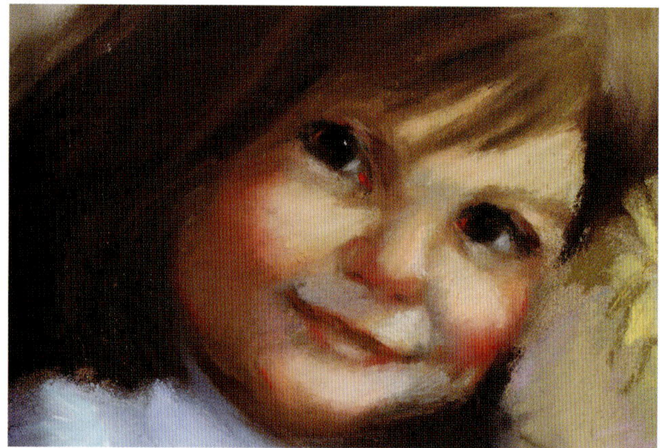

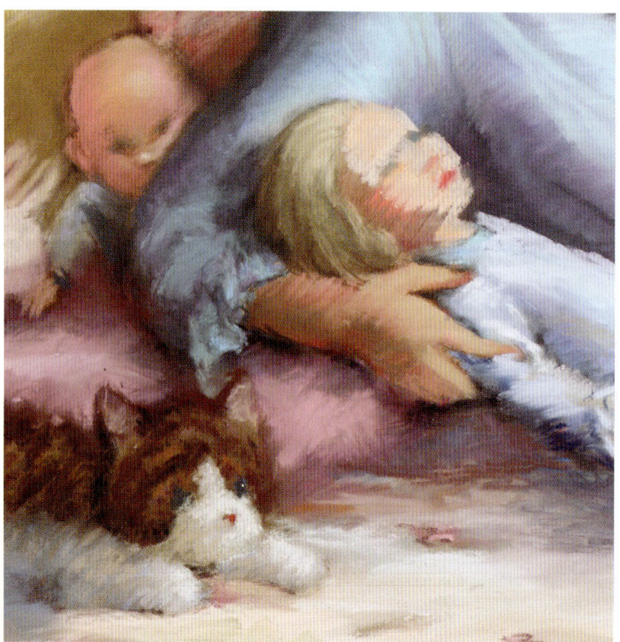

6 ADJUST THE FEATURES

Do a little at a time, but keep solid on the fundamentals. The warmth is most intense at the line where light and shadow meet. Keep the forehead slightly more golden. The center of the face from the eyebrows to the bottom of the nose is slightly more warm (red-oranges), and from the nose to the shin slightly more cool (blue/green).

7 USE THE HARD PASTELS

After layers of the creamy soft pastels from both the Brunette and Blonde charts have been built up, go back to hard pastels, in both stick and pencil forms, to push some of the details around in small areas. Use the hard pastels with an extremely light touch to push some of the pastel around as you would use a stump or tortillion. Leave just enough color to modify the temperature or hue of the underlying color. Use a light hand to place a whisper of color to make only the most subtle of adjustments.

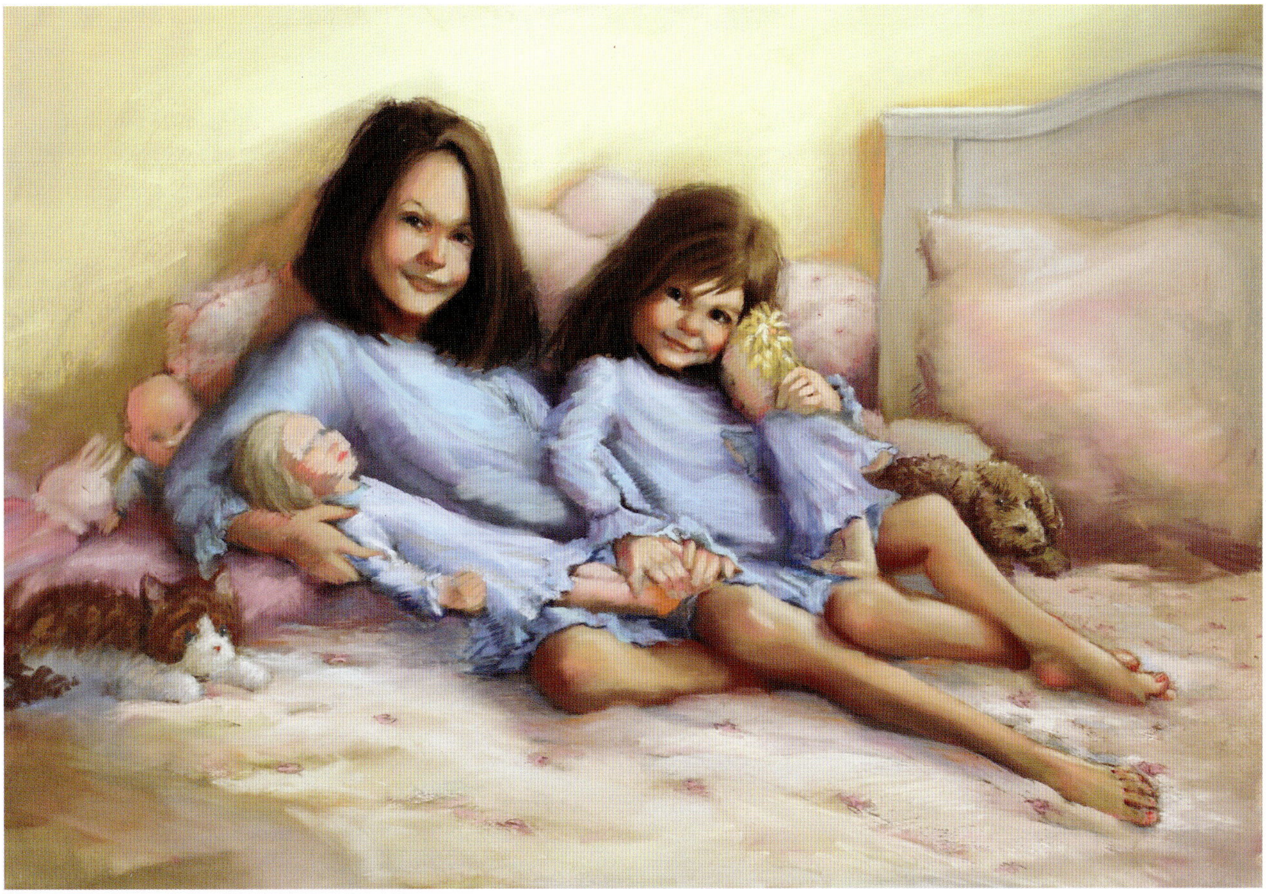

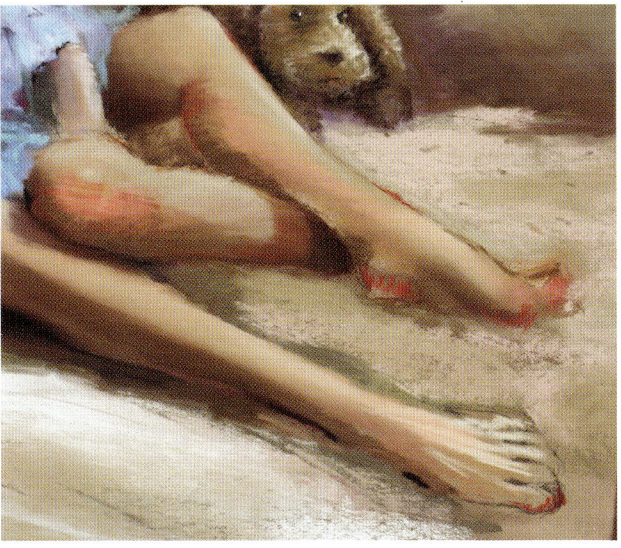

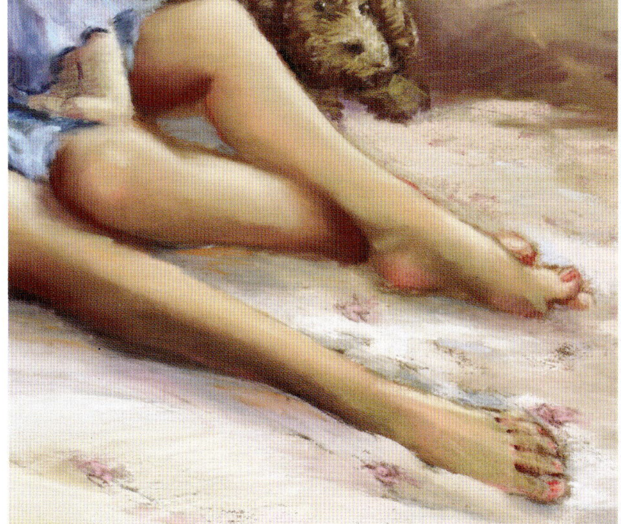

Tendons for Realism

Notice the tendons on the foot near the toes and the warmth added to the toes, heel, calves and knees. These are important at this stage to maintain a realistic feel. Additional layers of color will fit the tendons back into the skin.

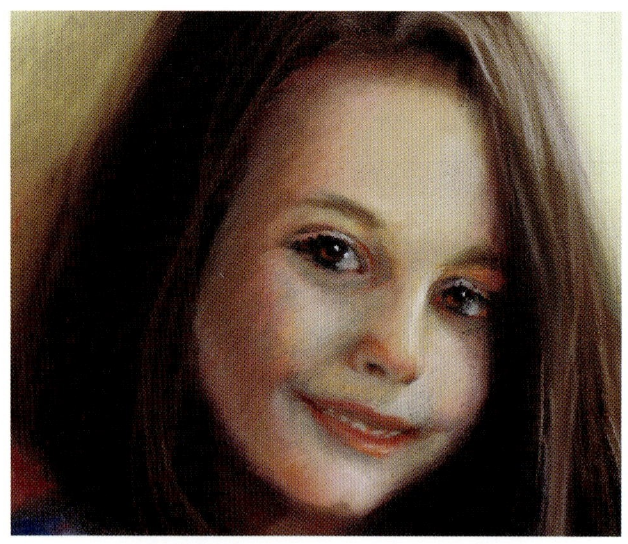

8 CLARIFY DETAILS AND CONSIDER EDGES

Examine the edges, making certain nothing is too sharp in any one area. Examine color temperatures to make certain that things that need to go back into the picture plane are cool enough and things that need to come forward are warm enough. Examine the hues to make certain no one area is so saturated with brilliant color that it stands alone instead of staying as an integral part of the whole. In this painting, check the confluence of hands, dolls and legs to make certain all make sense.

Is the personality present in the eyes? Beyond having made a likeness, has the painting represented the real personalities of these children? Is there a sense of the quiet, poetic, artistic, dreamer in the older child and the charming, clever and impish in the younger child? Check the eyes. Use pastel pencils for control and ease of maneuvering in those small areas. The slightest change of direction or hue can affect the expression. Viewers look into the eyes of portraits just as they look into the eyes of people in their presence and with whom they are conversing. The portrait is done when it can speak back to you.

ADDING THE POLISH

The fear of mentioning polish is that artists equate that with blending every square inch of the pastel completely flat. That would produce a much less interesting surface. Leaving the marks is one of the appealing qualities of pastel—this unusual medium that is the best combination of drawing and painting.

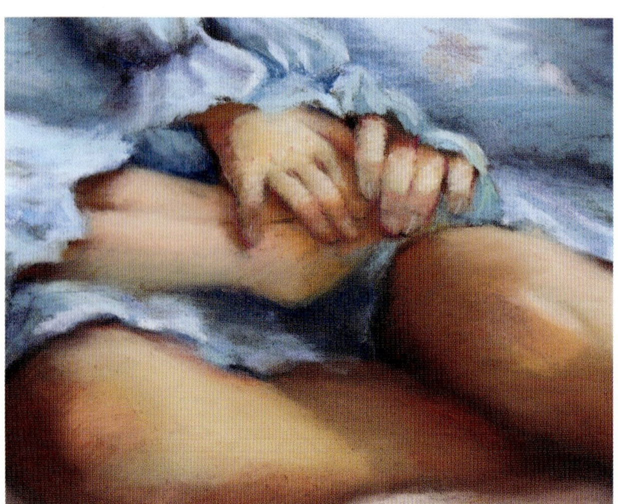

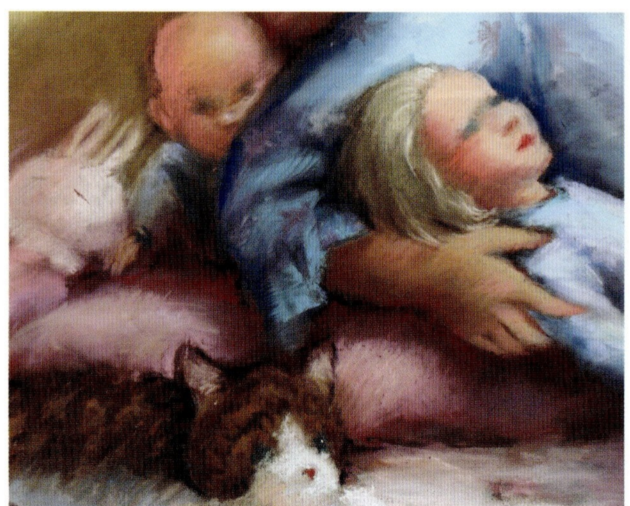

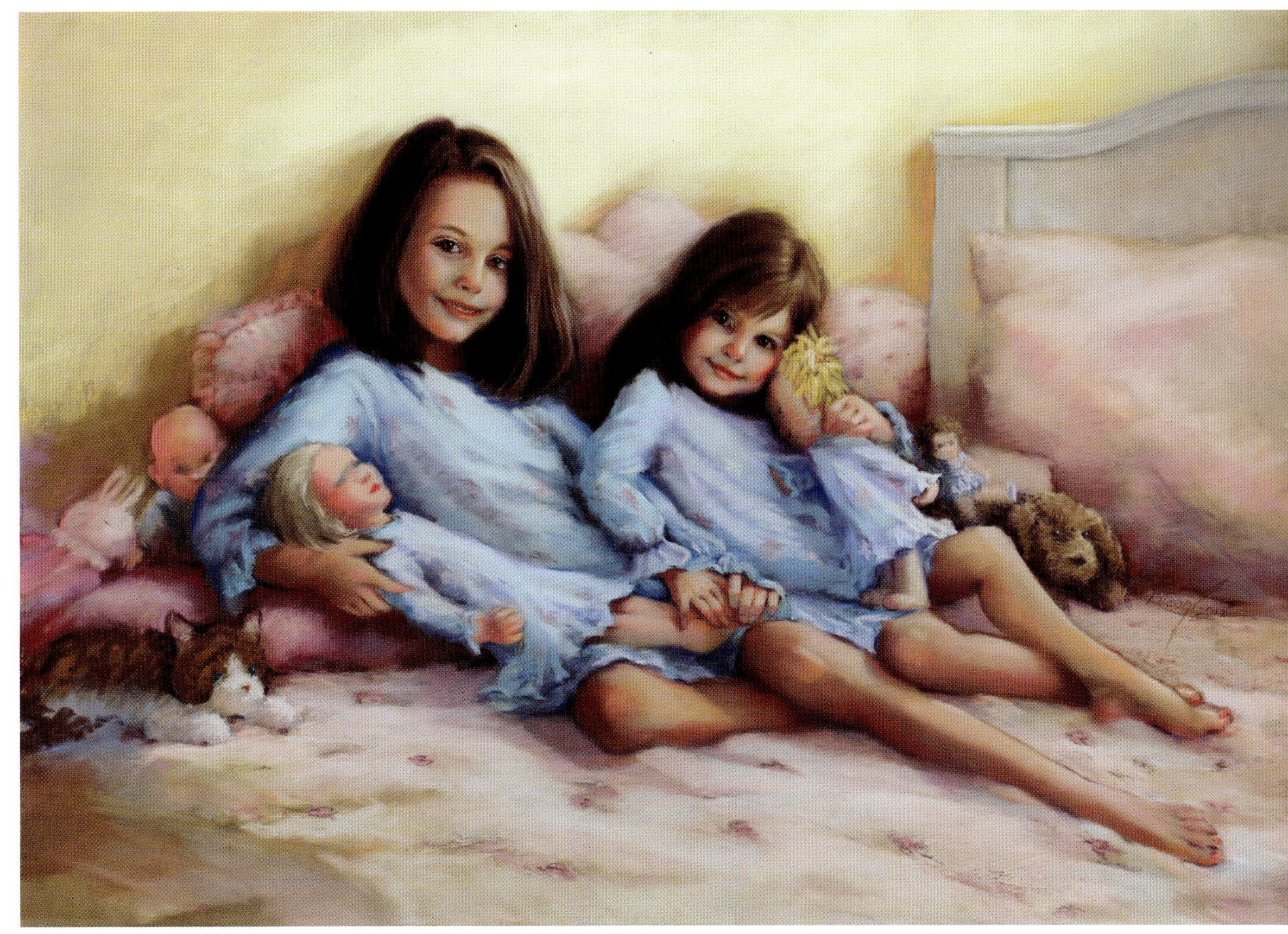

Leyna and Kiersten
Pastel on Ampersand Pastelbord
24" × 30" (61cm × 76cm)

PARTING NOTES

- Do the work. Put in the time. Cover miles of paper and canvas. Draw and paint with joy, rhythm and with love. Your style will evolve and become uniquely yours over time.
- Study the masters. Go to museums. Study the art of many centuries. No one does this alone. Speaking of advancements in the world of science, Isaac Newton spoke of "standing on the shoulders of giants." Art is the same. Learn from those past giants and move forward.
- "Art is never finished, only abandoned." — Leonardo da Vinci.
- If the artist creates every day, improvement will be seen with every stroke, and as the painting develops where little else can be or should be changed, it will tell you it is approaching finished.
- As an instructor, I expect great things from you. Every day is a new adventure. Now go paint!

COLOR REFERENCE CHART FOR PASTEL

ETHNICITY/HAIR COLOR	HAIR	SKIN	LIPS
Brunette	**In shadow:** *Terry Ludwig D40, Unison DK2, Sennelier 45* **In light:** *Rembrandt 538.7* **Highlights:** *Unison RE7, Nupastel 376*	**In shadow:** *Terry Ludwig EM6, Unison RE17, Sennelier 194* **In light:** *Unison RE7, Nupastel 376* **Highlights:** *Terry Ludwig EM2, Rembrandt 339.10, Sennelier 706*	*Terry Ludwig L22, Sennelier 684*
Redhead	**In shadow:** *Terry Ludwig D10, Unison RE6, Sennelier 405 or 406* **In light:** *Rembrandt 318.3 or 343.5, Nupastel 213* **Highlights:** *Sennelier 86 or 77, Rembrandt 370.9*	**In shadow:** *Rembrandt 343.3, Unison RE12 Sennelier 4 or 76, Nupastel 273* **In light:** *Unison 06, Nupastel 286* **Highlights:** *Sennelier 12, 21, 31 131, 244, 274 Unison BE19, Rembrandt 231.10*	*Sennelier 933 or 94, Unison RED6*
Blue blood/Porcelain	**In shadow:** *Terry Ludwig D20 with black as necessary* **In light:** *Terry Ludwig D20* **Highlights:** *Terry Ludwig D17*	**In shadow:** *Unison BE24* **In light:** *Unison RED18* **Highlights:** *Sennelier 315, Rembrandt 397.10*	*Rembrandt 371.8*
Blonde	**In shadow:** *Terry Ludwig G31, Terry Ludwig G36, Sennelier 528* **In light:** *Unison BE25, Grey23 or YGrey13* **Highlights:** *Sennelier 103, Unison Grey27 or LT2, Rembrandt 202.2, Nupastel 277*	**In shadow:** *Terry Ludwig MS10, Sennelier 465 or 406, Unison RE6, Nupastel 363* **In light:** *Sennelier 934, Unison RED12* **Highlights:** *Sennelier 308 or 387, Unison LT7*	*Terry Ludwig MS20, Sennelier 686, 705, 925, 935, Unison RE2*
Hispanic/Latino	**In shadow:** *Holbein 13, Girault 45* **In light:** *Girault 266, 298* **Highlights:** *Terry Ludwig EM18, Girault 122, Blockx 211*	**In shadow:** *Terry Ludwig D17* **In light:** *Terry Ludwig EM18, Girault 122, Blockx 211* **Highlights:** *Terry Ludwig EM24, L27, Unison RE8, Girault 28, Schiminke 021H*	*Terry Ludwig P6, Girault 92, Schminicke 022M*
Black (Warm Tones)	**In shadow:** *Unison Grey 13, Girault 265* **In light:** *Sennelier 397* **Highlights:** *Terry Ludwig D16, Unison A24, Rembrandt 409.5, Nupastel 223*	**In shadow:** *Terry Ludwig D19, Sennelier 75, Unison BE6, Rembrandt 538.3, Nupastel 353* **In light:** *Terry Ludwig MS10, Girault 406, Blockx 351, Schiminke 024D* **Highlights:** *Rembrandt 538.8*	*Rembrandt 343.8, Blockx 274*
Black (Cool Tones)	**In shadow:** *Unison DK16 add black, Cretacolor 251, 252* **In light:** *Unison DK16* **Highlights:** *Terry Ludwig D23, D45, Girault 376*	**In shadow:** *Terry Ludwig D55* **In light:** *Rembrandt 347.3* **Highlights:** *Sennelier 405, 406, Unison RE6, Girault 441, 46, Nupastel 363*	*Rembrandt 343.8, Blockx 274, Schiminke 024M*
East Asian	**In shadow:** *Sennelier 464 add black, Unison DK16, Cretacolor 250* **In light:** *Sennelier 464* **Highlights:** *Rembrandt 505.3, Nupastel 345*	**In shadow:** *Blockx 423, Nupastel 283* **In light:** *Sennelier 11,19, 73, 371, Rembrandt 236.9, Blockx 153, 154, Schiminke 0180* **Highlights:** *Terry Ludwig DB2, DB3, MS33, Sennelier 43, 44, 117, 126, 132, Unison LT4*	*Unison RE4, Rembrandt 343.7, Schiminke 023H, Blockx 273*
Native American	**In shadow:** *Terry Ludwig D52, D20, Sennelier 478* **In light:** *Sennelier 463, 365, Terry Ludwig D17, Holbein 137* **Highlights:** *Sennelier 419, 515, Terry Ludwig D27, D37*	**In shadow:** *Sennelier 75, Terry Ludwig D15, D17, Holbein 13, Unison BE6, Dk3* **In light:** *Sennelier 89, Terry Ludwig D35, Unison Dk1* **Highlights:** *Terry Ludwig EM40, Unison BE22, Schmincke 038H, 038M*	*Terry Ludwig P6, Unison R34, Schmincke 024H, 024 M*
Indian (Continental)	**In shadow:** *Terry Ludwig D17, Unison Grey36, Holbein 13* **In light:** *Sennelier 514, 526 Schmincke 095B* **Highlights:** *Terry Ludwig L28, Schmincke 092B, 092H, 092D*	**In shadow:** *Sennelier 397, Terry Ludwig L13, D19, Unison DK3* **In light:** *Sennelier 430, 63, Terry Ludwig 4845, Holbein 18, 19, Schmincke 037H* **Highlights:** *Sennelier 431, Terry Ludwig P30, Holbein 48*	*Sennelier 405, 406, Terry Ludwig MS10, Schmincke 024P, 024H*

INDEX

Acrylics, 79
Alla prima, 65-66, 112
Backgrounds, 16, 30, 104–105, 109–111, 118
Charcoal, 8, 24
Chiaroscuro, 27
Children, 48, 57–58, 61, 71, 75, 81, 133
sketching, 25, 27, 29, 58, 132
Clothing, 25, 107, 116, 124, 134
Color, 9, 14–15, 27, 57, 78
keys, 27, 121, 134–135
local, 20–21, 43
mixing, 31, 77–79
planning, 26–27, 30–31
surrounding, effects of, 15, 81, 87
See also Hair color, Skin color
Color charts, 7, 77–99, 140
hair, 77, 79–92, 94–99, 140
skin, 77–99, 140
Color temperature, 30, 78, 135
hair, 85, 91, 95
skin, 83, 85, 87, 89, 91, 93, 97, 99
Corrections, 119, 130
Design, 15–16, 22–23, 101–113
See also Golden Mean
Drawings, transferring, 125–126
Ears, 53–55
Edges, 15, 39, 61, 112–113
Eyebrows, 71
Eyeglasses, 109, 129
Eyes, 13, 39–43, 138
Asian, 39
baby, 57–58
catch-light, 41, 43
edges, 39
front view, 40–41
placing, 56
in profile, 39, 42–43
sockets, 39–40, 42–43, 57, 63, 135
Features, 129
placing, 56–59
baby, 57
in fifths, 59
in halves, 56–57
as a kite, 56
in thirds, 57–58
Feet, 137
Fixative, 11, 134
Focal point, 16, 22–23
Form, 15–17, 20–21, 38
Glazing, 66, 112
Golden Mean, 22, 38, 50, 73
Hair, 65–70
Hair color, 67, 70, 77, 79
Asian, 94–95, 140
black, 90–91, 140
blonde, 67, 86–87, 140
blue blood/porcelain, 84–85, 140
brunette, 67, 80–81, 134, 140
gray, 76–77, 91, 97
Hispanic/Latino, 88–89, 140
Indian continent, 98–99, 140
Native American, 96–97, 140
redhead, 82–83, 140
Halftones, 16–17
Hands, 22, 72–75
Heads, 38, 56–59
Highlights, 20–21, 43, 81
Jewelry, 74, 108, 122–123
Lighting, 30, 95, 97, 106
reflected, 20–21, 89, 93
stage, 116, 118, 122
Likeness, 20, 47, 71, 116, 130, 132
Mood, 26, 106
Mouths, 48–52, 58, 80–99
Noses, 44–47, 58, 63
constructing, 45–46
light and shadow on, 44–45
in profile, 47
shapes within, 45–46
Oil, 8–10, 111
brushes, 10, 117, 121
knives, 10–11, 113
studies, 26–27
Outlines, creating, 15–16
Painting, sculptural, 38, 60–61
Palettes, 9, 111
Pastels, 10–11, 27–29, 111, 125
Pencils, 8, 25, 132
Pets, 133
Photography, 32–35, 99, 103, 108, 110, 117
Planning, 7, 113, 116, 124
color, 26–27, 30–31
Poses, 74–75, 107, 109
Props, 102, 104–105, 109–110, 133
Settings, 107, 109, 111, 124–131
Shadows, 15–17, 20–21, 23, 78, 120
Shapes, analyzing, 15–16, 19
Sight sizing, 15–16, 18, 56
Sitters, 7, 13, 37, 102–103, 110
Sketches, 7–8, 13–17, 22–23, 64, 109–110
alla prima, 112
color, 26–31
graphite, 25
multiple, 30, 102–103, 118, 124–125, 133
oil, 119
watercolor, 11, 64
See also Studies
Skin, 97, 120
Skin color, 7, 77, 79, 81, 129
Asian, 94–95, 140
black, 90–93, 140
blonde, 86–87, 140
blue blood/porcelain, 84–85, 140
brunette, 80–81, 121, 140
Hispanic/Latino, 88–89, 140
Indian continent, 98–99, 140
Native American, 96–97, 140
redhead, 82–83, 127, 140
Skulls, 57, 62–63
Storytelling, 7, 22–23, 101–105, 107, 109–111
Studies, 24–29, 91, 93, 116, 125, 132
Surfaces
board, 11, 27, 116–117, 132
canvas, 79, 119, 124, 126
paper, 8
Teeth, 50, 63
Values, 14–17, 20–21, 34–35
Viewer, leading the, 14, 39
Watercolor, 11, 27–28, 79

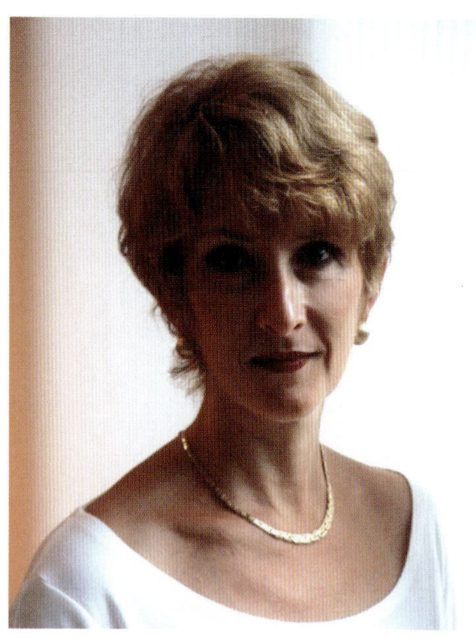

 Published by North Light Books, an imprint of F+W Media, Inc., 10151 Carver Road, Suite # 200, Blue Ash, OH 45242. (800) 289-0963. First Edition.

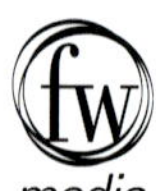

Other fine North Light Books are available from your favorite bookstore, art supply store or online supplier. Visit our website at www.fwmedia.com.

17 16 15 14 13 5 4 3 2 1

DISTRIBUTED IN CANADA BY FRASER DIRECT
100 Armstrong Avenue
Georgetown, ON, Canada L7G 5S4
Tel: (905) 877-4411

DISTRIBUTED IN THE U.K. AND EUROPE BY F&W MEDIA INTERNATIONAL, LTD
Brunel House, Forde Close, Newton Abbot, TQ12 4PU, UK
Tel: (+44) 1626 323200, Fax: (+44) 1626 323319
E-mail: enquiries@fwmedia.com

DISTRIBUTED IN AUSTRALIA BY CAPRICORN LINK
P.O. Box 704, S. Windsor NSW, 2756 Australia
Tel: (02) 4577-3555

Edited by Stefanie Laufersweiler and Vanessa Wieland
Designed by Amanda Kleiman
Cover Design by Julie Wallace
Production Coordinated by Mark Griffin

Painting on page 2–3: *Robert Case in Maggie Valley*,
Pastel on Ampersand Pastelbord
20" × 16" (51cm × 41cm)

ABOUT THE AUTHOR

A founding member and North Carolina Ambassador of the Portrait Society of America, Luana Luconi Winner was trained in Rome, Florence, Switzerland and the United States. Her portraits and paintings in various mediums have won national and international recognition and awards, including a Silver Medal at the International Association of Pastel Societies and Best in Show at the Richeson International Figure/Portrait Competition. She recently served two elected terms as president of the Pastel Society of North Carolina and sits on several art boards.

In demand as an instructor, Luana has served as faculty for the Portrait Society of America International Conference in Boston, Dallas and Washington, D.C. Art centers, museums and private art schools have hosted her workshops from California to Boston, Chicago to Florida. Her Italian workshops have been sellouts. Students particularly enjoy experiencing Italy with an instructor who lived in Rome and whose family originated in small Tuscan towns near Florence.

Luana has written articles for International Artist, The Artist's Magazine, American Artist, The Art of the Portrait, Signature, The Folio, *Strathmore's online web magazine, as well as for many regional publications and periodicals. She has authored four workbooks. Jerry's Artarama and Cheap Joe's have produced eight of Luana's instructional DVDs on drawing and painting portraits in pastel, watercolor, acrylic and oil (with twelve more in post-production), and she self-produced a video on oil, pastel and watercolor: "Great Faces: Parts and Pieces Series: The Eye." Silver Brush markets three brush sets in Luana's name. Visit Luana's website at www.winnerstudios.com.*

METRIC CONVERSION CHART

To convert	*to*	*multiply by*
Inches	Centimeters	2.54
Centimeters	Inches	0.4
Centimeters	Feet	0.03
Yards	Meters	0.9
Meters	Yards	1.1

ACKNOWLEDGMENTS

My deepest heartfelt thanks to Doug, my husband, who has been my rock through both my most difficult loss this winter and my most exciting new challenge with this book. Love and thanks to my daughter, Teresa, and her family, who always help to inspire love, organization and inventive creativity, and to my son, Al, who is always available to lean on for support, love, idea development and technical expertise. To my father, brother and extended family, just a note: We will try to keep each other from being lonely without her.

Many thanks to publisher Jamie Markle, who found me doing a portrait demonstration in California; to editor Kathy Kipp, who initiated this journey with me; and to editor Stefanie Laufersweiler, who expertly led me to a concise and clear conclusion. And to editor Vanessa Wieland, all the copy, design and other editors and staff for their finishing touches who made the book read well and look great.

Thanks also to Vern to vent, Jutta to remember, and Charlotte, Brian, Janice and George for the weekly boost.

I am grateful to my friends at Askew Taylor Paints, Cheap Joe's, Jerry's Artarama and the Artspace Artists in North Carolina for years of friendship and support.

This book's illustrations were completed with the gracious and ongoing support of these manufacturers and suppliers with whom I am pleased to be associated:

Savoir Faire: Sennelier Pastels, Sennelier Watercolors and Sennelier Oils
Ampersand: Gessobords, Pastelbords and Aquabords
Terry Ludwig: Soft Pastels
Strathmore: Gray Scale Paper, Charcoal Paper, Vellum, Canvas Paper, Tracing Paper
Silver Brush: Grand Prix Bristles, Renaissance Sables, Ruby Satin Synthetics
Holbein: Hard Pastels, Extra Fine Oils, Finest Watercolor, Acrylic Gray Toned Gesso
Jack Richeson Art Supply: Unison Pastels, Grey Matters Palettes, Daniel Greene Oil, Brushes and Soaps
M. Graham: Artist Oils, Galkyd Lite

Thanks to one and all, and I can only hope that we have a long and productive future ahead of us—together!

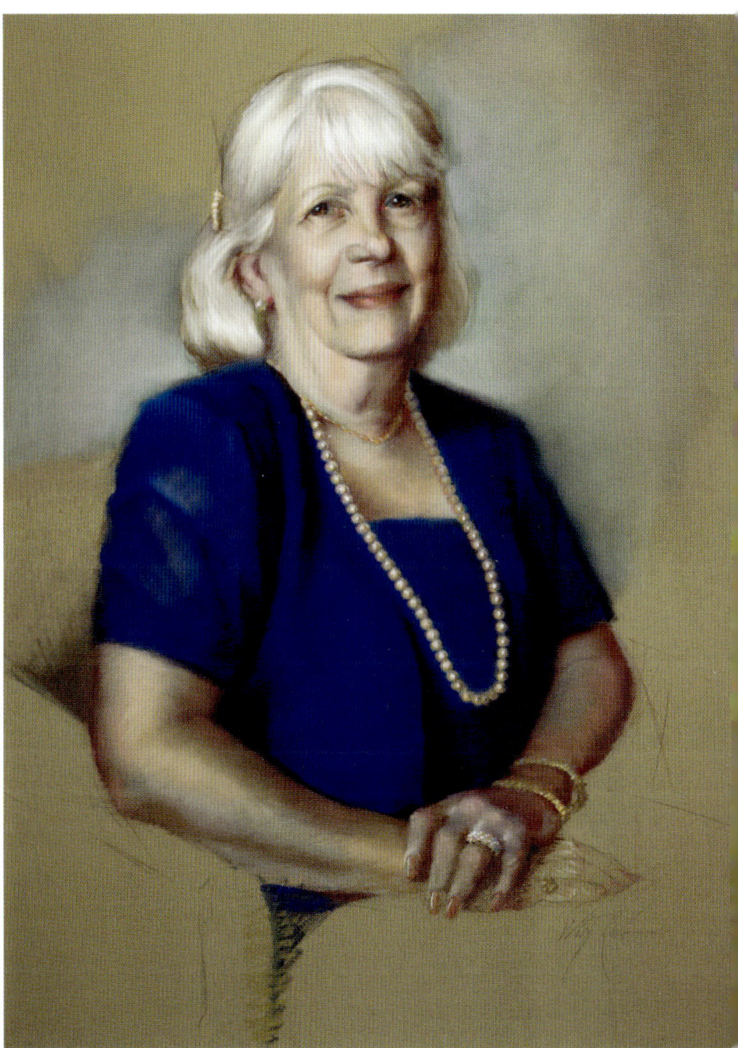

Dedication

This book is dedicated to Theresa Victoria Ciucci Luconi, whom we lost during the production of this book at 94 years old and just shy of celebrating her 72nd wedding anniversary. In life, she was a tiny Italian dynamo who never stopped teaching, cooking, caregiving or loving, and I will forever be grateful to her.

Mom on Her 90th Birthday
Pastel on Ampersand Pastelbord
24" × 18" (61cm × 46cm)

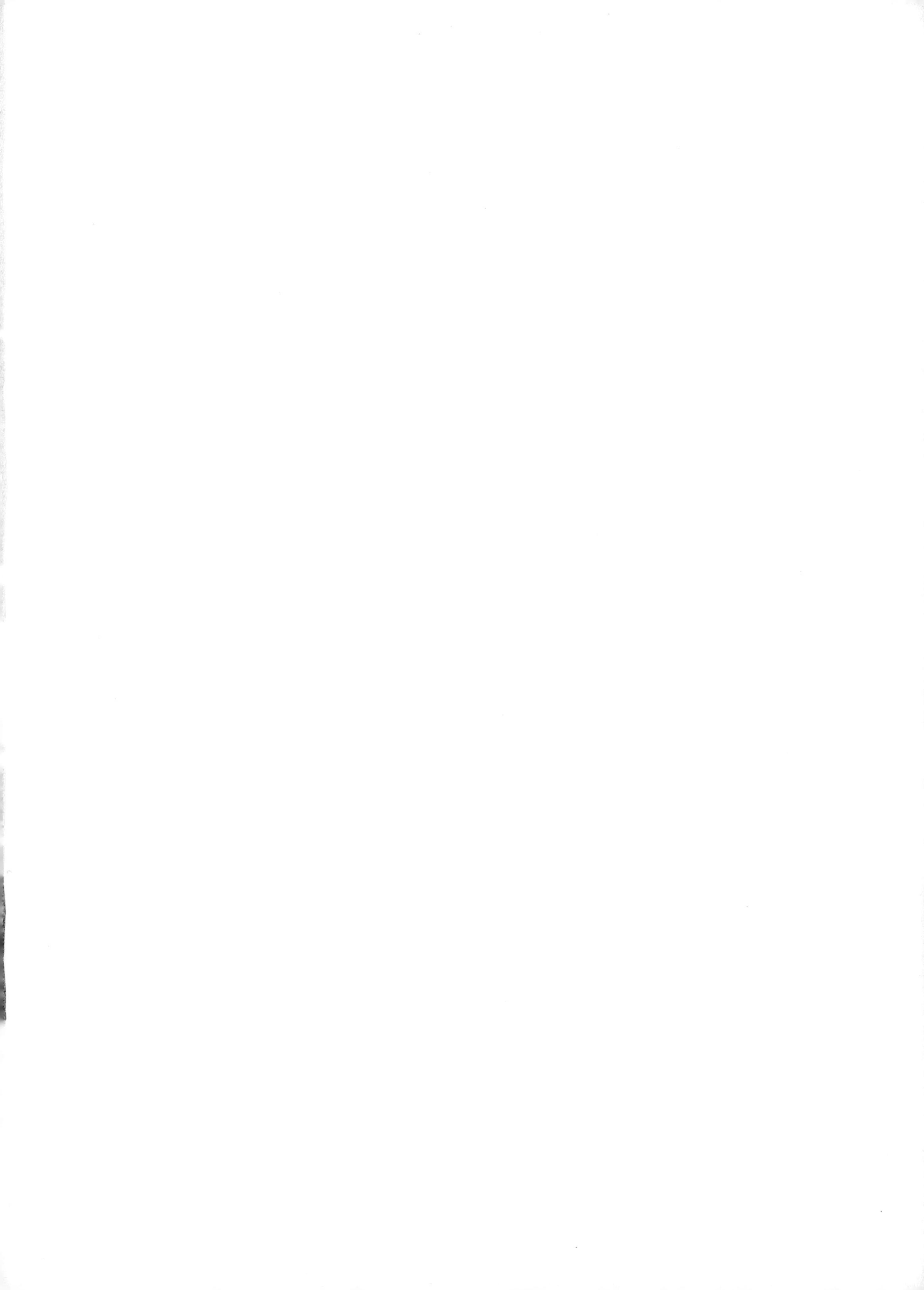